£29.95

STRATE IC MANAGEMENT IN TOURISM, 2ND EDITION

CABI TOURISM TEXTS are an essential resource for students of academic tourism, leisure studies, hospitality, entertainment and events management. The series reflects the growth of tourism-related studies at an academic level and responds to the changes and developments in these rapidly evolving industries, providing up-to-date practical guidance, discussion of the latest theories and concepts, and analysis by world experts. The series is intended to guide students through their academic programmes and remain an essential reference throughout their careers in the tourism sector.

Readers will find the books within the CABI TOURISM TEXTS series to have a uniquely wide scope, covering important elements in leisure and tourism, including management-led topics, practical subject matter and development of conceptual themes and debates. Useful textbook features such as case studies, bullet point summaries and helpful diagrams are employed throughout the series to aid study and encourage understanding of the subject.

Students at all levels of study, workers within tourism and leisure industries, researchers, academics, policy makers and others interested in the field of academic and practical tourism will find these books an invaluable and authoritative resource, useful for academic reference and real world tourism applications.

Titles available

Ecotourism: Principles and Practices
Ralf Buckley

Contemporary Tourist Behaviour: Yourself and Others as Tourists
David Bowen and Jackie Clarke

The Entertainment Industry: an Introduction
Edited by Stuart Moss

Practical Tourism Research
Stephen L.J. Smith

Leisure, Sport and Tourism, Politics, Policy and Planning, 3rd Edition
A.J. Veal

Events Management
Edited by Peter Robinson, Debra Wale and Geoff Dickson

Food and Wine Tourism: Integrating Food, Travel and Territory
Erica Croce and Giovanni Perri

STRATEGIC MANAGEMENT IN TOURISM, 2ND EDITION

Edited by

Luiz Moutinho

Department of Management
University of Glasgow
Glasgow, Scotland
UK

www.cabi.org

CABI is a trading name of CAB International

CABI Head Office
Nosworthy Way
Wallingford
Oxfordshire OX10 8DE
UK

Tel: +44 (0)1491 832111
Fax: +44 (0)1491 833508
E-mail: cabi@cabi.org
Website: www.cabi.org

CABI North American Office
875 Massachusetts Avenue
7th Floor
Cambridge, MA 02139
USA

Tel: +1 617 395 4056
Fax: +1 617 354 6875
E-mail: cabi-nao@cabi.org

A catalogue record for this book is available from the British Library, London, UK.

Library of Congress Cataloging-in-Publication Data

Strategic management in tourism / edited by Luiz Moutinho. -- 2nd ed.
      p. cm.
   Includes bibliographical references and index.
   ISBN 978-1-84593-588-7 (alk. paper)
   1. Tourism--Management. I. Moutinho, Luiz. II. Title.
   G155.A1S68 2010
   338.4'791–dc22

                                                                    2010026877

ISBN-13: 978 1 84593 588 7

Commissioning editor: Sarah Hulbert
Production editors: Tracy Head, Simon Hill

Typeset by SPi, Pondicherry, India.
Printed and bound in the UK by Cambridge University Press, Cambridge.

Contents

Contributors

Ronnie Ballantyne, Caledonian Business School, Glasgow Caledonian University, Cowcaddens Road, Glasgow G4 0BA, UK

Enrique Bigné, Universitat de Valencia, Departamento de Comercialización e Investigación de Mercados, Avda de los Naranjos S/N, 46022 Valencia, Spain

Dimitrios Buhalis, Deputy Director, International Centre for Tourism and Hospitality Research (ICTHR), School of Services Management, Bournemouth University, Talbot Campus, Fern Barrow, Poole, Dorset BH12 5BB, UK

Paul Cronje, General Manager, Clyde Travel Management, Kintyre House, 209 Govan Road, Glasgow G51 1HJ, UK

Larry Dwyer, Qantas Professor of Travel and Tourism Economics, School of Economics, University of New South Wales, Sydney, NSW 2052, Australia

Wayne Dwyer, 54 Hillcrest Parade, Miami, Queensland 4220, Australia

Vanessa Yanes Estevez, Dpto Economía y Dirección de Empresas, Universidad de La Laguna, Cº de la Hornera S/N. La Laguna, 38071, Tenerife, Spain

Peter Forsyth, Department of Economics, Monash University, Clayton, Victoria 3800, Australia

Anne-Mette Hjalager, Advance/1, Forskerparken/Science Park, Gustav Wiedsvej 10, DK-8000 Aarhus C, Denmark

Kun-Huang Huarng, Department of International Trade, Library Director, Feng Chia University, 100 Wenhua Road., Seatwen, Taichung 40724, Taiwan, ROC

Jithendran Kokkranikal, Department of Marketing, University of Greenwich Business School, Old Royal Naval College, Park Row, Greenwich, London SE10 9LS, UK

Luiz Moutinho, Foundation Chair of Marketing, Department of Management, University of Glasgow, Gilbert Scott Building, West Quadrangle, Glasgow G12 8QQ, UK

Mercedes Melchior Navarro, Dpto Economía y Dirección de Empresas, Universidad de La Laguna, Cº de la Hornera S/N. La Laguna, 38071, Tenerife, Spain

Eduardo Parra-López, Dr Profesor de Organización de Empresas, Dpto Economía y Dirección de Empresas Universidad de La Laguna, Cº de la Hornera S/N. La Laguna, 38071, Tenerife, Spain

Shirley Rate, Caledonian Business School, Glasgow Caledonian University, Cowcaddens Road, Glasgow G4 0BA, UK

Geoff Southern, Department of Management, University of Glasgow, Gilbert Scott Building, West Quadrangle, Glasgow G12 8QQ, UK

James Wilson, Department of Management, University of Glasgow, Gilbert Scott Building, West Quadrangle, Glasgow G12 8QQ, UK

Jonathan Wilson, Senior Lecturer, Department of Marketing, Events and Tourism, Business School, University of Greenwich, Park Row, Greenwich, London SE10 9LS, UK

Stephen F. Witt, School of Hotel and Tourism Management, The Hong Kong Polytechnic University Hung Hom, Kowloon, Hong Kong

Tiffany Hui-Kuang Yu, Department of Public Finance, Feng Chia University, 100 Wenhua Rd, Seatwen, Taichung 40724, Taiwan, ROC

Preface

Here we are with the second edition of *Strategic Management in Tourism*. It has been a long time, and I would like to apologize to the adopters of the book. Nevertheless, the long wait has meant that the second edition has been able to be designed in terms of new insights, updated concepts and a new articulation of themes.

Part I is now an enlarged element of the text and combines an analysis of the new tourism environment, economic development, tourism forecasting and new trends in tourism. Chapter 1 is reinforced not only by analysing new trends in tourism but also by placing a lens on the new business environment. I also very much welcome a new team of co-authors – R. Ballantyne and S. Rate. With this new team of co-authors, Chapter 2 brings in a new set of concepts and paradigms that are changing the face of the tourism industry. This is a brand new chapter. Chapter 3 is also a new addition to the book, co-authored by three new contributors and led by a prominent scholar in the field. It brings in a much needed appraisal of economic development in tourism. New co-authors have added the application of fuzzy time series to the chapter on tourism forecasting (Chapter 4).

Part II now involves consumer behaviour, strategic innovation, distribution channels, human empowerment, operations management, as well as two new chapters on financial management. Chapter 5 contains new material on consumer behaviour in tourism with a new set of contributors. A whole new chapter is added to the book tackling a very important and 'refreshing' topic – strategic innovation management in tourism (Chapter 6) – by a new contributor, Anne-Mette Hjalager. Another new chapter by Enrique Bigné covers the transformation of distribution channels (Chapter 7). Human resources issues are transformed into human empowerment and are encapsulated in Chapter 8 written by new contributors Jithendran Kokkranikal, Jonathan Wilson and Paul Cronje. Operations management in tourism (Chapter 9) has been revamped and updated by Geoff Southern. Two new chapters on financial management (Chapters 10 and 11) have been added with a new co-author – James Wilson. The new Chapter 11 focuses on the financial impact of tourism marketing.

Part III deals with strategic vision and management in tourism. Chapter 12 combines the areas of strategic planning and performance management. Once again, S. Rate and R. Ballantyne are the new co-authors. Chapter 13 is another brand new chapter on eTourism strategy, authored by the tourism supremo Dimitrios Buhalis. Chapter 14 is yet again a new additional chapter authored by Geoff Southern, covering the critical area of process-based management in tourism. Finally, Chapter 15 is the last novel addition to *Strategic Management in Tourism* and this chapter, written by E. Parra-López, V.Y. Estevez and M.M. Navarro, discusses international strategies in tourism. So, as you can see, apart from updating all the chapters, this new edition contains ten brand new chapters out of a total of 15! It is almost a totally new text.

As a final word, I would like to thank all of those academics who have adopted the book for their classes, as well as the book translations (e.g. into Macedonian and Croatian).

I sincerely hope you enjoy reading and using this brand new edition of *Strategic Management in Tourism*!

Finally, I would like to profusely thank Sylvia Kerrigan for all her help, dedication and friendship over many years, including putting together this text. Furthermore, I would very much like to thank my commissioning editor at CABI, Sarah Hulbert, for all her patience, understanding and assistance related to the completion of this new edition of *Strategic Management in Tourism*.

Many thanks, of course, to all the contributors and my co-authors. You have done a splendid job! My very best to all of you.

Luiz Moutinho
Glasgow, April 2010

To Catriona

chapter 1

The New Business Environment and Trends in Tourism

Luiz Moutinho, Ronnie Ballantyne and Shirley Rate

Understanding the business environment is pivotal to the formulation, development and maintenance of successful management strategy. The new business environment is constantly in flux, ever changing and dynamic in nature. The already rapid pace of change is accelerating – prompted and amplified by a variety of interrelated factors including technological innovations, consumer expectations and the rise of competition. Moreover, although the recent economic downturn coupled with regional uncertainties has impacted upon consumer spend on tourism products the world's economic and social climate is generally predicted to produce a strong increase in tourism over the next 10 years. New markets will emerge due to changing economic conditions, modified consumer behaviour and new technologies. The composition of the tourist population will alter, with increasing proportions of senior citizens, for example. There will be greater emphasis on individual and self-determined holidays and on educational and active recreational pursuits. On the one hand, increasing environmental awareness will affect planning policies and tourist demand. On the other hand, nature, which is the critical resource of tourism, will become more scarce and fragile. An ecological and more sustainable long-term approach to tourism planning is postulated. This chapter provides a rationale for appropriate frameworks to better understand this complex and challenging arena.

Successful new strategic tourism planning initiatives will require that decision makers not only understand historical and contemporary trends and movements in the business environment but will require the ability to predict new key emerging developments and shifts – this will lead to the development of innovative and effective strategies. This chapter then covers recent and probable future trends in tourism. The aim is not to present a definitive picture of developments over this period. It is far more important for this scenario to help the planners concerned with tourism to come to terms with future changes than merely to describe future conditions. Thus, we must examine any distinguishable and important trends with a view to answering the question: 'What decisions have to be taken now or in the coming years to make adjustment to these trends possible and in good time?'

In terms of the tourism arena, the relationship between the providers of tourism and travel services and the marketing environment in which they operate is unique. For most other businesses, the boundary between the company and the 'world outside' is distinct. For manufacturers, there is one world within the factory gates, and another beyond them. For most service providers there is a distinct location at which the service encounter takes place and can be managed. Changes in the world outside will affect such companies together with their customers and their competitors; but usually, with a little planning and some juggling of the marketing mix when necessary, the effect of external change can be diluted enough to allow most businesses to continue 'as usual' within their own four walls. In contrast, within tourism, the service encounter with a customer can occur within a journey which stretches from one side of the globe to the other and back again. The whole planet is the 'factory floor' of the tourism industry. While for other industries factors such as the physical environment or culture of a region may influence the nature of demand, they are a vital component of the **tourist** product itself. For tourism and travel providers there is no place to hide from the turbulent and unpredictable world in which we live (Gee *et al.*, 1994).

The special relationship between the tourism industry and its marketing environment means that the depth of understanding needed concerning the influence of the environment goes far beyond that which suffices for many other industries. The external environment of any industry contains a myriad of interdependent factors which need to be somehow separated out and categorized to make analysis of them possible. One of the simplest but most enduring frameworks for this analysis is the PEST framework which prompts companies to consider Political, Economic, Social and Technical factors which may affect their company. This is a traditional methodology and is rather a broad-brush form of analysis which, although adequate for industries less vulnerable to environmentally related disruption, is scarcely adequate for tourism providers.

To fully understand the new business environment, a more comprehensive approach is required. It is proposed that a new framework which better fits the nature of the tourism industry is applied to tourist environments. SCEPTICAL analysis considers environmental influences in terms of:

Social factors
Cultural factors
Economic factors
Physical factors
Technical factors
International factors
Communications and infrastructure factors
Administrative and institutional factors
Legal and political factors

This framework provides a more robust structure for understanding the complex business environment in which tourism providers operate.

Each of these categories may be the source of changes which present tourism operators with significant opportunities and threats. As with any form of environmental analysis, the difficult part is not in seeing what is happening in the world beyond the industry's doors. The real challenge lies in disentangling the elements of threat from the elements of opportunity within the changes in the wider world and in distinguishing the temporary 'blips' from the significant environmental shifts. Finally, and above all, it lies in deciding what to do in the face of a changing and uncertain environment.

SOCIAL FACTORS

Tourism is essentially a social phenomenon and, although like all industries it is influenced by the society in which it exists, tourism is unusual in that it involves a large-scale, if temporary, transfer of individuals between different societies. This can create social change of both a temporary and a longer-term nature. Anyone who has visited Paris regularly will know that the city's character changes radically in August, when vast sections of the Parisian population go on vacation and are replaced by a mass influx of tourists. In other industries, customers and their needs shape the nature of companies' marketing strategies and the product offerings. In tourism, customers and their needs can actually shape the society which they visit.

Demographic change

Currently some 78 million people are added to the global population each year. There are now around 6 billion people sharing the planet, and many population experts predict that this will increase to at least 8–10 billion (some time between 2020 and 2050) before global growth stabilizes. The startling reality is that over 90% of this growth will be in developing countries. As the populations of North America, Europe and Japan grow relatively smaller and older, the rest of the world is increasing rapidly and is getting younger. Very soon over 80% of those between 15 and 24 years of age will live in developing countries; in contrast, in Western Europe, one in three adults will be over 55. This 'developing countries boom–developed countries bust' demographic scenario has a wide range of societal, economic and environmental implications, and also significant implications for tourism. In particular for tourism marketers:

1. Global demographic changes must be reflected in planning and decision making with respect to the design, development, delivery and utilization of tourism facilities and services.
2. There is a need to encourage and support research to evaluate the needs of the growing population of older people worldwide. Mass market tourism has grown up with the assumption that the majority of its potential customers are relatively young, active and healthy. Demographic change will inevitably shift the age profile of the customer base, and may require substantial modifications to facility design, tour packaging and event organization. It may also require new initiatives to link tourism services to other services such as health care requirements. The level and nature of demand for tourism and travel are currently being affected by a number of demographic influences, discussed below, most of which seem set to continue or intensify in the foreseeable future.

The democratization of tourism

One of the most important demographically related changes is the 'democratization' of tourism. On a global scale, the socio-economic categories applied to individual nations become relatively meaningless since there are effectively two social groups: (i) the enfranchised members of the consumer society; and (ii) the disenfranchised poor (Durning, 1992). For the poor of the world, travel is usually undertaken for survival, and tourism is not an option. Among consumers, the opportunities for tourism have spread widely. The global economy is evolving in such a way that each of the industrialized nations has a solid, prosperous 'middle-class' core population. That in turn is being joined by significant middle-class populations in virtually every other country of the world. This middle class is relatively well educated and prosperous, and increasingly has discretionary money for recreation and leisure. In countries such as India or Indonesia, this middle-class 'crust' is quite thin, but its absolute numbers are large enough to offer plenty of potential tourism business. So, although many in the world are excluded from opportunities for travel and tourism, a process of 'democratization' of tourism is under way as it reaches many new consumers.

Global urbanization

Global urbanization is another significant demographic shift starting in the 20th century, and one that has a variety of effects for tourism providers. In 1950 there were around 600 million city dwellers. United Nations (UN) Population Fund estimates suggest that by 2030 more than 60% of the population will live in urban areas. Formerly rural countries such as India, parts of Latin America and Africa are rapidly urbanizing, throwing off-balance their farm economies and wreaking havoc on physical and social support systems. The millennium begins with around half of all humanity residing in urban areas; UN figures suggest that they are increasingly living in 'megacities' of over 10 million people. The number of such cities has grown from two in 1960 to 17 today and is projected to reach 26 by 2015, 22 in less-developed regions and 18 in Asia.

This rapid urban influx of millions in search of work does not provide ideal conditions for tourism services and resources. Resulting increases in congestion, pollution, poverty, unemployment and crime can all have a significant impact on the demand for tourism. Relatively affluent tourists traditionally have not been taught to notice or understand the economic realities of poverty around them (as witnessed by the contents of conventional travel guides and literature). Will tourists themselves demand a better understanding of the life that lies so close to their luxury hotels and beaches? Will they wish to be educated as well as entertained? Perhaps instead they will simply try to stay away from the megacities with their 'belts of human misery' that make well-to-do visitors feel unsafe and uncomfortable.

The outflow of people from rural areas typically contributes to the stagnation of local rural economies which has the effect of increasing the pressures for tourism development to compensate. Many rural areas are seeking to integrate tourism with more traditional rural activities such as farming. Certain government policies are now providing economic incentives for citizens to move back to the countryside. Tourism will aid this redistribution by offering more travel experiences in rural and out-of-the-way places as yet untapped for their tourism potential.

CULTURAL FACTORS

Research carried out in several countries, in particular a large-scale study by the Stanford Research Institute in California, USA, indicates that there is a clearly defined trend away from an 'outward-directed' lifestyle towards 'inward-directed' and 'integrated' values. Several recent studies indicate that 'post-materialistic values', in other words, growing non-materialistic needs, environmental care, diminishing concerns about career, prestige and status, etc., will gain in importance. In effect, the classic 'It's all about me' philosophy of consumption is increasingly being challenged by 'it's all about us', for example volunteerism and 'giving back'. Within traditional product-based marketing we are witnessing an ever-growing trend towards societal marketing whereby the corporation and the brands it represents wish to be perceived as wholesome and caring – this is a key trend that has been mirrored and will also continue to grow in the consumption of tourism-related products. A process of rehumanization and philanthropy is replacing the pursuit of physical beauty, material possessions and hedonism. Increasingly, we are witnessing the rise of altruistic consumption where more consumers experience a change or shift in 'awareness' or indeed consciousness. In response to this we will see the rise of voluntary simplicity: a move towards a way of life that is outwardly simple and inwardly rich, a trend towards simplification in lifestyles. After many years of being oppressed and obsessed with acquiring things, a large population segment has grown tired of this and may be ready to slow down and simplify. New luxuries will become time and simplicity, 'stillness' and peace of mind – intangibles like purpose, meaning, fulfilment and quality of life are gaining importance. These intangible luxuries are a response to the longing for an island of calm in a turbulent word. This movement will need to be reflected in the type of tourism products offered.

It must be stressed that classic materialistic lifestyles will not vanish, but an increasing polarization between exponents of material and non-material values is likely to take place. At the other end of the spectrum, uber premium or 'ultraluxe' will continue to develop. The rise of a global elite should ensure that the ultraluxe will grow and grow. These status-craving consumers are hunting down the next wave in uber-exclusive goods, services and experiences that are truly out of reach of the masses now that massclusivity has commoditized all but the most luxurious products on earth. Recent emerging examples of 'ultraluxe' include Virgin's out-of-atmosphere flights or Dubai's seven star luxury hotels with underwater suites.

In terms of the masses, there is a strong trend leading away from standardization towards an ever-greater diversity in lifestyles inciting new approaches to life and recreation and the rise of customization in tourist product offerings. The limits of mass tourism are recognizable not only from the quantitative but also from the qualitative point of view. The following trends are apparent and are probably of a long-term nature:

- Further increasing differentiation and pluralization of demand.
- The emergence of new specialized markets and market segments.
- A decrease of physically and culturally passive forms of vacation in favour of more active pastimes, such as high adrenalin, fantasy adventure or thrill-seeking activities and a shift towards maximizing individual liberty in recombining elements to produce custom-made holiday packages (modular product design). This has been mirrored in the shift and evolution of the travel agent towards travel adviser – offering expertise and counselling.
- The growing need for non-standardized services and individualized tourist behaviour is directly linked to the quest for self-determination (emancipation) and 'do-it-yourself' or 'maxi marketing' whereby customized, tailored solutions are developed for the individual – this is a key trend that is likely to accelerate and intensify.
- The advanced level of travel experience in the population, which goes hand in hand with more selective, critical and quality-oriented approaches to individual holiday planning as well as growing sophistication of demand and rationality of choice.
- An increasing desire to relate to nature, to gain first-hand experience and to engage in active pastimes (e.g. hobby holidays, trekking holidays, farm tourism).
- Higher levels of environmental consciousness and sensitivity to the quality of life in general.
- The increasing effort to learn, which often manifests itself in serious attempts to get to know foreign cultures.

The suppliers of tourist services will increasingly offer service packages that directly address specific customer problems and provide travellers with more opportunity to shape their holidays as they wish. Activities, experiences, participation and learning will all be key elements in the future. Adventure holidays, sports and health trips, sabbaticals and learning holidays will all become more popular. This desire for the experiential will give rise to a new tribe of consumers – 'transumers'. Transumers are consumers driven by experience instead of the 'fixed' traditional tourism offerings, driven by entertainment, by discovery, by fighting boredom, increasingly living a transient lifestyle, freeing themselves from the hassles of permanent ownership and possessions. The demand for 'soft' forms of transport and tourism, including 'back-to-nature' activities, will show a marked increase. An increasing number of tourists will look for a holistic type of recreation, in search of an 'overall balance' of body, soul and mind. More and more travellers will define their concept of a 'rich holiday' in terms of the depth rather than in terms of the diversity of their travel experiences.

Not only will the worldwide travel market itself be characterized by an ever-greater range of possible types of travel and destinations, but substitutional competition will also continue to increase. The range of alternative uses to which free time can be put is constantly expanding, a trend which is likely to continue over the next 20 years. Apart from travel, these options can be characterized by leisure within the home or in the vicinity. Of particular interest are the Internet and gaming pursuits. Also leisure-oriented design of living space, children's playgrounds near to dwellings, public leisure facilities in residential areas, centres or leisure parks, green belt areas around cities will all be central to current education and further training. To a certain extent, and an ever-increasing one, life is becoming a permanent learning process owing to the rapid rate of change in professional structures and technologies. The spectrum of educational facilities and opportunities is being continually enriched, even though the educational and professional routes are being further formalized under the direction of public institutions. Nevertheless, there is a clear trend towards the pluralization and liberalization of education and training in general, thanks to private initiatives. This applies to all levels, from primary school to university, but especially to training in specific technologies, skills or professional profiles. Schools of the future will not be institutions for imparting knowledge so much as integrated centres for education, culture and leisure. Leisure time will be used much more for productive purposes, in which context the following variants are relevant:

1. Paid work to increase disposable income.
2. Home-based production, which means not only a greater degree of tasks 'delegated' by industry to the consumer (such as collecting, assembling, repairing and maintaining products) but also increased production of an agricultural or handicraft type. This type of production is often carried out on a community basis.
3. Sociocultural involvement: this category includes all types of social, political and cultural involvement. The social cooperation networks, which even today are expanding rapidly and which in 20 years are likely to supply a significant proportion of social services, are a prominent example.

In view of the expansion of the 'informal' economy and a certain shift, for technological reasons, of professional activities to the traditional domicile, the boundaries between leisure time, work and living are becoming increasingly hazy. Innovations in the Internet, wireless laptop technology and mobile phone technology and the continuing convergence of technology platforms (e.g. the Apple iphone 'Apps') allow for a 'flow society' – the 21st-century consumer has increased flexibility to work and play while on the move. Also, the individual will have more opportunities to arrange his or her working hours and leisure time as required.

Reinforcing that, there are increasing signs that a shift away from a work-obsessed lifestyle is becoming a significant trend – time is the new currency. Flexitime, job-splitting, job-sharing, individual arrangements regarding holidays and pensions, etc., will become more common-place. There is a growing recognition of the value of cultural diversity (possibly a reaction to globalization and increasingly cosmopolitan societies). Parallel with this recognition is a desire to maintain and foster the special and unique characteristics of ethnic groups and host societies as a fundamental principle of tourism development and promotion.

ECONOMIC FACTORS

Tourism as an industry can and does have significant impacts on an economy's growth. For governments, foreign exchange earnings, income and employment generation are the key drivers of economic growth which influence and encourage investment in the industry. However, the growth of the industry is reliant on a number of factors.

Global economic conditions

Disposable income level is the economic factor seen as the most important, but other economic factors are also important. Tourism expenditure has been shown to be affected by levels of employment in service industries and links have been made between tourism expenditure and house prices. Shifts within the global economy will appreciably influence the level of tourism and travel demand, particularly within the triad of major world markets, the USA, Japan and Europe, home to the majority of the world's tourists. Thus, the strength of these economies, their currency and stock market volatility drives the conditions for global tourism.

Inevitably, demand and production of supply are highly dependent on the conditions of the global economy. As mentioned, global economic downturns tend to have a direct impact on expenditure on personal travel and tourism. Recent economic pressures have resulted in many countries, including emerging markets, experiencing a contraction in tourism demand.

Under such conditions, world trade declines, travellers cut costs by choosing to holiday in their own countries for shorter periods of time. This has produced a new form of holiday type – the 'staycation' whereby consumers are utilizing leisure and tourism services close to or indeed in the home. Alternatively, consumers will choose international destinations with the most attractive exchange rate. Thus international demand particularly suffers. Nevertheless, predictions for the growth of the global tourism industry are optimistic. According to the World Travel and Tourism Council (WTTC) the industry will experience a steady phase of growth, 4.4% per annum to 2018 at which point the industry will represent 10.5% of global gross domestic product (GDP) supporting 297 million jobs. They forecast an 86.5% increase in personal travel and tourism expenditure in the decade to 2018 (WTTC, 2010).

Yet currently in developed countries the economic perspective is generally one of greatly decelerated growth and plateauing disposable per capita incomes. The desire to travel in these countries is approaching saturation levels and sensitivity to price levels is therefore increasing. The limits to tourist expansion are already detectable. Furthermore, the problems of the major world markets, higher fuel costs and increasing demands to address fossil fuel consumption and climate change will persist in challenging growth in an energy-reliant industry. Despite this, emerging countries will continue to expand, both as tourism destinations and as traveller markets, thus it is these regions which will contribute to overall growth. Africa, Asia Pacific, in particular China, and the Middle East are experiencing higher growth rates than the world average while the USA and Europe will fall below that average and will continue to do so in the following decade. While long-haul flights by Europeans will expand less than forecast, this is unlikely to jeopardize the growth of these emerging markets due to the enormous 'internal' potential of these regions. This 'unfolding fan' of opportunity will spur transnational travel and hotel companies to expand to nearly every major gateway city in the Asia-Pacific region.

Demand and supply

As well as determining the growth and size of the industry, economic conditions will drive the level and nature of personal spending on travelling and tourism activity and in turn the nature of demand and supply. Personal expenditure on tourism is driven by cost-to-income comparisons. As such, factors such as GDP, inflation, interest rates, unemployment and disposable income all affect consumption and thus demand and supply of the industry. Despite recent economic pressures, the industry remains one of the biggest contributors to global GDP and optimistic forecasts suggest it will continue to grow. Thus, the competition for international tourists will almost certainly intensify in the coming years with more people having the time, money and preference to travel, and more governments around the world seeking to maximize the potential of the tourism industry through attracting international tourists. Such forecasts of increased tourism activity are based on the assumption that tourism facilities such as attractions, accommodation and transport are expanded and upgraded to meet demand.

Current and forecasts of future competition from new developing destinations and facilities has led to the increased power of the buyer which has dictated the nature of supply. In any market, choice leads to buying power; however, this is compounded further through technological advances allowing consumers to share assessment of tourist experiences worldwide. Such power and access to information have inevitably led to decreases in prices and as such the industry has experienced significant structural changes. There has been an exponential increase in the budget accommodation and airline sectors while first-class passenger numbers are falling. The concept of the package holiday continues to decrease as consumers demand to arrange holidays independently – the new 'prosumer' demands and enjoys more control over their consumption. Destination figures would imply that choice is driven by favourable exchange rates. A price-elastic tourist demand need not necessarily imply an end to all travel – after all travel has come close to being a 'basic need' – but it will continue to drive the demand for cheaper holidays and will inevitably result in significant shifts in market shares among various countries.

PHYSICAL FACTORS – ECOLOGICAL ASPECTS

Concern for the environment will in the future be far more widespread among the population than it is today. A growing awareness of environmental factors and sustainability will continue to increase and intensify. Over time this will become a dominant factor in terms of influencing consumer decision making and ultimate consumer choice. This growing appreciation that humankind and the natural environment share a common fate is promoting a conservationist approach at many levels. Even today, we can see an increasing environmental awareness in public opinion. This manifests itself in a growing tendency to reject those foreign tourist spots which have already exceeded their tolerance levels, not only in the opinion of the experts but also from the point of view of the consumer.

The implication is then clear – the tourism industry must begin to integrate these environmental concerns into their planning, operations and policies. Individual strands of tourism such as 'ecotourism' or 'ecological tourism' already exist and will continue to prosper – the growing awareness of environmental concerns coupled with a strong consumer movement towards a more ecological and socially conscious consumer-based standpoint will clearly nurture the continued development of low impact, responsible travel to fragile destinations. However, the implications are broader – as this movement becomes the norm there is increased need to factor in ecological aspects in mainstream mass tourism planning.

The inhabitants of mass tourist areas, some of whom have exchanged their initial euphoria at the influx of tourists for blatant resistance, will increasingly adopt realistic strategies to retain their independence and protect their environment. For example the dilemma facing mountain regions, concerning the balance between destruction of the landscape by tourist monoculture and desolation on account of depopulation, will be handled better than it is today, by means of multifaceted development, that is revalorization of mountain farming, including unconventional methods such as game farming, vegetable cultures and blending with other branches of the economy. The planning authorities and political institutions, thanks largely to the pressure of public opinion, will contribute to development in the interests of humans and the environment, by defining appropriate planning guidelines and ensuring that they are followed.

Destruction of natural resources vital to tourism will not be stopped immediately. As a consequence, decline of some traditional destination areas (due to gradual spoilage or, in some cases, due to environmental catastrophes) and rise of 'substitutes' in unspoiled surroundings will probably continue to a certain extent. Furthermore, artificial leisure environments will be created as a partial (and weak) compensation for the degraded natural milieu. Such developments will continue until society has implemented tourism strategies which reconcile man and nature. On the other hand, growing environmental sensitivity is likely to stimulate substantial efforts to protect, conserve and upgrade the natural as well as the sociocultural milieu. The demand for 'soft' forms of tourism will continue to grow as the environment spreads across the consciousness of the wider population.

Hopefully, on the supply side, a change towards a long-term planning mentality, which should substitute for short-sighted profit maximization, will take place. In recent times some tourism providers have utilized misguided strategies such as 'greenwashing', to exploit the raised awareness of environmental factors – where particular tourism initiatives are positioned as sustainable and environmentally friendly. These disguised tourism schemes only lead to short-term profit. Responsible future tourism programmes must seek to move away from conventional tourism modelling towards a more sustainable perspective. Even the best hotels and restaurants in tourist resorts can only thrive if they are part of an intact and sustainable environment. An ecologically viable strategy is the prime requisite for success. As far as the provision of accommodation facilities is concerned, a dramatic rearrangement of priorities, due to growing environmental awareness, has already begun. If in the past the emphasis was on the erection of new buildings, the future should see a comprehensive programme of renovation. The transformation of historic buildings or other old buildings into training and leisure establishments, and the shaping of the environment to accommodate leisure activities, both in the home and in its close proximity, will continue to gain considerably in importance.

International travel has grown by more than 500% in the past 25 years, according to the WTTC. As a consequence, there has been a substantial increase in the number of hotels built across the globe. But there is also evidence of a growing concern among both leisure and business travellers about the damage being done to the environment by tourism. And, increasingly, travellers are taking these concerns into account when they book holidays or business trips. When the world's biggest hotel chain, Holiday Inn, surveyed its guests, 78% of them said they were very concerned about the environment and 28% said they took environmental policies into consideration when choosing their hotel.

TECHNICAL FACTORS – TECHNOLOGICAL ASPECTS

A new 'marketsphere' has emerged – a technology-driven borderless world with fragmenting media and diverse customers resistant to traditional push marketing is now a reality. There are now endless opportunities for increased integration, synthesis and synergies between marketing and technology. Technological developments are changing the way that tourism providers are interacting with customers and are indeed altering the intrinsic make-up of the tourism product – we are witnessing the birth of a new age in tourism. This social revolution needs to be understood, but what needs to be driven home even more is that tourism operators and related companies who continue to deliver mediocre or bad experiences will find themselves in a downward spiral, fuelled by a digital revolution that has empowered the consumer.

In particular tourism operators must pay attention to the rise of the prosumer. The prosumer is one who is actively involved in the design of the product – ever-increasing levels of Internet interactivity have underpinned and nurtured this movement. Consumers can now actively and deliberately take part in the process of design, shaping or even producing a product or service knowing it is for them. Increasingly consumers are becoming active participants instead of passive audience members. This development may necessitate a shift in thinking in terms of how tourism providers build and nurture relationships with their customers, moving away from classic customer relationship management (CRM) towards customer managed relationships whereby the consumers' leverage and ability to influence control on the design and delivery of the tourism product challenge the balance of power between provider and consumer.

In terms of the provision of current tourism products, new technologies have given rise to new business models utilizing new sales and distribution systems. Electronic distribution has led to dramatic structural change including substitution of existing traditional sales channels. Historically, the Imholz travel agency, which a few years ago almost completely replaced the traditional booking of holidays in branch offices by telephone bookings, was a precursor of this development. Online bookings over the Internet are now commonplace. The emergence of low-cost airlines such as Easyjet or Ryanair in Europe – where further computerization has stimulated innovation and dictated structural changes among airlines and travel agents – has allowed consumers to develop and manage their own itineraries and in effect become their own travel agent. Furthermore, it is now commonplace for all airlines to offer this facility. 'Traditional' airlines such as British Airways now offer online booking. Clearly benefits exist for both providers and users in terms of accessibility and reduction in costs. Nevertheless the rise of the click culture seriously challenges the role of the traditional travel agent – the travel agent must market expertise and knowledge and in particular trust and security; the ability to provide solutions if things go wrong – stressing the human element. In effect, computerized services will also breed new opportunities for those travel agents who are willing to change and evolve – they must succeed in counselling their customers better. The new technologies will enable further specialization. New types of travel agencies will emerge, these pioneers will have the character of consulting rather than of booking agencies, using information systems to design individualized travel packages from available offers (Buhalis and Licata, 2002).

The digital revolution has also primed changes in consumer expectations regarding the acquisition of information. Consumers are in a demanding 'ready-to-go, ready-to-know' state of mind, expecting any information deemed relevant to be available instantly, in their own terms. Think of it as the Google effect (demanding and getting instant answers) permeating all aspects of daily life. This ready-to-know state of mind has induced **'infolust'** whereby experienced consumers are lusting after detailed information on where to get the best of the best, the cheapest of the cheap, the first of the first, the healthiest of the healthy, the coolest of the cool or on how to become the smartest of the smart. Instant information gratification is upon us. This technology-driven trend has serious implications for all strands of tourism – Web presence must be maintained and constantly updated. Of particular importance is website optimization – the order of retrieval or recall by browsers must be managed carefully as it is unlikely that 'ready-to-know' consumers will venture much further than the first ten 'hits' returned by Google or other search engines when undertaking information searches or choosing tourism products. As such, tourism operators must invest in this arena to ensure salience within the virtual domain.

Classically when one considers tourism one imagines experience and travel within the physical world – and the associated acquisition, usage and disposal of products and services that facilitate this. However, as we progress through the 21st century we must pay attention to the ongoing outputs of the 'digital revolution'. The rise of social networking platforms including Facebook, Twitter, YouTube, bebo and My Space allows individuals to interact and share their views and experiences with potentially unrestricted virtual communities (Stepchenkova *et al.*, 2007). There are important implications here for viral marketing – word of mouth/word of net – and for shifts in perceptions of leisure time. One step further is the virtual world of second life – where one can adopt another identity – cultivating another personality via an avatar and interacting with other virtual beings. The implication is clear: these modes of substitutional competition are becoming more desirable – home is hot! The home increasingly will offer a multidimensional point of experience – no longer simply a place of shelter but a decompression zone, where a variety of leisure and virtual tourism pursuits can be enjoyed – including virtual tourism, virtual gaming and virtual reality (VR) shopping. Enhanced three-dimensional representation coupled with the ease of use and 24 hour access will have considerable attraction to particular groups – those that have already moved towards cocooning or hiving in response to the fear of terrorism will gravitate even more towards these virtual innovations in leisure and tourism products (Wang *et al.*, 2002). Put simply, why leave home to experience 'tourism' if you can experience it in the safety of your home at your convenience? Furthermore, as many consumers are increasingly 'time-and-effort' starved, solutions that offer satisfaction via a combination of time minimization and effort minimization will continue to intensify in demand. The utilization of the Internet and ultimately VR technology are and will continue to be seen as important tools in 'time minimization' and 'evaluation of alternatives' factors within the consumers' decision-making process. Furthermore an increasing proportion of professional work will not be site-dependent. This leads not only to new forms of social organization and interaction but also to a certain shift of professional activity to the home of the working individual. Thus, the boundaries between work, living and leisure time become less rigidly defined (Cheong, 1995). As a consequence, significant groups of consumers who historically would have little or no motivation to participate in virtual forms of leisure and tourism may now utilize these new platforms to gain respite from work. In terms of the structure, technology has played a significant role in altering the shape of various tourism industries (Buhalis, 2003). This is particularly the case for the airline business, where further technological advances will stimulate innovation and dictate structural changes among airlines and travel agents. The quest for more efficient distribution has led to new alliances within and between firms of this sector. Others who have not kept up with the digital revolution have suffered. Technology has also led to increasing integration between the different sectors of the industry. It has fostered the growth of bigger organizations covering more aspects of tourism creating a new '**transpitality**' industry. Although considerable vertical and horizontal integration does now exist, it is likely that further consolidation of companies in all sectors will continue with increasing economic concentration in a small number of large companies. Furthermore, some of these companies will combine across sectors creating new '**diagonal marketing systems**'. These large corporations are likely to secure greater shares of the markets in which they operate, and there is no evidence that limits to economies of scale have yet been reached.

INTERNATIONAL FACTORS

The tourism industry is one of the oldest in the world and its evolution has largely been dictated by developments in travel and transport. The concept of international travel turned the industry into a global entity where international operations dominate. Inevitably, all industries that span international boundaries are concerned with international relations. Now the most international of all industries, the relationship between different countries around the entire globe should be of great concern to those in travel and tourism. As such, the developments and changes in relations between countries often form a critical aspect of continuous environmental scanning for those in the tourism industry. This is because of the significant impact relationships between countries can have on the operation of tourist organizations. International tensions between governments can deter tourists from venturing to particular destinations and can create barriers to travel, in the form of visa restrictions, for example. Additionally, terrorist activities in the USA and Indonesia and more recently in London and Turkey have placed extraordinary pressure on international relations. In contrast, recent years have witnessed some extraordinary changes within regions such as Eastern Europe and the Middle East, providing many opportunities for growth in new markets. Over the years, political change has played a significant role in international relations and global tourism. We have witnessed the opportunities for realizing the demand for travel to Eastern European countries and the former Soviet Union as the Cold War thawed. Similar growth has been seen in destinations which have survived political instability and conflict such as Vietnam, the former Yugoslavian states and South African countries. As barriers to trade and overseas investment are removed and the free movement of labour has been instigated, tourism in such areas has thrived. General political approaches to tourism have also dictated the nature of international relations and global travel. Governments can have a positive influence on tourism with the implementation of policies and infrastructure making countries attractive to tourists and allowing citizens to travel. The opening up of Eastern Europe has increased the potential for their citizens to travel, but it has also seen the birth of a new form of cultural and urban tourism. In the European Union (EU) and the USA there are many people with roots in Eastern Europe who find it appealing to engage in tourism in order to rediscover the lands of their ancestors. These are exciting opportunities and often attractive in terms of cost as new destinations are in the early stages of development. The last decade has witnessed many changes in international relations which have tended to promote tourism, as countries have come together either driven by political will or by economic forces. International cooperation is an increasingly important aspect of tourism development. Sometimes this comes in the form of reciprocal marketing alliances between countries, while in other cases it is part of the pattern of international aid and development support, exemplified by the EU's support for tourism development in Africa, the Caribbean and the Pacific. The benefits of these alliances to such regions include access to investment for education as well as infrastructure with the long-term opportunity to increase employment and grow their economies. Meanwhile, those tourism organizations which involve themselves in developing countries gain access to new and exciting destinations and opportunities to grow their international markets as well as globalizing their brands. Evidence of the true benefit of these international relations for developing countries has yet to be shown; however, it is clear that the growth of the tourism industry is tied to the nature of global relationships.

COMMUNICATION AND INFRASTRUCTURE FACTORS

Tourism providers are typically very dependent on an existing infrastructure to handle travel, hospitality and communication. Although tourism is viewed as an intangible service business, the investment in infrastructure needed to support many tourism products would dwarf the capital expenditure of all but the most global manufacturers.

Transport

In tourism terms, transport can have a variety of functions such as the destination itself in the case of rail and cruise travel. However, in the context of developing tourism destinations and the critical role of infrastructure, transport takes the meaning of derived demand; it is a necessary means of moving from origin to destination. Although travel and tourism are services, the importance of physical distribution within the industry makes it much more akin to those involving physical products. The requirement to move people around the world and within their destination areas, quickly, punctually and comfortably requires considerable support in terms of infrastructure. Infrastructure to serve all major forms of transport continues to expand with the network of cities and towns served by air travel and high-speed road and rail links. Recent developments have involved the move towards integration of infrastructure in a bid to manage the quality and communication between providers and to provide a seamless travel experience for the tourist.

Infrastructure development generally tends to lag behind the expansion of tourism and travel, which can lead to bottlenecks and overloads. With respect to air travel, congestion in the skies and on the ground already exists and is increasing. This is due to the accessibility of air travel, the growth of business travel and the increase in the low-cost airline sector. But, while the popularity of air travel has significantly increased, the growth of the world's airports has, in comparison, proceeded very slowly. Destination management requires government policies which allow growth and reduce congestion. However, pressures on governments continue to grow with respect to sustainability, carbon emissions and security and safety. In addition, developments in communications technology are expected to impact upon business travel demand in the longer term. Thus, the concept of transport infrastructure is a constantly changing one which will continue to evolve due to technology and global concerns for sustainable travel.

Accommodation

Accommodation, including location, facilities and related services, plays a substantial part in the overall tourist experience; thus it can have a positive or negative impact on the variety of other organizations involved in the tourism infrastructure. While the destination itself plus its attractions tends to be the driving motivator to travel, there are few factors that can deter future tourists as easily as stories of unavailable, half-finished or inadequate accommodation. The new age of technology and service review is such that people have access to and motivation for disseminating stories about their travel experiences – good and bad. Nevertheless, the growth of the industry has demanded the growth in bricks and mortar. The development of accommodation, however, is not necessarily straightforward. The industry is restricted by the governmental policies for growth in that specific area of the economy. Furthermore, legislation often places restrictions on the specific construction and location of buildings and facilities. Nevertheless, the industry has prospered on a global scale due to emerging economies and destinations such as China, India and Eastern Europe. Also, the industry has long utilized technology, more recently the Internet, in offering the consumer a cohesive experience in terms of reservations and communications. This, added to mergers and acquisitions, management approaches such as franchising, strategic alliances and joint ventures and more sophisticated segmenting, branding and pricing strategies, has allowed the industry to prosper.

Facilities/attractions

Far more than accommodation, destination choice is influenced by the availability, reputation and quality of the tourist attractions offered. Attractions and other specific facilities also play a key role in determining purchasing decisions during the stay, and many regions are recognizing the importance of such infrastructural developments in the local economy. As such, a robust and integrated set of attractions is a critical element for a tourism infrastructure to provide the combination of offerings the consumer demands as well as fostering related spending within the local community. As the networks of transport improve and general lifestyles change, there is a distinct trend of tourists taking more but shorter breaks per year and fewer long holidays. This trend is driven by population changes, changes in lifestyle and leisure patterns and a general growth in disposable income. As such, the demand for breaks to be interesting and entertaining will mean that the number and variety of attractions will have to increase to satiate this need.

ADMINISTRATIVE AND INSTITUTIONAL FACTORS

For any form of business the environment will contain a wide range of institutions which can influence the operation and development of their business. For tourism the number of institutions with an interest in, and potential influence on, the industry is vast and includes:

- *Trade unions.* Within the tourism industry, trade unions have not had a great deal of influence in relation to hospitality where wage rates, skill levels and union bargaining power are typically low, but they have exerted considerable influence on the transport services which tourism depends on. Strikes among airline or airport staff at peak holiday times have been a common occurrence over the last 20 years and responses to the global recession such as pay cuts and redundancies have amplified trade union activities and the ensuing problems for the tourism industry.
- *Academic institutions.* As an academic discipline, tourism is still relatively young and thus in its infancy in terms of development compared with some disciplines and sectoral research. That said, already the work of academics is influencing the decision-making processes within tourism, covering issues of planning, service delivery and marketing.
- *Local government.* Although national governments take considerable interest in tourism as a contributor to the economy, the onus for the promotion, control and management of tourism development is frequently devolved to local government level. Local government administrators have the particularly difficult task of trying to attract tourists into their region in pursuit of the economic benefits that they bring, while protecting the quality of life of the local population that elected them (Hall and Jenkins, 1996).
- *National tourism organizations* (NTOs). Although there are some very large players within the airline, tour-operator or hotel-chain sectors of the industry, tourism is a complex and fragmented industry. For this reason issues of planning, research and promotion for specific destinations are typically handled by NTOs at a national level, and often by similar smaller-scale agencies at a local and regional level.

- *Consumer groups.* Travel is a major item of expenditure for many households, and it also offers almost unprecedented opportunities for the creation of consumer dissatisfaction. A holidaymaker is, by definition, away from home and is therefore deprived of the comforts and support networks that 'home' entails. This tends to exacerbate holiday problems since they cannot easily be escaped and can render a major investment something to be endured instead of enjoyed. For this reason, groups such as the Consumers' Association have taken an increasing interest in tourism and travel products, and there are now numerous published guides, online reviews and television programmes which provide consumers with information to assist their purchasing decisions.
- *Special interest groups.* The size of the tourism and travel industry means that it attracts the attention of an enormous number of special interest groups. Other types of group will try to influence the tourism industry on an issue-by-issue basis, and will include groups relating to the environment, rights for specific sections of the population, cultural heritage and local businesses.
- *Law enforcement agencies.* The potential for tourists to become targets for criminal activities, combined with a desire among tourism operators and agencies to prevent crime levels acting as a deterrent to tourists, has tended to bring tourism operators and law enforcement agencies closer together.
- *Organized religion.* Although the influence of organized religion has lessened in the majority of developed countries, it continues to be an important sociocultural influence. Policies and pronouncements that encourage pilgrimage or which designate places as sacred can stimulate tourism, but religion can also react against the influence of tourism in an area where it is perceived to be threatening.

LEGAL AND POLITICAL FACTORS

The nature and development of tourism in any country are largely the result of its government's ideology on this facet of economic activity. While the private sector can and does play a significant role across a broad spectrum of sectors including transport, accommodation and attractions, a government will control its growth and development through its investment, infrastructure and regulation. Government intervention is necessary to ensure that the associated benefits of tourism are maximized and any potential problems are minimized for the benefit of the economy, society and environment, as well as for the long-term interest of the tourism industry itself. Whether the government opts merely for the creation of a climate conducive to the growth of a successful tourism industry, or decides to become more actively involved, perhaps even assuming an entrepreneurial role, intervention by the government should not merely be a manifestation of political rhetoric, but rather an organized, sustained and flexible approach to tourism planning with the aim of optimizing its social and economic returns.

Tourism is simply too important for governments to leave to market forces, as both the positive and the negative economic and social impacts of tourism are such that there is a necessity for some form of intervention (Lickorish and Jenkins, 1997). Nevertheless, levels of intervention as well as the nature of intervention can vary widely across countries.

There are many factors affecting the nature of a government's involvement in its country's tourism activities. Its particular ideology, its dependence upon tourism for economic survival, where tourism has recently grown to become a significant factor in its economy, where a country's community, heritage or environment requires protection are all factors which dictate the level of public intervention. Often, the sudden and uncontrollable impact of external forces, such as the destruction of the World Trade Center in New York in 2001, the Bali bombing in 2002, the outbreak of severe acute respiratory syndrome (SARS) in 2003 and the Indian Ocean tsunami in 2004, will determine the shape of state intervention in salvaging a tourism industry. Tourist destinations such as South Africa, Berlin and Northern Ireland are testament to the success of rejuvenation programmes. Equally, the shared goal of winning a bid to host an event such as the Olympic Games will often encourage governments to invest heavily in building a public–private partnership such as that for London 2012 or FIFA World Cup 2010 in South Africa. As the environment changes and the political tide ebbs and flows in different parts of the world, the tourism industry can do little but respond to the changes as best it can.

Recent global trends have altered general governmental approaches to tourism. The political shift to market-driven economies is bringing about a global economic restructuring in which market forces rather than ideology are used to guide decisions and develop policy. Recently, entire political systems have undergone dramatic changes in response to the pressure from their populations to provide the goods and services which they desire rather than those which are determined by the state. Although history warns that we must anticipate swings and counter-swings over time, it is probable that the next decade will see a continuation of the increasing role of market forces in determining the shape of world economic activity in general, and tourism in particular. While policy makers in tourism cannot do much to affect this trend, there are two areas for policy action, namely: (i) the need to encourage efforts to establish public–private partnerships that will ensure tourism development that is economically viable and yet socially responsible; and (ii) the need to encourage responsible and responsive research and development to support these partnerships.

Changes to subsidies and regulations

The trend towards market economies and shrinking government budgets is creating strong pressures for privatization and deregulation of tourism facilities and services. While the decade of the 1970s saw governments become increasingly involved in many areas of social and economic development, the 1980s witnessed changing attitudes to tourism moving towards passive encouragement rather than financial support with an increased focus on regulation. By the early years of the 21st century, economic realities began to force a drastic retrenchment of government activity. Policies of deregulation, privatization, the elimination of tax incentives and a move away from discretionary forms of intervention have been the norm for governments in many developed countries. The reality is that governments in many countries have simply found they are unable to support the many programmes and initiatives that were put in place in earlier years.

Tourism is only one economic sector facing reductions in government subsidies, in levels of regulation and a transfer of management responsibility into the private sector. One of the first indications of this was the process of liberalization and deregulation of airline and commercial transportation, first in the USA, and increasingly on a worldwide basis. The key effects are:

- Government subsidies to support tourism development are declining. Increasingly fees are being imposed for the use of tourism facilities and services that were previously 'free'.
- Government investment in tourism facility development is also declining with increasing pressures for privatization of all forms of tourism development. This trend is causing a marked change in the structure of investment portfolios in tourism-related projects.
- The trend to government decentralization of its structures and programmes is pushing responsibility for tourism planning and development to the regional and local level.

Policy makers in tourism can no longer count on government support for tourism development as a form of social development or as a mechanism for the redistribution of income and employment. Tourism facilities and supporting services will increasingly have to be competitive in the marketplace and economically viable to survive in the 21st century.

Government attitudes to tourism

Despite recent progress, recognition by governments of the tourism industry and its importance to social and economic development and well-being of regions is still far from satisfactory. During the 1980s, tourism made substantial progress in gaining this recognition. Despite this, tourism is still viewed in many quarters as a marginal industry, largely due to the fact that its impacts are poorly documented and poorly understood.

As such, there is a need for further effort to develop industry support for an integrated tourism lobby. In a related vein, there is a need to focus the attention of public international organizations on issues of significance to the tourism industry. Only in this way will governments acknowledge tourism as a foreign policy issue as well as a domestic one. This in turn should strengthen efforts to stimulate governments and internal lending institutions to increase the flow of resources to projects in various sectors of tourism. Similarly, greater recognition would stimulate governments to consider tourism needs in the course of public infrastructure development. It would also encourage the direct allocation of a portion of tourism taxes and fees to be used for tourism promotion, destination development and infrastructure development. In the future, the tourism industry will probably become more involved in collaborative relationships with governments to lessen the problems that plague overpopulated urban areas. By encouraging innovations in urbanization that strengthen the infrastructure of megacities – such as the recycling of waste, new and cheaper housing materials and alternative energy sources – the industry will in turn preserve its own tourist markets.

Political instability

Political instability and conflict between and within countries will always have a devastating effect on the tourist trade. Those in the tourism and travel industry must always be in touch with the political risks that exist across the world, but in recent years this has become more difficult than ever. As governments continue to reinvent themselves all over Eastern Europe, the former Soviet Union and other parts of the world, the tourism industry will face great challenges. On the one hand, democratization brings tremendous opportunities for growth. On the other, increasing gaps between the rich and the poor and the volatility of political alliances may put tourism policy makers in the business of serious risk analysis. Strategic planners will need to become more adept at 'mapping' zones of instability based on population and poverty projections, and at assessing other indicators of vulnerability that influence the levels of risk associated with tourism investments.

The size and international scope of the tourism industry have unfortunately made it and the tourists within it potential targets for politically motivated acts of terrorism. Episodes of fundamentalist violence directed against tourists in Egypt and Bali have caused these destinations to be re-evaluated by governments, tourism providers and consumers alike. Acts of terrorism, riots and political aggression are felt immediately with declining arrivals and lower hotel occupancy. These realities have led to a heightened need to protect tourists from terrorists and other forms of political instability. Recognizing that the tourism industry can only thrive in a peaceful world, it is essential that it takes a proactive role in collaborating with other organizations in promoting international understanding and goodwill at all levels.

SUMMARY OF TRENDS AND GLOBAL TOURISM ISSUES FOR THE FUTURE

- Environmental concern has reached an all-time high and will continue to grow. This will bring increasing pressure on all tourism initiatives to demonstrate that they contribute to environmentally friendly and sustainable development.

- Broad-based political movements, in which the populations of many countries are attempting to establish more participatory forms of government, are impacting on tourism. As a consequence, the residents of travel destinations will increasingly demand that tourism first and foremost serves their interests by providing benefits that outweigh its costs.

- World economic order is changing. Relentless pressure for almost all countries to adapt their economies to market forces is bringing about a major restructuring of wealth and income patterns, which will be reflected in global travel patterns.

- The 'globalization' of political and economic structures has initiated movement towards the 'borderless' world. In this new world the transnational corporation is a powerful force. Superior access of financing, technology and information provide this stateless entity with strategic and operational strengths which give it clear competitive advantages (see Go and Pine, 1995).

- World demographics will continue to evolve very predictably with wealthy nations experiencing ageing and stabilizing populations and this will be countered by a strong growth in the populations of developing countries. The impact of this on global travel patterns will need to be carefully monitored.

- Technology, in particular the linkage between (and interdependence of) telecommunications, transportation and tourism, is receiving increasing attention. The movement of information, goods and people is being examined with respect to both complementarity and substitutability.

- The role of tourism in developing countries poses serious questions. While many developing economies desperately need the financial receipts from tourism, the social and environmental costs imposed by inappropriate forms of tourism development simply cannot be ignored (see Oppermann and Chon, 1997).

- The issues of environment and developing countries are manifestations of broader concern relating to ethics and responsibility in tourism policy formation and management. Tourism is now so significant that it must seriously examine the values on which it is based in order to ensure that they continue to reflect those of the society it serves and affects.

- Concerns related to health, security and legal liability are very much at the forefront of the minds of both tourists and industry suppliers. International conflicts and wars, growing crime and terrorism levels and the spread of deadly communicable diseases will be very real factors in the development of tourism.

- Concerns related to the availability of an appropriate workforce in the growing global tourism industry will intensify. A broad range of social and economic policies – particularly those impacting on population planning, education, immigration, labour relations and the use of technology – will greatly influence the availability of the industry in each country to meet its human resource needs.

CONCLUSION

Essentially, the whole process of tourism strategic planning boils down to planning on uncertainty. Uncertainty is the complement of knowledge: the gap between what is known and what needs to be known to make correct decisions. Dealing sensibly with uncertainty is not a byway on the road to responsible tourism management decisions, it is central to it. To cope with future tourism planning, management and research, tourism professionals need to be Renaissance men and women. The ability to imagine, perceive and gauge the future is a paramount professional attribute of the tourism professionals of tomorrow. The future tourism phenomena will be managed by today's professionals who look to the future and shape it into a strategic vision. The information presented in this chapter has been aimed at helping to create that vision and was designed to show that 'we must not expect the expected!'

REFERENCES

Buhalis, D. (2003) *eTourism: Information Technology for Strategic Tourism Management*. Pearson (Financial Times/Prentice Hall), London.

Buhalis, D. and Licata, M.C. (2002) The future eTourism intermediaries. *Tourism Management* 23(3), 207–220.

Cheong, R. (1995) The virtual threat to travel and tourism. *Tourism Management* 16(6), 417–422.

Durning, A.T. (1992) *How Much Is Enough?* Earthscan, London.

Gee, C.Y., Makens, J.C. and Choy, D.J.L. (1994) *The Travel Industry*, 2nd edn. Van Nostrand Reinhold, New York.

Go, F. and Pine, R. (1995) *Globalization Strategy in the Hotel Industry*. International Thomson Business Press, London.

Hall, C.M. and Jenkins, J.M. (1996) *Tourism and Public Policy*. International Thomson Business Press, London.

Lickorish, L.J. and Jenkins, C.L. (1997) *An Introduction to Tourism*. Butterworth-Heinemann, Oxford.

Oppermann, M. and Chon, K.S. (1997) *Tourism in Developing Countries*. International Thomson Business Press, London.

Stepchenkova, S., Mills, J.E. and Jiang, H. (2007) Virtual travel communities: self-reported experiences and satisfaction. In: Sigala, M., Mich, L. and Murphy, J. (eds) *Information and Communication Technologies in Tourism 2007*. Springer Wien, New York, pp. 163–174.

Wang, Y., Yu, Q. and Fesenmaier, R.D. (2002) Defining the virtual tourist community: implications for tourism marketing. *Tourism Management* 23(4), 407–417.

World Travel and Tourism Council (WTTC) (2010) *Travel and Tourism: Economic Impact*. WTTC, London.

chapter 2

Futurecast Applied to Tourism

Luiz Moutinho, Ronnie Ballantyne and Shirley Rate

The tourism industry continues to push forward, ever expanding in importance to the global economy and increasingly involving more and more participants. It has become the world's largest industry. Chapter 1 identified that the tourism arena is in constant change and that the pace of change continues to accelerate. Utilizing SCEPTICAL analysis, salient trends in today's and the future market were identified. Key emerging trends were identified and their current and likely impact on strategic tourism decision making discussed. This chapter will further illuminate those elements that continue to gain in size and momentum on the tourism radar. In addition, and importantly, the chapter traces some of the more novel trends and developments that are now beginning to emerge. These new developments may only be present as 'weak signals' in terms of the environmental scanning at present; however, they are likely to accelerate and dominate in the coming years.

This chapter will focus on the future – bridging the gap between more traditional management approaches and the exploration of new paradigms of thought. By isolating and exploring these new paradigms and techniques in conjunction with tracing and understanding key trends and developments in the new business environment the tourism strategist gains invaluable decision-making intelligence that allows him or her to 'futurecast'. In effect tourism operators will have the ability to 'see' events before they occur – allowing strategic decision makers to develop innovative and effective strategic tourism initiatives. Moreover, this approach allows companies not only to anticipate major shifts in the environment but also to try to influence these changes.

The chapter is broken into three sections and identifies three topics for consideration: (i) 'New Social Values and Paradigm Shifts'; (ii) 'The New Consumer'; and (iii) 'Evolutions and Revolutions in Branding'. The implications for strategic management in tourism and specific future developments in the provision of tourism service will also be discussed. The chapter ends with projected examples of potential tourism innovations.

NEW SOCIAL VALUES AND PARADIGM SHIFTS

To protect and survive the future, tourism operators must anticipate the evolving nature of strategic management and marketing approaches and the environmental shifts that have led to new perspectives. Developments in technology have revolutionized the marketplace and are forcing tourism operators to reconsider the old and outdated business models of the past. Technology is one of the major catalysts to a pace of change unlike any other that has previously been experienced and demands the ability to operate with rapid decision cycles. Futurecasting will allow tourism operators to incorporate the new paradigms of consumer-centricity and customization within their business models. Equally it will allow them to anticipate and manage the impact of new social values such as 'cocooning' and 'affluenza' as well as trends in markets such as the 'Golden Mafia' and 'feminization'.

Neomarketing

New paradigms of marketing will threaten the traditional approaches and frameworks and the very ethos of old-school marketing and its techniques. Adopting neomarketing will see a move towards customer-centricity which will fix the 'broken' marketing function but will demand an entire and revolutionary change in the approach to the consumer. The evolution of technology and communications has transformed the concept of the consumer and as this entity changes, becomes more powerful, more cynical, more passionate and more involved in their brands so traditional business models become less relevant and less effective. There has been a seismic shift in the balance of power from the brand powerhouses to the uber-savvy consumers who know what they want and how to get it. In an era where the customer has control, they expect to participate in the decision making about their future. Customer-centricity then is when customers lead the design of business processes, products, services and business models. To achieve this demands a transformation in corporate culture, a challenge in itself. Businesses models must be designed with customers around their goals with a resulting organizational structure which is a vibrant ecosystem of partners and suppliers all aligned around the same outcomes.

For the tourism industry, marketer-created content whereby a one-fits-all approach resulted in offerings for the masses is irrelevant and unusable. Only a consumer-centric, neomarketing approach will allow tourism operators to identify and relate to the new 'prosumer', one who has taken control from the marketer in designing unique and customized offerings matching his or her own specific requirements. These requirements have evolved into a sophisticated and complex set of needs centred on achieving a depth and authenticity of experience, the 'transumer', no longer accepting materialistic, repetitive or staged tourist experiences. The rise of customer power largely thanks to technology means consumers can reveal the truth, share stories on a global scale about products and service through online forms of communication. Ultimately, they are the authors of brands and marketers have been left no option but to join forces to maintain some form of control. Consumer-generated marketing is a new approach which has led the tourist industry towards developing products and services which are authentic and experience-based and which are flexible, giving the customer control to design their own unique offering in a pick-and-mix, build-your-own style.

Particle marketing

Just as mass marketing became extinct as a concept due to pressures of the evolving competitive environment and increasing demands of the consumer, so too its successor, market segmentation, will soon be a relic of a bygone marketing era. Particle marketing represents a new way of thinking beyond the boundaries and restraints of traditional market segmentation approaches held dear by marketers for some decades. Recent consumer trends have seen a fragmentation of markets and individualization and fluidity of behaviours (Firat and Shultz, 1997). As such, conceptualizing consumers as members of homogeneous market segments is becoming increasingly difficult. Traditional segmentation variables such as age, gender, family life cycle and even more recent constructs of personality and lifestyle are less effective at predicting behaviour as people placed in such distinct groupings are behaving in more individualistic and inconsistent ways. Thus, marketers using segmentation strategies that try to define consumers via variables which lack discriminatory power and assume a single, consistent, stable way of behaving are likely to face failure.

Instead, marketers are being forced to focus on the needs and wants of smaller and smaller groups in a market resulting in the targeting of multiple market segments. However, the digital revolution of the marketplace will allow marketers to reduce their audiences even further. Particle marketing is a concept borrowed from physics which suggests the use of personal technologies to customize micro-individual offerings. Many companies now have access to technologies which provide enough data on customers to understand their individual tastes and preferences and how they evolve. However, data are only useful if they are used creatively. Not enough companies understand how to utilize customer data to deliver customer-valued propositions. Marketers can become so focused on the data that they retain a company- rather than customer-centric bias. Underlying the concept of particle marketing is the notion that the future of targeting relies on marketers embracing the philosophies of relationship marketing, in other words, securing enough information about consumers, a deeper, richer understanding, to attract, maintain and enhance relationships with them. Technologies should not be tools used to just blast out more marketing, more promotions, more newsletters which they can certainly do. The ethos of particle marketing is to use technologies to make interactions and offerings relevant to the customer. Indeed, the best executed relationship marketing is not about marketing at all, it is about relationship mediation. It is about making an advance that says: 'I value you, I want to understand (with you) you better'. Ultimately, it is about facilitating customization.

The Golden Mafia

One of the most dramatic social trends facing the tourism industry is that of the ageing population. The demographic shifts towards lower fertility and falling mortality, added to improvements in life expectancy, have created an increase in the proportion of populations over the age of 60. Worldwide, this cohort currently represents an estimated 10% of the population with an increase to 22% by the year 2050. In developed regions, however, these figures can be more than double the global average (Mirkin and Weinberger, 2001). In the UK, for example, the cohort over 50 years old is growing twice as fast as the population as a whole (Office for National Statistics, 2009a). Within these population bursts exists a group of consumers which represent significant potential and yet have largely been ignored by the tourism industry. The 'Golden Mafia' is those consumers who are enjoying more wealth and health and longer retirements than their predecessors. Indeed, their disposable income will be an increasingly important determinant of the structure of demand as the much-targeted youth market continues to steadily decline. But it is the nature of this group, its expenditure patterns, activities and lifestyles indicating increasing participation in hedonist and consumerist behaviours, that should be of most interest to tourism operators.

As well as wealth and disposable income, the Golden Mafia, by the time they reach retirement age, is likely to have reached the empty nest stage of the life cycle, resulting in fewer costs related to dependents and a wealth of leisure time. Thus, distinct growth in participation in sporting, leisure and other physical activities is already being witnessed. Additionally, the group are better educated and more interested in travel and tourism than previous generations, with travel being a major element in most retirement plans. More than any other age group, the Golden Mafia is an anti-materialistic generation moving away from a lifetime of consumption to focus on their keener appreciation of life experiences. They are motivated more by the capacity of a product or service to serve as a gateway to experiences, the 'transumers' of the future. The implications for the tourist industry are thus wide-reaching. The Golden Mafia, though, is no ordinary group of consumers. They have a more youthful outlook, feeling and acting younger than their chronological age, leading to an increased demand for holidays typically associated with younger people. These cognitively young consumers are more innovative in their consumer behaviour and this can be seen in their demand for more flexibility in length of stay, holiday extensions and off-peak offerings as well the nature of the travel product such as scuba diving, skiing, adventure cruises in Antarctica and climbing holidays in South-east Asia.

The feminization of markets

Women are playing an increasingly important role within decision-making units. This is largely due to the fact that more women have entered and continue to enter the workplace and more women are obtaining higher-paid senior roles. Thus, the general wealth of women is continuing to grow, albeit at a slower pace than men. Perhaps more importantly, though, is their financial independence and control. Increases in women's incomes have resulted in shifts in the family structure. This has meant further sharing not only of the household workload but also of decisions related to household finance. This is further compounded by the fact that, of the genders, women remain the predominant buyers of groceries, toiletries and cosmetics, clothing and magazines (Keynote, 2008) and are almost equal spenders in tourism activities (Office for National Statistics, 2009b). The idea of feminization of markets has originated from the demographic growth and power of the market as well as the idea that feminine marketing is a trend which both genders are responding to. Indeed, the very masculine approaches or patronizing 'pink' feminine approaches to marketing products such as cars and electricals is resulting in this powerful market boycotting brands which do not demonstrate a deeper understanding of them. A movement Popcorn (2001) has termed 'eveolution' suggests that 'essential truths' should be sought out to properly connect with this market. She suggests that organizations must understand the multiple lives of women in order to invest in long-term relationships and also that they should foster greater bonds between female consumers as a means of connecting them to brands.

The Why Generation

The 'Why Generation' reflects the wave of millennium youth who are technologically literate, marketing and media savvy and more affluent than any preceding generations. They are better educated than previous generations and more are entering higher education than ever before. However, patterns of study are changing, with many students delaying their entry into higher education. Instead, the Why Generation, true to their very nature, want to travel the world, learn about new cultures and meet new people. Having grown up with the Internet and other interactive technologies, this generation has a global collective consciousness born from the international and virtual communities in which they communicate and live. These experiences as well as increasing affluence have encouraged a hedonistic generation who exploit opportunities to gain instant gratification. They have also fostered a curiosity and fearless thirst for new experiences and exploring the world. The implications for the tourism industry are vast.

The new socioquake

Within any business context, operators are at the mercy of social and cultural forces that influence the basic values, perceptions, preferences and behaviours. However, facing the tourist industry now is the 'new socioquake' which reflects the future of social values, but also the pace in which they infiltrate borders and become global trends. The diffusion of information for events and trends across global locations is becoming shorter due to technological innovations in communications technology. Popcorn (2002) describes a number of future trends which will produce a socioquake effect. One of these trends which will inevitably impact upon the tourist industry is that of '**cocooning**', whereby the stresses of life are leading to people retreating to what is seen as the protection and shelter of the home. The availability of new technologies has to some extent allowed people to replace former activities which demanded travel outside the home and, as such, the restaurant, cinema, other entertainment and leisure industries will be impacted. Similarly, the tourist industry will feel the effect of the 'near-to-home syndrome' whereby the need to feel the security of home and job is leading to the decline of longer holidays and increased short and local breaks.

Another trend producing a socioquake is that of '**vigilantism**', which is largely due to increasing perceived control and power of the consumer. Consumers will no longer accept misbehaviour and demand that organizations respect the community in which they function as well as the consumers whom they serve. The tourist industry has long been accused of patronizing the 'Golden Mafia' both in their predominant marketing activities of price discounts due to the assumption they are thrifty and in their communications in which they depict the market as feeble, helpless or infirm. The industry has felt the effects of the power of this group of consumers who would rather boycott brands than endure such demeaning behaviour. A related trend is that of '**icon toppling**', reflecting not only the power of the consumer but their hunger for equality, justice and authenticity from organizations. We will see a continuing resistance to overpaid celebrities endorsing products they do not use as well as to boardroom salaries that do not reflect the realism consumers are striving for. The more distance that chief executive officers (CEOs) place between themselves and their consumers, the less engaged their consumers will become.

Finally, changes within the family structure and its income will significantly impact upon social values and consumer trends. The socioquake generated will be that consumers feel more and more stretched in terms of the roles they play and confused in terms of their inner values. People are living '**99 lives**' whereby they are expected to play a plethora of roles within their family unit as well as within the context of friendships and work. As consumers, then, people are expected to be dextrous in terms of buying skills. The more affluent people become, the more complex life becomes and the more roles people must play. This causes pressure and the result is the disillusionment of wealth and all that it brings. The movement of '**affluenza**' is the disorientation which consumers are increasingly experiencing due to a dichotomy of desires (Hamilton and Denniss, 2006). The unending search for happiness through products and services and demand for infinite choice are conflicting with the inner need for a simpler life, producing the fast-spreading virus, affluenza.

THE NEW CONSUMER

The development of the new consumer or indeed the new tourist is a significant trend – tourists are increasingly knowledgeable, more experienced and have higher expectations than ever before. The emerging consumer is not easily categorized by a classic segmentation typology but is an individual, a human being who has become a sophisticated 'high frequency' traveller, who is technologically literate and who has the ability to adapt and function in multicultural environments. The new empowered tourist, enabled by the Internet, will seek out authentic, customized, environmentally aware and friendly tourism experiences – specialist niche interest activities and independently customized tourism will flourish. Some of the key futurecast trends now follow.

Sense and respond

In our already present 24-hours-a-day, 7-days-a-week consumer culture the real-time organization must always be available to all customers all of the time. Time to market for products and services is becoming shorter, there is a mass expectation of constant innovation and company response to consumer queries and needs should be given on time. The already rapid pace of change in the business environment is set to continue to accelerate. Keeping pace with changing consumer behaviour, markets, social values and technologies will be one of the biggest challenges for tourism providers over the next 20 years. The high-velocity marketplace makes it difficult for managers to absorb, process, make decisions and take appropriate actions in real time. Flexibility and adaptability will become key ingredients for business success in the future. Moreover, the ability to forecast consumer needs even before consumers themselves are aware will become a significant contributor to obtaining and sustaining competitive advantage.

Insperiences

The **insperiences** trend is a natural progression on from the cocooning and hiving phenomenon. In a consumer society dominated by experiences in the public domain – often branded, designed, themed and curated – insperiences represent consumer desire to bring top-level, professional grade experiences into their domestic domain. The insperience is evolving. It will continue to be about consumers wanting to 'domesticize' any interesting experiences they have in the public space, at times treating every surrounding like a giant catalogue. This movement may occupy significant amounts of consumer spend traditionally allocated for tourism-related products and as such positions itself as serious substitute. Moreover, moving beyond the 'physical' the current wave of 3D-technology-driven entertainment will begin to bleed into the consumer domain in a variety of ways (e.g. the utilization of virtual reality (VR) shopping – 'helmet and glove' – to stimulate the experience of 'tailoring' the products and services to the individual consumer). These are already recognized as important tools of 'time minimization' and 'evaluation of alternatives' and innovative tourism operators will seek to promote their products and services in this way – stimulating more consumer senses and allowing greater customization of product offering.

In the fullness of time the virtual experience may indeed become a key tourism product – VR tourism – not simply being used as a sophisticated promotional mechanism to aid and prompt consumer choice of a 'real-world' tourism activity or destination, but offering a fully realized three-dimensional sensory experience within the comforts of one's own home. Furthermore, as technological innovations continue to accelerate, individuals will be able to experience virtual tourism not only by themselves but with their friends and family in the virtual domain. The gaming industry already engages in this activity, promoting and building online gaming communities; this type of activity is the natural successor to the already well-established social networking phenomenon. In addition, it is now recognized that consumers assume many roles in our society from the family unit, with friends, at the workplace and at play. As discussed in the previous chapter innovations such as second life already allow consumers to adopt other identities and cultivate other personality traits – as the technology becomes more sophisticated and the consumer becomes more fully immersed in the virtual experience they may desire more than to simply 'visit and interact' with other 'virtual tourists' in virtual tourism pursuits and destinations – they may indeed desire to 'holiday' from themselves and play other roles.

Attentioning and microscopic attention spans

With infomercials and branded entertainment continuing to pay for advertising space the 'info smog' phenomenon will only increase. Consumers will find their experience of reality so fragmented that their ability to concentrate will be drastically reduced – moreover, the type of information search that the Web encourages is a lateral search jumping from chunks of information – never concentrating on one element for any length of time. Securing consumer attention and involvement in tourism products will become increasingly challenging. New modes and methodologies of connecting and communicating with consumers such as tryvertising and the rise of the twinsumer will appear (see below).

Tryvertising

Companies are already utilizing search-based advertising via the online platform and are also initiating 'word-of-mouth'- or indeed 'word-of-net'-based presence to stimulate buzz, interest and hyperbole via blogs and discussion forums as new and more relevant ways to replace mass advertising, but there is a third alternative – tryvertising. Tryvertising is all about consumers becoming familiar with new products by actually trying them out – in effect experimentation over message – experienced consumers will continue to 'tune out' from commercials, ads, banners and other fancy wording and imagery that is forced upon them. Tryvertising bypasses these outdated modes, allowing consumers to make up their minds based on the experience, not the company's message. The consumers can then become advocates, true ambassadors and endorsers of the brand – this trend can be utilized and cultivated in harmony with the growth of consumer-generated marketing. Consumer content is already having a huge impact on certain sectors (e.g. the entertainment industry). The concept of the influential consumer has taken on a whole new level of importance. It can be argued that the influential consumers have become the true gatekeepers of success. The biggest shift powered by the digital lever is that the average consumer has become the new storyteller and digital experiences are becoming more important to an empowered consumer, who now has more options than ever before. Consumer-generated marketing via blogs, discussion forums or indeed YouTube reviews and testimonials is the most revolutionary concept in marketing to come along for a long time. As the role of trust and source credibility becomes heightened in consumer decision making, bias-free reviews and recommendations will carry great influence in generating awareness and facilitating consumer choice of tourism choice alternatives. Consumer-generated marketing is a fact of life to which all of us will have to adapt.

Twinsumer

Consumers trust other consumers more than advertisers across virtually every global geography. Consumers looking for the best products will inceasingly not connect to 'any other consumer' any more; they are hooking up with their taste twins (i.e. their **twinsumers**) – fellow consumers somewhere in the world who think, react, enjoy and consume the way they do.

Prosumpton: the rise of the prosumer

As stated in the previous chapter, the consumer is no longer content in terms of simply waiting for new products and services to arrive. The new consumer – the prosumer – will continue to demonstrate a more active behavior in consumption. The rise of the prosumer blurs the traditional boundaries of producer and consumer and importantly allows for shifts in business thinking – facilitating developments of new paradigms of marketing such as the aforementioned neomarketing and particle marketing.

Prosumption is viewed as a megatrend; 'customer-made' products and experiences will continue to accelerate in the 21st century. The phenomenon of corporations creating goods, services and experiences in close cooperation with experienced and creative consumers, tapping into their intellectual capital, and in exchange giving them a direct say in what actually gets produced, manufactured, developed, designed, serviced or processed (and rewarding them) will increasingly become the norm across many business sectors. The Web has given consumers greater power, liberating and empowering them, but at a deeper level there is a consciousness paradigm. The new consumer is searching for real value and needs to know what is behind the brand name and promise. By encouraging and facilitating co-creation the dimensions of the brand become more transparent to the consumer and indeed the consumers themselves become the authors of the brand experience – this will lead to greater trust and more involved, stronger relationships between organizations and individuals.

The continued growth of prosumers challenges traditional business logic where:

- firms create value unilaterally;
- consumers are passive; and
- products and services represent the value.

Prosumption brings a new frame of reference by:

- focusing on the customer–company interaction as a new value creation;
- co-creating value through customer and company;
- taking into consideration that value is unique to each customer and is associated with personalized experiences; and
- products and services area being only a means to an end.

Prosumption is, then, transforming the customer–company relationship by allowing the consumer to co-construct their own unique value. This new type of operation is turning the 'supply chain' into a 'demand value chain', by reversing the flow of marketing from 'company to customer' to 'customer to company'. Enlightened providers of tourism will collaborate with consumers to build a dialogue and exchange process that creates value for both parties. This shift in thinking moves the emphasis from what marketers do to consumers to what consumers want from marketing.

Rehumanization

As stated in the previous chapter, a process of rehumanization is already present. This is viewed as a significant trend that will continue to accelerate – the search for meaning in a technological, rapidly moving, pressure-filled society will become a dominant trait in many consumers. We will see the continued rise of 'chadventures' – adventure pursuits that also raise money for charitable causes – and other tourism pursuits that enable and nurture learning and growth will prosper. Authentic emotional connection between provider and consumer will be amplified – the importance of trust will become increasingly salient in terms of how consumers think and feel about different market offerings. Moreover, building on consumer concerns for environmental sustainability, it must be stressed that consumer access to information is now heightened. The Internet has revolutionized the distribution of tourism information and sales – not only can consumers compare prices with the click of a mouse, they can also look at a tourism operator's ethical or environmental policies and find out what is being said about them anywhere in the world.

Minipreneurs

The digital revolution also encouraged consumers to set up their own microbusinesses. Minipreneurs are consumers who are increasingly involved with the creation, production and trading of goods, services and experiences instead of merely consuming them. A vast army of consumers are turning into entrepreneurs; including small and microbusinesses, freelancers, weekend entrepreneurs, Web-driven entrepreneurs and so on. This megatrend will manifest in a variety of ways within the tourism arena – we are already witnessing simple but effective innovations such as house swapping and the launch of tourism initiatives based upon individuals' own leisure and tourism pursuits, activities and passions. Again, the emergence of the new technology-driven market sphere encourages the consumer to become an active participant as opposed to a passive audience member. Today's aspiring and established minipreneurs truly have a highly developed network of intermediaries, tools, resources and processes at their disposal. It is an ecosystem on a much more elaborate scale than anyone foresaw. This new breed of minipreneur has access for very little cost, if not for free, to:

- hardware, software and information communications technology (ICT) skills;
- design, production and manufacturing;
- monetizing existing assets;
- marketplaces;
- advertising;
- travel;
- talent; and
- finance, payment, logistics, etc.

Consumer decision making

As stated in the previous chapter, consumers are increasingly becoming 'time and effort' starved – solutions that present minimum cognitive effort and are easily and readily accessible will prosper. Consumer desire for simplicity, immediacy, customization and emotional authenticity challenges traditional typologies of consumer decision making. Implications in terms of decision-making process and the rise of simplifying choice heuristics will be further explored in Chapter 5, 'Consumer Behaviour in Tourism'.

Zones of tolerance

Zones of tolerance can be described as the difference between desired and adequate consumer expectations. Consumers will continue to become increasingly demanding as such zones of tolerance will continue to shrink. Zones of tolerance and their impacts on consumer experience must be monitored and explored by tourism providers. To over-promise and under-deliver is a very risky business and can have serious impacts on retaining customers and repeat purchasing behaviour.

Consumer emulation

It is the age of consumer emulation – across the marketplace we are now seeing strategists aggressively borrowing from consumer behaviour as they develop their own theories (e.g. borrowing from consumer best practices to build their own external blog). Starbucks and Dell are currently asking consumers to contribute ideas for future products via Internet research blogs.

New and novel … now!

Building on the key emerging trends of 'infolust' and the 'ready-to-know, ready-to-go' state of mind of the 21st-century consumer, we will see the rise of consumer tribes who desire the 'new and novel … now!'. These consumers are dissatisfied with what they have, the current state of their lives, and believe 'something else' would be better and far more satisfying. Ironically for this group the product offering does not necessarily have to be good, it has to be *new*. Implications for innovation management and time to market are clear – certain tourism providers will be encouraged to constantly innovate and will be under increased pressure to reduce time to market.

EVOLUTIONS AND REVOLUTIONS IN BRANDING

Brands have become omnipresent in today's marketplace. Consumers have become accustomed to using brands as essential guides to help navigate the over-cluttered multiple-choice world in which we live. Brands have historically facilitated short cuts in consumer decision making, reducing time and effort by identifying reputable and trusted sources of consumer value. Within the tourism arena, destinations, travel companies, accommodation, food and entertainment providers alike (hospitality) have all come to be marketed very much like traditional product-based brands with particular brand dimensions and personality traits highlighted and exaggerated in advertising claims. Tourism operators have sought to position their brands distinctively in the hearts and minds of their target audience, thus facilitating the development and maintenance of the brand tribe or brand community. Nevertheless, the classic branding paradigm is becoming tired and may now be beginning to lose its edge. As stated above, the rise of the empowered consumer suggests that in the future the most successful brands will be those that abandon the traditional top-down approach – 'we market to you' – in favour of bottom-up strategies – adopting true consumer-centricity whereby the consumer is an active participant in the design of the overall brand experience. In effect, tomorrow's megabrands will be the consumer's as opposed to the producer's agent, pioneering a transformation from trademarks to trust marks using trust-based marketing.

    The challenge for strategic decision makers is that consumers in the future will want less not more, sense not nonsense and above all they want companies to inject simplicity marketing. This means repositioning tourism brands to survive in an environment of savvy, cynical, marketing-literate consumers no longer seeking solace in false brand gods, hype and spin. In a society where brands are now becoming 'mental pollutants' and the traditional 'marketing medicine' (e.g. I buy therefore I am and to buy is to be perceived) is increasingly diagnosed as a 'disease', we are now witnessing the era of the demarketing chic. Brands can become negative baggage as they are undermined by the very values they own in the mind of the consumer. The deferential consumer, conditioned to 'salivate' and desire upon being 'buzzed' by brands, has been buried along with the golden era of marketing. Consumers are already becoming increasingly brand immune and in some cases they are developing 'brand allergies'. The classic model of interruption and annoyance is ending – consumers are no longer willing to be forced to absorb brand messages. As a consequence brands may be losing control of their own image but they can also take advantage of content creations via the aforementioned methodologies of neomarketing, particle marketing and prosumption and the associated buzz generated between consumers (e.g. tryvertising and twinsumers).

The new realities of branding are, then, upon us – innovative companies are dispensing with the mass economy tactics of old and replacing them with tactics more suited to the consumer economy. Strategic tourism planners must, then, recognize that markets consist of human beings and not segmentation typologies. Markets can no longer be treated as pure demographics, geodemographics or psychographics in terms of segmentation bases with brands to fit. Markets actually consist of human beings each with unique needs and desires. This awareness coupled with less passive and more savvy consumers prompts the need for a new model of brand relations – the 'brain to brain' model. Companies must adopt an intelligent and integrated marketing and management approach that seeks to establish and nurture 'intelligent dialogue' with customers. Ironically this may mean a return to classical marketing: solving people's problems at a profit. As brands evolve to ensure an intelligent dialogue with customers, ever greater demand for (emotional) authenticity and value will be desired by consumers. The emotional value is the economic value or momentary worth of feelings when consumers positively (or negatively) experience branded products and services. Emotional value, as much as quality or any other product attribute or dimension of an organization's worth, can make or break a business. If companies do not handle well consumers' emotional needs and wants, brands are at risk. Incorporating emotional design into the development and branding of the tourism product is becoming a necessity for tourism and travel providers. Today and in the future, marketers want to extend their contact with customers through time. In effect the brand must become not a product but an invitation, an invitation to an emotionally satisfying and enduring relationship. The brand promise is about the quality of that relationship.

CONCLUDING REMARKS

We are only at the very beginning of a new journey from 'brand building' and 'customer relationship management' to the consumer agency. This new vision of strategic tourism management is driven less by knowing about consumers and more by understanding (learning from) them. Consumers are now beginning to view themselves as citizens not only of countries but of corporations and as citizens they have a 'say' in how that organization behaves. The expected key 'futurecast trends' coupled with transformations in consumer behaviour and industry structures will necessitate that new emerging visions of strategic tourism management evolve and develop. The new emerging realities of the tourism arena present many challenges and opportunities for strategic management in tourism. Initially we will witness a continued re-engineering of established tourism products and destinations. The adaptation of current tourism enterprises will influence and shape the values of the present products and services towards new paradigms and techniques.

FUTURE FORECASTING – INNOVATIONS OF TOURISM

- Holidays of the future will be customized trips of a lifetime or 'sabbaticals' which feature some aid to self-actualization through a personal challenge or some process of self-growth. For example, 'creative', 'volunteer' and 'spiritual' tourism will fulfil long-held but unachieved goals of altruism, skills development or creative expression. The new consumer will increasingly co-create and author his/her own tourism experience. Tourism with true emotional reach and power will prosper.

- As international travel and immigration increase, the market of 'global nomads' increases. This will create a significant growth in 'visiting friends and family' travel as well as 'family reunion' travel.

- Unique selling propositions (USPs) will become unique experiential selling propositions and unique symbolic selling propositions. The brand promise will be about the quality of the relationship between tourism provider and consumer.

- A third of the population in developing countries will be over the age of 60 by 2050. This age cohort will dictate the shape of market demand. Demand for spirituality based on inner experiences as well as concern for health and longevity will lead to a boom in well-being, spa and fitness-related tourism. Medical services will become globalized and commoditized and countries will compete for incoming medical tourism in specific niche markets.

- As people become increasingly concerned with their carbon footprints, rail travel will become the sustainable alternative and as high-speed rail technology advances it will become a faster alternative for some trips. Other alternatives such as reinvention of the carbon-free airship will displace current types of air travel. There will be increased equilibrium between tourism, environmental concerns and technology in terms of fulfilling tourist wishes and expectations.

- Such will be the focus on carbon emissions, the airline industry will dramatically revolutionize the fuels they utilize and, as price no longer becomes a viable USP, consumers will be choosing between airlines according to their impact on the environment.

- New search and mapping technology will allow tourists to develop more sophisticated pre-visit knowledge and expectations. Tourism operators will be able to track consumers in real time identifying specific patterns of behaviour.

- Ultimately the new consumer will be able to create their own virtual tourism experiences utilizing state-of-the-art 3D technology. The virtual tourist will be able to simulate just about anything; for example, if a person wanted to experience a raft trip down the Grand Canyon of the Colorado River it will be possible to replicate this experience – with the technology delivering the same sensations. The consumer's sensory receptors will be stimulated to see, touch, hear, taste and smell! The more adventurous virtual tourist will also be able to role play – experiencing different tourism scenarios as different characters. Moreover, virtual tourism will not be restricted to replica tourism experiences in this world but it will give us access to artificial worlds to explore outside normal space and time.

- Although a more socially and environmentally aware consumer will rise there will still be desire and demand for the uber premium – the obscure and the exclusive will still attract the global elite (e.g. space tourism).

- Conference tourism and event-based tourism will accelerate. Competition and tendering for world interest events such as the Olympic Games and the Commonwealth Games will intensify. These events offer the hosts the ability to showcase destinations in a reputable and respected format to the world.

REFERENCES

Firat, A.F. and Shultz, C.J. (1997) From segmentation to fragmentation: markets and marketing strategy in the postmodern era. *European Journal of Marketing* 31(3/4), 183–207.

Hamilton, C. and Denniss, R. (2006) *Affluenza: When Too Much Is Never Enough*. Allen & Unwin, Sidney.

Keynote (2008) *Men and Women's Buying Habits*. Keynote Ltd, Middlesex.

Mirkin, B. and Weinberger, M.B. (2001) The demographics of population ageing. *United Nations Population Bulletin* Special Issue No. 42/43, 41–48.

Office for National Statistics (2009a) *Population Trends*, No. 138, Winter. Palgrave Macmillan, Richmond, UK.

Office for National Statistics (2009b) *Travel Trends 2009*. Palgrave Macmillan, Richmond, UK.

Popcorn, F. (2001) *Eveolution: the Eight Truths of Marketing to Women*. Hyperion, New York.

Popcorn, F. (2002) *Dictionary of the Future*. Hyperion, New York.

chapter 3

The Travel and Tourism Competitiveness Index as a Tool for Economic Development and Poverty Reduction

Larry Dwyer, Peter Forsyth and Wayne Dwyer

INTRODUCTION

Travel and tourism (T&T) is a key sector in the world economy and is a catalyst for economic growth and development in many countries. The United Nations Environment Programme (UNEP) regards a growing tourism industry as supporting economic development through improved infrastructure such as better water and sewage systems, roads, electricity networks, and telephone and public transport networks, as well as improved education, health and communication services, all of which can enhance a country's development prospects and the quality of life of residents. Tourism also has the potential to play an important role in promoting sustainable development, through the preservation of natural and cultural heritage (UNEP, 2002). In particular, T&T is taken to create important backward linkages with products and services sourced locally, producing beneficial effects for the local economy as a whole (Blanke and Chiesa, 2008).

Tourism is growing rapidly in many developing countries. The United Nations World Tourism Organization (UNWTO) estimates that less developed countries (LDCs) derive over 43% of their total services trade revenue from tourism exports, with the least developed countries deriving more than 70% (Lipman and Kester, 2007). The UNWTO estimates that up to 40% of GDP and jobs in the least developed countries are generated by T&T (Lipman and Kester, 2007).

In the LDCs in particular, tourism development is regarded as important for poverty reduction. As the World Economic Forum (WEF) has recently stated:

despite the current difficulties, the T&T sector remains a critical economic sector worldwide and one that provides significant potential for economic growth and development internationally. A growing national T&T sector contributes to employment, raises national income, and can improve a country's balance of payments. The sector is thus an important driver of growth and prosperity and, particularly within developing countries, it can play a leading role in poverty reduction.

(Blanke and Chiesa, 2009: xiii)

With its ability to generate employment, to provide economic linkages and to contribute to both the formal and the informal economies, tourism is considered to have more potential to help the poor than do other sectors of the economy. Although low-income countries suffer from a number of disadvantages, such as low skill levels, poor infrastructure and poor transport services, they also have important comparative advantages, such as excellent natural and cultural attributes, relatively unspoiled environments that can be attractive for nature-based tourism and abundant, low-cost labour. Revenues generated through the T&T sector can be invested in other sectors, and its growth will have spillover effects into other markets.

The UNWTO also states that tourism can help to reduce world poverty, especially in the light of United Nations (UN) World Millennium Goal No. 1 (halving the number of people living in poverty by 2015) (ESCAP, 2005). Among other advantages, it is claimed that tourism can help to: (i) improve economic conditions for the poor by unlocking economic opportunities and diversifying income sources; (ii) enhance social development in poor regions by providing new and improved infrastructure; (iii) transfer economic and social power to the poor by encouraging increased participation by poor local communities in tourism decision making; and (iv) promote environmental protection in poor regional areas, especially where many natural and human tourism environments are owned or serviced by local poor communities (Ashley and Roe, 2003).

And yet we must ask the question: is tourism development helping to reduce poverty in developing countries? Ashley *et al.* (2000) remind us that tourism is an industry driven by commercial interest, and does not include objectives to help the poor. Indeed, many activities associated with present-day tourism actually impoverish weaker groups through displacement of locally owned businesses, increased local prices, loss of access to resources, cultural disruption, adverse social and environmental impacts and so on. Clearly, the growth of tourism can be expected to raise aggregate income as with any export boom, and in this sense the sector may indeed offer pro-poor outcomes if indeed 'a rising tide raises all boats' (Wattanakuljarus and Coxhead, 2008). But whether tourism growth reduces the *relative* deprivation of the poor is not clear. If it does not, then government efforts to promote tourism growth may thus be inconsistent with the goal of reduced income inequality.

Given the potential significant benefits of fostering strong national tourism (and transport) sectors worldwide, the WEF in close collaboration with Booz Allen Hamilton, the International Air Transport Association (IATA), the UNWTO, and the World Travel and Tourism Council (WTTC) has developed a Travel and Tourism Competitiveness Index (TTCI) in an effort to better understand the drivers of T&T competitiveness and the challenges that face the industry at the present time (Blanke *et al.*, 2009). The TTCI is intended to provide a platform for multi-stakeholder dialogue to ensure the development of strong and sustainable national T&T industries capable of contributing effectively to international economic development including poverty reduction.

Comprehensive models of destination competitiveness have been developed by tourism researchers (Crouch and Ritchie, 1999; Dwyer and Kim, 2003), but these have provided frameworks for including relevant variables rather than actual measures of the competitiveness of different destinations.

The explicit aim of the TTCI, which covered 133 countries in 2008, is to provide a comprehensive strategic tool for measuring the factors and policies that make it attractive to develop the T&T sector in different countries. By highlighting success factors and obstacles to T&T competitiveness in these countries, the TTCI will serve as a useful tool for the business community and for national policy makers to work in developing tourism within destinations. By providing detailed assessments of the T&T environments in countries worldwide, the results can be used by all stakeholders to work together to improve the industry's competitiveness in their national economies, thereby contributing to national growth and prosperity (Blanke et al., 2009). The UNWTO claims that the TTCI can serve as a tool to support the global development agenda, with potential to enhance the competitiveness of the poorest countries and contribute to the Millennium Development Goals (Lipman and Kester, 2007).

Against this background, this chapter has several aims. First, it sets out to understand the role that LDCs play in tourism at the present time and the potential for tourism to be a catalyst for growth. Secondly, it discusses the TTCI and the method of its construction. If the TTCI is to have policy significance, it is essential that its components be identified and analysed as to their appropriateness. Thirdly, it explores the potential effectiveness of some initiatives in support of the TTCI as a tool to help reduce poverty in LDCs. These initiatives include recommendations for widespread adoption of the UN Tourism Satellite Accounts (TSAs), that tourism services should be reinvigorated in the World Trade Organization's Doha Development Round and that tourism should be mainstreamed for development. Fourthly, the chapter explores the role that these initiatives can play in enhancing tourism's potential to be an engine for growth in LDCs. In particular, the initiatives will be discussed in the context of recent research indicating that inter-industry effects can limit tourism's potential as a catalyst for economic development even in the face of elimination of barriers to tourism sector development. This research shows that tourism does not reduce poverty in some developing countries under present conditions. The findings of these studies need to be considered in any attempts to manage T&T to reduce income inequalities in less developed economies.

INTERNATIONAL TOURISM AND DEVELOPING COUNTRIES

T&T is currently one of the world's largest economic activities. It is the leading industry in many countries, as well as the fastest growing economic sector in terms of job creation worldwide (Blanke and Chiesa, 2008: xi). According to the UNWTO, international tourist arrivals reached 924 million in 2008, representing a growth of 2% compared with 2007 (tourism demand slowed in the second half of 2008, however, attributable to the deteriorating international economic situation). From 1950 to 2005, international tourism arrivals expanded at an average annual rate of 6.5%, growing from 25 million to 806 million travellers. The income generated by these arrivals grew at an even stronger rate, reaching 11% during the same period, outgrowing the world economy. Tourism has become one of the major players in international commerce, and represents at the same time one of the main income sources for many developing countries. The WTTC estimates that, from direct and indirect activities combined, the T&T sector now accounts for 9.9% of global GDP, 10.9% of world exports and 9.4% of world investment. Most new jobs in developing countries are created in tourism industries (WTTC, 2007).

The TTCI distinguishes four types of economies. These are:

- high-income economies: US$10,726 or more income per capita;
- upper-middle-income economies: US$3466–10,725 income per capita;
- lower-middle-income economies: US$876–3465 income per capita; and
- low-income economies: US$875 or below income per capita.

A comparison of average GDP growth with increase in GDP specific to the T&T sector confirms that low-income and lower-middle-income countries show proportionally higher than average sector growth rates compared with the other country segments (see Fig. 3.1). This growth is associated with an increasing diversification and competition among destinations. In 1950, the top 15 destinations absorbed 97% of international arrivals; in 1980 the share was 70%, decreasing to 58% in 2005 (Ringbeck and Gross, 2007).

Table 3.1 shows tourism numbers, market shares and growth rates for world tourism in the period 1990–2005 while Table 3.2 shows the corresponding statistics for tourism expenditure (see Lipman and Kester, 2007). The figures indicate that tourism expenditure shares of the LDCs are less than their shares of tourism flows, posing challenges to these countries to increase inbound tourism expenditure.

Despite their competitive weakness in absolute terms, many of these poorest economies have been advancing significantly in relative terms: between 1990 and 2005, developing economies' market share of international arrivals grew from 28.6% to 40.3% (Table 3.1), while their share of tourism expenditure grew from 18.1% to 30.1% over the same period (Table 3.2). For LDCs, between 2000 and 2005, the number of arrivals in the 50 poorest countries, most of which are in Africa, grew by 48%, almost three times the global growth rate. During the same period, LDC international tourism receipts grew by 76%, compared with a worldwide growth of 41%.

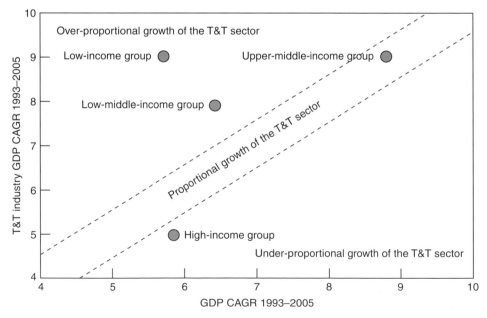

Fig. 3.1. Travel and tourism (T&T) industry versus overall economic growth. CAGR, Compound annual average growth rate.

Table 3.1. International tourist arrivals for the period 1990–2005 (Miller, 2007).

	Million arrivals			Market share (%)			Average annual growth (%)	
	1990	**2000**	**2005**	**1990**	**2000**	**2005**	**1990– 2000**	**2000– 2005**
World	439	689	808	100	100	100	4.6	3.3
Developing economies	126	243	326	28.6	35.2	40.3	6.8	6.1
Fifty least developed countries	2.9	6.4	9.5	0.7	0.9	1.2	8.4	8.2
Other low- and low-middle-income economies	46.7	111.4	163.5	10.6	16.2	20.2	9.1	8.0
Upper middle-income economies	76.0	124.7	152.7	17.3	18.1	18.9	5.1	4.1
High-income economies	313.4	446.2	482.6	71.4	64.8	59.7	3.6	1.6

While tourism arrivals and expenditure are growing in the LDCs, there are concerns about the barriers that reduce the potential of tourism to fulfil the role of a catalyst for growth. According to Ashley *et al.* (2000) these barriers include:

- lack of human and financial capital for development;
- lack of organization to coordinate activities of the private and public sectors;
- exclusion of large numbers of the community from decision making;
- remote locations;
- lack of market power and control over tourism supply or demand;
- bureaucracy, regulations and red tape;
- inadequate links between local suppliers;
- lack of language skills;
- poor understanding of tourist values, attitudes and expectations;
- lack of fit of tourism with existing livelihood strategies and aspirations;
- inadequate access to current and potential tourism markets;
- limited capacity to meet the requirements of the international tourism market;
- underdevelopment of domestic tourism sector;
- government focus on formal tourism sector to the neglect of the informal sector;
- relatively poor access to tourism infrastructure and assets; and
- lack of tourism market knowledge.

Table 3.2. International tourism receipts for the period 1990–2005 (Miller, 2007).

	US$ (billion)			Market share (%)			Average annual growth (%)	
	1990	**2000**	**2005**	**1990**	**2000**	**2005**	**1990– 2000**	**2000– 2005**
World	273	483	682	100	100	100	5.9	7.1
Developing economies	50	126	205	18.1	26.1	30.1	9.8	10.2
Fifty least developed countries	1.1	3.0	5.3	0.4	0.6	0.8	10.5	12.0
Other low- and low-middle- income economies	22.7	63.0	102.1	8.3	13.0	15.0	10.7	10.2
Upper- middle- income economies	25.8	60.1	97.5	9.4	12.5	14.3	8.8	10.1
High-income economies	223.8	356.8	476.6	81.9	73.9	69.9	4.8	6.0

Unless such barriers are overcome tourism will not achieve its potential as a driver of economic growth in LDCs. As we shall discuss below, tourism development is unlikely to reduce poverty if the poorer people in society work in export-oriented or import-competing industries.

TTCI AND ITS CONSTRUCTION

The objective of the TTCI has been to provide benchmarking tools that enable countries to identify key obstacles to competitiveness, and to provide a platform for dialogue among government, business and civil society to discuss the best ways of removing them. Within this context, its fundamental objective is to help to explore the factors driving T&T competitiveness worldwide, thus providing a basis for implementing policies on a country-by-country basis.

The TTCI is composed of a number of 'pillars' of T&T competitiveness, of which there are 14 in all. The pillars are organized into three subindexes capturing broad categories of variables that facilitate or drive T&T competitiveness. These categories are: (i) T&T regulatory framework; (ii) T&T business environment and infrastructure; and (iii) T&T human, cultural and natural resources.

Figure 3.2 summarizes the structure of the overall index, showing how the 14 component pillars are allocated within the three subindexes. Each pillar comprises a number of individual variables.

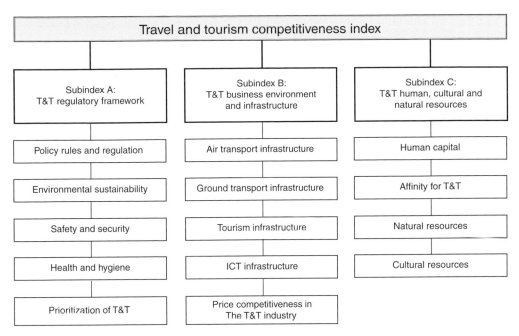

Fig. 3.2. Composition of the three subindexes of the Travel and Tourism Competitiveness Index (TTCI) (Blanke *et al.*, 2009: 6).

Subindex A: T&T regulatory framework

This subindex captures those elements that are policy related and generally under the purview of the government.

Pillar 1: *Policy rules and regulation*: Foreign ownership restrictions; Property rights; Rules governing foreign direct investment (FDI); Visa requirements; Openness of bilateral Air Service Agreements.

Pillar 2: *Environmental sustainability*: Stringency of environmental regulation; Clarity and stability of environmental regulations; Government prioritization of sustainable T&T.

Pillar 3: *Safety and security*: Business costs of terrorism; Reliability of police services; Business costs of crime and violence.

Pillar 4: *Health and hygiene*: Government efforts to reduce health risks from pandemics; Physician density; Access to improved sanitation; Access to improved drinking water.

Pillar 5: *Prioritization of T&T*: Government prioritization of the T&T industry; T&T government expenditure; Effectiveness of marketing and branding to attract tourists; T&T fair attendance.

Subindex B: T&T business environment and infrastructure

This subindex captures elements of the business environment and the infrastructure of each economy.

Pillar 6: *Air transport infrastructure*: Quality of air transport infrastructure; Available seat kilometres; Departures per 1000 population; Airport density; Number of operating airlines; International air transport network.

Pillar 7: *Ground transport infrastructure*: Road infrastructure; Railway infrastructure; Port infrastructure; Domestic transport network.

Pillar 8: *Tourism infrastructure*: Hotel rooms; Presence of major car rental companies; Automated teller machines (ATMs) accepting Visa cards.

Pillar 9: *ICT infrastructure*: Extent of business Internet use; Internet users; Telephone lines.

Pillar 10: *Price competitiveness in the T&T industry*: Ticket taxes and airport charges; Purchasing power parity; Extent and effect of taxation; Fuel price levels.

Subindex C: T&T human, cultural and natural resources

This subindex captures the human and cultural elements of each country's resource endowments.

Pillar 11: *Human capital*: Primary education enrolment; Secondary education enrolment; Quality of the educational system; Local availability of specialized research and training services; Extent of staff training; Availability of qualified labour; Hiring and firing practices; Ease of hiring foreign labour; Workforce wellness; Human immunodeficiency virus (HIV) prevalence; Malaria incidence; Tuberculosis incidence; Life expectancy.

Pillar 12: *Affinity for T&T*: Tourism openness; Attitude towards tourists; Recommendation to extend business trips.

Pillar 13: *Natural resources*: Carbon dioxide damage; Nationally protected areas; Business concern for ecosystems; Risk of malaria and yellow fever.

Pillar 14: *Cultural resources*: The number of United Nations Educational, Scientific and Cultural Organization (UNESCO) World Heritage Sites; Sports stadiums seating capacity; Number of international fairs and exhibitions in country.

The data set used to construct the TTCI includes both hard data and survey data from the WEF's annual Executive Opinion Survey. The hard data were obtained from publicly available sources, international T&T institutions and T&T experts (for example IATA, the International Civil Aviation Organization (ICAO), UNWTO, WTTC and UNESCO). The survey is carried out among CEOs and top business leaders making the investment decisions in each of the 133 economies covered in 2008.

The survey data comprise the responses to the WEF's Executive Opinion Survey, with additional questions relevant to tourism. The responses range from 1 to 7. A standard formula is used to convert each hard-data variable to the 1-to-7 scale. Each of the pillars has been calculated as an unweighted average of the individual component variables. The subindexes are then calculated as unweighted averages of the included pillars. The overall TTCI is then the unweighted average of the three subindexes (Blanke *et al.*, 2009).

TOURISM COMPETITIVENESS OF TWO DEVELOPING COUNTRIES: BRAZIL AND THAILAND

Performance in respect of T&T competitiveness remains varied, with some economies demonstrating diverse strengths but also substantial weaknesses. The WTTC suggests that the TTCI can be used to determine both a rationale and a strategy for how countries at various stages of economic development can make their T&T sectors more competitive.

Although some of the factors are a 'must have' for high-income economies to maintain destination competitiveness, they might not yet be essential for developing countries. Indeed, the importance of the various factors that make up the TTCI is likely to vary depending on each country's stage of development. Political stability, for instance, is a prerequisite for any country looking to attract foreign business and international travellers. Government investment in environmental protection and new technologies, on the other hand, might become relevant only once basic infrastructure is in place (Dwyer and Kim, 2003). A less-developed country that is in the process of building up its air and ground transport network may consider environmental regulations a secondary priority. In this respect, the growing pressure for all countries to initiate mitigation and adaptive measures to combat global warming will be of particular relevance to LDCs as such measures will inevitably involve costs to tourism suppliers.

T&T naturally increases as a country's economic and social welfare improves, and, as it does so, it becomes more important to its government and business leaders. That is why the TTCI naturally ranks advanced economies higher than countries at lower stages of development.

It is instructive to consider the T&T competitiveness of two developing countries, Brazil and Thailand. These countries are selected because they have been independently assessed recently for the potential of their tourism industries to reduce poverty. The discussion is based on that of Blanke and Chiesa (2009).

The TTCI of Brazil

Brazil is ranked fifth in the Americas and 45th overall. Brazil is ranked second out of all countries for its natural resources and 14th for its cultural resources, with many World Heritage Sites, a great proportion of protected land area and the most diverse fauna in the world. There is a substantial focus on environmental sustainability (ranked 33rd). However, the ground transport network remains underdeveloped, with the quality of roads, ports and railways ranked 110th, 123rd and 86th, respectively. Safety and security continue to be of serious concern, ranked 130th overall, just behind South Africa and Russia, and only just ahead of Bangladesh, Pakistan and Nigeria. Brazil also suffers greatly from a lack of price competitiveness (91st), attributable in part to high ticket taxes and airport charges in the country, as well as high prices and high taxation more generally. Further, the overall policy environment is not particularly conducive to the development of the sector (ranked 95th), with discouraging rules on FDI and too much time and red tape required for starting a business (Blanke and Chiesa, 2009: xvii).

The TTCI of Thailand

Thailand is ranked just behind Malaysia in the Asia Pacific at eighth place and 39th overall. It is endowed with rich natural resources and a strong affinity for T&T (ranked 24th and 22nd, respectively), with a very friendly attitude of the population towards tourists (ranked 13th). This is buttressed by the sector's strong prioritization by the government (ranked 12th) with, similar to Malaysia, excellent destination-marketing campaigns and good price competitiveness. However, some weaknesses remain: despite the prioritization of the sector by the government, some aspects of the regulatory environment – such as stringent foreign ownership restrictions, visa restrictions for many travellers and the long time required for starting a business in the country – are not particularly conducive to developing the sector (ranked 62nd). In addition, given the importance of the natural environment for the country's tourism, environmental sustainability should be a greater priority (ranked 99th) (Blanke and Chiesa, 2009: xx). More recently, Thailand's political stability has deteriorated and this is substantially affecting tourism flows.

The brief overview of the TTCI for the two countries reveals that both have potential to increase destination competitiveness. Brazil's weaknesses involve its policy rules and regulations, safety and security, health and hygiene, ground tourism infrastructure, ICT infrastructure, price competitiveness, human resources and affinity for tourism. Thailand shares some of these weaknesses particularly as regards policy rules and regulations, safety and security, health and hygiene, ICT infrastructure and human resources. It is these weaknesses that need to be addressed if each country is to move up the TTCI rankings list.

A key element of a successful tourism industry is the ability to recognize and deal with change across a wide range of key factors and the way they interact. Key drivers of global change within the external environment can be classified as: (i) economic; (ii) political; (iii) environmental; (iv) technological; (v) demographic; and (vi) social (Dwyer *et al.*, 2009). Achieving competitive advantage in times of rapid change requires tourism stakeholders to have a clear understanding of the direction of change and its implications for business or destination management. Since tourism is essentially integrated with other sectors in the economy, tourism trends cannot be considered in isolation from key drivers that will shape the world of the future. The challenge for tourism stakeholders in both private and public sectors is to account for these changes proactively to achieve and maintain competitive advantage for their organizations. One implication is that governments need to create an environment that best prepares their economies for the opportunities arising from the T&T sector. The TTCI can play an important role in highlighting areas of strength, weakness, opportunity and threat. In the next section we address some important management implications of the TTCI for LDCs. However, as we shall discuss below, the solution to improving destination competitiveness while at the same time reducing poverty is not easily achieved.

MANAGEMENT IMPLICATIONS FOR DEVELOPING COUNTRIES

The WTTC emphasizes three main initiatives that should be pursued in association with production of the TTCI, in order to enhance the economic development and reduce poverty worldwide. These three recommendations are (Lipman and Kester, 2007):

1. There should be widespread adoption of TSAs to ensure routine provision of data on the macroeconomic importance of the sector for policy making.
2. Given tourism's importance for developing countries, there is a window of opportunity for tourism services to be taken more explicitly into account in the Doha Development Round of trade negotiations, and this opportunity should be pursued.
3. Tourism should be integrated more explicitly into development processes – particularly by including the sector in the national poverty reduction strategy and in the overall support strategies of international aid agencies.

We now discuss each recommendation in turn, providing additional perspectives on various issues.

Widespread adoption of TSAs

Since it is not possible to identify tourism as a single 'industry' in the national accounts, its value to the economy is not readily revealed. Tourism activity is 'hidden' in other industry activities (accommodation, transportation, telecommunications and so on). This suggests that any attempt to examine the economic contribution of tourism that is focused on systems of national accounts only, and which highlights only tourism-related sectors, is likely to seriously underestimate the overall expenditure by tourists and thus its economic significance (Spurr, 2006).

Because of this accounting issue, governments may underestimate the benefits that tourism brings to their economies. This issue is of particular concern to LDCs, many of which are now following the high-income countries in developing TSAs. TSAs enable the relationships between tourism and other economic activity to be explored within the national accounts framework, extracting all the tourism-related economic activity which is included in the national accounts but not identified as tourism. All of the relevant activity is identified in a separate but related account, that is, an account which is a satellite of the core national accounts. By highlighting tourism within the national accounting framework, TSAs allow the tourism industry to be better included in the mainstream of economic analysis. As a statistical tool that is compatible with international and national accounting guidelines, TSAs can enhance the credibility of tourism as a main economic sector, help to identify critical elements in sector success or failure, enable valid comparisons between regions, countries or groups of countries, and facilitate comparisons with other internationally recognized macroeconomic aggregates and compilations.

TSAs provide policy makers with insights into tourism and its contribution to the economy, providing an instrument for designing more efficient policies relating to tourism and its employment aspects (Spurr, 2006). A TSA can serve as a tool for enhanced strategic management and planning for the tourism industry. Indeed, the Organisation for Economic Co-operation and Development (OECD) has described the purpose of the TSA as being to 'improve the effectiveness of tourism policies and actions and to improve existing measures for evaluation of these policies in the context of a broader policy agenda' (OECD, 2001).

Increasing numbers of countries have developed or are developing TSAs consistent with the *Tourism Satellite Account: Recommended Methodological Framework* (UNWTO, 2008a) developed by the Commission of the European Communities, the OECD, the UNWTO and the UN, and approved by the United Nations Statistical Commission. TSAs have now become the unifying framework of most of the components of the System of Tourism Statistics (UNWTO, 2008b). Over 70 countries have developed or are developing TSAs (Libreros *et al.*, 2006). Unfortunately many of the LDCs are yet to develop TSAs.

TSAs can be used to derive measures of tourism yield and tourism productivity (Dwyer *et al.*, 2007; Dwyer and Forsyth, 2008). Both types of measures provide opportunities for LDCs to improve the economic contribution of the tourism industry by monitoring the effectiveness of its inputs in producing the types of goods and services demanded by tourists.

Reinvigorating tourism services in the Doha Development Round

The World Trade Organization conducts negotiations through what are called **rounds**. The Doha Development Round commenced at Doha, Qatar in November 2001 and is still continuing. Its objective is to maintain the process of reform and liberalization of trade policies, thus ensuring that the multilateral trading system plays its full part in promoting recovery, growth and development of all countries. In this context, enhanced market access, balanced rules and well-targeted, sustainably financed technical assistance and capacity-building programmes have important roles to play in industry development including tourism.

While tourism services are under discussion in the Doha Round, the WTTC and other bodies are concerned that policy makers have failed to grasp the full development potential of the sector. Some specific concerns of the WTTC centre on the failures:

- to cover T&T services in a comprehensive way given that it deals with transportation issues separately despite the evident linkages with T&T competitiveness;
- to link T&T with development and poverty alleviation and thus to consider the range of capacity-building support measures available for poor countries' competitiveness enhancement;
- to link T&T with sustainable development, despite the clear interrelationship with the sector and particularly despite its importance for developing countries;

- to recognize effectively the links between T&T and infrastructure such as roads, ports, airports and telecommunications channels, which are vital for effective T&T competition in developing states; and
- to capitalize on the links between T&T and agriculture and the way in which rural tourism development can help to support agricultural communities, where poverty levels are often very high.

The Doha Round explicitly recognizes the particular vulnerability of the least developed countries and the special structural difficulties they face in the global economy. Participants are committed to addressing the marginalization of least developed countries in international trade and to improving their effective participation in the multilateral trading system. In this context, it is to be regretted that tourism is not being given more attention on the UN's world development agenda. Perhaps the progressive development of TSAs in developing countries will help to generate an increased awareness of the economic contribution of tourism in LDCs.

Mainstreaming tourism for development

The WTTC states that, to make a significant difference in enhancing the competitiveness of the poorest countries, LDCs must highlight T&T in their national Poverty Reduction Strategies (Lipman and Kester, 2007). At the same time, the WTTC has encouraged development-financing institutions – the World Bank Group, the regional development banks and bilateral aid agencies – to recognize in their support strategies the potential in T&T for stimulation programmes to create jobs and reignite growth. The conviction is that tourism has more capacity for job creation and economic regeneration than virtually any other sector, and is a fast entry vehicle into the workforce for young people and women.

Emphasizing the strong linkage of T&T to other sectors, the WTTC states that there needs to be an explicit awareness that T&T is the major services export for so many developing countries and has the potential to provide capacity building, job creation, economic diversification and a genuine competitive advantage for all poor countries. It is claimed that those countries that mainstream tourism squarely in their stimulation priorities will be enhancing their socio-economic competitiveness generally and in the sector specifically (Lipman and Kester, 2009: 107, 108).

Already, steps have been undertaken to place tourism development more firmly within the wider development agenda of LDCs. The UNWTO has developed a number of programmes to help states generally use T&T in their development projects. They have created a dedicated programme, Sustainable Tourism for Eliminating Poverty (ST-EP) to link sustainable tourism and alleviate poverty in a disciplined way and to tap global funding for identified tourism activities, focusing on community-based actions (Sofield *et al.*, 2004).

One approach that promises to help reduce poverty in LDCs is pro-poor tourism (PPT). PPT is an approach to tourism rather than a specific tourism product or tourism sector. It consists of a set of principles, strategies and initiatives that seek to help the poor tap into and gain benefit from tourist activities (Ashley and Roe, 2003; ESCAP, 2005). To this end, PPT is focused more on unlocking opportunities for the poor than on expanding the overall size of tourism. Driving the push for PPT also is the realization that the alleviation of poverty is now an essential condition for world peace.

The principles that underlie PPT include the following (Ashley *et al.*, 2000):

- Incorporation of PPT into the wider tourism framework, putting poverty reduction into the minds of tourists and adding poverty concerns to tourism's existing commercial, environmental and ethical objectives.
- Enhancement of economic opportunities for the poor by including them in tourism decision making and reducing barriers to their economic participation in tourist activity.
- Placement of poverty at the centre of the tourism sustainability debate. To date, the sustainable tourism debate has tended to focus on environmental concerns and mainstream destinations, neglecting the links between poverty, the environment and development. The elimination of poverty, though, is increasingly seen as critical for sustainable development.

The effectiveness of PPT strategies has not yet been demonstrated, if only because they are relatively new and largely untried. The action agenda to eliminate poverty is obviously complex. Benefits to the poor from tourism depend on whether and how they can participate economically in the industry. Until strategies are in place and have had a chance to work, there is uncertainty as to exactly how and to what extent tourism will reduce poverty.

The WTTC argues that extending the TTCI to integrate the principles of PPT and to remove bias towards wealthy countries will make the index more meaningful and can better link up with the aim of emphasizing quality of life. Although the WTTC provides no guidance as to precisely how this is to be done, we suggest that there are two ways to proceed. One way is to consider, for each of the identified indicators under the identified pillars, the extent to which the poor benefit relative to the rest of the population. A second way to proceed is to extend the range of variables comprising the TTCI to include those that specifically relate to the poor. An example of this is the extension of measures of tourism yield to include the development of pro-poor yield measures (Dwyer, 2007). The issues deserve further attention from tourism researchers.

While tourism may have the *potential* to reduce poverty in developing countries, some recent investigations of the effects of tourism development reveal that it makes poorer people relatively worse off in certain circumstances. These findings lend support to the PPT view that simply increasing the volume of tourism does not reduce poverty per se. We next discuss some of these findings.

INTER-INDUSTRY EFFECTS OF TOURISM GROWTH

The effects of tourist expenditure on the economy are estimated using economic models that identify and quantify the linkages between the different sectors of the local economy and the linkages with other regions. The greater the extent to which tourism development generates production in the primary, secondary and tertiary sectors, the greater is the tourism multiplier and consequent impact of injected expenditure on gross regional product and employment. Ideally, when there is an increase in tourism expenditure, the tourist industry can expand output to meet the additional demand by employing additional labour, land and capital plant and equipment. This will allow multiplier effects to ripple through the economy (Fletcher, 1994).

We should be wary, however, about attributing large tourism multipliers to this process. The multiplier mechanism implicitly assumes that there are unused resources available to meet any extra demand. When the economy is at or near full employment, however, with no spare capacity in some key sectors, increased tourism demand imposes cost pressures as the prices of scarce resources are bid up. In such circumstances, tourist expenditure will result in increased prices rather than increases in output, income and employment. Moreover, if other industries employ the same resources as does the tourist industry, they also face cost pressures resulting from the increased tourism demand. In the absence of offsetting productivity improvements, price increases attract resources into tourism, increasing the industry's costs and making the destination less price competitive. The size of the cost increases depends on the supply of different factors, whether these factors account for a significant proportion of the tourist industry total production costs, and how quickly extra supplies can be made available.

In reality, economies experiencing an increase in tourism expenditure, particularly developing countries, will face labour, land and capital constraints. In the competition for scarce resources, increased costs will tend to reduce the competitiveness of other sectors in the economy, particularly export-oriented and import-competing industries. Price increases may particularly affect trade-exposed sectors that face world prices for their products. They will be unable to pass on cost increases without losing market share. Any loss of market share by domestic producers means that the net gain to the economy from further tourism will be lower. Indeed, the additional tourism may result in losses to traditional export and import-competing industries.

The nature of the exchange rate regime is also a crucial determinant of the economic impacts of inbound tourism. Under the floating exchange rate system that characterizes most of the world's economies, an expansion of international tourism will strengthen a country's real exchange rate, leading to a reduction in other exports and/or an increase in demand for imports at the expense of the demand for domestic import-competing commodities. If tourism expands at the expense of other tradable industries, there is a reduced multiplier effect on income and employment, although there may be a small positive impact on employment if tourism is more labour intensive than other industries which it replaces.

In many less developed countries with small open economies, the most obviously affected sectors will be the traditional export sectors such as agriculture, mining and manufacturing, which suffer reduced competitiveness on world markets due to exchange rate appreciation. If increased tourism demand leads to increased investment, foreign borrowing will increase and so too possibly FDI for a period, pushing the exchange rate even higher. This will further reduce traditional exports and increase imports.

The study of the economic impacts of tourism shocks has recently undergone a 'paradigm shift' as a result of the use of computable general equilibrium (CGE) models in place of the standard approach using input-output models (Dwyer *et al.*, 2004). The development and application of this superior technique have major implications for the way that tourism economists think about the economic impacts of tourism and for the policy advice they give to decision makers in both the public and the private sectors.

Simulations of increased inbound tourism in LDCs using CGE models suggest that an expansion of tourism may be at the expense of a reduction in some traditional export and import-competing industries and that, on balance, the economy-wide effect may not be as great as destination managers have tended to believe. These results cover both developed economies and LDCs such as Zimbabwe (Mabugu, 2002), Fiji (Narayan, 2004) and Indonesia (Sugiyarto *et al.*, 2003). To illustrate the issues we herein present two brief case studies, one for Brazil and the other for Thailand. The TTCI for each of these countries was set out above.

Tourism and poverty reduction in Brazil

Poverty is widespread across Brazil. The Brazilian government sees tourism as a major potential source of job creation and reduction of economic disparities, and long-term policies to improve the industry in the country have been established. The number of tourist arrivals increased from 1.1 million in 1990 to 4.1 million in 2003. The government expects that about 1.2 million jobs will be created in tourism businesses in 4 years should the growth trend continue.

Blake *et al.* (2007) provide an economy-wide analysis of the distributional effects of tourism expansion, providing a means of answering the question of whether and how tourism can contribute to poverty relief. Tourism may be expected to reduce poverty via three channels:

- The first channel is prices, by which tourism spending leads to changes in prices for goods that poor households purchase.
- The second channel relates to the effects that tourism spending has on the earnings of employed and self-employed labour and in returns to capital.
- The third channel is government, by which the expenditure changes government revenues and can thus affect government spending, borrowing or tax rates.

Blake *et al.* (2007) use a CGE model for Brazil to quantify the effects on income distribution and poverty relief that occur via changes in prices, earnings and government revenues following an expansion of tourism. The CGE model is calibrated using a social accounting matrix (SAM) that shows the payments that take place among the different industries, products, factors, households, firms, the government and the rest of the world. The model incorporates the earnings of different groups of workers within tourism, along with the channels by which changes in earnings, prices and the government affect the distribution of income among rich and poor households. The model has the advantage of incorporating the entire range of activities undertaken in the Brazilian economy, thereby permitting analysis of the interrelationships between tourism and other sectors.

The model assumes a 10% increase in demand by foreign tourists in Brazil in order to investigate the effects of this on income distribution in the economy. Table 3.3 shows changes in the composition of real earnings resulting from the 10% increase in foreign tourism demand, by household.

Column 1 shows the direct earnings effects, which are the earnings by household in the sector from which foreign tourists are purchasing goods and services.

The figures in column 2 show that the indirect earnings effects are highly significant for the high-income household, which earns more through the indirect than through the direct effects.

Table 3.3. Distribution of earnings by households (US$ million) (Blake *et al.*, 2007).

	1	2	3	4	5	6
	Direct effect	Direct plus indirect effect	Total effect simulation 1			
Household	Earnings	Earnings	Earnings	Prices	Government	Firms
Lowest-income household	11	15	12	1	0	5
Low-income household	25	35	25	4	5	0
Medium-income household	14	22	3	1	6	4
High-income household	18	39	7	−6	11	29

In columns 3 to 6, the CGE model results are decomposed into earnings, prices and government channels as well as the effects of increased firm investment.

The results show that the total earnings effects (column 3) are often lower than the direct plus indirect earnings effects, and that, for the medium- and high-income households, the total earnings effects are small. Other export sectors are much more intensive in their use of factors of production – capital and skilled labour – that are owned by the richer household groups than are tourism businesses. Therefore, the greatest burdens of the crowding out activities fall on the medium- and high-income households.

The price channel (column 4) is shown to have a moderate effect, increasing the real income of the poorest household groups but reducing the real income of the richest group. The government channel (column 5), in this simulation, acts to increase the incomes of all households except the poorest as they receive very low levels of transfers. The firms' effect (column 6) comes through the fact that establishments invest more in response to the tourism shock, and the additional holding of capital (with future earnings potential) is allocated to households in proportion to their ownership of firms.

The simulations indicate that tourism benefits the lowest-income sections of the Brazilian population and has the potential to reduce income inequality. The lowest-income households are not, however, the main beneficiaries, as households with low (but not the lowest) income benefit more from the earnings and price channel effects of tourism expansion.

High- and medium-income households, followed by the low-income group, benefit most from the government channel effects, with the exception of the case when government directs the revenue from tourism expansion specifically towards the lowest-income group. The latter type of revenue distribution could double the benefits for the lowest-income households, giving them around one-third of all the benefits. The implication is that policies directed specifically towards benefiting the lowest-income group are required if the poorest are to achieve the greatest gains.

The results suggest caution when generalizing the effects of tourism growth on poverty within a country. In the case of Brazil, there is a strong reinforcement effect whereby the industries that reduce their output following a tourism demand increase are export industries that employ factors of production from the richer households. Therefore, the structure of earnings in non-tourism export sectors plays a significant role in determining the net poverty effects of tourism. Blake *et al.* (2007) emphasize that this type of earnings structure may not apply in other countries. Hence, it would be important to apply the model to tourism expansion in other countries, in order to investigate the effects that would occur under different types of earnings structures.

Tourism and poverty reduction in Thailand

Wattanakuljarus and Coxhead (2008) use a CGE model for Thailand and simulate the effects of tourism growth. Their stated goal is to take account of general equilibrium adjustment mechanisms in answering the question: is tourism growth pro-poor?

Foreign tourism is by far Thailand's largest export industry. 'Visitor exports', or sales of tourism goods and services to foreign visitors, averaged US$10.2 billion (12% of total exports) in 1998–2005 on more than 10 million annual visitor arrivals. The next largest category of exports, computers and parts, averaged US$8.5 billion in the same period. On average during 1998–2005, Thai tourism directly and indirectly accounted for 13% of GDP, 10% of employment (3 million jobs) and 12% of investment. Successive Thai governments have placed great store in earnings from tourism, and have supported a range of promotional programmes in the past decade.

Wattanakuljarus and Coxhead assume that inbound tourism increases by 10%. Depending on the assumptions regarding factor constraints, this induces growth in real GDP of between 0.88% and 2.06%, leading households to increase consumption by between 3.81% and 4.11%. Due to increased household and tourism consumption, total domestic absorption increases by between 2.90% and 3.25%.

Wattanakuljarus and Coxhead distinguish the following categories:

- LowAg the poorest 80% of households in agriculture;
- HighAg the richest 20% of households in agriculture;
- LowNag the poorest 80% of households in non-agriculture; and
- HighNag the richest 20% of households in non-agriculture.

On these definitions, pro-poor growth is characterized by a relatively faster rate of increase in the incomes of households in the LowAg group, since that is where most poor Thai households are found.

Table 3.4 shows the additional factor income accruing to each of the four sectors following a 10% increase in tourism to Thailand. Owners of the factor that gain most from a given shock will benefit most from tourism growth. Table 3.4 indicates that a 10% tourism expansion generates an extra 75,413 million baht of income for owners of non-agricultural labour. Of this, 2115 million baht goes to LowAg, 1087 million baht goes to HighAg, 21,197 million baht goes to LowNag, and 51,014 million baht goes to HighNag. Other factor income changes can be read in the same way. The largest percentage increase in factor earnings goes to capital in non-agricultural sectors, and the largest part of this gain is earned by the HighNag group. As a result, just over 55% of the total increase in factor incomes accrues to this group.

The simulations indicate that capital and labour in non-agriculture are the factors that gain the most. In Thailand, corporations are the major owners of capital in non-agriculture, and corporate income accrues mainly to wealthy non-agricultural households. Similarly, since

Table 3.4. Distribution of additions to factor incomes across households (million baht) (Wattanakuljarus and Coxhead, 2008).

Household[b]	Income[a]							Distribution (%)
	LabAg	LabNag	Land	CapAg	CapNag	Forest	Total	
LowAg	4,229	2,115	1,616	2,196	14,499	79	24,734	14.04
HighAg	240	1,087	1,612	908	4,636	33	8,516	4.83
LowNag	717	21,197	841	125	22,435	4	45,319	25.72
HighNag	188	51,014	1,162	28	45,223	1	97,616	55.41
Total	5,374	75,413	5,231	3,257	86,792	117	176,185	100
Distribution (%)	3.05	42.80	2.97	1.85	49.26	0.07	100	

[a] LabAg, agricultural labour; LabNag, non-agricultural labour; Land, income from land; CapAg, agricultural capital; CapNag, non-agricultural capital; Forest, income from forests.
[b] LowAg, the poorest 80% of households in agriculture; HighAg, the richest 20% of households in agriculture; LowNag, the poorest 80% of households in non-agriculture; HighNag, the richest 20% of households in non-agriculture.

high-income non-agricultural households are the major owners of labour in non-agriculture, they are the next biggest beneficiaries. As a result, given the distribution of factor ownership across household groups, the inbound tourism expansion raises incomes across the board, but the main share of the gains accrues to the non-poor.

Wattanakuljarus and Coxhead (2008) conducted sensitivity analysis with different assumptions regarding factor constraints. In every scenario, however, although tourism growth benefits all household classes, the biggest gains accrue to high-income and non-agricultural households. It is concluded that tourism growth in Thailand is not pro-poor or pro-agriculture.

The study has interesting policy implications. One is that a tourism promotion campaign leading to increased international visitation may increase the gap between rich and poor. To address this increased inequality, additional policy instruments are required to correct for the inequalities occasioned by tourism growth.

CONCLUSIONS

The results of CGE modelling of the effects of increased tourism flows do not imply, of course, that tourism cannot be an engine for growth. But they do imply that gaining extra tourists is only one element that needs to be addressed by destination managers. Unless factor constraints can be overcome and unless strong links can be forged between local industries, tourism expansion will not fulfil its promise as a strong engine for economic growth. Destination managers with a good understanding of the above issues can use the TTCI productively to indicate priority areas that can be addressed so as to enhance the economic effects of increased inbound tourism expenditure.

While tourism makes a valuable contribution to the economies of LDCs, there is generally a potential for much improvement in this respect. Growth rates in tourism are higher in LDCs than in higher income economies implying that LDCs are gaining a greater share of world tourism flows and the associated expenditures. If LDCs are to enhance tourism's contribution to their economies they will need to address certain barriers that they have in common. In respect of what issues need to be addressed to improve destination competitiveness, the TTCI is a useful initiative that allows different countries to assess their performance against other countries at various levels of development. While the TTCI is a useful basis for policy making to enhance tourism's potential as an engine for growth and as a means of reducing poverty, other initiatives can be undertaken to leverage the benefits to individual countries. These initiatives include developing TSAs and reinvigorating services within the Doha Development Round. While LDCs face formidable challenges to growth, such initiatives can help tourism to play a more important role in their economic development. Of wider significance is the reduction of structural and regulatory impediments to growth that seem to bedevil LDCs. It is here that the TTCI can provide important input into tourism strategy development and management.

REFERENCES

Ashley, C. and Roe, D. (2003) *Working with the Private Sector on Pro-Poor Tourism. Opinions and Experience from Two Development Practitioners.* Overseas Development Institute (ODI), London.
Ashley, C., Boyd, C. and Goodwin, H. (2000) *Pro Poor Tourism: Putting Poverty at the Heart of the Tourism Agenda.* UK Government Overseas Development Institute, London.

Blake, A., Arbache, J.S., Sinclair, T. and Teles, V. (2007) Tourism and poverty relief. *Annals of Tourism Research* 35(1), 107–126.

Blanke, J. and Chiesa, T. (2008) The Travel and Tourism Competitiveness Index: measuring key elements driving the sector's development. In: *The Travel & Tourism Competitiveness Report 2008: Balancing Economic Development and Environmental Sustainability.* World Economic Forum (WEF), Geneva, Switzerland, pp. 3–26.

Blanke, J. and Chiesa, T. (2009) The Travel and Tourism Competitiveness Index 2009: measuring sectoral drivers in a downturn. In: *The Travel & Tourism Competitiveness Report 2009: Managing in a Time of Turbulence.* World Economic Forum (WEF), Geneva, Switzerland, pp. xiii–xxvi [Executive Summary].

Blanke, J., Chiesa, T. and Trujillo Herrera, E. (2009) The Travel and Tourism Competitiveness Index 2009: measuring sectoral drivers in a downturn. In: *The Travel & Tourism Competitiveness Report 2009: Managing in a Time of Turbulence.* World Economic Forum (WEF), Geneva, Switzerland, pp. 3–38.

Crouch, G.I. and Ritchie, J.R.B. (1999) Tourism, competitiveness, and societal prosperity. *Journal of Business Research* 44, 137–152.

Dwyer, L. (2007) Relevance of tourism yield to impact measurement in tourism chain development. Paper presented at the meeting Poverty Alleviation through Tourism – Impact Measurement in Tourism Chain Development, 12–13 December, International Finance Commission, Mekong Private Development Facility, Phnom Penh, Cambodia.

Dwyer, L. and Forsyth, P. (2008) Economic measures of tourism yield: what markets to target? *International Journal of Tourism Research* 10, 155–168.

Dwyer, L. and Kim, C.W. (2003) Destination competitiveness: a model and indicators. *Current Issues in Tourism* 6(5), 369–413.

Dwyer, L., Forsyth, P. and Spurr, R. (2004) Evaluating tourism's economic effects: new and old approaches. *Tourism Management* 25, 307–317.

Dwyer, L., Forsyth, P. and Spurr, R. (2007) Contrasting the uses of TSAs and CGE models: measuring tourism yield and productivity. *Tourism Economics* 13(4), 537–551.

Dwyer, L., Edwards, D., Mistilis, N., Scott, N. and Roman, C. (2009) Destination and enterprise management for a tourism future. *Tourism Management* 30, 63–74.

Economic and Social Commission for Asia and the Pacific (ESCAP) (2005) The contribution of tourism to poverty alleviation. *ESCAP Tourism Review* No. 25 ST/ESCAP/2380, 1–89.

Fletcher, J. (1994) Input-output analysis. In: Witt, S. and Moutinho, L. (eds) *Tourism Marketing and Management Handbook,* 2nd edn. Prentice Hall International, London, pp. 480–484.

Libreros, M., Massieu, A. and Meis, S. (2006) Progress in tourism satellite account implementation and development. *Journal of Travel Research* 45, 83.

Lipman, G. and Kester, J. (2007) Tourism competitiveness and the development agenda. In: *The Travel & Tourism Competitiveness Report 2007: Furthering the Process of Economic Development.* World Economic Forum (WEF), Geneva, Switzerland, pp. 55–66.

Lipman, G. and Kester, J. (2009) Strengthening the Travel and Tourism Competitiveness Index. In: *The Travel & Tourism Competitiveness Report 2009: Managing in a Time of Turbulence.* World Economic Forum (WEF), Geneva, Switzerland, pp. 107, 108.

Mabugu, R. (2002) Short-term effects of policy reform on tourism and the macroeconomy in Zimbabwe: applied CGE analysis. *Development Southern Africa* 19, 419–430.

Miller, R. (2007) Tourism competitiveness and the development agenda. In: *The Travel & Tourism Competitiveness Report 2007: Furthering the Process of Economic Development.* World Economic Forum (WEF), Geneva, Switzerland, pp. 45–54.

Narayan, P. (2004) Economic impact of tourism on Fiji's economy: empirical evidence from the computable general equilibrium model. *Tourism Economics* 10(4), 419–433.

Organisation for Economic Co-operation and Development (OECD) (2001) *Tourism Satellite Account Recommended Methodological Framework*. OECD co-edition with the United Nations Statistics Division (UNSD), EUROSTAT Tourism Unit, Paris and the United Nations World Tourism Organization, Paris.

Ringbeck, J. and Gross, S. (2007) Taking travel and tourism to the next level: shaping the government agenda to improve the industry's competitiveness. In: *The Travel & Tourism Competitiveness Report 2007: Furthering the Process of Economic Development*. World Economic Forum (WEF), Geneva, Switzerland, pp. 27–44.

Sofield, T., Bauer, J., De Lacy, T., Lipman, G. and Daugherty, S. (2004) *Sustainable Tourism Eliminating Poverty (ST-EP)*. Sustainable Tourism Cooperative Research Centre, Gold Coast, Australia.

Spurr, R. (2006) Tourism satellite accounts. In: Dwyer, L. and Forsyth, P. (eds) *International Handbook on the Economics of Tourism*. Edward Elgar, Cheltenham, UK.

Sugiyarto, G., Blake, A. and Sinclair, M. (2003) Tourism and globalization: economic impact in Indonesia. *Annals of Tourism Research* 30(3), 683–701.

United Nations Environment Programme (UNEP) (2002) *Global Environment Outlook 3 – Past, Present, and Future Perspectives*. UNEP, Madrid.

United Nations World Tourism Organization (UNWTO) (2008a) *Tourism Satellite Account: Recommended Methodological Framework*. Jointly presented by the United Nations Statistics Division (UNSD), the Statistical Office of the European Communities (EUROSTAT), the Organisation for Economic Co-operation and Development (OECD) and the UNWTO, Madrid.

United Nations World Tourism Organization (UNWTO) (2008b) *2008 International Recommendations for Tourism Statistics*. UNWTO, Madrid.

Wattanakuljarus, A. and Coxhead, I. (2008) Is tourism-based development good for the poor? A general equilibrium analysis for Thailand. *Journal of Policy Modeling* 30(6), 929–955.

World Travel and Tourism Council (WTTC) (2007) Executive summary. In: *Travel and Tourism, Navigating the Path Ahead*. The 2007 Travel and Tourism Economic Research of the WTTC and Accenture. WTTC, London, pp. 1–10.

chapter 4

Demand Modelling and Fuzzy Time Series Forecasting

Stephen F. Witt, Luiz Moutinho, Kun-Huang Huarng and Tiffany Hui-Kuang Yu

INTRODUCTION

In science, and even in everyday life, many things are highly predictable, but in other circumstances prediction is often difficult. Furthermore, in making predictions, we are often unsure about the outcome. Forecasting assists tourism managers to improve decision making. In an organizational design context, forecasting should not be regarded as a self-contained activity, but should be integrated within the planning context of which it is a part. The role of forecasts in the tourism planning process was noted by Gunn (1994: 5):

> Of interest to many tourist businesses is increasing the ability to make forecasts. Decisions on the purchase of new generations of equipment, new sites, and new technology may rest on predictions of increased demand for a specific tourism service or product.

It is often stressed that accuracy is the critical characteristic of a forecasting method, as noted by Archer (1994: 105):

> The accuracy of the forecasts will affect the quality of the management decision … In the tourism industry, in common with most other service sectors, the need to forecast accurately is especially acute because of the perishable nature of the product.

Martin and Witt (1988b), in a study which reported the views of tourism academics and practitioners on the desirable characteristics of forecasts, confirmed that forecast accuracy is regarded as the most important property of a forecasting method. The purpose of this chapter is to examine several more advanced forecasting methods (qualitative and quantitative) and provide examples which illustrate potential applications of the various methods. The main methods described are:

- Delphi and jury of executive opinion;
- cross-impact analysis;
- probability forecasting; and
- econometric forecasting.

More substantial textbooks dealing with forecasting are Frechtling (1996), Wilson and Keating (1998) and Makridakis *et al.* (1998).

DELPHI FORECASTING/JURY OF EXECUTIVE OPINION[1]

The Delphi method of forecasting has attracted considerable attention in the tourism literature since the late 1970s (Robinson, 1979; Seeley *et al.*, 1980; Kaynak and Macaulay, 1984; Var, 1984; Liu, 1988; Yong *et al.*, 1989; Moeller and Shafer, 1994; Taylor and Judd, 1994). This technique aims to obtain expert opinion about the future through questionnaire surveys of a group of experts in the field, and is particularly useful for long-term forecasting. The respondents provide their estimates of the probabilities of certain specified conditions or events occurring in the future, and also estimate when the events would be likely to occur. Delphi studies are carried out anonymously in order to minimize conforming influences; thus, rather than meeting physically to debate the various issues under consideration, the experts are kept apart so that their views are not affected by dominant personalities, social pressure, etc. Delphi studies involve several iterative rounds, and at each stage the derived group opinion is fed back to the participants in the form of the range and distribution of responses. The panel members are requested to re-evaluate their previous replies in the light of the summary group opinion and to justify any answers which would still differ greatly from the overall group opinion. The experts are thus able to try to convince one another about their views. Eventually a group consensus emerges and it is possible to draw up a forecast. The distinguishing characteristics of Delphi forecasting are the aim – to generate aggregate expert opinion about the future – and the method used – maintenance of strict anonymity within the group of experts and iterative polling of participants with feedback of group opinion between polls.

One example of the use of the Delphi technique to predict future tourism trends in the Province of Nova Scotia, Canada to the year 2000 was described by Kaynak and Macaulay (1984). Subsequently, Liu (1988) carried out a Delphi study to forecast tourism to Hawaii by the year 2000. Also, Yong *et al.* (1989) used the Delphi method to forecast the future of the tourism industry in Singapore, with the most distant time horizon for the year of probable occurrence being '2000 and beyond'.

The above three cases are all examples of standard Delphi forecasting applications in tourism involving postal questionnaires, strict anonymity and iterative polling of participants. However, Robinson (1979) and Seeley *et al.* (1980) presented a 'symposium Delphi' approach which they suggest can be used at conferences to generate forecasts. The methodology was applied at the International Symposium on Tourism and the Next Decade which was held in Washington, DC during 1979, and was used to forecast international tourism conditions up to the year 2000. A two-round 'symposium Delphi' study was undertaken, with the sample group comprising 25 people (all of these participated in round 1, but only 19 in round 2). The questionnaires were administered in a face-to-face situation with the whole group present, and the mean results for each question were displayed immediately. Clearly therefore, the usual Delphi anonymity condition did not hold. On the other hand, 'the interpersonal environment provided an opportunity to clarify responses'

(Robinson, 1979: 271). A further major advantage of the symposium Delphi approach can be the existence of a captive audience with the resultant possibility of a 100% response rate within a minimal time period. Whether the forecasting approach adopted at the Tourism and the Next Decade Symposium can be correctly termed a 'Delphi' forecast is questionable; it is a 'consensus of expert opinion approach', but does not satisfy all the Delphi requirements.

The advantage of the Delphi approach over other consensus of expert opinion forecasting approaches where participants do meet – that the views of the experts are not affected by social pressure, etc. – needs to be balanced against the disadvantages of being unable to engage in debate with the other experts in order to exchange ideas, clarify points, etc. and the fairly long time period required to carry out the exercise.

In this next section, the particular consensus forecasting approach examined is **jury of executive opinion**. Results of a jury of executive opinion forecasting exercise carried out in 1992 are presented in which the distinguishing characteristics were: (i) that a specific time horizon far into the future (2030) was considered as opposed to the more usual year 2000 time horizon; (ii) that the emphasis was specifically upon the impacts of developments in science and technology upon tourism; (iii) that the forecast focus was not destination specific (e.g. Nova Scotia, Singapore); and (iv) that the tourism experts were mainly European, but with some Central Americans also present, compared with the more usual non-destination specific forecasting situation in which the views of North American tourism experts predominate. The focus on the impacts of developments in science and technology stems from: first, the fact that they have 'come to dominate the economy and society in the developed world'; and, secondly, the expected rapid pace of technological development as exemplified in the statement that 'All the technological knowledge we work with today will represent only 1% of the knowledge that will be available in 2050' (Cetron and Davies, 1991: 5). Clearly, however, there are also many economic, social and environmental factors which will have a substantive influence on the future nature and evolution of the field of tourism. The objective of the study was to help to create a strategic vision of the future of tourism up to the year 2030. Underlying this objective is the premise that future tourism phenomena can be managed by looking at futuristic scenarios which are based on the impact of science and technology. In this way management by anticipation and proactive strategies can be translated into competitive advantage.

Future developments affecting tourism

Twenty-five possible future developments affecting tourism were selected from a framework developed by Shafer and Moeller (1988, 1994), in which they describe possible developments in science and technology that may strongly impact tourism planning and development. Shafer and Moeller's visions of future developments resulted from a review of over 100 popular and scientific articles, and cover such areas as: (i) video; (ii) transportation; (iii) recreation equipment; and (iv) computers and robotics. The questions included in the present study were selected on the basis of their direct relevance and importance to tourism development over the period to 2030. In addition, it was realized that the spread of knowledge among the tourism experts would be sketchy in some of the areas covered by Shafer and Moeller. Hence, attention was restricted to those facets in which the experts were expected to have a high degree of interest/involvement: areas that they could visualize, relate to and respond to. The questions selected for inclusion in this study cover the areas of tourism superstructure, robotics, computers/artificial intelligence, recreation and transportation. These possible future developments are listed and described in Table 4.1. It was specifically on account of the rather innovative/radical nature of several of the possible tourism developments under consideration that it was felt important in this case to permit full discussion among the tourism experts before a forecast was generated, and thus to follow a non-Delphi consensus approach.

Table 4.1. Possible future developments and consensus forecasting results.

Possible development	Impact importance (1 = low, 5 = high)	Mean probability of occurrence (%)	Most likely year of occurrence (1992–2030)
Tourism superstructure			
Floating hotels	2.6	57	2000
Multi-storey floating hotels moored offshore, containing shopping, gymnasiums and glass-enclosed elevators carrying tourists to the sea floor			
Underwater hotels	2.8	26	2030
Built completely underwater, visitors will be able to study and watch undersea life through their bedroom windows			
Theme parks	3.2	67	1997
Individual experience centres where technology lets people role play … Life in Victorian England, Early America or French Revolution			
Robotics			
Robots play a large part in planning facilities and services: restaurants, landscaping, park design and entertainment	2.6	50	2000
Robots will be built in the form of buildings, providing most services of modern hotels, and these hotels will be run by an administrative computer	4.0	73	2000

(Continued)

Table 4.1. Continued.

Possible development	Impact importance (1 = low, 5 = high)	Mean probability of occurrence (%)	Most likely year of occurrence (1992–2030)
Computers/artificial intelligence			
Programs which can make judgements will be used by tourism managers to design the best programme mix for differing clientele and to manage natural resources for a multiplicity of uses	4.0	69	2000
Computers with artificial intelligence will mimic human senses and attitudes	2.5	24	2030
Recreation			
Artificial environments	3.1	60	2000
Specially created and commonly used for recreational facilities and outdoor activities			
Skill training in recreation	3.5	78	1995
Video tapes used on location to train tourists, e.g. skiing, scuba diving, sailing			
Videocycles	2.9	63	1995
Combination of stationary exercise bike and TV/VCR used to tour scenic routes in forested and urban environments			

(Continued)

Table 4.1. Continued.

Possible development	Impact importance (1 = low, 5 = high)	Mean probability of occurrence (%)	Most likely year of occurrence (1992–2030)
Night vision	2.6	51	2000
Glasses to allow participation in outdoor recreation in the dark. Other devices to improve hearing, touch, sense of smell, strength and coordination instantly			
Sunpods	2.8	62	2000
Solar-powered bubbles for all-over tan and relaxation even in freezing temperatures			
Simulations and image libraries	2.9	75	1996
Creation of own desired images and sensations through home-based wall-size TV screens, e.g. rafting on Colorado River. Inexpensive flat-panel display devices to view the world's art treasures, with resolution so good as to look like the real painting			
Digital TV	2.7	74	2000
Allows viewers to participate in production, superimposing and altering events			
Sensavision TV	2.8	49	2000
Whole room is part of TV set, allowing viewer to feel temperature and humidity, and to smell, i.e. to be part of the scene			

(Continued)

Table 4.1. Continued.

Possible development	Impact importance (1 = low, 5 = high)	Mean probability of occurrence (%)	Most likely year of occurrence (1992–2030)
Transportation			
Air travel	4.2	48	2020
New York to Tokyo: 2 h scheduled flight			
Paris to Tokyo: 1 h scheduled flight	3.5	28	2030
Skycycles: one-person light aircraft flying 40 km and more by pedal power (24 km/h)	1.5	16	2030
Jet powered backpacks: individual flight propulsion within reach of middle-income families	3.3	25	2030
Two-person aircraft: for touring and soaring, at an accessible cost	3.4	60	2010
Magnetic trains	3.9	52	2015
Flying on cushions of electromagnetism make short trips between cities faster than airlines manage today, e.g. Los Angeles to Las Vegas			
Supersubs	3.2	53	2000
Undersea tour buses, like undersea planes			
Multiple transportation cars	3.8	58	2020
Usable on land and in flight, at an accessible cost			
Space travel			
Shuttle services to orbiting hotels	3.5	4	2030
Space resorts	3.4	20	2030

Procedure

The fieldwork was conducted in June 1992 in Valencia, Spain, at a tourism seminar, where 25 tourism experts were asked about their views on possible future developments in tourism. The tourism experts were selected to achieve a broad spectrum and comprised approximately 40% academics (drawn mainly from the areas of marketing, management, economics and accounting/finance), 40% from the commercial tourism industry (mainly managers of hotel chains and travel agencies, and consultants), and 20% from central and local government and tourist offices. The latter group size was restricted to 20% as it was felt that tourism authorities would generally be more distant from the effects of technological change than academics and the commercial tourism industry. A time span of 4 hours was allowed for the exercise. First, the objectives of the study were explained, and then the questionnaire was distributed. Next, the 25 possible future tourism developments were explained in detail, and participants were allowed to ask clarification questions. The tourism experts were then split into groups of five to discuss the various issues. A lunch break followed, during which the experts were encouraged to continue exchanging views. Then a final question clarification session took place before participants filled in the questionnaires individually. Thus, in addition to the non-observance of the anonymity condition necessary for a Delphi study, iterative polling of participants was not carried out. However, the instant feedback which occurred in the discussion groups obviated the potential benefits of iterative polling. The 25 tourism experts were asked to rank the importance/impact of each of the 25 possible future developments affecting tourism on a scale of 1 (low importance/impact) to 5 (high importance/impact); to assess the probability of occurrence (0–100%); and to forecast the most likely year of occurrence (over the period 1992–2030). Many of the developments predicted to occur by the year 2000 have in fact taken place.

Empirical results

The mean scores of the responses by the group of tourism experts regarding the impact/importance of each development, its probability of occurrence and its most likely year of occurrence are presented in Table 4.1.

CROSS-IMPACT ANALYSIS[2]

In this section we focus upon a less well-known forecasting method, cross-impact analysis, and examine its potential application within a tourism context. Although cross-impact analysis has received some attention in the general forecasting literature (e.g. Helmer, 1981), the technique appears to have been largely overlooked in the tourism forecasting literature. However, there are a few documented examples of the application of cross-impact analysis to recreation (Bonnicksen, 1981; Becker *et al.*, 1985, 1986). Cross-impact analysis is a technique used for examining the impacts of potential future events upon each other. It identifies groups of reinforcing or inhibiting events, and unfolds relationships between events which may appear unrelated. In brief, cross-impact analysis provides a forecast, making due allowance for the effects of interacting forces on the shape of things to come. The technique is suitable for projects which involve environmental scanning, which is tracking broad trends appearing in the environment. A tourism organization may use cross-impact analysis to study, for example, the impacts of technological trends in transportation capability, automation, communications and information processing. Essentially, cross-impact analysis consists of selecting a group of five to ten people to serve as project participants. These would normally be top decision makers – the managing director, marketing manager, operations manager, etc. – as well as possibly outside consultants. They are asked to specify critical events relating to the subject of the project. For example, in a tourism marketing project the events may fall into any of the following categories:

1. Corporate objectives and goals.
2. Corporate strategy.
3. Markets or customers (potential volume, market share, possible strategies of key customers, etc.).
4. Competitors (product, price, promotion and distribution strategies).
5. Overall competitive strategic posture, whether aggressive or defensive.
6. Internally or externally developed strategies which might affect the project.
7. Legal or regulatory activities having favourable or unfavourable effects.
8. Other social, demographic or economic events.

The initial attempt is likely to generate a long list of alternatives which needs to be consolidated into a manageable size (e.g. 25–30 events) by means of group discussion, concentrated thinking, elimination of duplication, and refinement of the essence of the problem. Management's creativity and far-sightedness play an important role in an organization's ability to pinpoint the relevant areas of concern, and hence tourism organizations should seek to develop within their managers the habit of creative thinking. The project coordinator/moderator plays a crucial role in facilitating and directing the discussion among participants, and hence in determining the effectiveness of the discussion group. His or her role involves stimulating discussion among all the participants, while at the same time ensuring that the focus of the discussion does not stray too far from the subject. The coordinator must have good observational, interpersonal, communication and interpretative skills in order to recognize and overcome threats to the discussion process. He or she should attempt to develop the following three stages in the group discussion:

1. Establish a rapport with the group, structure the rules of group interaction and set objectives.
2. Provoke intense discussion in the relevant areas.
3. Summarize the group's responses in order to determine the extent of agreement.

The selected n events are represented in an $n \times n$ matrix for developing an estimated impact of each event on every other event. This is done by assuming, for each specific event, that it has already occurred and will have an enhancing, inhibiting or null effect on other events. The project coordinator seeks the impact estimates from each project participant individually, and displays the estimates in the matrix in consolidated form. The project participants then vote on the impact of each event. If the spread of votes is too wide, the coordinator will ask those voting at the extremes to justify their positions. The participants are encouraged to discuss differences in the hope of clarifying the problem. Another round of voting takes place. During this second round the opinions usually converge and the median value of the votes is entered in the appropriate cell in the matrix. This procedure is repeated until the entire matrix is complete. In the process of matrix completion, the review of occurrences and interactions identifies those events that are strong actors and significant reactors, and provides a subjective opinion of their relative strengths. This information then serves as an important input in formulating strategy.

Case study example

The application of cross-impact analysis to a tourism example is now considered. The case is real, but artificial data are used to illustrate application of the technique. The Azores are situated in the Atlantic Ocean, 1230 km from Lisbon and 3380 km from New York, and include nine different islands aggregated into three major groups. They are volcanic mountains, with varied character and landscape. The existence of nine dispersed islands makes access to the region difficult. At present, only three of the islands have airports with the capacity to receive intercontinental flights, but recently there has been an increase in the number of inter-island flights. During the recent past there has been rapid growth in the supply of tourist accommodation; for example, between 1988 and 1989 capacity grew by 20%. By the mid-1990s, the total number of tourist beds in the region had grown to approximately 4000, about 50% being located on São Miguel, 25% on Terceira and 20% on Faial. Five other islands account for the remaining 5%, with no tourist accommodation on one of the islands. The evolution of tourist demand for the Azores is illustrated in Table 4.2.

The market grew fairly rapidly throughout the mid-1980s, but declined in 1989. The average tourist length of stay during the period was stable at just over 3 days, and the average occupancy rate in all tourist accommodation was 35%. The major tourist origin markets for the Azores were Portugal (67% of nights), followed by Germany (11%) and the USA (6%). A complete breakdown is presented in Table 4.3. From 1988 there was a decline in the number of American and Canadian tourists (two of the more traditional markets for the Azores), and an increase in the number of tourists originating from less traditional European markets, such as Holland, Belgium and Spain. Geographically, the two direct competitors to the Azores are Madeira and the Canary Islands. The average length of stay and spending level by tourists in the Azores were well below the levels recorded at these destinations.

Situation analysis

The Azores' strengths and competitive advantages in the tourism sector, as perceived by Azores Tourist Board (ATB) managers on the basis of market research studies, were described as follows:

1. High quality of life, absence of pollution and the provision of close contact with nature.
2. Excellent location for deep-sea fishing, snorkelling and scuba diving.
3. Good conditions for walking and hiking trips, as well as bird watching, and 'scientific' tours to study the flora, vegetation and volcanic nature of the islands.

Table 4.2. Tourist arrivals and growth rates for the Azores (1983–1989).

Year	Tourist arrivals	Growth rate (%)
1983	227,682	7.5
1984	245,430	7.8
1985	254,605	3.7
1986	282,451	10.9
1987	306,255	8.4
1988	323,214	5.5
1989	317,114	−1.9

Table 4.3. Total shares of nights spent in the Azores by foreign tourists (1990).

Country	Share of nights spent (%)
Portugal	67.3
Germany	11.4
USA	5.6
Switzerland	2.4
UK	2.3
Canada	2.0
France	1.7
Scandinavian countries	1.3
Spain	1.2
Belgium	0.9
Holland	0.6
Other countries	2.7

4. Ideal stopover location for yachting and good facilities for golfers.
5. Potential for the development of cultural and rural tourism.

Some of the major weaknesses which might hamper the development of tourism in the region were as follows:

1. Distance from the most important origin markets, cost of travel and the reduced number of scheduled flights to the Azores.
2. Lack of superstructure, particularly in the area of entertainment: improvements here could increase tourists' average spending levels and length of stay in the islands.
3. Inadequate professional qualification and training skills provided for staff employed in the tourism industry, which has a negative impact on the quality of tourist services offered to visitors.
4. Seasonality effects which create marked underutilization of facilities during the low season and overutilization during the high season.

   The tourism sector plays a crucial socio-economic role in the development for the Azores in terms of its contribution to the GDP, balance of payments, employment and payment of reasonable salaries. The ATB forecast a cumulative annual growth rate of 10% for foreign tourist arrivals until the year 2000. It aimed to increase tourists' average length of stay and reduce seasonality through the implementation of promotional programmes and by improving the entertainment facilities on the islands. The ATB was particularly interested in encouraging tourism investment designed to develop new tourist products, activities and facilities such as spas, convention centres and sports centres, which would enable foreign teams to come to the islands for training periods, tourist trails, footpaths, scenic points and nature parks.

Use of cross-impact analysis
Being aware of the global trends in the tourism industry and tourist flows worldwide, and taking into consideration the internal situation of the Azores, tourism authorities considered which marketing strategies would be most effective in striking a balance between the role of tourism as a catalyst for sustainable socio-economic development in the region and the

preservation of the local cultural heritage, quality of life and the physical environment. The ATB recognized that continued growth and development in the future stem from current strategic planning and decided to use cross-impact analysis in order to enable its managers to map out a strategic plan more effectively. In addition to competition, the ATB was concerned with the analysis of four main environmental factors (events):

A. A further decline in the number of tourist arrivals originating from the more traditional markets.

B. Increased dependency on a limited number of airlines and specialized tour operators and travel agents.

C. Increased cost of international travel.

D. A general increase in domestic (internal) tourism.

These events are arranged in matrix form as shown in Table 4.4. The arrows show the direction of the impacts. For example, the occurrence of event D (a general increase in internal tourism) is likely to bring about a decrease in the cost of international travel (event C). Hence, an inhibiting arrow is placed in the cell at the intersection of row D and column C. The increased dependency on a limited number of airlines and specialized tour operators and travel agents (event B) is likely to raise the cost of international travel (event C). Therefore, an enhancing arrow is placed in the cell where row B and column C intersect. It is not expected that the occurrence of event B would have any effect on event A, so a horizontal line is placed in this cell. The other cells are completed in accordance with similar judgements. The completed matrix shows the direction of impact of rows (actors) on columns (reactors). If interest focuses primarily upon event D, for example, then column D should be studied for actor events. Each of these actor events should be examined in turn to determine what degree of influence, if any, it is possible to have on these actors in order to bring about/prevent the occurrence of event D.

Next, the impact should be quantified to show linkage strengths (i.e. to determine how strongly the occurrence of one event would influence the occurrence of each of the other events). To assist in quantifying the interactions, a subjective rating scale may be used (Table 4.5). Table 4.6 shows how the basic cross-impact matrix can be modified to show linkage strengths. Consider, for example, the impact of event D on event B. It is felt that the occurrence of event D would have a critically enhancing impact on the likelihood of occurrence of event B. Both the direction and degree of enhancing impact are shown in Table 4.6 by the +8 rating in the appropriate cell. On the other hand, event A's occurrence would make event B less likely; the consensus rating is –4, and this is entered in the appropriate cell. This process is continued until all interactions are evaluated and the matrix is complete.

Another approach involves the use of probabilities of occurrence. Once the probability of occurrence of each event is assessed, then the change in that probability can be assessed for each interaction. The probabilities of occurrence can be entered in an information column preceding the matrix, and then the matrix may be constructed in the conventional manner. However, in many instances the degree of impact is not the only important information to be gathered from a consideration of interactions. The time relationships are often critical and can be shown in a number of ways. For example, time information can be added (within parentheses) to each probability of occurrence depicted in the matrix.

Table 4.7 illustrates the use of a cross-impact matrix incorporating interactive probabilities of occurrence and time relationships. Consider the impact of event D on the probable occurrence of event B. It is judged to have a critically enhancing effect and the consensus is that the probability of occurrence of event B will change from 0.60 to 0.80. (In this particular case study example, it was assumed that the participants' consensus judgement was that a value of +2 on the

Table 4.4. Basic format for the ATB cross-impact matrix.

If this event were to occur		Then the impact on this event would be[a]			
		A	**B**	**C**	**D**
A	A further decline in the number of tourist arrivals originating from the more traditional markets	✕	↓	↓	↑
B	Increased dependency on a limited number of airlines and specialized tour operators and travel agents	—	✕	↑	↑
C	Increased cost of international travel	↑	↓	✕	↑
D	A general increase in domestic (internal) tourism	↑	↑	↓	✕

[a] Up arrow, enhancing effect; horizontal line, no effect; down arrow, inhibiting effect.

Table 4.5. Example of subjective rating scale.

Voting scale	Subjective scale	Effect	Overall effect
+8	Critical	Essential for success	Enhancing
+6	Major	Major item for success	
+4	Significant	Positive, helpful, but not essential effect	
+2	Slight	Noticeable enhancing effect	
0	No effect	No effect	
−2	Slight	Noticeable inhibiting effect	Inhibiting
−4	Significant	Retarding effect inhibiting	
−6	Major	Major obstacle to success	
−8	Critical	Almost insurmountable hurdle	

Table 4.6. The ATB's cross-impact matrix showing degrees of impact.

If this event were to occur	Then the impact on this event would be			
	A	B	C	D
A A further decline in the number of tourist arrivals originating from the more traditional markets	✕	−4	−4	+8
B Increased dependency on a limited number of airlines and specialized tour operators and travel agents	0	✕	+8	+6
C Increased cost of international travel	+2	−6	✕	+6
D A general increase in domestic (internal) tourism	+4	+8	−6	✕

voting scale in Table 4.5 translated into an increase in the probability of occurrence of 5 percentage points in Table 4.7, a value of +4 into an increase of 10 percentage points, and so on. Similarly, a value of –2 translated into a decrease in the probability of occurrence of 5 percentage points, and so on.) The new probability is, therefore, entered in the appropriate cell. Event B is judged to have no effect upon event A; therefore, the original probability, 0.70, is unchanged. Event B is strongly inhibited by the occurrence of event C, and the resulting probability of occurrence is lowered from 0.60 to 0.45. The occurrence of event B will increase the probability of occurrence of event D from 0.70 to 0.85. This procedure is followed until all of the cells are completed.

The time relationships in Table 4.7 can be interpreted as follows. If event B were to occur it would have a major enhancing effect on event D, raising D's probability of occurrence from 0.70 to 0.85; this enhancement would occur immediately. If event C were to occur, it would raise the probability of occurrence of event A from 0.70 to 0.75; it would take 2 years for the enhancement to be completed. The information provided by the cross-impact matrices should have proved very useful for strategic planning by the ATB. It may be that the ATB was particularly concerned about a further decline in the number of tourist arrivals originating from the more traditional markets and had plans to deal with the situation should it occur. Various marketing strategies could be employed to halt the decline. By studying column A in Table 4.7, the tourism authorities could pinpoint those events which were likely to have a marked impact on the likelihood of occurrence of event A. Thus, for example, if there was a noticeable general increase in domestic tourism, the probability of occurrence of a further decline in the number of tourist arrivals originating from the more traditional markets would increase from 0.70 to 0.80. Hence, the ATB would need to step up its marketing efforts accordingly. The idea underlying cross-impact analysis is that the probability of occurrence of an event is directly related to the occurrence/non-occurrence of other events. By analysing correlations between events, it is possible to estimate the likelihood of future events occurring. This information

Table 4.7. The ATB's cross-impact matrix showing interactive probabilities of occurrence.

If this event were to occur	Having this probability of occurrence	Then the new probability of occurrence of this event would be			
		A	B	C	D
A A further decline in the number of tourist arrivals originating from the more traditional markets	0.70	✕	0.50 (+2 years)	0.40 (+1 year)	0.90 (immed.)
B Increased dependency on a limited number of airlines and specialized tour operators and travel agents	0.60	0.70	✕	0.70 (immed.)	0.85 (immed.)
C Increased cost of international travel	0.50	0.75 (+2 years)	0.45 (immed.)	✕	0.85 (immed.)
D A general increase in domestic (internal) tourism	0.70	0.80 (+2 years)	0.80 (+1 year)	0.35 (+2 years)	✕

immed., immediate.

can then be incorporated into the strategic planning process. Thus, cross-impact analysis can lead to improved strategic vision and allow management to follow a more proactive approach. Cross-impact analysis provides a framework for the analysis of a range of possible events and complex interactions. Given that tourism is characterized by a high degree of interdependence among events, cross-impact analysis is a forecasting technique that would seem to be particularly relevant for this field.

PROBABILITY FORECASTING

It may not be necessary to obtain *highly* accurate forecasts of specific values, but only to ascertain whether the probability falls within a particular range of values, in order to support good tourism management decisions. Furthermore, it is usually assumed that there is a cost trade-off when choosing a forecasting model. Fitzsimmons and Sullivan (1982: 118) noted that:

'Generally the less-expensive models yield less-accurate forecasts, and there are costs associated with inaccuracies in the forecast … Is it worthwhile to spend more on an accurate forecasting model than incur the potential costs of a less-expensive but poor forecast?' Although Martin and Witt (1988a, 1989a, b) have provided some empirical evidence to the contrary (i.e. that more expensive models do not necessarily lead to more accurate tourism demand forecasts), to the extent that the widely quoted trade-off stated by Fitzsimmons and Sullivan is true, it is important to identify an acceptable level of forecast accuracy. Decision theory can be used to determine optimal strategies when a tourism decision maker is faced with several decision alternatives and an uncertain or risk-filled pattern of future events (e.g. states of nature). (Risk is taken to mean a situation in which various outcomes to a decision are possible, but where the probabilities of the alternative outcomes are known. Uncertainty describes a situation in which there is no such probabilistic knowledge or where the information is fragmentary.) This section examines the precision required for probability forecasts and the use of skew loss functions as applied to tourism. For a general discussion of probability forecasting, the reader is referred to Wilson and Keating (1998), Delugio (1998) and Makridakis *et al.* (1998).

Required accuracy levels

Here we assess how accurate the forecasts of the probabilities associated with the occurrence of alternative states of nature need to be when we are considering problems involving few possible actions and few states of nature. As an example of this class of problem, suppose that a regional tourism authority is interested in marketing a multi-unit tourist pack comprising local dairy, wines and handicraft products in order to generate additional visitor arrivals and higher spending levels. The product is made by a batch process which, through equipment indivisibilities, is restricted to the following annual capacities:

A_1: 1 million units
A_2: 2 million units
A_3: 3 million units

The conditional opportunity losses under S_1 (high sales) and S_2 (low sales) are shown in Table 4.8.

As can be seen from Table 4.8, in this example if S_1 obtains then act A_3 is the best course of action and is accordingly assigned a conditional opportunity loss of zero. If S_2 obtains, however, act A_1 becomes the best course of action. Act A_2 is a kind of 'hedging' act in the sense that the conditional opportunity losses associated with it are not extreme under either S_1 or S_2. The problem facing tourist product planners is to estimate the probabilities of occurrence of S_1 and S_2, and in particular they need to know how precise these estimates should be.

Suppose that $P(S_1)$ denotes the probability that S_1 occurs. Then $P(S_2)$ is equal to $1 - P(S_1)$. If $P(S_1)$ were equal to 0.1, then the expected opportunity losses (EOLs) of the three acts would be:

$EOL(A_1) = 0.1(6) + 0.9(0) = £0.6$ million
$EOL(A_2) = 0.1(3) + 0.9(3) = £3.0$ million
$EOL(A_3) = 0.1(0) + 0.9(8) = £7.2$ million

Clearly, under these conditions act A_1 (the low-capacity facility) would be preferable to the other courses of action. By assuming various values that $P(S_1)$ could take, we can construct the chart of expected opportunity losses shown in Fig. 4.1.

If $P(S_1)$ is less than 0.5, then act A_1 is best, whereas, if $P(S_1)$ is between 0.5 and 0.625, act A_2 is best. If $P(S_1)$ exceeds 0.625, then act A_3 is best. If $P(S_1)$ is exactly 0.5, either A_1 or A_2 could be

Table 4.8. Conditional opportunity losses: new multi-unit tourist pack problem (£ million).

Act	State of nature	
	S_1	S_2
A_1	6	0
A_2	3	3
A_3	0	8

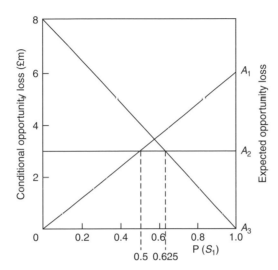

Fig. 4.1. Expected opportunity losses: new multi-unit tourist pack problem (£ million).

chosen, and, if $P(S_1)$ is exactly 0.625, either A_2 or A_3 could be chosen. These 'indifference' points are determined by finding the points on the abscissa where the lines of expected opportunity loss intersect, that is where:

$$EOL(A_1) = EOL(A_2)$$

Letting $P(S_1) = P$, we have:

$$6P + 0(1 - P) = 3$$

$$P = 0.5$$

Similarly:

$$EOL(A_3) = EOL(A_2)$$

$$0P + 8(1 - P) = 3$$

$$P = 0.625$$

The implication of these calculations is that the new tourist product planner does not need to know the precise value of $P(S_1)$ but only that it falls within specific ranges. In terms of the assumptions of this tourism problem, the same act (act A_1) would be chosen if $P(S_1)$ were, say,

0.1, as would be chosen if $P(S_1)$ were, say, 0.4. Although the illustration is simple, it does serve to demonstrate that, in some tourism marketing problems, forecasts do not need to be made with high precision.

Skew loss functions

In more realistic cases a greater number of states of nature and courses of action are possible. For example, in accommodation capacity problems some 'best' level of accommodation may exist for each possible sales level. In tourism demand capacity planning problems, the quantity of beds allocated may vary more or less continuously within a certain range. Let us now suppose that the same regional tourist authority is interested in determining the 'best' (optimum) number of beds to offer for distribution to tour operators and travel agents. If travel intermediaries' requests for suitable accommodation exceed the quantity available, unfilled requests will result. If the number of beds available in the region exceeds the demand, there will be costs associated with the excess supply of accommodation. For purposes of illustration, suppose that the imputed 'cost' for each unfilled tour operator's/travel agent's request per night is £12.00, and suppose that the cost associated with each bed vacant per night is £3.00. The regional tourist authority is interested in recommending some best level of accommodation capacity that minimizes expected cost under an uncertain tourist demand. The regional tourism planners should define the probability distribution of the possible tourist demand levels for accommodation in the area. As an example, suppose that the planners are willing to believe that tourist demand for accommodation in the region will exceed 20,000 beds but will be no higher than 80,000 beds. Their 'most probable' estimate of tourist demand is that it will be between 30,000 and 40,000 beds. The cumulative probability distribution can then be derived from a histogram chart. The smooth curve should be used to approximate cumulative probabilities within the histogram intervals. For example, the estimated probability of tourist demand being less than 35,000 beds can be seen to be approximately 0.45 (Fig. 4.2). To determine the optimal number of beds to be offered to the market, tourism planners would like to

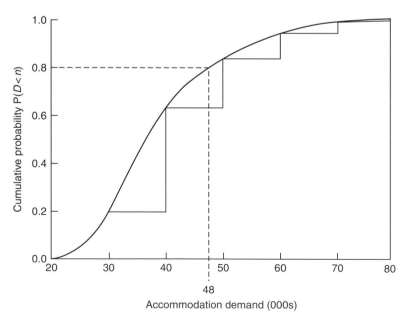

Fig. 4.2. Probability distribution: tourist demand for regional accommodation (000 units).

find the appropriate balance point where the expected cost of under-construction just equals the expected cost of over-construction. Both these costs are proportional to the difference between the amount offered and the amount requested. Fortunately, however, it is not necessary to construct a pay-off table for each possible act and tourist demand level. Instead, the following principle may be adopted. Keep increasing the accommodation capacity until the highest level n is reached for which the expected incremental cost of adding the nth unit is still less than the expected incremental cost of not adding the nth unit to the accommodation capacity level.

If we let D = tourist demand level, C_o = £3.00 = cost per night of over-construction and C_u = £12.00 = cost per unit per night of under-construction relative to tourist demand, then we have by application of the principle above:

$$C_o P(D < n) < C_u [1 - P(D < n)]$$

$$[P(D < n)] (C_o + C_u) < C_u$$

$$P(D < n) < \frac{C_u}{C_o + C_u}$$

$$P(D < n) < \frac{£12.00}{£3.00 \ + \ £12.00}$$

$$P(D < n) < 0.80$$

From Fig. 4.2, it can be seen that the largest n for which $P(D < n) < 0.80$ is approximately 48,000 beds. This represents the graphical solution to the tourist capacity problem. Had the planners not considered the asymmetry in the costs of over- versus under-construction, they might have planned for either:

- a capacity level equal to the midpoint of the bar in the histogram with the greatest incremental height (i.e. 35,000 beds), the modal forecast; or
- a capacity level equal to the median or 0.5 cumulative probability level of the distribution (i.e. 36,000 beds).

In either case, they would have considerably 'under-produced' relative to the solution that takes into account the conditional costs of over- versus under-production.

Although the need for accurate forecasts is often stressed, there are situations in which highly accurate point forecasts are not particularly useful. In particular, in the case of probability forecasting it is often necessary only to know whether or not the probability falls within a particular range of values. Even if increased accuracy can be obtained, it is often not the case that the additional cost entailed is justified. When knowledge regarding error costs is available, this should be incorporated in the forecast-generating procedure. In particular, cost asymmetries will affect the level of demand to plan for.

ECONOMETRIC FORECASTING[3]

The econometric approach to forecasting tourism demand involves the use of regression analysis to estimate the quantitative relationship between tourism demand and its determinants; the estimation is carried out using historical data, and future values of tourism demand are obtained by using forecasts of the demand determinants in conjunction with the estimated relationship. See, for example, Smeral et al. (1992) and Smeral and Witt (1996). The group of variables that influences international tourism demand will depend on the purpose of visit under consideration. As by far the majority of international tourist trips take place for holiday purposes, and it is only for holiday trips that individuals are completely free to choose the destination, transport mode, and so on, we shall just concentrate on those factors that influence the demand for international *holiday* tourism.

Tourism demand function

The variables involved in tourism demand forecasting are discussed below.

Forecast variable

Tourism demand is generally measured in terms of the number of tourist visits from an origin country to a foreign destination country, or in terms of tourist expenditures by visitors from the origin country in the destination country. Tourist nights spent in the destination country are an alternative measure.

Population

The level of foreign tourism from a given origin is expected to depend on the origin population. In some studies population features as an explanatory variable, but more often the effect of population is accommodated by modifying the dependent variable to become international tourism demand per capita.

Income

In tourism demand functions, origin country income or private consumption is generally included as an explanatory variable and commonly enters the demand function in per capita form (corresponding to the specification of demand in per capita terms). The appropriate form of the variable is private consumption or personal disposable income.

Own price

The appropriate form of the price variable is by no means clear. In the case of tourism there are two elements of price: (i) the cost of travel to the destination; and (ii) the cost of living for the tourist in the destination. In certain studies where econometric forecasting models have been developed for international tourism demand, a specific destination tourist's cost of living variable is incorporated in the models. Usually, however, the consumer price index in a country is taken to be a proxy for the cost of tourism in that country. In general, this procedure is adopted on the grounds of lack of more suitable data. Whichever destination price variable is used, it needs to be adjusted by the rate of exchange in order to transform it into origin country currency. Exchange rates are also sometimes used separately to represent tourists' living costs. The usual justification is that consumers are more aware of exchange rates than destination costs of living for tourists, and hence are driven to use exchange rate as a proxy variable.

Substitute prices

Economic theory suggests that the prices of substitutes may be important determinants of demand. For example, an increase in holiday prices to Spain may increase demand for holidays to Portugal. Mostly, those substitution possibilities allowed for in international tourism demand studies are restricted to tourist destination living costs. Substitute prices may be incorporated by specifying the tourists' cost of living variable as destination value relative to a weighted average value calculated for a set of alternative destinations, or by specifying a separate weighted average substitute destination cost variable.

Just as tourists' living costs in substitute destinations are likely to influence the demand for tourism to a given destination, so travel costs to substitute destinations may also be expected to have an impact, and can be allowed for in a similar manner. Furthermore, if the data are disaggregated by transport mode, then travel cost to the same destination by alternative transport mode(s) would influence tourism demand to a particular destination by a given transport mode.

Qualitative effects

Dummy variables can be included in international tourism demand functions to allow for the impact of 'one-off' events. For example, when governments impose foreign currency restrictions on their residents (e.g. the £50 annual limit introduced in the UK during late 1966 to late 1969), this is expected to reduce outward tourism. Similarly, the 1973 and 1979 oil crises temporarily reduced international tourism demand; although the impacts of the oil crises on holiday prices and consumer incomes are incorporated in these explanatory variables, a further reduction in international tourism demand is likely because of the psychological impact of the resultant uncertainties in the world economic situation. Witt and Martin (1987) discussed a range of one-off events which have been accommodated by dummy variables.

Trend

A trend mainly represents a steady change in the popularity of a destination country over the period considered, as a result of changing tastes. It also, however, captures the time dependent effects of all other explanatory variables not explicitly included in the equation, such as changes in air service frequencies and demographic changes in the origins.

Marketing

National tourist organizations engage in sales-promotion activities specifically to attempt to persuade potential tourists to visit the country, and these activities may take various forms including media advertising and public relations. Hence, promotional expenditure is expected to play a role in determining the level of international tourism demand. Much tourism-related marketing activity is not, however, specific to a particular destination (for example, general travel agent and tour operator advertising) and therefore is likely to have little impact on the demand for tourism to that destination. The promotional activities of national tourist organizations are destination specific and are therefore more likely to influence tourist flows to the destination concerned.

Lagged dependent variable

A lagged dependent variable (i.e. an autoregressive term) can be justified on the grounds of habit persistence. Once people have been on holiday to a particular country and liked it, they tend to return to that destination. There is much less uncertainty associated with holidaying again in the country compared with travelling to a previously unvisited foreign country. Furthermore, knowledge about the destination spreads as people talk about their holidays and show photographs, thereby reducing uncertainty for potential visitors to that country. In fact, this 'word-of-mouth' recommendation may well play a more important role in destination selection than does commercial advertising. A type of learning process is in operation and, as people are, in general, risk averse, the number of people choosing a given alternative in any year depends on the numbers who chose it in previous years.

A second justification for the inclusion of a lagged dependent variable in tourism demand functions comes from the supply side. Supply constraints may take the form of shortages of hotel accommodation, passenger transportation capacity and trained staff, and these often cannot be increased rapidly. Time is also required to build up contacts among tour operators, hotels, airlines and travel agencies. Similarly, once the tourist industry to a country has become highly developed it is unlikely to dwindle rapidly. If a partial adjustment mechanism is postulated to allow for rigidities in supply, this results in the presence of a lagged dependent variable in the tourism demand function (Gujarati, 1988: Chapter 16).

Empirical results

Examples of estimated econometric models are presented in Table 4.9. The most comprehensive study in terms of the variety of origins/destinations covered is by Martin and Witt (1988c), and the first ten models are taken from this study. The four models selected from other studies were specifically chosen because they include explanatory variables not covered in the Martin and Witt study. Thus model 11 incorporates population as a demand determinant, models 12 and 13 incorporate marketing expenditure and model 14 incorporates a lagged dependent variable and travel time. (The elasticity values presented in model 14 are impulse estimates.) All the models are specified in log-linear form.

Population features as an explanatory variable only in model 11, but the estimated elasticity of 4.4 seems far too high to be realistic. (The population elasticity is expected to be fairly close to unity.) Furthermore, an 'incorrect' coefficient sign is estimated for income. It appears, therefore, that multicollinearity between population and income may well be a problem in this model, which is why population does not, in general, feature as an explanatory variable in tourism demand models. The results from model 11 are not included in the discussion which follows.

Income appears in each model in Table 4.9, but the values of the estimated elasticities vary considerably, ranging from 0.4 to 6.6. However, other than the 0.4 value, the estimated income elasticities exceed unity, showing clearly that foreign tourism is generally regarded as a luxury. The median value of 2.4 strongly supports a priori expectations about the luxury nature of foreign tourism. Many of the differences in elasticity estimates can be readily explained. For example, although the income elasticity obtained in model 5 (0.4) is somewhat lower than expected, travel from the USA to Canada is likely to be regarded in a similar manner to domestic (USA) tourism (i.e. a necessity, rather than a luxury), whereas overseas travel from the USA to the UK (model 6) is viewed as a luxury (income elasticity is 2.4). In contrast, the value of the income elasticity for travel from France to Switzerland (model 1) is similar to that for travel from France to the UK (model 2) at 2.8. Again, this makes sense as Switzerland is a destination with a very high cost of living for tourists, whereas visiting the UK involves a high cost of travel because of the sea border, and therefore holidays to Switzerland and the UK are likely to be regarded as being at about the same luxury level by the French. (However, the income elasticity for travel from France to neighbouring cheap destinations (such as Spain) would be expected to be much lower; see, for example, the difference in income elasticities for travel from Germany to Switzerland (high cost) and Austria (low cost).)

As far as own price is concerned, travel cost appears in 11 of the 14 models, and the elasticity estimates range from –0.04 to –4.3, with the median value being –0.5. The three cases where demand is most responsive to own travel cost are those models which incorporate statistically significant substitute travel costs. Destination cost features in 12 models, and the elasticity estimates range from –0.05 to –1.5, with the median value being –0.7. Tourists thus seem to react in a fairly similar manner to destination cost changes and travel

Table 4.9 Examples of estimated econometric models.

Authors	Ref date	Model no.[a]	Method of est[b]	R^2	Pop	Inc	Trav cost	Dest cost	Exch rate	Comb cost	Subst TC	Subst DC	Subst CC	Dummy variables	Trnd	Mark	Lag DV	Travel time
Martin and Witt	1988c	1	OLS	0.969		2.819*		-1.242*				1.053		-0.022[1]	-0.150*			
														-0.034[2]				
	(data 1965–1980)	2	CO	0.953		2.756*	-0.708				0.600			-0.204*[1]				
		3	CO	0.987		1.292*	-0.037	-0.755*						-0.109*[2]				
		4	CO	0.896		4.923*	-C.932	-1.250			2.803*			-0.040[1]	-0.122			
		5	OLS	0.776		0.372	-C.355	-0.364			0.156			-0.042[2]	-0.018			
		6	CO	0.897		2.431*	-0.198	-0.428										
		7	CO	0.991		4.550*		-0.235	1.859*			0.130		-0.258*[1]				
														-0.619*[2]				
														-0.061*[3]				
		8	CO	0.911		1.775	-0.155		0.637		0.921			-0.022[1]				
		9	CO	0.972		1.331	-1.122*	-1.403*	2.258*		6.305*			-0.604*[2]				
		10	CO	0.978		1.743	-4.337*	-0.679	1.827*		2.226*	3.308*		-0.374*[1]				
														-0.367*[2]				
Chadee and Mieczkowski	1987 (data 1976–1985)	11	OLS	0.95	12.40*	-2.90+		-1.52*	1.26*					0.69+[4]				
														1.90+[5]				
														0.50+[6]				

Explanatory variables[c,d]

(Continued)

Table 4.9 Continued.

Authors	Ref date	Model no.[a]	Method of est[b]	R²	Pop	Inc	Trav cost	Dest cost	Exch rate	Comb cost	Subst TC	Subst DC	Subst CC	Dummy variables	Trnd	Mark	Lag DV	Travel time
Papadopoulos and Witt	1985 (data 1972–1982)	12	CO	0.996		3.346*	−0.458	−0.721*						−0.515*[7]		0.175		
		13	OLS	0.939		6.645*	−0.475	−0.706						−0.552*[7]		0.041		
Witt	1980 (data 1964–1972)	14	OLS	0.969		1.386	−0.199	−0.049						−0.055[8]			0.908*	−0.165
														0.091[9]				
														0.157[10]				
														0.152[11]				
														0.145–1.015[12]				
Median values[e]						2.4	−0.5	−0.7	1.8		1.6	1.1		−0.1[1]	−0.1	0.1		
														−0.2[2]				
														−0.5[7]				

[a] Model 1, France to Switzerland; Model 2, France to UK; Model 3, Germany to Switzerland; Model 4, Germany to Austria; Model 5, USA to Canada; Model 6, USA to UK; Model 7, UK to Austria; Model 8, UK to Spain; Model 9, UK to Austria by air; Model 10, UK to Austria by surface; Model 11, USA to Canada; Model 12, Austria to Greece; Model 13, Switzerland to Greece; Model 14, denotes UK to multiple destinations.

[b] OLS, ordinary least squares; CO, Cochrane–Orcutt.

[c] Pop, population; Inc, income; Trav cost, travel cost; Dest cost, destination cost; Exch rate, exchange rate; Comb cost, combined cost (travel + destination); Subst TC, substitute travel costs; Subst DC, substitute destination costs; Subst CC, substitute combined costs; Trnd, trend; Mark, marketing (promotional) expenditure; Lag DV, lagged dependent variable.

[d] *, significant at 5% level; +, significant at 10% level; 1, 1974 oil crisis; 2, 1979 oil crisis; 3, UK currency restrictions 1967–69; 4, second quarter; 5, third quarter; 6, fourth quarter; 7, political disturbances/1974 oil crisis; 8, non-sterling area destination; 9, low cost of tourism of sterling area destination; 10, holiday type; 11, travel mode; 12, range of destination intrinsic characteristic values.

[e] Ignoring results from model 11.

cost changes. Exchange rate appears as an explanatory variable in only five of the 14 models and in only one case is it the sole representation of tourists' destination living costs. The estimated elasticities range from 0.6 to 2.3, with a median value of 1.8, indicating that, for those origin–destination pairs where exchange rate is important, there is a relatively high sensitivity of demand to exchange rate changes. The fairly high absolute values obtained for the price elasticities again support a priori expectations regarding the luxury nature of foreign tourism. With regard to substitute prices, travel cost appears in six of the 14 models but destination cost in only three. The travel cost values span the range 0.2 to 6.3 with a median value of 1.6, and the destination cost elasticity values vary from 0.1 to 3.3, with a median value of 1.1. A wide range of dummy variables features in the models, showing, in particular, that political events can have marked impacts on tourism demand. Models 12 and 13 indicate that marketing expenditure does have a positive impact on tourism demand, but that the estimated elasticities are low. Model 14 demonstrates the negative impact of travel time on tourism demand, and the importance of habit persistence and/or supply constraints (as represented by the lagged dependent variable).

The forecasting performance of econometric models of international tourism demand is mixed. In the earlier studies econometric models often generated less accurate forecasts than simple extrapolative methods. However, Witt and Witt (1995) and Lim (1997) suggested that this may have been caused by lack of diagnostic testing coupled with appropriate remedial action. The more recent studies, which incorporate a range of diagnostic tests, partially support this hypothesis. For example, Kim and Song (1998) compared the forecasting performance of econometric models with several univariate time-series models and discovered that the econometric models were the most accurate. On the other hand, Kulendran and King (1997) found that econometric models generated more accurate forecasts than some univariate time-series models but less accurate forecasts than others.

FUZZY TIME SERIES FORECASTING[4]

Fuzzy time series models refer to the procedures used to solve forecasting problems in which the historical data are linguistic values. The main difference between fuzzy time series and conventional time series is that the former consist of fuzzy sets while the latter are real numbers (Chen, 1996). Song and Chissom (1993) provide the concept of fuzzy time series as follows:

Let U be the universe of discourse, where $U = \{u_1, u_2 \ldots u_n\}$. A fuzzy set A of U is defined as $A = f_A(u_1)/u_1 + f_A(u_2)/u_2 + \ldots + f_A(u_n)/u_n$, where f_A is the membership function of A, and f_A: $U \to [0, 1]$. $f_A(u_i)$ is the degree of membership of u_i in A, where $f_A(u_i) \in [0, 1]$ and $1 \leq i \leq n$. The fuzzy time series can then be defined as follows:

Definition 1. Let $Y(t)$ ($t = \ldots, 0, 1, 2, \ldots$), a subset of R, be the universe of discourse on which fuzzy sets $f_i(t)$ ($i = 1, 2, \ldots$) are defined and $F(t)$ is a collection of $f_1(t), f_2(t), \ldots$ Then $F(t)$ is called a fuzzy time series on $Y(t)$ (Song and Chissom, 1993).

During modelling, if $F(t)$ is caused by $F(t - 1)$ only, the relationship can be expressed as $F(t - 1) \to F(t)$, where $\to$ can represent any operation to formulate the fuzzy relationship between $F(t - 1)$ and $F(t)$. During forecasting (after obtaining all the fuzzy relationships), $F(t - 1)$ can be used to forecast $F(t)$. People are used to conducting in-sample estimation as well as out-of-sample forecasting. In this case, the data are separated into in-sample and out-of-sample data, where the in-sample data are used for establishing the fuzzy relationships and out-of-sample data are for out-of-sample forecasting.

Many previous fuzzy time series studies have focused on proposing different operations to improve forecasting results (Song and Chissom, 1993, 1994; Chen, 1996; Hwang *et al.*, 1998; Huarng and Yu, 2006). Hereafter, we take the study of Huarng *et al.* (2007) (here-after, referred as neural network based model) as an example to illustrate the forecasting process of a fuzzy time series model, where neural networks are used as the operation to train the fuzzy relationships and to forecast. Meanwhile, that study compares the perform-ance of the proposed model with a conventional econometric model and a fuzzy time series model (Chen, 1996).

Data

The data are taken from Executive Information System, Tourism Bureau Ministry of Transportation and Communication, Taiwan (Republic of China). The monthly data are from 1984/01 to 2005/09, where those from 1984/01 to 2000/04 are used for neural network train-ing and those from 2000/05 to 2005/09 are for forecasting. Taiwan tourist number at time $t - 1$ is taken as the input and that at time t is taken as the output (the forecast target).

Model

Step 1. Fuzzification

First, we fuzzify all the actual tourist numbers (*actual*) at time t into fuzzy tourist numbers, $F(t)$. The length of interval (*LOI*) is set to 1000. Because the minimum of all the tourist numbers is 40,256, we round the minimum by the *LOI* to *MIN* = 40,000. Following Song and Chissom (1993) and Chen (1996), an equation is proposed to fuzzify each *actual* as follows:

$$F(t) = rounddown \left(\frac{(actual - MIN)}{LOI} \right) + 1.$$

For example, the actual tourist number in 1984/01 was 120,080, whose corresponding fuzzy tourist number is $F(1984/01) = rounddown \left(\frac{(120,080 - 40,000)}{1000} \right) + 1 = 81$. Similarly, the actual tourist number in 1984/02 was 133,994: $F(1984/02) = rounddown \left(\frac{(133,994 - 40,000)}{1000} \right) + 1 = 94$.

Step 2. Neural network training

The fuzzy relationship between two consecutive fuzzy tourist numbers is then modelled as $F(t) \rightarrow F(t+1)$, where $F(t)$ is the input and $F(t + 1)$ is the output of the neural networks. The neural network structure is depicted in Fig. 4.3, where there are one input layer with one input node, one hidden layer with two hidden nodes, and one output layer with one output node.

Following the above examples, $F(t) = F(1984/01) = 81$, and $F(t + 1) = F(1984/02) = 94$. Hence, 81 is the input and 94 is the output for neural network training, respectively.

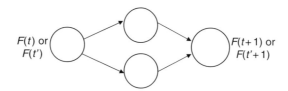

$F(t)$ or
$F(t')$

$F(t+1)$ or
$F(t'+1)$

Fig. 4.3. The neural network structure for training and forecasting.

Table 4.10. The comparison of performance among different models.

	Models		
	ARIMA (1, 1, 1)	**Chen (1996)**	**Huarng *et al.* (2007)**
RMSE[a]	32,948.83	32,759.31	30,938.78

[a] RMSE, root mean squared error.

Step 3. Forecasting

After training, the trained neural network is used for forecasting. Suppose t' represents the time point for out-of-sample forecasting. Different forecasting processes are proposed for the two conditions of $F(t')$.

> **Case 1:** If $F(t')$ ever appears in the training data, we take the corresponding output from the neural network as $F(t' + 1)$. For example, the actual tourist number in 2000/08 was 220,227; $F(t') = F(2000/08) = 181$. Because 181 appears in the in-sample data, we take 181 as the input for the neural network forecasting. From the neural network based model, the output for 2000/09 (or fuzzy forecast for the next time point) is 178.11. In other words, $F(t' + 1) = F(2000/09) = 178.11$.

> **Case 2:** If $F(t')$ never appears in the training patterns, we set $F(t' + 1)$ equal to $F(t')$ (Huarng and Yu, 2006). For example, $F(t') = F(2000/10) = 210$. However, 210 never appears in the in-sample data. Hence, 210 becomes the fuzzy forecast for the next time point, 2000/11. In other words, $F(t' + 1) = F(2000/11) = F(t') = F(2000/10) = 210$.

Step 4. Defuzzification

For each fuzzy forecast, an equation is proposed for defuzzification:

$$forecast(t' + 1) = (F(t' + 1) - 0.5) \times LOI + MIN.$$

For example, $F(t' + 1) = F(2000/09) = 178.11$.
$forecast(2000/09) = (178.11 - 0.5) \times 1000 + 40{,}000 = 217{,}607.36$.

Empirical results

The root mean squared error (RMSE) is used to compare the performance of the neural network based model with others, as in Table 4.10. The RMSE from a conventional model, ARIMA (1, 1, 1), is 32,948.83; the RMSE from another fuzzy time series model (Chen, 1996) is reported as 32,795.31; and the RMSE from the neural network based model (Huarng *et al.*, 2007) is 30,938.78. Obviously, the neural network based model outperforms the other two models.

CONCLUSION

Forecasts of tourism demand are crucial for planning purposes. In this chapter, a range of tourism forecasting methods has been outlined which can be applied in a wide variety of situations.

NOTES

[1] Material in this section has appeared previously in Moutinho and Witt (1995).
[2] Material in this section has appeared previously in Moutinho and Witt (1994).
[3] Material in this section has appeared previously in Witt and Witt (1995).
[4] Material in this section has appeared previously in Huarng *et al.* (2007).

REFERENCES

Archer, B.H. (1994) Demand forecasting and estimation. In: Ritchie, J.R.B. and Goeldner, C.R. (eds) *Travel, Tourism and Hospitality Research: a Handbook for Managers and Researchers*, 2nd edn. Wiley, New York, pp. 105–114.

Becker, R.H., Dottavio, F.D. and Bonnicksen, T.M. (1985) Conventional wisdom and qualitative assessment. In: Wood, J.D., Jr (ed.) *Proceedings of 1985 National Outdoor Recreation Trends Symposium 2*, vol. 1. Science Publications Office, National Park Service, US Department of the Interior, Atlanta.

Becker, R.H., Dottavio, F.D. and Menning, N.L. (1986) Threats to coastal national parks: a technique for establishing management priorities. *Leisure Sciences* 8(3), 241–256.

Bonnicksen, T.M. (1981) Brushland fire management policies: a cross impact simulation of Southern California. *Environmental Management* 5(6), 521–529.

Cetron, M.J. and Davies, O. (1991) *50 Trends Shaping the World*. World Future Society, Bethesda, Maryland.

Chadee, D. and Mieczkowski, Z. (1987) An empirical analysis of the effects of the exchange rate on Canadian tourism. *Journal of Travel Research* 26(1), 13–17.

Chen, S.-M. (1996) Forecasting enrollments based on fuzzy time series. *Fuzzy Sets and Systems* 81, 311–319.

Delugio, S. (1998) *Forecasting Principles and Applications*. McGraw-Hill, Maidenhead, UK.

Fitzsimmons, J.A. and Sullivan, R.S. (1982) *Service Operations Management*. McGraw-Hill, New York.

Frechtling, D.C. (1996) *Practical Tourism Forecasting*. Butterworth-Heinemann, Oxford.

Gujarati, D.N. (1988) *Basic Econometrics*, 2nd edn. McGraw-Hill, New York.

Gunn, C.A. (1994) A perspective on the purpose and nature of tourism research methods. In: Ritchie, J.R.B. and Goeldner, C.R. (eds) *Travel, Tourism, and Hospitality Research: a Handbook for Managers and Researchers*, 2nd edn. Wiley, New York, pp. 3–11.

Helmer, O. (1981) Reassessment of cross-impact analysis. *Futures* 13(5), 389–400.

Huarng, K. and Yu, T.H.-K. (2006) The application of neural networks to forecast fuzzy time series. *Physica A* 363(2), 481–491.

Huarng, K., Moutinho, L. and Yu, T.H.-K. (2007) An advanced approach to forecasting tourism demand in Taiwan. *Journal of Travel and Tourism Marketing* 21(4), 15–24.

Hwang, J.-R., Chen, S.-M. and Lee, C.-H. (1998) Handling forecasting problems using fuzzy time series. *Fuzzy Sets and Systems* 100, 217–228.

Kaynak, E. and Macaulay, J.A. (1984) The Delphi Technique in the measurement of tourism market potential: the case of Nova Scotia. *Tourism Management* 5(2), 87–101.

Kim, S. and Song, H. (1998) Analysis of inbound tourism demand in South Korea: a cointegration and error correction approach. *Tourism Analysis* 3, 25–41.

Kulendran, N. and King, M.L. (1997) Forecasting international quarterly tourist flows using error-correction and time-series models. *International Journal of Forecasting* 13, 319–327.

Lim, C. (1997) An econometric classification and review of international tourism demand models. *Tourism Economics* 3, 69–81.

Liu, J.C. (1988) Hawaii tourism to the year 2000. *Tourism Management* 9(4), 279–290.

Makridakis, S., Wheelwright, S.C. and Hyndman, R. (1998) *Forecasting – Methods and Applications*, 3rd edn. Wiley, Chichester, UK.

Martin, C.A. and Witt, S.F. (1988a) An empirical analysis of the accuracy of forecasting techniques. In: *Proceedings of Travel and Tourism Research Association 19th Annual Conference*. Travel and Tourism Research Association, Salt Lake City, Utah, pp. 285–298.

Martin, C.A. and Witt, S.F. (1988b) Forecasting performance. *Tourism Management* 9(4), 326–329.

Martin, C.A. and Witt, S.F. (1988c) Substitute prices in models of tourism demand. *Annals of Tourism Research* 15(2), 255–268.

Martin, C.A. and Witt, S.F. (1989a) Forecasting tourism demand: a comparison of the accuracy of several quantitative methods. *International Journal of Forecasting* 5(1), 1–13.

Martin, C.A. and Witt, S.F. (1989b) Accuracy of econometric forecasts of tourism. *Annals of Tourism Research* 16(3), 407–428.

Moeller, G. and Shafer, E.L. (1994) The Delphi Technique: a tool for long-range travel and tourism planning. In: Ritchie, J.R.B. and Goeldner, C.R. (eds) *Travel, Tourism and Hospitality Research: a Handbook for Managers and Researchers*, 2nd edn. Wiley, New York, pp. 473–480.

Moutinho, L. and Witt, S.F. (1994) Application of cross-impact analysis in tourism: a case study of the Azores. *Journal of Travel and Tourism Marketing* 3(1), 83–95.

Moutinho, L. and Witt, S.F. (1995) Forecasting the tourism environment using a consensus approach. *Journal of Travel Research* 33(4), 46–50.

Papadopoulos, S.I. and Witt, S.F. (1985) A marketing analysis of foreign tourism in Greece. In: Shaw, S., Sparks, L. and Kaynak, E. (eds) *Marketing in the 1990s and Beyond: Proceedings of Second World Marketing Congress*. University of Stirling, Stirling, UK, pp. 682–693.

Robinson, A.E. (1979) Tourism and the next decade: a look to the future through 'A Return to Delphi'. In: *Proceedings of Travel and Tourism Research Association Tenth Annual Conference*. Travel and Tourism Research Association, Salt Lake City, Utah, pp. 269–282.

Seeley, R.L., Iglars, H. and Edgell, D. (1980) Utilizing the Delphi Technique at international conferences: a method for forecasting international tourism conditions. *Travel Research Journal* 1, 30–35.

Shafer, E.L. and Moeller, G. (1988) Science and technology: the wild cards in tourism strategic planning. Paper presented at Benchmark 1988: a National Outdoor Recreation and Wilderness Forum, Tampa, Florida, 13–15 January.

Shafer, E.L. and Moeller, G. (1994) Science and technology. In: Witt, S.F. and Moutinho, L. (eds) *Tourism Marketing and Management Handbook*, 2nd edn. Prentice-Hall, Hemel Hempstead, UK, pp. 120–125.

Smeral, E. and Witt, S.F. (1996) Econometric forecasts of tourism demand to 2005. *Annals of Tourism Research* 23(4), 891–907.

Smeral, E., Witt, S.F. and Witt, C.A. (1992) Econometric forecasts: tourism trends to 2000. *Annals of Tourism Research* 19(3), 450–466.

Song, Q. and Chissom, B.S. (1993) Forecasting enrollments with fuzzy time series – Part I. *Fuzzy Sets and Systems* 54, 1–9.

Song, Q. and Chissom, B.S. (1994) Forecasting enrollments with fuzzy time series – Part II. *Fuzzy Sets and Systems* 62, 1–8.

Taylor, R.E. and Judd, L.L. (1994) Delphi forecasting. In: Witt, S.F. and Moutinho, L. (eds) *Tourism Marketing and Management Handbook*, 2nd edn. Prentice-Hall, Hemel Hempstead, UK, pp. 535–539.

Var, T. (1984) Delphi and GSV techniques in tourism forecasting and policy design. *Problems of Tourism* 3, 41–52.

Wilson, H. and Keating, B. (1998) *Business Forecasting*, 3rd edn. McGraw Hill, Maidenhead, UK.

Witt, S.F. (1980) An abstract mode-abstract (destination) node model of foreign holiday demand. *Applied Economics* 12(2), 163–180.

Witt, S.F. and Martin, C.A. (1987) Measuring the impacts of mega-events on tourism flows. In: *The Role and Impact of Mega-Events and Attractions on Regional and National Tourism Development: Proceedings of International Association of Scientific Experts in Tourism (AIEST) 37th Congress*. AIEST, St Gallen, Switzerland, pp. 213–221.

Witt, S.F. and Witt, C.A. (1995) Forecasting tourism demand: a review of empirical research. *International Journal of Forecasting* 11, 447–475.

Yong, Y.W., Keng, K.A. and Leng, T.L. (1989) A Delphi forecast for the Singapore tourism industry: future scenario and marketing implications. *International Marketing Review* 6(3), 35–46.

chapter 5

Consumer Behaviour in Tourism

Luiz Moutinho, Ronnie Ballantyne and Shirley Rate

INTRODUCTION

Consumer behaviour refers to the process of acquiring and organizing information in the direction of a purchase decision and of using and evaluating products and services. This process encompasses the stages of searching for, purchasing, using, evaluation and disposing of products and services. The tourist buying decision presents some unique aspects: (i) it is an investment with no tangible rate of return; and (ii) the purchase is often prepared and planned through savings made over a considerable period of time. That is, the vacation tourist will invest with no expectation of material and economic return on his or her purchase of an intangible satisfaction.

As travellers become more sophisticated in their vacationing behaviour, research must continue to become more sophisticated to explain this behaviour. Consumers want their real experiences reflected and connected to their very specific and personal needs – not a generally perceived notion of their needs. Tourism providers must then become truly customer centric – they must adopt research that listens to the 'voice of the consumer' – it has to be about understanding them implicitly, in real time and moreover on their schedule. Only then will they be able to deliver experiences that consumers truly value. Old-style marketing is outbound by its nature – inbound marketing involves listening to the consumer. As highlighted in the previous chapters consumers can no longer simply be classified by segmentation typologies but are indeed individual human beings – reading consumers is becoming more complex and multi-dimensional – as such a deeper understanding and insight into what drives individual tourism behaviour is necessary.

There are many factors that influence an individual's behaviour. To take adequate actions in the area of tourism marketing, one must understand: (i) how people perceive such things as destination areas, air travel, travel distances and travel advertising; (ii) how they learn to consume and to travel; (iii) how they make travel decisions; and (iv) how personality affects those decisions. One must also analyse: (i) what motivations influence the individuals' travel decisions; (ii) how attitudes are formed; and (iii) how various groups affect travel behaviour. Considering factors of a broader nature, the tourism marketing context requires an appraisal of the effect of economic, technological and social changes, generating factors that will increase certain types of leisure activities and decrease others. The rise in the cost of energy, the trend to smaller family units and to live in smaller spaces, the improvement of forms of communication – in particular advances in Internet technology – the mass adoption of the Internet and digital networks is transforming the way in which consumers share and manage information between themselves and corporations. It presents an interactive platform where consumers can build meaningful dialogue with tourism providers – challenging the classic 'top-down' approach of 'we market to you' or 'telling and selling' to a 'bottom-up' experience whereby the consumer can become a more active participant in the overall brand experience as opposed to a passive receiver of information and products.

Travel decisions, therefore, are very much affected by forces outside the individual, including the influences of other people. The forces that other people exert are called social influences. As Fig. 5.1 shows, these social influences can be grouped into four major areas: (i) role and family influences; (ii) reference groups; (iii) social class; and (iv) culture and subculture.

The analysis of consumer behaviour requires the consideration of various processes that are internal and external to the individual (see Engel *et al.*, 1995). Hence, to understand the purchasing behaviour one needs to examine the complex interaction of many elements, present at different stages, from arousal to decision, as well as from purchase to post-purchase experiences. Figure 5.2 shows the interaction of elements that are involved in consumer behaviour. In the consideration of all these processes, this chapter will first deal with determinants of a broader nature, the cultural and reference group influences. Next, concepts concerning the individual and his or her relationship with the environment will be presented with a focus on: (i) personality factors and self-concept; (ii) perception and cognition; (iii) motivation; and (iv) attitude and intention. Then other important determinants of tourist decision making, perceived risk and the family decision process, will be discussed. This set of concepts will permit an integrated analysis of the decision-making process. The final section will present an illustration of tourist behaviour modelling.

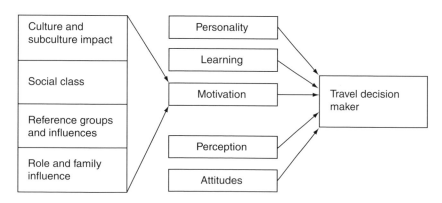

Fig. 5.1. Major influences on individual travel behaviour.

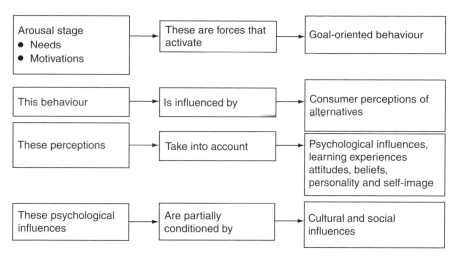

Fig. 5.2. Interaction of elements in the psychological field of the consumer that influence behaviour.

CULTURAL INFLUENCES AND REFERENCE GROUPS

Cultural influences

Culture is the complex abstract and material elements created by a society. It refers to values, ideas, attitudes and meaningful symbols, as well as artefacts elaborated in a society. These elements are transmitted from one generation to another and serve to shape human behaviour, implying explicit or implicit patterns of and for behaviour. The concept of culture is broad and it is not easy to analyse the culture determination of behaviours. Its influence is natural and subtle, and often the individuals are neither conscious nor aware of it. The multiple cultural factors taken together will characterize a given society, such as its language, religion, technology, etc. In the context of consumer behaviour, one can regard culture as the total of learned beliefs, values and customs, including the material elements, which serve to regulate the consumption patterns of members of a particular society. A form of investigation of this broad factor is cross-cultural analysis, consisting of a systematic comparison of similarities and differences in the material and behavioural aspects of cultures. These analyses may be statistical, when describing the structure of the culture, or functional, when dealing with factors determining behaviours and activities in different cultures. Within a society, an important broad factor influencing consumer behaviour is *social class*. This constitutes a relatively permanent division of categories in a society, a division that brings about some restrictions of behaviour between individuals in different classes; individuals in a given social class share similar values, lifestyles and behaviour standards. However, it must be emphasized that there are many ways of establishing such a classification. Researchers may use different categorizations, resulting in three, four, five, six social classes, and so forth. Social classes tend to be hierarchical but they may be dynamic. It is very likely that members of a social class will follow the standards of behaviour of that class; nevertheless, individuals may vary in the degree of congruence as to their class insertion. The behaviour patterns of an individual are related to the beliefs and values that were incorporated. *Beliefs* constitute a person's particular knowledge and assessment of something (another person, a store, a product, a place, etc.), and are often expressed as mental or verbal statements (i.e. 'I believe that …'). *Values* may have the characteristics of beliefs but they are not directed towards a specific object: they serve as standards for appropriate behaviour; and they are widely accepted by the members of a social group. Stemming from the fact that there are values specific to a social group, some standards of behaviour are established and members are expected to conform to them. These are norms and they consist of concepts or generalizations which guide behaviour.

Reference groups

People turn to particular *groups* for their standards of judgement. Any person or group – real or imaginary – that serves as a point of reference for an individual is said to stand as a reference group. It exerts a key influence on the individual's beliefs, attitudes and choices.

The family is a very important reference group in a particular culture. Different values and expectations are built in the individual through the family. Other examples of reference groups are religious and ethnic groups, the trade union and the neighbourhood. Reference groups may interact and overlap. They can be classified in terms of different criteria. Those groups with which the individual has interpersonal contact are called affiliative groups. Taking the criterion of degree of interpersonal contact, two categories can be identified: (i) primary groups, with which the person has a regular contact; and (ii) secondary groups, with which the person interacts inconsistently or on few occasions. Also depending on their degree of defined structure and organization, groups may be classified as formal (such as a trade union) or informal (such as a neighbourhood).

Groups that influence general values and the development of a basic code of behaviour are qualified as normative, while those that serve as points of reference or influence specific attitudes and behaviour are designated as comparative. As stated in Chapters 1 and 2, technology has dramatically changed the way in which consumers now interact with each other and businesses – as well as the aforementioned traditional modes of reference group we are now in the age of the virtual reference groups – the rise of social networking and consumer blogging literally gives the user unlimited access and exposure to other 'trusted' opinions, views and attitudes to every manner of products and services available. As such the Internet poses its own unique challenges in the way that it has liberated consumers to share their personal experiences and opinions about brands – from tribal brands to brand boycotts. For example a primary branding driver is the recognition of the power that blogs and wikis have in fuelling word of mouth, which accounts for 30–50% of brand switching (a wiki is a website that allows visitors to add, remove, edit and change content, typically without the need for registration). As discussed in earlier chapters innovative companies are now developing and implementing new methodologies that recognize the importance of virtual reference groups (e.g. twinsumers, tryvertising and consumer emulation). Brands are seeking to build platforms which enable them to engage with their customers. Increasingly these platforms such as discussion forums or blogs get consumers to be part be part of the narrative or story – building the brand community. It is a totally different approach from the traditional advertising strategy based around intervention – reflecting the changing nature of consumer behaviour in the marketplace.

Opinion leadership

The final social influence to be considered is *opinion leadership*. An opinion leader is a person who influences the actions or attitudes of others. Individuals may be opinion leaders, opinion seekers or opinion recipients. Considering the person's tendency to lead or seek for opinion, four categories of interpersonal communication result:

1. The socially integrated: a person whose score is high in opinion leadership as well as in opinion seeking.

2. The socially independent: a person whose score is high on opinion leadership and low on opinion seeking.

3. The socially dependent: a person whose score is low on opinion leadership and high on opinion seeking.

4. The socially isolated: a person whose score is low on opinion leadership as well as on opinion seeking.

Interpersonal communication relative to opinions may be initiated either by the leader or by the receiver. Also, in relation to the four categories described above, it must be remembered that the characterization of an individual is not absolute and may vary according to different social contexts. Again the ability of the opinion leader to influence others' attitude is amplified by the Internet – the potential 'reach' is almost unbounded. Furthermore, as consumers wish to reduce the amount of perceived risk involved in the purchase decision – trust becomes an increasingly dominant factor in terms of influencing consumer choice – more and more consumers will seek out authentic and credible accounts regarding experience and opinion from valued opinion leaders. Consequently the views of virtual opinion leaders will become increasingly important to the tourism provider.

PERSONALITY AND SELF-CONCEPT

Personality can be defined as the configuration of a person's characteristics and ways of behaving, which determines his or her adjustment to the environment in a unique way. Personality is a concept that emphasizes the effect of an individual's past history on his or her current behaviour. Trait theorists view personality as a collection of traits, which are defined as relatively enduring characteristics. The trait concept implies a more quantitative approach, with assessments effected through personality tests and inventories. More holistic approaches make use of personal observation, self-reported experiences or projective techniques.

The consideration of personality types is important to appraise vacation behaviour trends. Psychocentric persons are more concerned with themselves, anxious and inhibited. Allocentric persons tend to be self-confident, outgoing and adventurous. These differences must be taken into account since they will mean diverse vacationing behaviours.

Tourist self-image

Within the consumer's conceptual structure there are concepts that the individual believes characterize him or her. They constitute the consumer's *self-image*. There is not only one kind of self-image. Usually self-image is described as what the individual believes himself or herself to be but there is also the ideal self, referring to what he or she would like to be. Purchase intentions relating to some products tend to be correlated with self-image, while those relating to other products are correlated with the ideal self-image. The activated self-image consists of the expectations a person holds about himself or herself and his or her behaviour in relation to an object or product. A similar interpretation also assumes the existence of three categories: (i) the present self, that is, the individual's self-image at a given time; (ii) the past self; and (iii) the future self. Another suggestion of these categorizations emphasizes a kind of 'others' self-image', which is how an individual thinks others see him or her.

The concept of self-image is important to marketers mainly for marketing segmentation and positioning of products: for example, as consumer awareness of environmental concerns and sustainability increase, there will a drive to reflect these values in the branding of tourism products. Conversely at the other end of the spectrum those consumers still interested in the obscure and elite will seek out brands that reinforce and position themselves as 'ultraluxe'. In either case the brand proposition must seek to reflect actual and desired dimensions of the self. In these tasks the self-image of individuals belonging to a target group must be taken into account. The tourist may prefer destinations and services that match his or her self-image – the 'looking glass' concept.

The attitudinal dimensions of tourist products can be classified into three classes: (i) those related to ego-involvement with the symbols associated with the product; (ii) those concerning the sensory character of the product attributes; and (iii) those concerning the functional aspects of the product. When a person wants to change his or her current image in order to gain entrance into a reference group, a whole new pattern of purchases may result. This may lead to the trial of new products and to a different level of purchasing. Marketers must be aware of these tendencies. Appeals based on certain desires of the tourist, such as to improve health and attractiveness, can have a strong influence on individuals aiming to change their self-concept.

The relation between self-image and product image is important to predict tourists' behaviour towards destinations and services. There are several ways of assessing the congruity between these two images. One of them involves the use of the semantic differential technique, with scales having bipolar adjective end points. The tourist is required first to identify the position on the scales of his or her self-concept and, following that, to go through the same procedure with respect to product image. Next, the discrepancy of the two images is calculated by the following equation:

$$Dkj = \sqrt{\sum_{i=1}^{m} (Sij - Pij)^2}$$

where Dkj is the overall linear discrepancy between the jth tourist's self-image and his or her perception of the image of the kth destination; i is the specific image component used to assess destination and self-image; m is the total number of image components; Sij is the jth tourist's self-perception on the ith image component; and Pij is the jth tourist's destination perception on the ith image component.

PERCEPTION AND COGNITION

The comprehension of the process of knowledge acquisition and incorporation of experiences will permit better predictions of actual vacation behaviour. Perception and learning strongly influence evaluation and judgemental processes. *Perception* is the process by which an individual selects, organizes and interprets stimuli in a meaningful and coherent way. A stimulus is any unit of input affecting any of the senses. Perceiving stimuli involves exposure, reception and assimilation of information. Our sensory system is sensitive to different modalities of external stimuli: auditory, visual, tactile, olfactory and taste. When inputs are transmitted, information reception will depend on the cues from the source of the stimuli (a product, a message, etc.) and the individual's reactions based on current knowledge.

An individual tends to organize his or her perceptions and knowledge in order to produce meaningful relationships among separate elements. What an individual perceives in many situations is determined not only by the intrinsic nature of the stimulus object or sensations, but also by his or her own system of values and needs determined by the social context.

The first stage of perception is the attention filter. One does not perceive all the stimuli arriving but grasps information selectively through a process of comparison of inputs with previous information. Furthermore, most stimuli to which one is exposed are screened out if they are uninteresting and irrelevant. The second stage is the interpretation process, whereby the stimulus content is organized into one's own model of reality, resulting in awareness and interpretation of the stimulus, that is, in cognition.

Selective perception

Perception is selective in two ways: attention and distortion. Selective attention refers to the fact that individuals usually attend to those stimuli which are regarded as relevant to his or her needs and interests, and neglect or distort inconsistent stimuli. Since we cannot perceive everything, we become selective in our attention, blocking perception when an excessively high level of stimuli are affecting us (stimulus bombardment – media are now so fragmented and consumers are so overloaded with brand messages that they are getting harder to reach), when arriving stimuli are irrelevant, or when they are culturally unacceptable, damaging or incompatible with our values and beliefs. We have now entered an age of stimuli bombardment, visual saturation, sound bites and microscopic attention spans. The number of images and voices shouting for consumer attention has accelerated beyond critical mass, and the resulting explosion has fragmented the public mind. As a consequence consumers have developed mental filters – 'tuning in and tuning out' via selective perception to guard against 'hypercommunication'. This is the reason why selective attention is also seen as a form of perceptual defence. Today's consumers are bombarded with 60% more advertisements than they were a decade ago and as such there is now a tendency for consumers to avoid or ignore traditional advertising rather than to process it. Classically the degree of complexity of stimuli will determine different levels of attention: moderately complex stimuli are more likely to attract our attention than simple or too complex ones – however, as more and more companies compete for our attention the modes of communication used must become more and more innovative and in some cases 'novel' to rise above the clutter and noise (e.g. branded entertainment). The line between entertainment and branding has blurred – a hot subspecies of branding dubbed 'advertainment' is now commonplace in response to selective perception.

Perceptual bias or selective distortion is a tendency for people to modify information in the direction of personal meanings. Involvement in the object or message can be a function of self-perception, which, in turn, is a function of need and social conditions; the result is selective distortion and selective retention of available information. The information obtained from a specific message is the sum of the relevant statements as perceived by the receiver. The audience receives the message and relates the symbols it holds by relating it to prior learning. Integration of information implies different processes in the audience, resulting in acceptance or rejection of the message, retention or modification, belief or disbelief.

Vacation destination comprehension is related to the halo effect, which is the tendency of a tourist to be biased by his or her overall opinion in the process of evaluating distinct attributes of a destination or service. This is a form of generalization and it minimizes the effort required to make travel decisions.

Information search

An important question is: how sensitive is the average vacation tourist regarding the information received about a tourist product? Perceptual effects may be examined at three levels: (i) the amount of information available to the tourist; (ii) the amount of information the tourist is exposed to; and (iii) the amount of information actually retained.

Information seeking is the expressed need to consult various sources prior to making a purchasing decision. Initially, there is the recognition of the problem, which is the result of a perceived imbalance or need to shift to a desired state. It activates the decision process, through the search for information about alternatives. One type of search is internal, that is, the retrieval of information about alternatives, stored in memory. However, and especially in the case of vacation travel, the search is often external, involving active processes and a variety of information sources. There are individual differences in terms of the likelihood of a tourist to be involved in a search, but the level of active search is usually dependent on the degree of balance between expectation of predicted benefits and costs, or on the degree of certainty about the merits of alternative destinations and services. The concept of overt search includes all the activities of a potential tourist directed at collecting information about a product. In terms of external search the Internet has dramatically impacted upon external search strategies, and the immediacy of information online regarding different tourism options promotes the 'Google effect'. Internet browsing has trained consumers to disregard 'empty' words and claims – message relevance has become more important than repetition: online content full of unsupported claims and over-worked 'image-building' phrases is rejected more quickly today than ever before. As such, meaningful, relevant information is now desired by consumers in the online domain. One reason for the occurrence of a limited external search is that tourists often have available a large amount of information, previously acquired – prior knowledge and experience can be retrieved and consulted through internal search, thus minimizing time and cognitive effort in terms of decision making. The role of consumer memory is discussed in greater detail in the next section.

The mechanism of the use of information by the tourist comprises four stages: (i) exposure (contact with the sources of information); (ii) awareness (interest in the product); (iii) assimilation (attitude towards the product attributes); and (iv) attitude change (awareness of the product and association of product and attributes).

Memory

Memory plays a major role in consumer choice. There are three stages involved in memory. First the information enters the memory and is encoded. Then the information is stored. The third stage is retrieval. Storage is said to be a function of the level of information processing at the time the message is received so that retention will depend on how information is processed. One influential approach to memory assumes it to be a multiple-store process, with different types of memory storage systems, each with specific functions and properties. A typical model of this type assumes a set of sensory stores, a short-term and a long-term store.

For an advertisement to be remembered, it must be encoded and stored in the long-term memory system. Information stored can be of two types: that actively acquired and that passively absorbed from the environment. The quantity of information that will be retained in long-term memory (data considered relevant or useful) is only a fraction of the total information communicated. The stored information can be retrieved (i.e. recovered for use). With respect to recall, an inappropriate context as well as new and old learning may interfere and reduce the possibility of retrieving given material. Forgetting is mainly the result of interference of new information and experiences occurring between the time of encoding and that of retrieval.

The process of response to communication begins with a state of unawareness. The initial response is to become aware of a message. This response is followed by comprehension or knowledge, when the receiver must relate the message to prior learning experiences so as to give meaning to it. The subsequent states are liking, preference, conviction and action.

Learning process

Comprehension or knowledge about the tourist product consists of the facts acquired about it that are used as the basic material for decision making. To understand the acquisition of knowledge about a product, it is necessary to consider the learning process.

Learning refers to the establishment of new responses to the environment. *Cognitive learning theory* focuses on problem solving, that is, on mental processing, and considers the tourist as an active learner. This approach emphasizes the topics discussed above: information processing leading to comprehension and action. *Instrumental learning theory* emphasizes the role of reinforcement and repeated trials. Reinforcement is the process by which a consequence increases the likelihood of a specific response to certain cues. When cues are pertinent to expectations, they tend to activate certain drives (Evans *et al.*, 1996).

As mentioned above, in relation to the halo effect, generalization is an important aspect of the learning process to be taken into account in the analysis of vacation behaviour. Stimulus generalization is the process by which the same response is made to similar but different stimuli, such as when a person responds to a given travel situation in the same way he or she has responded to different but similar situations in the past. On the other hand, stimulus discrimination involves the learning of different responses to different but similar situations. The processes of generalization, emphasizing stimulus similarity, and of discrimination, emphasizing stimulus difference, are fundamental in consumer behaviour assessment. Tourists can discriminate between two similar products and show preference for one of them and they can generalize about different, not yet experienced, aspects of a destination on the basis of known stimuli.

Hence, careful attention has to be given to the stimuli related to travelling and the way they affect tourist behaviour. The expression 'travel stimuli display' refers to the different kinds of information presented to the tourist. Information may have a significative or symbolic character related to the product attributes such as quality, distinctiveness, prestige and availability. Tourists' behaviour is influenced by affective and by symbolic appeals.

Tourist sources of communication

Depending on the source of information, communication can be classified as: (i) primary (experiences derived directly from the product); (ii) secondary (mass communication); (iii) tertiary (information obtained from travel agencies or exhibitions); and (iv) personal. Tourists will actively process the information provided by the source but will not make judgements about the product based only on information; they combine it with other experiences and previous knowledge to develop attitudes and intentions and to reach a buying decision.

Messages received by the tourist are sometimes seen as ambiguous when confronted with previous experience. The filtration process serves to protect the tourist since it permits discrimination between facts and exaggerations in advertising. Communication is the determinant of much of vacation behaviour and an advertisement is intended to communicate, allowing the acquisition of knowledge, the formation or change of a product image, the arousal of needs and wants, the creation of interest in a product, and the inducement to action.

The primary form of communication is word of mouth – or indeed word of net. This conversation activity is a channel for both receiving and disseminating information concerning vacation destinations and tourist services. Product involvement is one of the motivations for word of mouth. When a tourist product is perceived to be central to the individual's self-image, there is a high probability of the product being used and focused on in conversation. The content of conversation depends on the assimilated communication, and the rate of word of mouth depends on the tourist's awareness and attitude.

Internalization of information occurs when the individual accepts the opinion because it is congruent with his or her existing values. Here, the factors 'credibility' of message and personal relevance of the information play an important role. Based on personal experience and expectations, the tourist uses a trade-off of all the alternatives to reach a decision to act. This process is shown in Fig. 5.3. Consumers use information in five different ways: (i) to evaluate alternatives in making a choice; (ii) to reinforce past choices as a rationalization process; (iii) to resolve conflict between buying and postponing; (iv) to remind them when to buy; and (v) to acquire knowledge for epistemic purposes.

The processes of exposure, perception and retention will be influenced by the advertisement in different ways: (i) in the cognitive domain, the extent to which it carries useful information, its relevance, its believability; and (ii) in the affective domain, its attractiveness and its likeability. Consumers are now seeking improvement in the relevance of advertising and are more likely to respond positively to those companies who utilize modes of 'social marketing' and cause related marketing programmes as opposed to traditional advertising formats.

Product image formation

After processing the information, the tourist will possess what is called 'total thoughts' about the product, encompassing positive, negative and neutral thoughts. Given the information

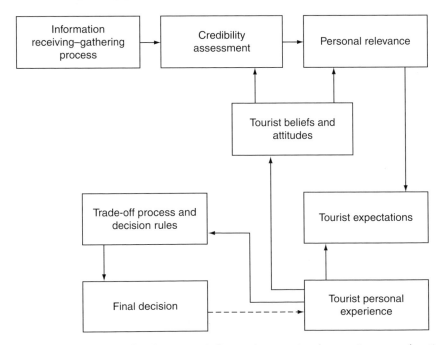

Fig. 5.3. A possible relationship between information received, experience and action.

possessed about a vacation destination, the tourist will form an image of it. This image is a description of the tourist's attitude towards a number of cues related to the destination attributes. This attitude is based partially on feelings, not solely on knowledge. The destination image tends to be an oversimplification in the mind of the tourist and, at the same time, a consistent configuration constructed according to the available information. To construct it the tourist may add missing information, generalizing information of known aspects to (other) unknown aspects.

Physical attributes of a vacation destination act only as stimuli inducing certain associations; thus, the image is not what the product actually is, but what the tourist's beliefs tend to construct. There are three components in image formation: (i) related to awareness, implying the information the tourist believes a tourist destination or service possesses; (ii) related to attitude, implying feelings and beliefs about the tourist product; and (iii) related to expectations, implying the benefits expected to be derived from the tourist product. The concept of image can be formulated as:

$$I = f(Aw, BA, Ex)$$

where I is the image of the destination or service; f is a function of; Aw is the level of awareness in relation to the product; BA is the beliefs and attitudes developed about the product; and Ex is the expectations created with the product. The attractiveness of a tourist destination and the choice of it will greatly depend on its image. It is an important fact to marketers that, in general, images tend to be easily modified.

MOTIVATION

Motivation refers to a state of need, a condition that exerts a 'push' on the individual towards certain types of action that are seen as likely to bring satisfaction. Vacation tourist motivation is greatly determined by social factors and is related to the need for optimal arousal. We have a need for stability as well as for novelty. In the case of travelling there are usually multiple motives, based on the tourist's expectations of what will be gained from the purchase.

There are two views in relation to the individual's logical consistency. Some theories stress the need for balance and harmony, considering the individual more likely to be satisfied with the expected and to be uncomfortable with the unexpected. However, other theories maintain that the unexpected is satisfying and that the individual will seek complexity, not sameness. In terms of travelling, the former theory would predict that the individual would visit well-known places, while according to the latter theory people would seek unknown places, restaurants and hotels. As a matter of fact, these theories explain different behaviours that do occur, and different individuals may behave more in accordance with one or the other assumption. The most likely is that people will seek for a balance between consistency and complexity.

In the case of leisure travel there is a search for variety, that is, for situations which offer a certain degree (variable among individuals) of incongruity, uncertainty, novelty and complexity, combined with a degree of familiarity: a contact with the familiar and the novel.

Travel motivators

Satisfaction associated with vacation travel includes relaxation of tension, which is a strong underlying element to different desires and expectations concerning a vacation. The search for a mental state of renewal always seems to be involved.

The answer to 'why do people travel?' is not a simple one. Two sets of motivations must be distinguished: general and specific. General motivations imply that people travel for many reasons, and many times they are not fully aware of them. Some general travel motivations are presented in Table 5.1. This range of motives is broad, in common with other classifications, for they are attempts to encompass basic classes of motivators.

A new generation of travellers is beginning to emerge, in the sense that the traveller has ceased to be a tourist and has become a searcher. For that reason, many travel folders and advertisements are still speaking a language of the past. The motivations include the discovering of oneself and psychological mobility, with the traveller willing to know different cultures, the psychological aura, fauna and flora of an area and a country. The challenge involved in travelling is based on the exploring instinct labelled the 'Ulysses factor' in reference to the hero of Homer's *Odyssey*. It is the need for exploration and adventure, involving an exciting and even (according to the individual's perception) risky action. It is a physical and intellectual need related to knowledge and curiosity.

ATTITUDE AND INTENTION

Attitude

An *attitude* is a predisposition, created by learning and experience, to respond in a consistent way towards an object, such as a product. This predisposition can be favourable or unfavourable.

Table 5.1. A list of examples of general travel motivations.

Educational and cultural
    To see how people in other countries live and work
    To see particular sights, monuments or works of art
    To gain a better understanding of current events
    To attend special cultural or artistic events

Relaxation, adventure and pleasure
    To get away from everyday routine and obligations
    To see new places, people, or seek new experiences
    To have a good time, fun
    To have some sort of romantic sexual experience

Health and recreation
    To rest and recover from work and strain
    To practise sports and exercise

Ethnic and family
    To visit places your family came from
    To visit relatives and friends
    To spend time with the family and children

Social and 'competitive'
    To be able to talk about places visited
    Because it is 'fashionable'
    To show that one can afford it

Attitudes are generally considered to have three components: cognitive, affective and conative. The cognitive component is sometimes called the belief or knowledge component, consisting of the beliefs and opinions, based on some evidence, that an individual holds about something (a place, an experience, another person); the affective component refers to the feelings and emotions about the destination or service and implies judgement on the basis of emotion; the conative is the action tendency, which can have a favourable or unfavourable character (Hoyer and MacInnis, 1997).

Tourist attitude change

In order to change attitudes, marketers can

- modify the characteristics of the tourist product (real positioning);
- alter beliefs about the product (psychological positioning);
- alter beliefs about competitive products (competitive depositioning);
- change the relevant weights of the product attributes;
- induce attention to certain attributes; and
- modify the tourist's ideal levels for certain attributes.

Inhibiting factors may lead the tourist to respond to a destination in a way different from his or her attitude towards it. The sense of uncertainty, of caution or indecisiveness is also present in vacation behaviour. Some inhibitors of a positive attitude are the availability of alternatives, problems of incompatible income, or other limiting factors such as the impact of other people's behaviour. Travel preferences are developed as a result of perception of benefits. When choosing a destination, the traveller assesses the level of different benefits in each alternative. The outcome of this assessment is the intention to buy one destination.

So, to influence a traveller's decision, one may increase the importance of one or some specific benefits. The perception of benefits will shape the overall attractiveness of a destination. Alternatives are regarded as viable, neutral or rejected. The viable alternatives will then be more carefully considered. Research has indicated that usually travellers will analyse no more than seven alternatives in a given vacation decision. So far we have discussed attitudes towards an object. However, an alternative interpretation holds that attitudes are actually related to 'behaviour towards' an object. The Fishbein (1967) attitudes-towards behaviour model is expressed by the following equation:

$$\text{Attitude (behaviour)} = \sum_{i=1}^{n} b_i e_i$$

where b_i is the strength of belief that ith specific behaviour will have a specific consequence, n is the number of specific behaviours and e_i is the evaluation of the outcome.

A multi-attribute object (e.g. a vacation destination) is viewed as a bundle of attributes leading to costs and benefits of differential desirability to individuals or segments of the market. Overall affect is posited to reflect the net resolution of an individual's cognitions (beliefs) as to the degree to which given objects possess certain attributes weighted by the salience (importance) of each attribute to the individual. Our general attitudes, interests and outlook towards life are related to our attitudes towards different kinds of vacation experiences and to what we would like to find in a vacation. Confidence generation is related to destination comprehension, intention and the degree of satisfaction gained in the purchase and utilization of a product. Confidence also implies the tourist's ability to judge the quality of the services offered.

Intention

Intention indicates the likelihood of purchasing a tourist product; it is the readiness-to-buy concept. Behavioural intention is said to be a function of: (i) evaluative beliefs towards the tourist product; (ii) social factors which tend to provide a set of normative beliefs for the tourist; and (iii) situational factors than can be anticipated at the time of the vacation plan or commitment. This function is expressed in the following equation:

$$BI_{ij} = b_1\ (Eb_{ijk}) + b_2(SE_{ij}) = b_3(AS_{ij})$$

where BI_{ij} is individual i's plan to behave in a certain way towards vacation destination j; b is the beta coefficient; Eb_{ijk} is individual i's belief k about vacation destination j; SE_{ij} is individual i's social environment influencing behaviour towards j; and AS_{ij} is individual i's anticipation of events at the time of his or her behaviour towards j.

The assessment of a market potential has to take into account that there are factors that can be anticipated and others that cannot. Variables that can be anticipated should be analysed (for instance, demographic and economic factors) before further study of behavioural variables is initiated. The relationship between attitude formation, intention and the travel decision-making process is summarized in Fig. 5.4.

A final issue to be considered concerning attitude and intention refers to their measurement. Social psychologists have attempted to create methods of assessment. Attitudes may be inferred from systematic observations of the individual's behaviour in social contexts or from responses to questionnaires. One problem with the questionnaire technique is that respondents

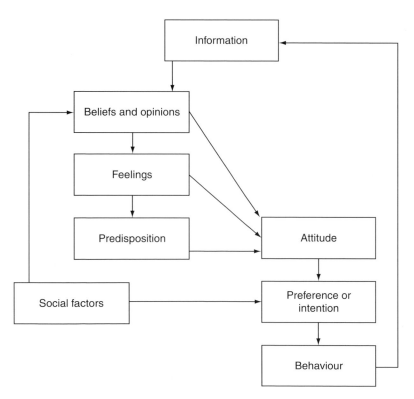

Fig. 5.4. Attitudes and the travel decision-making process.

may misrepresent their feelings in their statements. Researchers have been cautious about the power to predict subsequent buying behaviour from the assessment of attitudes and intentions. Actually, in real situations, there is a gap in time and space between the manifestation of an intention and buying behaviour. Several non-predicted factors may appear during this interval. Despite this fact, a useful technique for measurement is the rank-order scaling procedure.

PERCEIVED RISK

Being faced with a purchasing situation, a tourist has a certain degree of risk involved in the decision to be made. Perceived risk is a function of uncertainty and consequences. This may include: (i) uncertainty inherent in the product; (ii) uncertainty in place and mode of purchase; (iii) degree of financial and psychosocial consequences; and (iv) the subjective uncertainty experienced by the tourist. The degree of risk may vary with the costs involved in a decision and the degree of certainty that the decision will lead to satisfaction. Costs may concern time costs, ego costs, monetary costs and other costs resulting from the eventual failure of need satisfaction. For this last case the types of consumer (vacation tourist) loss can be defined as physical loss, loss in time, ego loss or financial loss.

Tourists can be risk neutral, risk avoiders or risk takers. The first types of risk to be perceived are connected with financial and social-psychological aspects. 'Overall perceived risk' includes performance, physical, social-psychological and time risks. The concept of perceived risk can be formulated as:

$$PR_x = f(PER_x, PSR_x, PPR_x)$$

where PR_x is perceived risk (the x relates to the individual product under consideration); f is a function of; PER is perceived economic risk; PSR is perceived social risk; and PPR is perceived psychological risk.

The origin of risk perception lies in the uncertainty of the congruence between self-image and product image. Researchers regard risk handling as a risk reduction process. Risk reduction methods are used until its level reaches one which is tolerable to the individual and consistent with purchase goals. Figure 5.5 describes the risk variables relationships. To understand how vacation tourists reduce risk, it is necessary to consider the major types of perceived risk:

1. Functional risk – the risk that the product will not perform as expected.
2. Physical risk – the risk that the tourist product will be harmful.
3. Financial risk – the risk that the product will not be worth its cost, in either time or money.
4. Social risk – the risk that a poor product choice may result in embarrassment before others.
5. Psychological risk – the risk that a poor product choice will harm the consumer's ego.

The different types of risk have to be considered by a tourist organization in order to help the tourist to reduce the perceived risk (Box 5.1). Some sources of perceived risk in a buying situation include uncertain buying goals, uncertain purchase rewards, lack of purchasing experience, the prediction of positive or negative consequences, peer influence and financial considerations (see Fig. 5.6).

For an assessment of tourist risk variables, one should study the relationship between the tourist's past behaviour and his or her learning process towards travel-related concepts, the tourist's intrapersonal characteristics, the type of information sources used by him or her before and after the tourist product purchase, the tourist's level of risk awareness and the tourist's evaluation of the product attributes. Several risk-reduction strategies can be used by tourists:

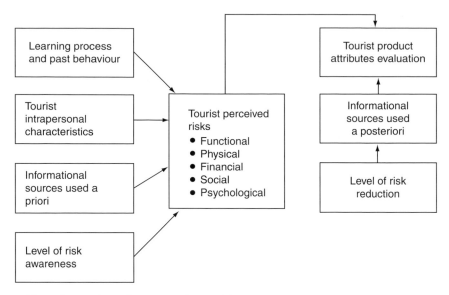

Fig. 5.5. The relationship of tourist risk variables.

Box 5.1. The buying behaviour process for airline products.

Airlines deal intimately with customers, selling a service that to many is threatening, that few profess to be able to evaluate objectively, and that constitutes a sizeable expenditure. Marketing-by-market promotional planning must continue the accent on reinforcing user 'loyalty'. Surveys indicate that individuals do not have clearly formed beliefs about most airlines (although frequent flyers generally prefer one above others), that utility for the 'product' is high, and that there is little emotional involvement when they discuss airlines. Companies in the airline business need a systematic, ongoing process of data collection to evaluate marketplace perceptions rather than awakening one day to find their position eroded by more astute competitors. Since airlines can seldom be tried out, inspected or tested without a purchase, and are intangible, testimonials are one method to signify that the 'product' performs well and that the 'quality' is high, adding to convenience value for air travellers. An airline that is marketing-oriented has to examine periodically its responsiveness to tactical needs in different markets as well as to frenzied price competition.

- expecting less from the product or service;
- regularly purchasing the same product (characterizing tourists' loyalty);
- acquiring tourist information;
- purchasing the most expensive product;
- relying on government or consumer travel reports; and
- relying on tourist guarantees.

When studying the problem of adequacy, the analysis of the cost–benefit equilibrium level for the prices paid by the vacation tourist should be taken into account. The consistency

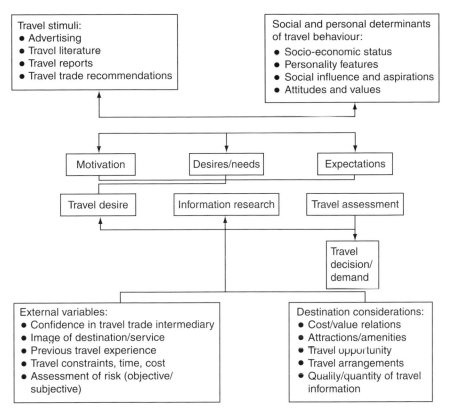

Fig. 5.6. Travel decision model.

of the product represents the sum of all real attributes perceived by the tourist when utilizing the tourist service. Product consistency follows a kind of ranking system in the tourist's mind, and it plays an important role for the vacation destination 'sold' to the tourist.

FAMILY DECISION PROCESS

Family goals and roles are major determinants of vacation decision making. Family influences are important in two major ways: (i) they affect individual personality characteristics, attitudes and values; and (ii) they affect the decision-making process that is involved in the purchase of tourism services.

One person in a family may be responsible for problem recognition, another for search and still another for making the decision. Family decision making varies in terms of social class. Decision making in families, with respect to product selection, may be described as syncratic, partially syncratic and autonomic. Syncratic decision making generally means joint decisions and partially syncratic decision making means that some decisions are made on a joint basis and some are made by either partner. Autonomic decision making means that approximately an equal number of separate decisions are made by each partner.

Family life cycle

Changes in family characteristics produce changes in lifestyle and dramatic changes in consumer behaviour. Family life cycle (FLC) is a form of classification of family, marital status, age and work status of family members. There are different FLC models. The one presented by Wells and Gubar (1966) can illustrate this form of classification. They considered the following five stages:

1. Bachelor stage.
2. Newly married couple with young children or no children.
3. Full nest I (youngest child under 6), full nest II (youngest children 6 or over), full nest III (older married couples with dependent children).
4. Empty nest I (no children at home, head in labour force), empty nest II (head retired).
5. Solitary survivor (in labour force or retired).

Joint decision making predominates when there is a great deal of perceived risk with regard to product attributes. An increase in role specialization occurs over the stages in the FLC, which is reflected by a decline in the degree of joint decision making. There is a suggestion that men strongly dominate decisions concerning the actual date of vacation, the amount spent, the length of stay and the price of lodging. Syncratic decision making prevails in relation to the choice of the actual destination and the type of lodging.

In Table 5.2, different aspects of travel decisions are considered in relation to family decision style. Although in general travel decisions are made jointly – a syncratic process – there are cases of only one-partner dominance. Joint decision making is strong with respect to the vacation destination and the amount to be spent. When there is a dominant decision-making role of the male partner, it is usually in two areas: lodging and destination point. Family vacation behaviour patterns are, thus, associated with the life stages of the family, and the trips are often the highlights of family life, especially when the family is growing.

Table 5.2. Family decision-making styles.

Family travel decision	Predominant family decision-making style
Type of lodging accommodation	Husband dominant
Vacation destination(s)	Husband dominant
Whether to take children along	Joint influence–individual decision
How long to stay on vacation	Joint influence–individual decision
Dates of vacation travel	Joint influence–individual decision
Mode of transportation on family vacation	Joint influence–individual decision
Vacation activities	Joint influence–individual decision
Whether to go on vacation	Joint influence–joint decision
How much money to spend on vacation travel	Joint influence–joint decision

Cosenza and Davis (1981) suggested six stages of FLC, each with a characteristic decision-making dominance:

1. Syncratic.
2. Husband dominant.
3. Wife dominant.

4. Wife dominant.
5. Syncratic.
6. Wife dominant.

In Stage 1, the couple is in the initial stage of marriage and willing to participate in vacation decisions. They tend to seek information actively. A change appears in Stage 2, with the husband playing a slightly dominant role, due to the fact that his career is at a critical stage and his work schedule is a major criterion. In Stage 3, there is a dramatic change to wife-dominant decisions. Role specialization leads the wife to take charge of planning in the area of vacations. This is a stage with a high level of vacation purchase. Stage 4 is marked by a slight shift to syncratic decision again, but decisions are still wife dominant. Stage 5 is one of syncratic decisions, although with a slightly higher influence by the husband. In Stage 6 decisions seem to be dominated by the wife again. This is the stage of the retired couple who have been married for more than 40 years. The frequency of vacation travel tends to diminish at this stage.

A final aspect that has to be included in the consideration of the family decision-making process is related to the children. The influence of children in the family decision is very important but usually indirect: children's needs as well as the benefits they can gain from the travel experiences are taken into account in the process. Also, travel is seen as an important opportunity to strengthen family bonds. During the vacation travel children still have little direct influence but they may direct choices of lodging and restaurants, or of certain activities. This influence by children will, of course, depend on the stage of family life.

VACATION TOURIST PROCESS

A decision is an outcome of a mental process whereby one action is chosen from a set of available alternatives. Decision-process models describe how information is acquired and related in order to make a decision. Most of the models deal with five different steps in the decision process: (i) problem identification; (ii) information search; (iii) evaluation of alternatives; (iv) choice; and (v) post-choice processes. The tourist decision process involves the tourist's motives and intentions, as well as the stimuli that turn intention into choice of product or destination. The tourist can make a decision through different approaches, from highly routine to very extensive. In the case of a routine decision-making approach, decisions are made quickly and with little mental effort; the perceived knowledge about the alternatives available is high. When an extensive approach is taken, there is need for considerable time and effort in the search for information and evaluation of alternatives.

THE INFLUENCE OF FRIENDS AND RELATIVES IN TRAVEL DECISION MAKING

Although there are numerous facets involved in the decision-making process, one area that has begun to receive more attention is the issue of who makes the decision within the travel group. This interest stems from a number of factors. First, a tourism experience appears to be a highly social event (i.e. involving two or more people in the travel group and the likelihood that many of these trips involve visiting family or friends). Secondly, destination and attraction marketers must design their advertising based on their knowledge of who will be using the information to make various types of decisions.

Most attempts to understand the dynamics of group decision making related to travel decisions have focused on the role of the spouse/partner or the children in the process; however, there have been few research efforts in this area. Further, there have been very few, if any, research efforts that have focused on the role of friends and/or relatives in the decision-making process, beyond the role this group plays in providing information for what are considered the primary decision makers. There would appear to be a number of reasons why this latter group should be considered as a more dynamic element of the decision process. First, if we are visiting an area for the first time, it would seem logical that we might defer at least some of the decision making to individuals who are more knowledgeable about the destination area. Secondly, the friends/relatives may in a number of instances become part of the group visiting a particular attraction.

Crompton (1981), in his research on pleasure travel, has suggested that friends and/or relatives influence behaviour throughout the recreation experience. From the perspective of providing information for decision makers, the influence of friends and/or relatives has been well documented (Jenkins, 1978; Bultena and Field, 1980; van Raaij and Francken, 1984). In fact, when asked what sources provide trip-related information, friends and/or relatives are usually listed as the most frequent and most credible source (Gitelson and Crompton, 1983; Capella and Greco, 1987). Reference groups, including friends and relatives, are also important factors in the overall decision-making process. According to Peter and Olson (1994), reference groups exert a major influence over most aspects of consumer behaviour, especially the decision-making process. They influence decision makers in three ways. The first type of influence involves the provision of information, which is used or not used by the decision maker based on the perception that the information is useful and the reference group member is credible. The second type of influence is utilitarian in nature. This occurs when a member of a reference group provides a reward or sanction for something that the decision maker has done. The third type of influence is exerted on the decision maker's self-concept and is called value-expressive influence (Hawkins *et al.*, 1997).

Results in Table 5.3 indicate that all of the travel-related decisions studied were influenced by friends and/or relatives. The extent to which friends and/or relatives played either the dominant or sole decision-making role ranged from 29% in the case of deciding how long the non-locals would stay to 39% in the decision process to decide what the non-locals would do while in the region. An additional 11–25% of the six decision areas were equally decided by friends and/or relatives and one or more other group members.

In slightly more than half of the decisions (54%), friends and/or relatives were not the dominant or sole decision maker. Of the six decisions included in the study, friends and/or relatives were involved in at least one decision as the sole or dominant decision maker in 47% of the cases. In approximately one-third of the groups (34%), friends and/or relatives dominated the decision-making process in at least four of the six types of decisions.

Past studies have restricted their focus to the role these friends and/or relatives play in providing decision makers with information. But these results indicated that friends and/or relatives shape behaviour in a more direct fashion and, in many cases, take on the role of 'sole' decision maker.

Thus, future research efforts need to include friends and/or relatives as potentially equal partners in the decision-making process, just as they have done with the spouse/partner and children. A number of important issues related to the decision-making process deserve attention in future research efforts. At what point in time do friends and/or relatives become influential? For example, do friends and/or relatives affect the decision-making process prior to or during the trip and/or after the trip has begun? Andereck (1992) suggests that information related to the timing of various decisions would allow researchers to better understand tourist behaviour

Table 5.3. Role played by friends and/or relatives in selected travel decisions (%) (Source: Gitelson and Kerstetter, 1994).

Level of influence	Which sites ($n = 67$)	Length of stay ($n = 66$)	What to do ($n = 67$)	Where to eat ($n = 64$)	Trip info ($n = 60$)	Where to stay ($n = 45$)
Sole decision maker	25	18	21	25	27	24
Dominant role	13	11	18	11	10	9
Equal role	12	20	16	25	12	11
Lesser role	6	5	5	3	2	2
No role	43	47	40	36	50	54

Number of decisions where friends and/or relatives played total or dominant role (%)

Did not play sole or dominant role in any decisions	54
Sole or dominant decision maker in at least one type of decision	5
Sole or dominant decision maker in two or three decisions	7
Sole or dominant decision maker in four or more decisions	34

and, as a result of this knowledge, help tourism marketers and suppliers to more effectively target their market(s).

EXTERNAL INFORMATION SEARCH

External information sources are employed by tourists and form the basis for vacation planning. For marketers it is relevant to know what kind of information should be used in tour brochures to stimulate the tourist's external search process.

Gathering tourist information

The problems of tourism marketing are different from the problems of traditional product marketing. The differences are the result of the characteristics of tourism supply and demand. Tourism is a *service*. An intangible experience is being sold, not a physical good that can be inspected prior to service (Mill and Morrison, 1985). Generalizations that have widespread acceptance among scholars and practitioners in the field as being characteristic of services include intangibility, simultaneity of production and consumption and non-standardization (see Zeithaml *et al.*, 1985). Services are not directly perceptible and are unpredictable in their outcomes for the buyer. This implies that they would influence the purchasing behaviour of consumers. The fundamental characteristics of services appear to create particular uncertain and risky purchase situations. In this context, Murray (1991) states that it is logical to expect that consumers acquire information as a strategy of risk reduction in the face of this specific uncertainty. Moreover, he argues that services are more difficult to evaluate than goods. As a consequence, consumers may be forced to rely on other cues and processes when evaluating services.

Tourism marketers may benefit from the improved knowledge of *search behaviour* in vacation planning. In general, knowledge of information acquisition strategies is important to marketing managers because information search is at an early influential stage in the purchase decision process. In fact, the information sources employed by tourists form the basis for vacation planning (van Raaij and Francken, 1984). Consumer information sources can be classified into two broad types – internal and external. Both types are used by consumers to gather information and cope with perceived risk.

Information sources

In this field of research, information importance is a significant determinant of both pre-purchase and ongoing external search. Furthermore, ongoing external search and the balance of pre-purchase search activities are also influenced by enduring involvement and previous experience (see Perdue, 1993). In general, sources of external information search can be classified in terms of whether the source is marketing oriented or whether information comes from personal or impersonal communication (Engel *et al.*, 1995). Non-marketer-dominated information sources such as personal media are expected to play a particularly important role in the consumer decision process for services. However, personal information sources and mass media are related in several ways. For example, tourism indicates that mass media (such as the Internet, tourist advertising and brochures) are consulted most in the beginning, and personal media (such as salespersons, friends, personal advice) are mainly used at a later stage of the vacation planning (van Raaij and Francken, 1984). Tour brochures and other sources of mass media initially play a significant role in determining choice of recreation and vacation destinations. Because consumers understand that the purpose of these mass media is to persuade as well as to inform, they discount the value of this 'biased' information and seek to verify its authenticity (see Maute and Forrester, 1991). The phenomenon is reflected in the fact that people in the vacation group usually share in the information search process, and often several sources of information are consulted in planning a trip. In general, the vacation search process involves one or more individuals along with a variety of sources for a multiple set of decisions (e.g. see Capella and Greco, 1987; Snepenger *et al.*, 1990). With regard to vacation decision making it is found that social information sources are the most important. Members of the immediate family rank first, relatives second and friends third (Jenkins, 1978). These facts are in line with Murray's (1991) conclusion that service consumers prefer the opinions and experiences of other comparable individuals in making service purchase decisions. This is reflected in the rise of 'twinsumers' and trusted online brand communities that offer valued and trusted opinion. This strategy helps to reduce perceived risk in the purchase decision.

Vacations are intangibles, which means that the prospective buyer can neither see nor feel them prior to purchase, nor can he or she return the product if dissatisfied. Mansfeld (1992) states that tourism marketers should follow two prevailing research strategies. One is the study of tourists' stated preferences; the other is the study of actual choice. He suggests that the second research direction should look into the information-gathering stage. In this case, the impact of promotional information material on touristic choice behaviour should be examined. Because this material is meant to create favourable images and to stimulate 'non-leading' motivations, it is important to evaluate its 'bias effect' on possible choice directions. More specifically, Perdue (1993: 184) states that research focusing on propensity to seek information as a dependent variable, particularly within the context of the growing body of hedonic consumption literature, may significantly improve external search theory. Also distinguishing between the decision or propensity to seek information and the actual selection and use of alternative sources of information may significantly improve our theoretical understanding of external search behaviour.

Brochures

Leisure studies demonstrate that tourists rely more on informational material while preparing their trip at home rather than after arriving at their destination (Mansfeld, 1992). In this context Manfredo (1989) points at the fact that so-called 'active information seekers' (i.e. individuals who are deliberately searching for external information) are of particular interest because of the possibility that they are ready to act (visit a given area) and because they may be susceptible to persuasive appeals. When we keep in mind that tourists prefer personal information, it is reasonable to assume that persuasive communication strategies should stress experiential or subjective rather than technical or objective dimensions of the trips on offer. This means that travel agencies and tour operators should make the description more tangible in brochures by providing visible or explanatory cues that prospective tourists can use to evaluate the ultimate (emotional) advantages and quality of the vacation. Potential inclusive tour buyers, although they can bear in mind word-of-mouth and published recommendations as well as their own past personal experience, still have to rely largely on what they read and see in operators' brochures; the tour operators' brochures have many similarities with commercial published leisure magazines. They are regarded by their users as being 'a good read', whetting the appetite for the vacation products on offer (see Hodgson, 1993). From this hedonic and motivational point of view it is important to stress experiential information in brochures. Promotional leisure information about feelings of pleasure, relaxation, excitement, adventure and fun will probably motivate tourists to plan a trip.

Actually there is no scientific study available in the travel-research and destination-marketing literature on whether advertising stimulates tourism (see Woodside, 1990). While tourism 'advertising conversions research' studies are helpful in comparing the performance of different advertisements, media vehicles and media, such advertising conversion studies do not address the more basic question: what kind of information should be used in brochures to trigger the external search behaviour of tourists?

Since tour brochures are infrequently effective in getting the attention of the information seeker, it is useful to examine the impact of different types of brochure information on external search behaviour.

MENTAL IMAGERY AND BEHAVIOURAL INTENTIONS

In general, consumer researchers suggest that the experiential aspects of consumption play an important role in consumer choice behaviour (see Hirschman and Holbrook, 1982). From this point of view, MacInnis and Price (1987) state that in the choice of many leisure services an important part of the choice involves assessing how it will feel (the sensation surrounding the anticipated leisure experience). Regarding the latter, experiential processes, such as imagining, daydreams and emotions, play an important role in vacation choice behaviour (see Mannell and Iso-Ahola, 1987). In this perspective, it is reasonable to assume that when consumers imagine tourist behaviour they direct their attention to desirable feelings and leisure experiences. It is self-evident that other, more economic and rational, aspects of holidays will also be regarded (e.g. modes of travelling, accommodation and expense). MacInnis and Price (1987) provide several propositions about the potentially unique effects of elaborated imagery on consumer behaviour, such as the stimulating influence of elaborated imagery on affective experiences, purchase intentions and purchase timing. This relationship between elaborated imagery and enhanced purchase desire is directly relevant to a promotional strategy that focuses on stimulating external search behaviour. Evidence suggests that imagery-producing advertisements result in superior recall and more positive attitudes towards the product. However, there has been limited examination of the relationship between imagery and behavioural intentions in a marketing context.

Enactive imagery

According to Aylwin (1990), adults can use three different though interconnected forms of representation: (i) verbal representation, or inner speech; (ii) visual imagery, or 'pictures in the mind's eye'; and (iii) enactive imagery, a kind of imagined action or role play. Enactive imagery is specialized, for representing the temporal perspective of enactive imagery extends to include the possible consequences of action. Enactive imagery provides an insider's perspective on situations, and allows access to subjective aspects opaque to subjects using verbal or visual representations. Aylwin (1990) states that affective and other subjective constructs are most frequent in enactive imagery. This fact is in line with Lang's (1984) work, which shows that representations involving active participation are accompanied by more affective arousal (as indexed by physiological indices such as heart rate) than purely visual representations.

Actually, enactive imagery is a form of cognitive representation in which the consumer is personally involved with stimuli, through 'do-it-yourself or experience-it-yourself' thoughts (see Goossens, 1994a). The conceptualization of enactive imagery is comparable with the concept of 'self-relatedness' (see Bone and Ellen, 1990) and Krugman's concept of high involvement. Krugman (1965) suggested that at the highest level of involvement consumers produce 'personal connections', or 'bridging experiences', whereby they relate the advertisement content to meaningful aspects of their own lives. Furthermore, enactive imagery is narrowly related to the concept of 'constructive processing'. Here, the consumer goes beyond the advertisement's content and connects it in some meaningful way to his or her own life. Examples of these constructive elaborations include thinking up novel uses for the product and/or imaging the product in use (see MacInnis and Jaworski, 1989; Buchholz and Smith, 1991).

Self-related imagery

Bone and Ellen (1990) reported a study which provides a stimulating contribution to the knowledge of the effect of imagery processing and imagery content on behavioural intentions. Based on the study of Anderson (1983), they empirically examined the relationship between self-related imagery and behavioural intentions in a radio advertising context. In this experiment radio was selected as the experimental medium because self-generated imagery should have a greater effect than other generated imagery. If a consumer is forced to create his/her own images, then mental processing is at a deeper level than if the images are created for him/her (e.g. through pictures). In their study Bone and Ellen (1990) found support for the hypothesis that self-related imagery creates more positive behavioural intentions than other-related imagery. Given the results of this self-relatedness factor, it appears that consumer researchers may wish to investigate other message characteristics, such as promotional texts with hedonic information, which could directly or indirectly affect behavioural intentions when imagery processing occurs (Antonides and van Raaij, 1998).

Brochure design

Although the Internet challenges may of the traditional modes of tourism communication, the tourism brochure is still viewed by many as a necessary element in the decision-making process. A search online for different tourism options can prompt consumer requests for further information – the brochure. Immediately the dialogue between provider and consumer has developed and become more involved. Both online and brochure content in terms of visual style, pitch and tone must complement each other and reinforce the same value propositions. Classically the brochure was seen as a key method of making the intangible more tangible. A characteristic of the medium 'tour brochure' is that pictures are used to generate mental imagery processing and emotional experiences. In this context it is relevant for tour operators to investigate the effect of the use of self-related imagery – instructions and verbal emotional information on external search behaviour. To be effective in stimulating the external information search of tourists, persuasive communication strategies need to focus on helping persons to imagine the positive sensory and emotional experiences of vacations. From this point of view the tourism industry should use emotional information in their promotion campaigns. By using information about feelings of pleasure and fun, advertisers actually try to tempt the consumer to plan a trip.

'The greater the use of cues that appeal to hedonic needs, the greater consumers' motivation to attend to the ad' (see MacInnis *et al.*, 1991). These emotional cues are essentially 'touch points' that trigger the recall of particular consumer associations that seek to convey the essence of the brand. Apart from verbal information, figural/prominent stimuli can be used to enhance the attention to tour brochures. Research indicates a strong impact of pictures on attention, elaboration and memory. Moreover, the size of the advertisement itself influences its prominence and consequent attention paid to it (Finn, 1988).

'The greater the use of figural/prominent executional cues, the greater consumers' motivation to attend to the ad' (see MacInnis *et al.*, 1991). Because of the widespread use of pictures in tour brochures, knowing the effect of picture size on all kinds of dependent variables (such as attitude towards the advertisement, behavioural intentions and overt behavioural responses) is of considerable importance to tour brochure design. Brochures with enactive imagery instructions, experiential texts and large pictures are supposed to be more attractive and will increase the return of the response card. Brochures without texts and small pictures will have a smaller impact.

According to MacInnis and Price (1987: 485) imagery instructions may be an important manipulation strategy when consumers are allowed the time to generate vivid imagery, when cues are concrete, when instructions focus on subjects' reactions to the image, and when consumers have sufficient knowledge to generate imagery about reactions. In a study, Goossens (1994b) found that both experiential text and large pictures did not affect the attractiveness of the cover and the overall information provided in the brochures. Besides, the emotional texts did not affect the degree to which the subjects could project themselves into the experience of the vacation situation (i.e. enactive imagery). There is reason to assume that a stated level of low involvement with the particular tourist information explains the unexpected results. On the other hand, it is possible that mere descriptive (verbal) experiential information is not effective in making brochures more attractive. This may be explained by the fact that people tend to respond to advertising with what van Raaij (1989) calls a primary affective reaction. Furthermore, he assumes that a cognitive elaboration of information does not change the first impression of an advertisement. According to van Raaij this phenomenon is especially valid for visual information. In this perspective Goossens (1993) argues that vacation pictures with people who express their positive feelings visually will have a positive effect on the attractiveness of tourist brochures. Moreover, visual information about emotional experiences, such as facial expressions of positive feelings, are cues which probably improve the consumer's motivation to attend to an advertisement.

In general, imagery processing is often used by consumers to evaluate marketing stimuli, and consumers differ with respect to their ability and desire to invoke imagery processes. Imagery may potentially improve the believability and memorability of a communication and influence consumer processing and responses. The understanding how individuals differ in their abilities to process imagery in various senses (see Gutman, 1988), and how use of enactive imagery influences the way consumers evaluate tour brochures, may help identify more effective ways to reach active vacation information seekers.

Communication effectiveness

Regarding this, Stern (1988) argues that creative and symbolic language may be used to endow the abstract service with sense appeal, and an analysis of figures of speech can help advertisers determine which kinds will most effectively reach consumers.

In communication messages, emotional information is often used to draw the attention of the target group, to intensify their interest and to communicate the essence of the message. These three functions of emotions in information processing are essential for advertising goals. Nevertheless, considerable research suggests that advertising executional cues may influence communication effectiveness. Related research indicates that communication effectiveness is in part driven by consumers' motivation to process information from an advertisement. However, little research has explicitly linked executional cues to communication effectiveness via their impact on motivation and levels of processing. The greater the use of visual cues that enhance the relevance of the vacation activities to the self, the greater consumers' motivation to process information from the adverts. Follow-up research is relevant because tourist organizations usually communicate with their target groups in an emotional manner, for example by using hedonic and sensory information in brochures, magazines, advertisements, and so on. An important part of this information concerns the consumption experience of leisure products. Information about feelings of pleasure, relaxation, excitement, adventure and fun meets consumers' hedonic needs; advertisers may motivate tourists with adequate pictures of travellers who express their satisfied (leisure) feelings. In terms of recent developments, technology continues to alter the ways in which tourism providers and consumers interact, and as such the nature of the commercial message is beginning to change. Consumers are moving from the mass to the multi-mediated world of interactive communication. Consequently, the message is becoming multidimensional with interactive advertising pods of product information now appearing that can be peeled like an onion. Messages are moving from an 'intrusive commercial' to an 'invited conversation'. This participative communication model is the very opposite of the long-established monologue approach in every way. Participative advertising is not arrogant but humble and inclusive. It does not barge in but asks to be invited. It trusts the consumers and puts their needs before its own; in effect, participative advertising is designed for a world in which consumers are in charge. Ultimately, the new media age revolves around consumer communications, whereby consumers are now taking control of what new media are developed and which will succeed.

Understanding search behaviour

The marketing implications of knowledge of search processing are diverse. For example, insight into search processes may assist in determining whether segmenting the audience may improve the efficiency of media communications. Knowledge of search processes may aid in the development of advertising appeals targeted at specific segments. Knowledge of search processes may also help to select appropriate marketing strategies for different market segments. Besides, knowledge of external information search may be quite useful in improving informational campaigns.

Various types of customer analyses identifying individuals' search behaviour have been used in tourism market planning (e.g. Manfredo, 1989; Perdue, 1993). In particular Havitz and Dimanche (1989) suggested that the relationship of the 'involvement' construct with search behaviour and promotional stimuli is relevant in tourism contexts. In addition, Bloch *et al.* (1986) noted that search behaviour is not always limited to pre-purchase events. Individuals engaging in an 'ongoing search' focus more on the recreational and enjoyment value of the search than on its information value. This so called 'ongoing search' concept is strongly related to 'enduring involvement'. In this case consumers gather information as a goal in itself. This means that the satisfaction (reward) stems from engaging in the search process itself. Thus, 'ongoing searchers' are primarily intrinsically motivated for (leisure) information, which means that the search process can be seen as an activity for its own sake, or even as a specific facet of their leisure lifestyle. For direct marketers, such consumers are important with respect to 'word-of-mouth information' to other customers. Influence exerted by those sources appears to confirm service marketing theory, which suggests that consumers desire subjective and experiential information.

On the other hand, a consumer's information search activity may be mainly extrinsically motivated, which means that the activity is satisfying in terms of its consequence of pay-offs. In fact these information seekers are of particular interest for direct marketers because they may be susceptible to the emotional benefits of hedonic appeals. Considerably more research is needed to develop communication strategies that *stimulate* vacation search behaviour. Tourist mass media, such as Web domains and tour brochures, play a significant role, especially in the beginning of the vacation planning process, in determining choice destinations. Since brochures are manageable sales tools for tourism marketers, more research should be done on the effects of different kinds of verbal and visual information on vacation search behaviour. Continued research along these lines will aid advertisers and media planners in their efforts to stimulate tourism (Goossens, 1994b).

TOURIST EVOKED SET

The specific destinations or tourist products that a tourist will consider in making a purchase choice are known as the *evoked set*. Within the evoked set different types of sets have to be taken into account in the various stages of a decision:

- The *total set* comprises all possible tourist alternatives in a particular tourist product category that are available in the market, even if the tourist is not aware of them or cannot recall them.
- The *unawareness set* is composed of all the tourist product alternatives that the tourist is not aware of in the market.
- Within the *awareness set*, one can find all the alternatives that the tourist can recall at a certain point in time.
- Among all the product alternatives that the tourist may recall, only some of them will be considered important in a purchase situation, and these will make the *consideration set*.
- Some of the alternatives may be important but can be considered infeasible (e.g. due to financial constraints). This is the *infeasible* or *inept set*.
- Within the *choice set*, one will find only those alternatives that will be subjected to a 'mental weight evaluation', in terms of the attributes considered important to the tourist and his or her belief that some of them can deliver the expected benefits.

- Based on this evaluation process, some of the alternatives will be placed in the *non-choice set*.
- Finally, the *decision set* will determine the overall best alternatives to purchase.

In some cases, we may find an inert set, consisting of alternatives that the tourist is indifferent towards because they are not perceived as having any particular advantages. The ways in which travellers evaluate and choose vacation destinations have critical implications in the planning and evaluation of destination tourism strategies. A central concern for the marketing strategist is to gain entry for his/her product and service (specific brand) into customers' abilities to retrieve such information into active memory when making product and service choices.

MENTAL CATEGORIZATION

As consumers are increasingly pressured in terms of time and the number of choice alternatives that now exist, they have developed decision-making heuristics that act as short cuts – in order to simplify the decision-making process. Sophisticated 'phased' or 'funnel' decision-making methods have emerged where consumers screen out unacceptable choice alternatives, preserving decision-making energy and time to evaluate between a smaller reduced subset of brands; as stated above this is commonly referred to as the 'choice set'. Travellers in reality are then likely to consider a rather limited number of travel destinations in planning their leisure travel behaviour. The rationale for the limited set is based upon Howard's (1963) concept of evoked set, which he originally defined as 'the collection of brands the buyer actually considers in the purchase decision process'. The concept of the evoked set was expanded by Narayana and Markin (1975), who also suggested the concepts of inert and inept sets. The inert set consists of those brands in the product category of which the consumer is aware but does not have sufficient information to evaluate one way or the other. The inept set consists of those brands the consumer has rejected from his or her purchase consideration, because of either an unpleasant experience or negative feedback from other sources. Spiggle and Sewall (1987) divided the evoked set into two: (i) an 'action set' of alternatives towards which a consumer takes some action, for example by travelling to a destination from which he or she has received information; and (ii) an 'inaction set'.

Destination awareness

A general model of traveller leisure destination awareness and choice has been provided by Woodside and Lysonski (1989). Destination awareness includes four categories: (i) consideration set; (ii) inert set; (iii) unavailable and aware set; and (iv) inept set. Affective associations are specific feelings (positive and negative) that are linked with a specific destination considered by the traveller. The affective associations are positive usually for destinations a consumer would consider visiting and negative for destinations a consumer has decided definitely not to visit. The learning of these associations between specific affective concepts and a specific destination indicate how the destination is positioned in the consumer's mind (Woodside *et al.*, 1999). In the model, categorization in the destination awareness set is shown as a one-way directional influence on affective associations because some minimal amount of destination recognition/memory recall and categorization may be necessary to activate positive, neutral or negative affective associations.

Travellers construct their preferences for alternatives based on destination awareness and affective associations. Preferences are the rankings assigned to destinations by relative attitude strength; that is, the ordering a consumer assigns to alternative destinations from most liked to least liked. Intention to visit is the traveller's perceived likelihood of visiting a specific destination within a specified time period. In the model, actual destination choice is predicted to be affected by both intention to visit and situational variables. Intention to act has been found to be significantly associated with actual behaviour, provided that the intention question is posed concretely and related to a specific time period and situation. The greater the involvement or importance of leisure travel for the consumer, the smaller the number of travel destinations considered. Previous travel to a destination relates positively to the destination being included in the consumer's consideration set versus other mental categories of vacation destinations (Swarbrooke and Horner, 1999).

Destinations in consumers' consideration sets are linked with more positive associations compared with destinations in other mental categories, while destinations found in consumers' inept sets are most likely to be linked with negative associations. Consumers' preference for specific destinations is associated positively with the rank order in which the destinations are mentioned in consumers' consideration sets. On average, the first-mentioned destination is preferred more than the second, the second more than the third. Intention to visit a specific destination is influenced positively by the consumer's preference towards the destination. While this preference intention may appear self-evident, the link between preference and intention may be stronger for some destinations than others. This general model is useful in planning for tourism marketing decisions and measuring performance in implementing such decisions for specific destinations.

Consideration set

Some researchers have found an average consideration set of 5.4, and others an average consideration set of 2.7. The average size of the consideration set tends to get larger with foreign travel destinations. Overall, the sizes of the consideration sets are relatively small and quite similar in size to sets found for brands of non-durables being considered for purchase by consumers. The average size of the respondents' consideration set is significantly greater than the average number of destinations mentioned in the respondents' inert, unavailable and inept sets.

Given that the set sizes are relatively small, being mentioned in a consumer's consideration set represents value, given that most respondents mention only a limited number of destinations and assuming that consumers are more likely to select final choice from alternatives mainly from their consideration set. Experience via previous visits to a travel destination is associated significantly with a subject's categorization of destinations in their consideration set.

Understanding destination awareness

Research results provide evidence that preference is associated strongly with consideration, that is, order of access of alternatives from long-term memory into working memory. Thus, using unaided awareness measurement is useful in learning how well a nation is faring in building a traveller franchise (i.e. preference over competing destinations). Vacation travellers are likely to consider a limited number of vacation destinations when planning trips and categorize these alternatives into different sets according to perception, preference and experience. Tracking potential customers' awareness, preferences and descriptions of competing vacation destinations is useful for measuring marketing performance and planning marketing actions.

Tracking studies which focus on the types of sets discussed above reveals if a particular nation often makes the traveller's mental 'short list' (the consideration set) and is therefore a contender for further evaluation and possible choice by travel customers. Such studies enable a marketing strategist to learn the principal associations with his or her brand (i.e. country) stored in long-term memories by potential customers. Learning such associations provides clues for the marketing strategist of what needs to be done for his or her nation to gain entry into travellers' consideration sets and how to convert consideration into purchasing action (Woodside and Ronkainen, 1993).

In the process of evaluating alternatives, the tourist uses two kinds of information: (i) the range of products available composing the evoked set; and (ii) the criteria for selection concerning the attributes of the alternatives. The procedures used to facilitate the final selection are called decision rules, decision strategies or heuristics. The compensatory form of decision rule implies an evaluation of each attribute of each alternative. The result of this will be a higher score for a particular alternative, which makes it likely to be purchased. When tourists do not make a balanced evaluation of the different alternatives, the decision rule is said to be non-compensatory.

The travel decision model

The travel decision model is based on motivational levels, needs and desires of the individual as well as his or her expectations when facing a travel decision. According to the level of overall travel desire, he or she will be more or less receptive to travel stimuli such as advertising and promotion, travel reports, brochures, etc. The decision process will be shaped according to social and personal determinants of travel behaviour such as personality, socio-economic status, attitudes and values, reference groups, and so on. The travel assessment of the different alternatives includes the analysis of a variety of factors, such as cost/value relations, attractions and amenities within each destination, travel opportunity and arrangements as well as the quality and quantity of available travel information. Other external variables, such as confidence in the travel agent, the overall image of the alternative destinations and services, the tourist's previous travel experience, travel constraints (time, cost, etc.) and the degree of perceived risks (financial, functional, social, physical and psychological), are also important determinants in the travel decision model.

Decision rules

Information-processing theory aims to describe and explain the means by which people absorb, structure and utilize information. In a marketing context, this is based on the recognition that consumers are constantly exposed to more information than they can meaningfully cope with. Consequently, they adopt *decision rules*, or strategies, in order to simplify the choice process. Five major types of strategies have been identified:

1. A *conjunctive* or threshold rule: options (e.g. vacation destinations) are eliminated from further consideration when they are perceived to have certain unacceptable features. Minimum acceptable levels exist for each attribute and each alternative is judged in relation to these cut-off points. An alternative that falls below the cut-off point on one or more alternatives is eliminated. A second strategy (such as the lexicographic process) may be used to make a final choice.
2. A *disjunctive* rule: options are chosen on the grounds that they are believed to possess a single overwhelming advantage, in terms of the features being considered. This is the simplest of all judgement models.
3. A *lexicographic* rule: this postulates that, on occasion, people may screen options by priorities, i.e. the first vacation destination to demonstrate an advantage on a subset of key attributes,

considered in order of importance, will be the one to be chosen. Alternatives are compared on the one attribute that is most important, and, if one is noticeably better, it is selected with no further evaluation. If two or more are judged about equal, they are compared on the second most important attribute.

4. A *compensatory* rule: the option chosen will be the one that is perceived to have the best overall balance of favoured characteristics across all attributes. This fourth rule is at the basis of most well-known multi-attribute models.

5. *Elimination by aspects*: like the conjunctive process, alternatives are evaluated against minimum cut-offs on attributes, but, like the lexicographic process, evaluation starts with the most important attribute. Those alternatives exceeding the cut-off point of the most important attribute are evaluated on the second most important attribute, and then the third, and so on

A tourist may, in a particular choice situation, adopt any one or more of these decision rules. For instance, he or she may, by means of the threshold rule, eliminate several available alternatives from consideration (e.g. they may all be regarded as too expensive); this process will leave a repertoire of alternatives for further consideration and the choice from within this repertoire may then be made by a compensatory balancing of pros and cons. Pre-decision information search acts as a filter for the available set of products and product attributes for each vacation tourist.

Modelling decision making

The trade-off model is based on the assumption that, on many purchasing occasions, tourists are faced with a series of imperfect options. In arriving at a decision, an individual will sacrifice (trade-off) a desired level of a particular attribute in order to obtain a certain level of a different attribute. In making choices between different levels of various attributes, the tourist will reveal the utilities, or the relative value, he or she attaches to these attributes. Stewart and Stynes (1994) explored the development of a model of decision making associated with long-term, complex purchase processes. The lengthy decision-making process associated with complex purchases creates more opportunities than usual for marketers to assist, direct and influence a buyer's choice, but to do so they must understand both how and when in an extended choice process potential buyers are most easily reached. The process of choosing one alternative over others involves making a series of decisions in which an individual's motivations, preferences, knowledge, cognitive processes, resources and constraints all play a role. Research into the behaviours and consequences of decision making is conducted in many fields, each with a slightly different theoretical and methodological emphasis. Structural models are frequently grounded in economic theories of consumer choice, while process models rely more heavily on psychological theories of perception, learning and judgement. The research objectives and methods used to test the two classes of models reflect these different origins.

Structural models

Most applications of decision research concerning recreation and tourism utilize discrete choice models, in particular multinomial logit models (Stynes and Peterson, 1984) used together with conjoint scaling methods (Louviere, 1983; Louviere and Timmermans, 1990a). Conjoint choice models predict a consumer's choice based on: (i) attributes of the alternatives in the choice set; (ii) assumptions about how perceptions of the attributes are combined to form overall evaluations; and (iii) the assumption that the individual will choose the alternative which maximizes his or her utility (Louviere, 1988). In recreation and tourism contexts, these models have been applied to studies of park visitation (Louviere and Timmermans, 1990b), the effect of park management options on park choice (Leiber and Fesenmaier, 1984) and vacation destination choice (Goodrich, 1978; Haider and Ewing 1990). Structural models are not considered useful as replica models of cognitive or behavioural processes, but rather as predictive tools.

Process models

In contrast to predictive structural models, process models focus on how a choice is made, and argue that this process has much to do with which choice is made. Behavioural decision theory states that decision making involves learning and adaptation to the decision environment. Learning can alter the decision maker's perception and judgement, and is most likely to occur when the decision maker is initially unfamiliar with the choice alternatives or the decision environment. Adaptation will be most important when the decision environment is unfamiliar, or when the environment changes over time. Both of these conditions, an unfamiliar task and a changing decision environment, are most likely to be associated with complex choice, implying that learning and adaptation will be most important when choice is most complex.

Other decision theories also support the concept of learning and adaptation during decision making. According to some researchers, each person needs to understand and interpret or frame the choice in their own terms before they begin trying to solve it. In these models of problem solving, framing is proposed as a first step in solving a problem or making a choice. The frame coordinates and directs other decision-making activities. Information processing research focuses on the ways people deal with large amounts of information, and has shown how people create and use a variety of methods for searching and processing information to avoid being burdened with too much information; an example of adaptive decision making.

While structural models treat decision making as a static or a temporal event, dynamics are an implicit element of most process models, as the notion of a process implies some sequence of events. The concept of adaptive behaviour, for example, assumes that the decision maker will react to perceptual and environmental changes, and their decision-making behaviour will reflect that reaction.

Decision theory has moved from its origins in microeconomic consumer theory to a more psychologically based, empirically supported perspective which adds recognition of the importance of both environmental constraints and human cognitive limitations. The basis for decision-making behaviour in process theory encompasses both the economic concept of subjective expected utility maximization and the psychological concepts of stimulus response behaviour and cognitive processing.

Simpler choices such as those widely studied in marketing and tourism can be seen as special cases or simplifications of more general decision processes. Time is perhaps the dimension that decision researchers have most neglected, explaining the general absence of learning, adaptation and feedback processes within decision models.

The importance of decision framing in complex choice, together with the prevalence of strategic and complex decisions related to tourism, has implications for conducting tourism choice research. Understanding how people frame tourism decisions would allow researchers to present subjects with choices that utilize frames like their own, improving the validity of decision experiments. The extent of individual variation in decision making makes reliance on a single choice model problematic. Because of their proposed link to decision behaviour, decision frames could be a useful tool for segmenting decision makers into groups, allowing succinct structural models to be developed for each.

EVALUATION OF ALTERNATIVES

Tourists interpret products as arrays of cues and select only a few cues which have a high informational value, based on predictive and confidence values. Cues can also be conceptualized in terms of whether they are part of the physical object (*intrinsic*) or augment it (*extrinsic*). Tourists show a preference for intrinsic cues, but in some situations (e.g. *quality* is difficult to evaluate) are more reliant on extrinsic cues. Due to the tourist's limited cognitive capabilities, perceptual selectivity results in the tourist becoming more attentive to a limited number of tourist product attributes and, consequently, tourists may not notice a difference when changes in a tourist product formulation do not reach a critical threshold. Tourism brand names are very important extrinsic cues. However, the focus of trust has begun to shift: historically trust in the product or service was enough – this was facilitated through the recognition of reputable brand names – but increasingly consumers want to be assured about not only the product/service itself but the people behind the product too. Quality research may benefit from a de-emphasis on price as the main extrinsic quality indicator.

A major difficulty in reaching value is the variety of different meanings of 'value' held by tourists. Building a model of value requires that the researcher understands which of many meanings are implicit in the tourists' expressions of value. Tourists form judgements based on samples of cues which they believe to be indicative of certain characteristics. Consumers assign information values to the available cues, selecting those with the highest values.

> A cue's information value is a function of its predictive value (accuracy of predicting an attribute) and its confidence value (consumer's confidence in the predictive value assigned to the cue).

Research shows that tourists base their decisions on a limited number of the available cues and that the predictive value of a cue has a dominant effect on cue utilization, with a moderating effect from the confidence value. The somewhat restricted level of information search undertaken by tourists can be explained within this framework. If a few cues offer high predictive and high confidence values, these will be selected. However, where none of the cues has high predictive and high confidence values, more cues would be consulted. Learning, through tourist product experience, would enable tourists to adjust their predictive and confidence values internally, which would stabilize over time and reduce the need for information. In other words, each tourist sees a tourist product as a bundle of product attributes with varying capacities for delivering those benefits which can be acquired by buying such tourist products or services. Consumers will pay the most attention to those attributes that better connect with their needs. Figure 5.7 shows a model which affords an overview of the relationships among the concepts of price, perceived quality and perceived value. Thus, according to this model, both intrinsic and extrinsic cues may determine both the quality and the perceived value. It is now time to discuss the circumstances under which these cues may affect the evaluation of tourist products from both their *perceived quality* perspective and *perceived value*.

Perceived quality

Figure 5.8 depicts the perceived quality component of the conceptual model in Fig. 5.7. First of all, a tourist product's quality is evaluated as high or low depending on its relative excellence or superiority among tourist products or services that are viewed as substitutes by the tourist. The fact that specific or concrete *intrinsic attributes* differ widely across tourist products, as do the attributes tourists use to infer quality – even within a tourist product category, may provide different signals about quality. As attributes become more abstract, there is more tourism product parity.

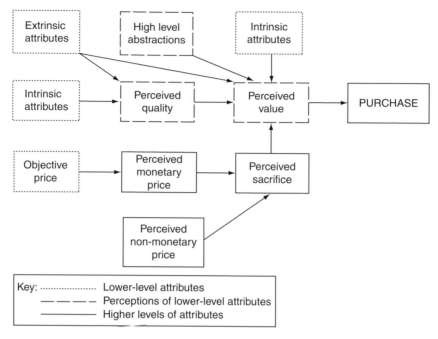

Fig. 5.7. The relationship between price, perceived quality and perceived value.

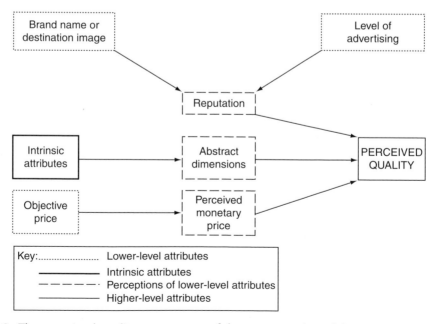

Fig. 5.8. The perceived quality component of the conceptual model.

Tourists represent the attributes in memory at abstract levels; this is seen in the way in which, for example, tourists compare non-comparable alternatives (e.g. how they choose between such diverse alternatives as a stereo and a Hawaiian vacation). Tourists may use informational cues to develop beliefs about products and the response to their choise or overall evaluation may be a direct function of these mediating beliefs. These beliefs may be of two types: (i) descriptive, which involves a restatement of the original information in more abstract terms; and (ii) inferential, which involves an inference to provide information missing in the environment.

Therefore, these distinctions illustrate the level at which dimensions of quality can be conceptualized. The intrinsic tourist product attributes that signal quality may be product-specific, but dimensions of quality can be generalized to tourist product classes or categories. Price, brand name and level of advertising are the extrinsic cues frequently associated with quality in research, yet many other extrinsic cues are useful to tourists.

Price

Price appears to function as a surrogate for quality although a multitude of experimental studies on the topic reveal that the relationship may not always be positive. However, the use of price as an indicator of quality may be used:

- when the tourist has inadequate information about intrinsic attributes;
- when intrinsic cues to quality are readily accessible, when brand names provide evidence of a tourism company's reputation, or when level of advertising communicates the tourism company's belief in the brand; the tourist may prefer to use those cues instead of price;
- when the tourist is aware of tourist product prices; and
- when consumers have not sufficient tourist product knowledge to detect quality variation among tourist products.

Thus, tourists appear to depend more on price as a quality signal in some tourist product categories than others. Facts like the difference in objective price–quality relationship by tourist product category may make the price relevant as a signal of quality or not; while the existence of little variation in prices within the same tourist product category may not attribute high quality to tourist products that cost less than those of the competitors.

Brand name

Similarly, brand name may serve as a 'shorthand' for quality by providing tourists with a bundle of information about the tourist product. It is accepted that tourists have limited cognitive capabilities and that to overcome this limitation they seek efficient means of processing and storing information. There is clear evidence that tourists recognize a brand name as an informational chunk. Thus, the brand names may enable stored information to be recalled from memory which then interacts with the intrinsic cues to produce different results.

Level of advertising

Level of advertising has been related to tourist product quality. The level of advertising, rather than actual claims made, informs tourists that the tourism company believes the tourist products are worth advertising (i.e. are of high quality). Supporting this argument is the finding that many consumers perceive heavily advertised brands to be generally higher in quality than brands with less advertising.

Thus, we can conclude by saying that extrinsic cues serve as generalized quality indicators across tourist brands, products and categories. Research shows that extrinsic cues serve as generalized quality indicators across tourist products (e.g. brand name as a surrogate for quality), but the nature of intrinsic cues as indicators of quality is tourist-product specific. Besides, tourists show a preference for intrinsic cues when they have a choice. However, when intrinsic cues are not available, if quality is difficult to evaluate or when the evaluation of intrinsic cues requires more effort than tourists perceive to be worthwhile, extrinsic cues will be preferentially sought.

Implications

All this consumer behaviour theory may be used to help tourism companies to decide whether to invest in tourist product improvements (intrinsic cues) or in marketing (extrinsic cues) to improve perceptions of quality. A single answer is unlikely to be given because of the difficulties involved. On the one hand, tourists depend on intrinsic attributes when the cues have high predictive value. On the other hand, tourists depend on extrinsic attributes more than intrinsic attributes when the tourist is operating without adequate information about intrinsic tourist product attributes. At the point of purchase, tourists cannot always evaluate relevant intrinsic attributes of a tourist product (insufficient time or interest or tourists have little or no experience with the tourist product). The last difficulty is that the signal quality changes over time because of the development of technically better tourist products (the features that signal superiority change), promotional efforts, and as a response of competence, changing tourist tastes and information.

The particular implications for tourism marketing researchers are that attention must be focused on finding the few key tourist relevant attributes, rather than relying on a managerially derived attribute list. As the intrinsic cues used by tourists vary by tourist product, a standardized attribute list cannot be contemplated. Thus, if tourism marketers want to assess tourists' appreciation of formulation changes, the use of trained panels may be of value. Besides, since tourists may develop categories and evaluate tourist products by deciding which mental category the tourist products are more similar to, and hence what their properties are likely to be, it could happen that these categories do not contain mental images of all competing brands but just those perceived as relevant to the tourist. Thus, if, for example, a tourism company wants to be good at developing new tourist products, given the rapid changes in preferences, technology and competition, a comparative, rather than monadic, analysis may be very useful.

Perceived value

In order to finish the whole picture, we add the last component of the model, before the purchase is completed: *value*. Value is proposed to be a higher-level abstraction and differs from quality in two ways. First, value is more individualistic and personal than quality and is therefore a higher-level concept than quality. Although value has been defined in many ways (as an 'emotional pay-off', an abstract, multidimensional, difficult-to-measure attribute, and as 'instrumental values'), the concept remains a high-level abstraction for all of them. Secondly, value, unlike quality, involves a trade-off of 'give' and 'get' components. Though many conceptualizations of value specify quality as the only 'get' component in the value equation, the tourist may include other factors, several that are in themselves higher levels of abstraction, such as prestige and convenience. Therefore, benefit components of value include salient intrinsic attributes, extrinsic attributes, perceived quality and other relevant high-level abstractions.

Tourists may sacrifice both money and other resources to obtain tourist products and services. To some tourists, the monetary sacrifice is pivotal and anything that reduces the monetary sacrifice will increase the perceived value of the tourist product. Less price-conscious tourists will find value even at the expense of higher costs because time and effort are perceived as more costly. Others may respond depending on the cues – often extrinsic cues – in forming impressions of value. Thus, tourists who may define value as low price, may not compare a reduced-price tourist product with the prices of other tourist brands.

Those tourists who define value as the quality that they get for the price they pay may mention either intrinsic or extrinsic attributes (level of service or brand name). Finally, the tourists who define value as what they get for what they pay may depend on intrinsic attributes. However, not all the intrinsic attributes of tourist products can be evaluated in the same way. One would expect to find a more rational evaluation in situations of high information availability, processing ability, time availability and involvement in the purchase.

All this goes to show that the diversity of meaning of the perception of value for tourists may depend on the frame of reference in which the tourist is making an evaluation. That is, at the time of purchase, value may mean low price or sale, etc. (extrinsic attributes). On the other hand, value may involve some calculation about the tourist product itself (intrinsic attributes: location and so on). Finally, it has also been suggested that not all tourists want to buy the highest quality product in every tourist product category. Instead, quality appears to be factored into the explicit or implicit valuation of a tourist product by many consumers. A given tourist product may be high quality, but, if the tourist does not have enough money to buy it (or does not want to spend the amount required), its value will not be perceived as being as high as that of a tourist product with lower quality but a more affordable price. The same principle may apply to tourist products that need more decision-making time than the tourist's time constraints allows.

Implications

Research is required that investigates which cues are important and how tourists form impressions of quality based on objective cues. Tourism companies may also benefit from research that identifies the abstract dimensions of quality desired by tourists in a tourist product basis. This process involves a careful look at situational factors surrounding the purchase and use of the tourist product. Identifying the important quality signals from the tourist's viewpoint and then communicating those signals, rather than generalities, are likely to lead to more vivid perceptions of quality. Linking lower-level attributes with their higher-level abstractions locates the 'driving force' and 'leverage point' for advertising strategy. The dynamic nature of quality suggests that tourism marketers must track perceptions over time and align tourist product and promotion strategies with these changing views. Because tourist products and perceptions change, tourism marketers may be able to educate tourists on ways to evaluate quality. Advertising, the information provided and visible cues associated with tourist products, can be managed to evoke desired quality perceptions. Tourism marketers should also acknowledge the existence of non-monetary costs, such as time and effort. Anything that can be built into tourist products to reduce time, effort and search costs can reduce perceived sacrifice and thereby increase perceptions of value. Reducing monetary and non-monetary costs, decreasing perceptions of sacrifice, adding salient intrinsic attributes, evoking perceptions of relevant high-level abstractions, and using extrinsic cues to signal value are all possible strategies that tourism companies can use to affect value perceptions. Thus, the selection of a strategy for a particular tourist product or segment depends on its tourists' definition of value. Strategies based on tourists' value standards and perceptions will channel resources more effectively and will meet customer expectations better than those based on tourism company standards. An understanding of what quality and value mean to tourists offers the promise of improving tourism brand positions through more precise market analysis and segmentation, tourist product planning, promotion and pricing strategy. An understanding of consumer behaviour can also help to design more realistic marketing procedures and evaluate a tourism company's strategy. Therefore, this line of thinking implies that tourism marketing researchers can better guide marketing decisions by applying these aspects of consumer behaviour theory to different aspects of tourism marketing procedures.

TOURIST BEHAVIOUR MODELLING

A vacation tourist behaviour model is presented in Fig. 5.9. It consists of a flow chart with three parts: (i) Part I – pre-decision and decision processes; (ii) Part II – post-purchase evaluation; and (iii) Part III – future decision making. Each part is composed of fields and subfields, linked by other concepts related to the tourist's behavioural processes.

Part I: Pre-decision and decision processes

This part is concerned with the flow of events, from the tourist stimuli to the purchase decision. The fields included are: (i) preference structure (as a major process in the pre-decision phase); (ii) decision; and (iii) purchase. As the two last phases are outcomes of pre-decision, the model is more detailed in respect to preference structure, and its analysis includes the following subfields: (i) stimulus filtration; (ii) attention and learning processes; and (iii) choice criteria.

Field 1: Preference structure

The tourist's preference structure for a particular destination is based on a set of factors, and, as additional objective information modifies that set, effective judgements for the destination can be expected to change over time. Among those factors are the internalized environmental influences, which include cultural norms and values, family and reference groups, financial status and social class. These are broad determinants of preference structure and, thus, will influence tourist product evaluation. Individual determinants of preference structure comprise concepts such as personality, lifestyle, perceived role set, learning and motives. Motives can be defined as the conscious recognition of a psychological need influenced by genetics, experience and situation.

Intention to purchase depends on confidence generation, that is, certainty and sureness towards the vacation destination or tourist service. Confidence generation is a 'summary' concept in the sense that it results from all the preceding elements. The consumer has a pervasive sense of uncertainty, caution, anxiety and indecisiveness. Those sentiments are no less present in travel than elsewhere, and are no less consequential. They are inhibitors which cause a tourist to respond differently from the way his or her attitude towards the destination or service dictates.

SUBFIELD A: STIMULUS FILTRATION

Travel stimuli display can appear via mass media or personal sources and it has either a significant or symbolic connotation related to attributes such as quality, price, distinctiveness, prestige, service and availability. Consumers do not use raw information provided by mass communication, but process it before using it. Stimuli may be intentionally or incidentally apprehended. Also, messages received by the tourist vary in degrees of stimulus ambiguity. This leads to a search for additional data and holds a confrontation between information received and real experience. Thus the filtration process comes to protect the tourist, since it implies the ability to discriminate facts from exaggerations in advertising.

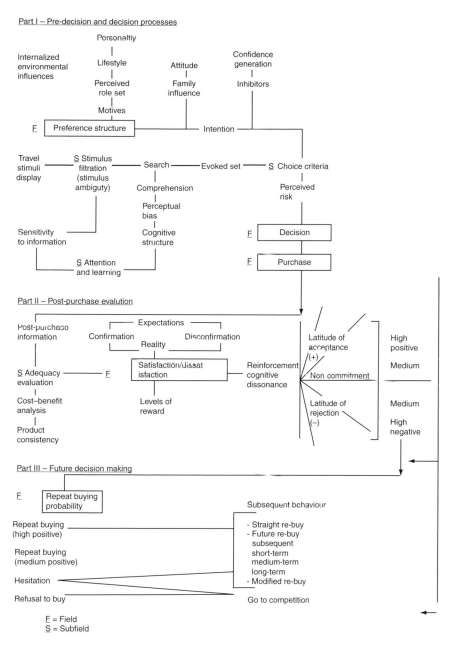

Part I – Pre-decision and decision processes

Personaltiy

Internalized
environmental
influences

Lifestyle

Attitude

Confidence
generation

Perceived
role set

Family
influence

Inhibitors

Motives

F   Preference structure

Intention

Travel
stimuli
display

S Stimulus
filtration
(stimulus
ambiguty)

Search

Evoked set

S Choice criteria

Comprehension

Perceived
risk

Perceptual
bias

Sensitivity
to information

Cognitive
structure

F   Decision

S Attention
and learning

F   Purchase

Part II – Post-purchase evalution

Post-purchase
information

Expectations

Confirmation

Disconfirmation

Reality

S Adequacy
evaluation

F

Satisfaction/dissat
isfaction

Reinforcement
cognitive
dissonance

Latitude of
acceptance
/(+)

Non commitment

High
positive

Medium

Cost–benefit
analysis

Levels of
reward

Latitude of
rejection
(–)

Medium

Product
consistency

High
negative

Part III – Future decision making

F   Repeat buying
probability

Subsequent behaviour

Repeat buying
(high positive)

- Straight re-buy
- Future re-buy
subsequent
short-term
medium-term
long-term
- Modified re-buy

Repeat buying
(medium positive)

Hesitation

Refusal to buy

Go to competition

F = Field
S = Subfield

Fig. 5.9. A vacation tourist behaviour model.

The concept of search includes all activities directed at collecting information about a
product. It may become stronger when the tourist is uncertain about the merits of alternative
destinations. One reason for the limited scope of external search is that tourists often have
available a wealth of previously acquired information, based on past experience and previous
knowledge, which can be retrieved through internal search.

The promotional information may arrive either from a tourist board/organization or from intermediaries or channels of distribution. Advertising of a vacation product results in a fraction of potential users becoming aware of the product and the remaining entering the non-aware class. The aware tourists then become either triers or non-triers.

SUBFIELD B: ATTENTION AND LEARNING PROCESSES

Assuming the system is active, the individual 'sizes up' inputs selectively through a process of comparison whereby inputs are compared with information stored in memory. Attention indicates sensitivity to information and deals with the magnitude of information intake by an individual at a specific time.

Learning can be considered as any systematic change in behaviour, and is measured by the increase in the probability of making a particular response. It holds an interrelationship with the cognitive structure, which is an organized system of knowledge and beliefs formed from sources of learning. The search for meaning, the need to understand, the trend towards better organization of perceptions and beliefs to provide clarity and consistency for the individual permit the comprehension of the tourist product.

SUBFIELD C: CHOICE CRITERIA

The criteria tourists employ in evaluating destinations or tourist services that constitute their evoked sets are usually expressed in terms of tourist product attributes that they feel are important to them. Sometimes the tourist would maintain in the long-term memory an overall evaluation of the alternatives in his or her evoked set. This would make assessment by individual attributes unnecessary. Instead, the tourist would simply select the alternative with the highest perceived overall rating. This type of synthesized decision rule has been labelled the 'Affect Referral Rule' and may represent the simplest of all decision rules.

Field 2: Decision

The decision process may be studied as a sequence of conflicts; the conflict situations constituting a decision process are those that precede the choice and are necessary to explain what is chosen. This decision results in a psychological predisposition in terms of intention towards the buying act.

A tourist's decisions may be based on perceived images, on information from tourism destination promotion, on previous experience, on image of potential destinations, on travel intermediaries, advice or on social interaction. The decision process is determined by the tourist's background awareness, which includes formation of beliefs and images (revised tourist terms of reference), the evaluation of vacation concepts and, finally, the travel decision (the merging of different beliefs and accommodation of opinions).

Field 3: Purchase

The preceding steps can lead to the act of buying a vacation destination. Purchase has been described as the outcome of psychic processes taking place more or less consciously. The total tourist product is generally purchased in a sequence (i.e. transportation, accommodation, tours, etc.) and not always as a tour package.

Purchases can occur out of necessity; they can be derived from culturally mandated lifestyles or from interlock purchases; they can result from simple conformity to group norms or from imitation of others.

Part II: Post-purchase evaluation

Post-choice evaluative feedback has a significant impact on the decision maker's set and/or subsequent behaviour. One of our key elements noted as affecting a tourist's expectations is the satisfaction with post-purchase. Post-purchase evaluation has three major purposes. First, it adds to the tourist's store of experiences and it is through post-purchase assessment that experience is taken into the tourist's frame of reference. Hence, it broadens personal needs, ambitions, drives, perceptions and understanding. Secondly, post-purchase assessment provides a check on market-related decisions. Thirdly, it provides feedback to serve as a basis for adjusting future purchase behaviour. Many tourism operators have a tendency to lose interest in the post-sale 'afterlife' – this is a missed opportunity and can be very costly in terms of building future relations with the consumer. Moreover, as suggested above, monitoring consumer satisfaction can illuminate current flaws in marketing decision making – this is a key driver for performance management and is discussed in later chapters.

SUBFIELD D: ADEQUACY EVALUATION

Adequacy evaluation is the factor related to the 'ideal' point of each attribute of the tourist product as perceived by the tourist. When evaluating adequacy, the tourist uses a mental cost–benefit analysis; this leads to an equilibrium level for the prices paid. Product consistency represents the sum of all real attributes perceived by the tourist when utilizing the service, and follows a kind of ranking system in the user's mind.

Field 4: Satisfaction/dissatisfaction

Gratification varies in terms of levels of reward, and these are key factors to benefit delivery and future decision making. The satisfaction/dissatisfaction dimension must also be considered in relation to the cognitive dissonance mechanism. Although commitment to repurchase will also depend on factors such as variety seeking, subsequent behaviour will be shaped by zones or latitudes of acceptance and of rejection in consumer perceptions. In the present model a third zone was introduced, the non-commitment latitude.

Part III: Future decision making

Future decision making is mainly related to the study of the subsequent behaviour of the tourist by analysing different probabilities for repeat buying a particular destination or tourist service.

Field 5: Repeat buying probability

Subsequent behaviour will, thus, depend on levels of return prospect and may result in: (i) 'straight re-buy'; (ii) re-buy in different time parameters (subsequent, short-term, medium-term or long-term); and (iii) modified re-buy behaviour, based on the change to new tourist products or on the search for a better quality of services.

The inclusion of post-purchase evaluation and future decision making in this model was an attempt to contribute to a global analysis of tourist behaviour and, as a practical outcome, to marketing decision planning. The development of the tourism industry requires generation of criteria for a better quality of services in order to match the changing needs and desires of the tourist population (Moutinho, 1987). It is not just about understanding your customers from the outside, but also about getting a real feeling for what it is like to lead their lives; only then will the tourism industry be in a position to create, design and deliver emotional experiences that go beyond mere customer satisfaction.

REFERENCES

Andereck, K. (1992) Comments on researching consumer information. In: *Proceedings of the 23rd Annual Conference of the Travel and Tourism Research Association*. Travel and Tourism Research Association, Minneapolis, Minnesota, pp. 50–52.

Anderson, C.A. (1983) Imagination and expectation: the effect of imagining behavioural scripts on personal intentions. *Journal of Personality and Social Psychology* 45(2), 293–305.

Antonides, G. and van Raaij, W.F. (1998) *Consumer Behaviour – a European Perspective*. John Wiley & Sons, Chichester, UK.

Aylwin, S. (1990) Imagery and affect: big questions, little answers. In: Hampson, P.J., Marks, D.E. and Richardson, J.T.E. (eds) *Imagery: Current Developments*. International Library of Psychology, Routledge, London, pp. 247–267.

Bloch, P.H., Scherrell, D. and Ridgway, N. (1986) Consumer search: an extended framework. *Journal of Consumer Research* 13, 119–126.

Bone, P. and Ellen, P. (1990) The effect of imagery processing and imagery content on behavioural intentions. *Advances in Consumer Research* 17, 449–454.

Buchholz, L.M. and Smith, R.E. (1991) The role of consumer involvement in determining cognitive response to broadcast advertising. *Journal of Advertising* 20(1), 4017.

Bultena, G.L. and Field, D.R. (1980) Structural effects in national park going. *Leisure Sciences* 3(3), 221–240.

Capella, L.M. and Greco, A.J. (1987) Information sources of elderly for vacation decisions. *Annals of Tourism Research* 14, 148–151.

Cosenza, R.M. and Davis, D.L. (1981) Family vacation decision making over the family life cycle: a decision and influence structure analysis. *Journal of Travel Research* 20(2), 17–23.

Crompton, J. (1981) Dimensions of the social group role in pleasure vacations. *Annals of Tourism Research* 8(4), 550–567.

Engel, J.F., Blackwell, R.D. and Miniard, P.W. (1995) *Consumer Behavior*, 8th edn. The Dryden Press, Fort Worth, Texas.

Evans, M., Moutinho, L. and van Raaij, W.F. (1996) *Applied Consumer Behaviour*. Addison-Wesley, Harlow, UK.

Finn, A. (1988) Print and recognition readership scores: an information processing perspective. *Journal of Marketing Research* 25 (May), 168–177.

Fishbein, M. (1967) A behavioural theory approach to the relations between beliefs about an object and the attitude toward the object. In: Fishbein, M. (ed.) *Reading in Attitude Theory and Measurement*. John Wiley, New York, pp. 389–400.

Gitelson, R. and Crompton, J. (1983) The planning horizons and sources of information used by pleasure vacationers. *Journal of Travel Research* 21(3), 2–7.

Gitelson, R. and Kerstetter, D. (1994) The influence of friends and relatives in travel decision-making. *Journal of Travel and Tourism Marketing* 3(3), 59–68.

Goodrich, J.N. (1978) The relationship between preferences for and perceptions of vacation destinations: application of a choice model. *Journal of Travel Research* 17 (Fall), 8–13.

Goossens, C.F. (1993) Picturing a holiday: a study on effects of emotional information. PhD Dissertation, Tilburg University, The Netherlands.

Goossens, C.F. (1994a) Enactive imagery: information processing, emotional responses and behavioural intentions. *Journal of Mental Imagery* 18, 11–19.

Goossens, C.F. (1994b) External information search: effects of tour brochures with experiential information. *Journal of Travel and Tourism Marketing* 3(3), 89–107.

Gutman, E. (1988) The role of individual differences and multiple senses in consumer imagery processing: theoretical perspectives. *Advances in Consumer Research* 15, 191–196.

Haider, W. and Ewing, G.O. (1990) A model of tourist choices of hypothetical Caribbean destinations. *Leisure Sciences* 12, 33–47.

Havitz, M.E. and Dimanche, F. (1989) Propositions for testing the involvement construct in recreational and tourism contexts. *Leisure Sciences* 12, 179–195.

Hawkins, D., Best, R. and Coney, K. (1997) *Consumer Behavior*, 7th edn. McGraw-Hill, Maidenhead, UK.

Hirschman, E.C. and Holbrook, M.B. (1982) Hedonic consumption: emerging concepts, methods and propositions. *Journal of Marketing* 46 (Summer), 92–101.

Hodgson, P. (1993) Using qualitative research to understand consumer needs in tour brochure design. *Journal of Travel Research* 32(1), 50–52.

Howard, J.A. (1963) *Marketing Management*. Richard D. Irwin, Homewood, Illinois.

Hoyer, W. and MacInnis, D. (1997) *Consumer Behaviour*. Houghton Mifflin Company, Abingdon, UK.

Jenkins, R.L. (1978) Family vacation decision-making. *Journal of Travel Research* 16(4), 2–7.

Krugman, H.E. (1965) The impact of television advertising: learning without involvement. *Public Opinion Quarterly* 29 (Fall), 349–356.

Lang, P.J. (1984) Cognition in emotion: concept and action. In: Izard, C., Kagan, J. and Zajonc, R. (eds) *Emotions, Cognitions and Behaviour*. Cambridge University Press, New York, pp. 193–226.

Leiber, S.R. and Fesenmaier, D. (1984) Modelling recreation choice: a case study of management alternatives in Chicago. *Regional Studies* 18, 31–43.

Louviere, J. (1983) Integrating conjoint and functional measurement with discrete choice theory: an experimental design approach. *Advances in Consumer Research* 10, 151–156.

Louviere, J. (1988) *Analysing Decision Making: Metric Conjoint Analysis*. Sage University Paper series on Quantitative Applications in the Social Sciences, Series no. 07-001. Sage, Beverly Hills, California.

Louviere, J. and Timmermans, H. (1990a) Stated preference and choice models applied to recreation: a review. *Leisure Sciences* 12, 9–32.

Louviere, J. and Timmermans, H. (1990b) Using hierarchical information integration to model consumer response to possible planning actions: a recreation choice illustration. *Environment and Planning* A 22, 291–308.

MacInnis, D.J. and Jaworski, B.J. (1989) Information processing from advertisements: toward an integrative framework. *Journal of Marketing* 53(4), 1024.

MacInnis, D.J. and Price, L.L. (1987) The role of imagery in information processing: review and extensions. *Journal of Consumer Research* 13, 473–491.

MacInnis, D.J., Moorman, C. and Jaworski, B.J. (1991) Enhancing and measuring consumers' motivation, opportunity and ability to process brand information from ads. *Journal of Marketing* 55 (October), 32–53.

Manfredo, M.J. (1989) An investigation of the basis for external information search in recreation and tourism. *Leisure Sciences* 11, 29–45.

Mannell, R.C. and Iso-Ahola, S.E. (1987) Psychological nature of leisure and tourism experience. *Annals of Tourism Research* 19, 314–331.

Mansfeld, Y. (1992) From motivation to travel. *Annals of Tourism Research* 19, 399–419.

Maute, M. and Forrester, W.R. (1991) The effect of attribute qualities on consumer decision making: a causal model of external information search. *Journal of Economic Psychology* 12, 643–666.

Mill, R.C. and Morrison, A.M. (1985) *The Tourism System: an Introductory Text*. Prentice Hall, Englewood Cliffs, New Jersey.

Moutinho, L. (1987) Consumer behaviour in tourism. *European Journal of Marketing* 21(10), 1–44.

Murray, K.B. (1991) A test of services marketing theory: consumer information acquisition activities. *Journal of Marketing* 55 (January), 10–25.

Narayana, C.L. and Markin, R.J. (1975) Consumer behaviour and product performance: an alternative conceptualisation. *Journal of Marketing* 39 (January), 1–6.

Perdue, R.R. (1993) External information search in marine recreational fishings. *Leisure Sciences* 15, 169–187.

Peter, J.P. and Olson, J.C. (1994) *Understanding Consumer Behaviour*. Irwin, Boston.

Snepenger, D., Meged, K., Snelling, M. and Worrall, K. (1990) Information search strategies by destination-naive tourists. *Journal of Travel Research* 28 (Summer), 13–16.

Spiggle, S. and Sewall, M.A. (1987) A choice sets model of retail selection. *Journal of Marketing* 51 (April), 97–111.

Stern, B.B. (1988) Figurative language in services advertising: the nature and uses of images. *Advances in Consumer Research* 15, 185–190.

Stewart, S.I. and Stynes, D.J. (1994) Toward a dynamic model of complex tourism choices: the seasonal home location decision. *Journal of Travel and Tourism Marketing* 3(3), 69–88.

Stynes, D.J. and Peterson, G. (1984) A review of logit models with implications for modelling recreation choices. *Journal of Leisure Research* 16(4), 295–310.

Swarbrooke, J. and Horner, S. (1999) *Consumer Behaviour in Tourism – an International Perspective*. Butterworth-Heinemann, Oxford.

van Raaij, W.F. (1989) How consumers react to advertising. *International Journal of Advertising* 8, 261–273.

van Raaij, W.F. and Francken, D. (1984) Vacation decisions, activities, and satisfactions. *Annals of Tourism Research* 11, 101–112.

Wells, W.D. and Gubar, G. (1966) Life cycle concept in marketing research. *Journal of Marketing Research* 3, 355–363.

Woodside, A.G. (1990) Measuring advertising effectiveness in destination marketing strategies. *Journal of Travel Research* 28 (Fall), 3–8.

Woodside, A.G. and Lysonski, S. (1989) A general model of traveller destination choice. *Journal of Travel Research* 27(4), 8–14.

Woodside, A.G. and Ronkainen, I.A. (1993) Consumer memory and mental categorisation in international travel destination decision making. *Journal of International Consumer Marketing* 5(3), 89–104.

Woodside, A.G., Crouch, G.I., Mazanec, J.A., Oppermann, M. and Sakai, M.Y. (eds) (1999) *Consumer Psychology of Tourism, Hospitality and Leisure*. CAB International, Wallingford, UK.

Zeithaml, V.A., Parasuraman, A. and Berry, L.L. (1985) Problems and strategies in services marketing. *Journal of Marketing* 49 (Spring), 33–46.

chapter 6

Strategic Innovation in Tourism Business

Anne-Mette Hjalager

INTRODUCTION

Being innovative has become a mantra for enterprises and individuals alike. The ability to control change in a way that is consistent with overall visions and goals for the future is accorded positive recognition. Compared with other industries, such as pharmaceuticals or information technology (IT), innovation in theory and practice is rarely associated with tourism. An important explanation is that tourism enterprises are, on average, small and less inclined to invest in formalized research and development (R&D) (Hjalager, 2002; Pikkemaat and Peters, 2005; Sundbo *et al.*, 2007). None the less, intrinsic development processes in the service industry – including tourism – are catching more attention as their economic importance increases. How to foster innovation and harvest the derived benefits is therefore becoming a key strategic management discipline.

Strategic innovation is defined as follows:

> Strategic innovation is the determined, targeted, planned, and measured pursuit of such changes in organizations that lead to the introduction of new product/services, new production processes, supply chain links, managerial revisions, communication changes, and institutional paradigm shifts. Strategic innovation is a dimension of the strategic management discipline, and thus innovation is included and embedded in comprehensive attempts of an organization to achieve and maintain a competitive advantage.

Strategic innovations can be distinguished from the incremental and 'accidental' changes, as strategy, by definition, includes a sustained choice (Goodstein *et al.*, 1992; Dess *et al.*, 2005).

The aim of this chapter is to provide an overview of the nature of innovation in tourism. Further, it discusses strategic matters in greater depth looking at the differences and the organizational implications of episodic and continuous change. In addition, it specifies important categories of driving forces that materialize for organizations as incentives in innovation processes.

WHAT ARE INNOVATIONS IN THE TOURISM BUSINESS?

In his seminal work, Joseph Schumpeter (1961) delivered a first thought-provoking classification of inventions and innovations. Inventions are major scientific, technological or cultural breakthroughs. Innovations are inventions brought further towards a stage of practical applicability and commercialization. Schumpeter contributed with a typology of innovations. The list below represents an elaboration of Schumpeter's original classification in order to grasp the particular circumstances of modern tourism businesses. Common to all innovations is that they are new to the customer and/or new to the organizations that implement them.

- **Product/service innovations** are the introduction of new artefacts or services that are substantially improved in comparison with previous versions. Alternatively, in order to count as innovations, an improvement may be original compared with a competitor's performance in the field. An innovation may include changes in functional characteristics, technical abilities and ease of use, image features, or any other dimension. In the tourist industry innovations often address emotional needs, or innovations ensure that tourists are offered experiences in new ways.
- **Process innovations** involve the introduction of notably improved production methods or new styles of delivering the product/service. Process innovations may be visible to the customer, and thus for example lead to a more expedient service, wider choice, more individualization, or other features. However, process innovations may also take place backstage and be invisible to tourists. Then they represent major cost-efficiency improvements, for example through investments in technology which increases productivity.
- **Supply chain innovations** occur when changes take place in sourcing of input from suppliers, regardless of whether these supplies classify as raw materials, technology or services. Normally in tourism, production and consumption of a product take place simultaneously. However, a division of labour is deepening in the tourist business as in other sectors, thus increasing the importance of intelligent logistics and consistent supply chain agreements.
- **Managerial innovations** will radically change the division of labour within the organization, for example by empowering employees through new managerial concepts. Managerial innovations can also consist of new employee incentives, competence development, or may imply a re-conceptualization of the relationship between employees and customers in the service encounter.
- **Communications innovations** refer to new ways of presenting products or organizing branding or marketing information, documentation and feedback to and from customers. Communications innovations can be concerned with establishing new categories of communication, dialogue with customers, suppliers or the general public, and using new technologies for this purpose.
- **Institutional innovations** are new business models that add value in other fields or in entirely new ways, for example by activating idle resources or hitherto unidentified needs. New paradigms of collaboration, for example between public and private sector, can lead to institutional reorientations. Institutional innovation may also imply the restructuring of the legal framework or procedures to raise capital and to organize ownership in tourism.

Examples of innovations in tourism are shown in Table 6.1.

In practice many innovations will combine effects from more than one field (Gallouj and Weinstein, 1997; Stamboulis and Skayannis, 2003). A hotel investing in new air-conditioning does not seem innovative in the first place. However, the system may be constructed in such a way that it saves energy and space simultaneously – a process innovation. And, at the same

Table 6.1. Examples of innovations in tourism.

Type of innovation	Examples
Product/service innovations	Themed attractions that may enhance personal identities or cater for specialized interests. Examples are found in relation to heritage cars or motorbikes, extreme sports experience packages, etc. Alternatively, holiday experiences may be connected to a faith, conviction or value set, such as bible camps or pro-poor travel activities. This includes products and services developed to address intrinsic features in the 'feel good' arena Opportunities also exist to connect with other people in new ways, for example in variations of partying on the move New comfort provisions, including napping areas in airports for example Repositioning 'everyday' products, such as hotel rooms or eatable items as designer products
Process innovations	Crowd management and queue control systems in theme parks, including for example VIP priority systems, self-service aggregates, speed management in rides, etc. Implementation of robots in cleaning or gardening Dispensing systems for drinks or food in restaurants, bars, etc.
Supply chain innovations	Certified, authenticity and quality controlled regional food deliveries to tourist catering Carbon footprint certifications and related supplier agreements Electronic issue of tickets, permits and after-sale services, etc.
Management innovations	Consistently themed catering facilities. Empowerment and commitment of staff by a combination of attractive career prospects and promising job titles, adequate talent training, fun with the customers, possibilities to invest in the company, etc.
Communication innovations	Internet check-in and privilege systems. Text messages with delays in transportation Feedback from customers through blogging. Viral marketing methods
Institutional innovations	Discount airlines – combined concept of Internet sales, no connecting flights, low levels of service on board, payment for extras. Related innovations in hub structures and airport management Pro-poor tourism – linking the tourism purchase with charitable actions or operations

time, the system may be redesigned for customers to operate easily for their comfort – a distinctive service innovation. In addition, the hotel may want to communicate the investment to the customers as part of an ecotourism profile, and thus add on a comprehensive marketing innovation. The aggregate effects of a simple and unsophisticated air-conditioning investment may, in an innovation perspective, initiate a chain process with wider value creation effects and impacts that are novel to the hotel operation as well as to the customers (Hallenga-Brink and Brezet, 2005).

Another spectacular example is the retail chain 'Build-A-Bear'. The shops can sell the highly priced soft toys, not because of a superior quality, but because the customers have to make the bear themselves from a wide selection of furs, designs, clothing and accessories. Part of the production process has been put in the hands of the customers, who have become 'prosumers' rather than consumers. These prosumers work enthusiastically on the 'assembly line' without getting paid for it (Addis and Holbrook, 2001).

The nature of the tourist product, where the consumption (most often) takes place at the same location as its production, renders combined innovations particularly imperative. Continuous value creation in operations with small economic margins will frequently require that any change introduced, or any investment made, is carefully analysed for potential supplementary innovations in other parts of the production chain (Buhalis, 1998). A comprehensive consideration is a key challenge for strategic management in the tourism business.

INNOVATION AND STRATEGY

It is helpful to keep in mind that organizations are not alike in terms of planning and implementing innovation processes. Nevertheless, carefully constructed flow charts (e.g. those elaborated excessively in Rothwell (2002) and Lynch (2006)) provide inspiration and logical frameworks which are relevant and to some extent feasible for most organizations. Hallenga-Brink and Brezet (2005) address a series of flow charts in a tourism context.

The main steps in the innovation process are:

1. To describe, understand and analyse the environment.
2. To determine the goals and visions for action.
3. To plan the course of action needed in the light of the analysis.
4. To implement the decided actions.
5. To assess and revise the strategy.

Linear recommendations like these do intuitively make sense, but in practice they are not uniformly applicable. On reflection of its shortcomings, writers have often distinguished between an incremental and a rational strategy for innovation (Tidd *et al.*, 1997). The disadvantage of established innovation literature is that rational models invariably appear to be more advanced and productive than incremental models, which is probably partly true (Mintzberg, 1994; Chesbrough *et al.*, 2006).

Weick and Quinn (1999) make an interesting alternative distinction between the two main modes of addressing change in organizations: episodic change and continuous change. The model could be useful as a 'think-piece' for many tourism enterprises. Table 6.2 elaborates on the two variants as preconditions for strategic management styles and actions. Neither variant (episodic change or continuous change) is consistently better than the other, as they tend to apply to different types of organizations. Contrary to other contributions in the literature, Weick and Quinn's model does not classify incrementally innovative organizations as unprofessional, but rather they understand incrementalism as a result of general 'generic' characteristics of these organizations. For innovation processes to be successful they must be consistent with the principal strategic approaches in an organization.

In tourism, as in other sectors, there are organizations of both categories. The changes that took place in Scandinavian Airlines led by the charismatic CEO, Jan Carlzon (Carlzon and Lagerström, 1987), could be mainly interpreted as an episodic version of the management and service innovation strategy. The pyramids of organization were turned upside down in a very orderly way, and the staff got used to a new active role where they are designated as developers on behalf of the company instead of just people in a machinery taking orders from others, and where the customers got a new role in the service delivery process. The lively biography by Sir Richard Branson (Jackson, 1994) demonstrates that the Virgin Group may, in retrospect, mostly resemble the continuous innovation behaviour in the right-hand column of Table 6.2.

Table 6.2. Comparison between episodic and continuous change and innovativeness.

	Episodic change and innovativeness	Continuous change and innovativeness
Metaphors	Organizations as cathedrals: inertia-seeking organizations, where changes are infrequent, discontinuous and intentional	Organizations as tents: organizations are emergent and self-organizing and change is constant, evolutionary and cumulative
Occurrence of change	Changes are seen as occasional interruptions from the equilibrium	Change is a pattern of endless modification – a work in process
Driving forces	External interruption	Internal instability, continuous interpretation
Perspective	Macro, all-comprising, integrated, holistic, global	Micro, close, partial, local
Emphasis	Adaptation	Adaptability
Main intervention logic	Intentional change: unfreeze, transition and refreeze in a new situation. Linear, progressive	Redirection of existing tendencies. Processional, cyclic change without an end state
Role of management in innovation processes	Goals and milestone setters, budget providers, project managers, controllers. Building new meaning and symbol systems. Building new coordination and commitment	Sense makers, narrators. Pattern recognizers and problem re-shapers. Roadblock movers. Improvisation motivators. Learning agents. Translators of external impulses. Creators of enriched dialogue
Role of the remaining organization in the innovation processes	Innovators dedicated to the task. R&D departments	Everyone is a legitimate actor in innovation processes

Branson places emphasis on the importance of both dreams and joy, and the organization is built to take chances whenever they materialize. Collaborating closely on what is important, and moving on if things are not succeeding as expected, is an integral part of all employment levels in the organization.

Traditionally, changes are often considered inconvenient and are forced by necessity, as Table 6.2 illustrates is typical of episodic changes. They may be the result of major technical modification, or transformed consumer behaviour, or major crises of an environmental nature, etc. (Carlsen and Liburd, 2007). In the case of travel agencies, the Internet made it necessary to rework overall business missions and concepts (Page, 2006). Accordingly, innovations are relatively infrequent in many organizations, but they may be radical in nature, and they are subject to distinct strategic decisions initiated at a high level in the organization. In rigid organizations changes can be difficult and create tension, and, for that reason, the top management's legitimization is essential. The organization may want to seek outside assistance in order to facilitate innovation processes and implement change in a new 'frozen' form and in resettled and renegotiated cultures.

Innovation strategies included under the episodic mode seek to adapt the organization to new situations, which are expected to last for some time. For example, new products or services will need to be developed in order to compensate for a declining demand from a demographically diminishing customer group. Many tourism enterprises try consistently to cater for the expanding senior traveller market, to such an extent that other customer segments are cut out of their programmes (Novelli, 2005).

In the continuous model, innovations are more incremental and cumulative, and they emerge in the course of daily performance. For example, the breakdown of some machinery leads to a search for replacements, but also for upgrades. New technology may offer advanced facilities, and eventually the customers may experience this as enhanced service. Backstage, the work processes can become more efficient. Some of these changes, however important, can be the result of a quite unintended – even chaotic – process, which includes agents at all levels in an organization.

Weick and Quinn (1999) describe these improvisations as taking place in 'pockets' of innovation with a high extent of self-organizing. The activities in the pockets are legitimized, but not included in a strategic plan. Rather, the strategy consists of a shared vision – for example, consisting of general goals for improved customer satisfaction – within which there is ample place for interpretation. Accordingly, strategies in this model of change focus on facilitating learning and making room for the individual and the work collective. There is a belief that problems and opportunities will trigger action in such ways that top management cannot possibly foresee and plan consistently for (Mattsson *et al.*, 2005).

Neither of the two strategies – the episodic and the continuous – are better than the other by definition. They operate under dissimilar circumstances and in different managerial and strategic climates. Over time, organizations may even shift from one style of change to the other. Formalized project organizations bring a certain amount of predictability into the continuous innovation model, thus attempting to adopt the best from both worlds. As organizations become larger, they may stiffen in structure and behaviour. However, even quite bureaucratic organizations can contain or develop subunits or projects where continuous innovation is prevalent, though exempted from the mainstream and only barely tolerated. For example, trail and visitor units in wildlife areas and nature parks may be far more 'playful' and flexible in their operations than their mother organizations, which are responsible for nature management and maintenance, logging, plantation, etc.

DRIVING FORCES AND INNOVATION STRATEGY

Table 6.2 suggests that innovation can definitely be a managed process, and even in tourism enterprises there is an inclination to innovate more consistently (Hallenga-Brink and Brezet, 2005; Sundbo *et al.*, 2007). Goals, agendas and structures are to be decided by senior management, and it is they who allocate resources for the efforts (Page, 2006). Likewise, management is responsible for the assessment of risks connected to change proposals and, eventually, to launch the innovation in practice. However, no matter the managerial power and persistency, external factors heavily influence the nature and direction of innovative endeavour. In this section, a number of driving forces will be analysed in greater detail.

External factors are often interpreted only as obstacles to smooth operation and annoying interruptions to established routines. However, seen with more unbiased eyes, the driving forces are petrol or inspiration for an innovation strategy. Any organization with innovation ambitions may account for driving forces although some may be considered more carefully than others.

It makes sense to distinguish between the following categories of driving forces, each of which has something to offer to the context of innovation strategy.

Technology-driven innovations

Much of the development in tourism is embedded in technology items and systems that enterprises purchase for their normal operations. In most recent years, information and communication technology (ICT) equipment has given way to myriads of process innovations (Buhalis and Law, 2008). Handling bookings, checking in of guests in hotels and processing their accounts have become substantially rationalized, and supplementary systems for housekeeping help to make the operations more flexible and adaptable and – potentially – to increase the employee involvement and satisfaction.

In broad terms, technology does not only consist of ICT. Technology also includes those building materials and fittings that go into swimming pools, amusement park rides, beach promenades, nightclub decorations, etc. Technologies come in the format of robots for lawn mowing, cooking equipment for catering, vehicles, drinks dispensers, etc., which are all tools in the operation of some important tourist facilities. Also technology comprises skis, kayaks, golf clubs, kites and other gear that tourists use to entertain themselves, and which are matters of intense development. For example, something as simple as the addition of waterproof storage compartments in sea kayaks has opened up the opportunity for longer trips and thereby new tourism experiences. As a consequence, the opportunities for local tour organizers are enhanced.

Every time a technology producer expands, develops and improves the functionality of its products, tourism enterprises are potentially faced with fresh prospects for their operations. Some tourist enterprises adopt new technology very rapidly. Cost- and labour-saving technologies in particular are soon implemented in tourist enterprises, but also technologies that can enhance the tourists' experience or increase their comfort are speedily taken on board (Sundbo *et al.*, 2007). A restaurant implemented a by-the-glass dispensing system for red wine and discovered, much to their surprise, that guests' behaviour changed immediately towards testing and tasting. Earnings – particularly on expensive wines – increased significantly.

It is very seldom that tourist enterprises are prime movers in the development of technology, although it does take place. The Viking museum in York in the UK, for example, started to collaborate with a chemicals supplier to find methods to enhance visitors' experience by disseminating smoke, food and animal smells towards visitors on the rides (Goldkuhl and Styvén, 2007). However, most often tourism enterprises limit themselves to purchasing the equipment, and only along with or after the implementation do they realize its innovative potential.

Information about technology-driven innovations can be obtained by:
- studying advertisements and product presentations in the trade press;
- visiting trade shows and fairs;
- observing competitors' use of technology; and
- getting inspiration from enterprises outside tourism, recognized for a faster implementation of advanced technology.

Research-driven innovations

A generic medical drug, or a new highly efficient computer chip, is the result of intensive scientific research efforts. It is very hard to relate tourism directly with such invention. As a matter of fact, hard-core science ingredients in tourism are normally very few, and research-driven laboratory innovation hardly takes place in tourism. However, that does not mean that science is absent in tourism innovation.

Take, for example, the development of museum exhibitions. Historical authenticity and accuracy depend on academic anthropological research. Groundbreaking research is in fact sometimes rapidly transformed into spectacular events (Sigala, 2005). Computed tomography (CT) scanning of mummies has added new dimensions to research, and historical museums have soon transformed this into an innovation for the tourist gaze as well.

Academic research also contributes greatly, but often somewhat unnoticed, to the essential infrastructures for tourism. Research in flora and fauna, geology and topography is the backbone of, for example, nature trails (Woodroffe *et al.*, 2005), and protective recommendations by researchers spill over on to destination websites, and even on the self-confessed image of business enterprises.

University–business collaboration does exist in tourism, and it is an upcoming phenomenon (Tribe, 2002). Nevertheless, many tourist enterprises have difficulties envisaging how researchers can benefit their innovation processes. There are, however, examples that research and tourism can meet on even terms, for example in medical and wellness tourism. There is a demand for openness and adjustment practice from both sides.

Information about research-driven innovations can be obtained by:
- taking in university staff and students on short-term placements, including PhD projects;
- screening new research and studies of popular science;
- participating in collaborative projects at the destination level; and
- organizing seminars and innovation workshops with invited researchers.

Supplier-driven innovations

As demonstrated above, much innovation in tourism is not undertaken by tourism enterprises themselves, but embedded in the supplies and raw materials purchased from suppliers.

Restaurant catering provides many examples. Precooked items are prevalent in numerous restaurants, and souse vide (cooked, chilled and vacuum-packaged dishes) is emerging. That means that innovation in restaurant menus is, in principle, pushed backward in the production chain (Hjalager, 1999).

Similar supplier-driven innovation is taking place in theme parks, where specialized 'ride producers' ensure that regular visitors will see new categories of entertainment and decoration every year.

Franchises and licences are widespread in tourism. Licence holders, or the franchiser, are in charge of innovation, not the local entrepreneur. A full package of supplies, which includes not only products but also management systems, marketing devices, staff training, etc., is delivered, and there are often rigid follow-up and control measures to ensure an uncompromised joint standard. For example, medical tourism and beauty surgery tours are increasingly included in franchised concepts for the sake of brand recognition and handling of pro-risks and safety matters.

However, tourist enterprises' collaboration with suppliers need not be a total surrender. Possibly, advanced tourism users may become test benches for new supplies (Von Hippel, 2005). Such supplier–user collaboration may be time consuming and cumbersome, but, when successfully pursued, it may offer a distinctive competitive advantage.

Information about supplier-driven innovations can be obtained by:
- studying advertisements and product presentations in the trade press;
- visiting trade shows and fairs;
- investigating franchise opportunities among franchise brokers; and
- requesting collaboration with key suppliers.

Price- and cost-driven innovations

Tourism markets can be very competitive, and large segments of economically restricted customers are keen on getting bargains or value for money. Most industrialized countries operate with a significant labour cost share, and they are in sharp competition with destinations in less developed countries. As a consequence tourist enterprises in many places around the world continually hunt for cost reductions.

Pricing policies are important management issues and a field in which innovations can be launched. Airlines, for example, increasingly regulate prices continuously, dependent upon demand. They have succeeded in persuading their customers to accept a concept where there is no such thing as a fixed price. In other segments of tourism, innovations in terms of yield management methods have been keenly adopted and developed by enterprises. Working with prices is also seen in the form of comprehensive loyalty programmes and upgrade policies. Such programmes and policies may include collaboration with many other enterprises in order to enhance the benefits for the consumers as well as for members in the joint enterprise partnership.

It is of major importance to understand tourists' behaviour in detail. Business customers on an allowance react differently to prices in various parts of a hotel product from leisure customers. They do not respond uniformly to issues such as upgrading, extra services, bargains, etc. For example, self-service is fully accepted by leisure tourists, who have plenty of time. If it is combined with a distinctive 'good price', the bargain is likely to be regarded favourably. Tourists gladly cook their own meals, clean their rented cabins, drive their hired car and check in and out without face-to-face contact with staff. Strategic self-service developments are therefore crucial elements in price- and cost-driven innovations.

Information about price- and cost-driven innovations can be obtained by:
- observing and interviewing visitors, organizing focus groups, etc.;
- visiting trade shows and fairs to screen self-service equipment; and
- observing competitors' and other service enterprises' cost-saving measures.

Employee-driven innovations

Service-sector employees are claimed to be the most valuable resource for their enterprises (Baum, 2007). Normally, services need a human touch, at least at some stage of their production and delivery. Theory is, however, often quite different from practice – especially in tourism: service deficiencies or productivity gaps are often found to be due to lack of appropriate training and management of staff. Tourism and hospitality generally suffer from a very high employee turnover with employees having a low skills average, and in this situation the inclination to invite employees into innovation activities may be very limited.

Fortunately, there are exceptions from the general and gloomy human resource management (HRM) profile in the tourist sector. It is widely recognized that committed and well-qualified employees, who can use their experience and observation from hands-on practice, are crucial for continuous service improvements and for gains in efficiency. Tapping the knowledge embedded in practice is a distinct means to ensure continuous development and innovation. But it has also become an indispensable ingredient in modern management practice and an element in recruiting and retaining staff.

Culture in the workplace and management style is crucial (Jones *et al.*, 2003). Autocratic workplaces with a significant power and prestige distance are less likely to be able to make the best out of employees' contributions to innovation than workplaces with less emphasis on hierarchy and formalization. Employees need openness and trust in order to confidently present vague ideas and unconsolidated proposals. McDonald's has a reputation for employee involvement in innovation, both at individual workplaces and more globally in the corporation.

Information about employee-driven innovations can be obtained by:
- organizing staff seminars and meetings;
- setting up proposal boxes and other systematic collections of ideas and hints;
- observing work processes and enquiring into work cultures;
- involving employees in development projects and experiments;
- constructing incentives to contribute with innovative ideas; and
- allowing free 'thinking time' for staff.

Customer-driven innovation

Customers are frequently an overlooked resource and inspiration for innovation. However, a carefully attended tourist can be a goldmine of information that can lead to changes in products, services and processes and information layout, etc. of great importance for the profitability and success of an enterprise.

One very simple method is to dig into the nature of customers' complaints. Comments can directly inspire improvement processes. In addition, observations regarding guest practices can also be of importance. Staff at a hotel in a hiking area, for example, observed that many guests 'secretly' made themselves a lunch pack from the items on the breakfast buffet. This created a lot of irritation due to increased costs. The food and beverage (F&B) manager used her observations to offer the customers a service: make your lunch pack for the price of a few dollars. She provided proper packaging, bags and foil for the purpose. The combined result was an enhanced service and better economy in the F&B function.

Some managers in tourism enterprises have inappropriate ways of handling customer complaints. Solving problems by compensating (upgrading, price reduction, etc.) may create satisfaction for the customers in the situation but managerial effort is necessary in order to draw attention to the innovation message and to follow up on it.

Most organizations can become better at taking on board observations made by the staff. Those in housekeeping, for example, have much to offer in terms of important information, but they are seldom asked. If cultures in the workplace place value on input from customers via all staff members, however troublesome, as opportunities for improvements, innovation behaviour is also likely to be positively influenced.

It is a challenge for tourist enterprises not only to grasp immediate customer needs but also to seek into their future desires, hidden aspirations and dreams, which are harder to come by. If 'lead customers' can in any way be identified, much knowledge can be gained from observation of what they say and do. Adventure tourist organizations, as an example, pay a great deal of attention to those customers who are best equipped or most courageous. It is likely that these early adapters will create followers. Innovations may include safety measures that can be essential in order to gain a larger customer base for such activities that are otherwise regarded as too dangerous.

Information about user-driven innovations can be obtained by:

- launching customer surveys;
- setting up proposal boxes and other methods for systematic collection of ideas and hints;
- observing and enquiring among (lead) customers;
- involving lead customers so that they contribute innovative ideas to innovation processes;
- interviewing customers in other facilities of similar categories, for example in other destinations; and
- inviting test users or 'mystery shoppers'.

Legislation-driven innovation

Understandably enough, tourism operators are often not keen on legislative burdens, and their associations' agendas are full of proposals for liberalizations expected to make life easier for business. However, legislation does not uniformly discourage innovation and change.

Tour operators are much in favour of legislation, particularly in the fields of planning, environmental control, safety, etc. Back in the 1990s the German Touristik Union International

(TUI) actively participated with Spanish governmental bodies to enhance protection of the natural environment and improve bathing water quality. Law enforcement and construction of an appropriate infrastructure improved the situation, environmental taxes were inaugurated and TUI gained a reputation as a sustainable tourism innovator (Hjalager, 1998). Climate change initiatives may alert tour operators and worldwide destinations alike to regard legislation as a factor in strategic innovation (Carlsen and Liburd, 2007).

Legislation can prohibit less-efficient tourism services providers and create more room for the professional ones: law-abiding restaurants, for example, keenly following all food hygiene standards, since they are less likely to be closed by the authorities, and side effects may occur as innovations in production flows, higher staff retention, etc.

Naturally some enterprises and their innovativeness rely on an under-regulation and lack of law enforcement. Destinations where for instance drug use and clubbing are major activities may thrive in such a clandestine environment, and these enterprises come up with continuous ranges of new service – all disadvantages unmentioned.

Information about legislation-driven innovations can be obtained by:

- following and interpreting legislative processes, nationally and internationally;
- inviting civil servants to comment on development processes; and
- tapping knowledge from industry associations.

CONCLUSION

Strategic innovation is facilitated by the ability to see connections, to spot potential and to take economic advantage of it. This chapter demonstrates that innovation in tourism is much more than the introduction of a new service or the publishing of a new pamphlet; it may also be a new way to produce or organize a service, a better link to suppliers or changes in the way that a message is communicated. Particularly radical innovations that change the entire agenda in the industry typically range across the innovation categories. Thomas Cook represents an early and visionary example of overarching innovations that included all elements in an extensive value chain. The World Wide Web has been a technological basis for numerous more recent innovations. One among many examples is the auctioning of holiday products, which turn the sales mechanisms upside down.

No matter whether the innovations are comprehensive or incremental the whole innovative exercise is not an easy process. A key risk is that painfully acquired organizational competences will become partly or completely obsolete. Another risk is that collaborative networks, where valuable trust and insight have been established, need to be reassessed and reworked in order to exploit new possibilities. Accordingly, innovation is always both a creative and a destructive effort. Managers are often the worst enemies of innovation strategies, particularly if their privileges and benefits are linked to institutional set-ups and internal procedures that are incompatible. As demonstrated in this chapter, the organizational side of the innovation processes is crucial, no matter whether it is a small or large organization, or whether it is voluntary/non-governmental organization (NGO) or in private or public ownership.

Many popular texts claim 'innovate or die'. This is partly true. The inclination to innovate may come in waves or reflect economic fluctuations or prerequisites. An economic crisis is devastating for the innovative ability in some enterprises, while others will see opportunities in it. Likewise, climate change will close some opportunities, but open others. This chapter has only marginally addressed the issue of entrepreneurship as a driving force in innovation. But the fact is that giants in the sector constantly leave openings for the innovative newcomers. If the large chain restaurants are reluctant to adopt organic products, for example, room is made for many different outlets that promote health and environmentally sustainable food concepts. Theoretically, the large chains could launch a new way of eating by focusing all their assets in terms of organizational infrastructure and marketing power on this objective. The constellation in industry would then change, but, again, new options would emerge.

Some segments of the tourism economy may actively innovate on a continuous basis, while others are relatively unaffected and passive for most of the time. Large groups of enterprises – and typically those in the small-and-medium enterprise (SME)-dominated tourism business – are predominantly second movers. They adapt when others have made the whole range of more-or-less fatal mistakes. They imitate, copy and move along in a way that may prove to be successful in its own way (Cano *et al.*, 2001). To reduce risks numerous enterprises rely on innovations that are already embedded in technology, equipment and supplies. It should be recognized that doing it safely on a second wave can also be a distinct and feasible business strategy in its own right.

This chapter warns the reader against believing that innovation can be planned by fancy flow charts alone. Specialized laboratories are not an obvious option either. Tourism is a business where people relate and interact to a wider extent than in many other segments of the economy. Tourism innovation is therefore dominantly a people process. Customers, suppliers, business partners, authorities and even competitors possess a wealth of knowledge. Tapping that knowledge, interpreting the information and recycling it in new contexts is what strategic innovation in tourism is all about. The challenge is for managers and employees to get the time and resources under daily work burdens to listen and reflect and to transform knowledge acquired into more systematic strategic processes.

REFERENCES

Addis, M. and Holbrook, M. (2001) On the conceptual link between mass customization and experiential consumption. *Journal of Consumer Behaviour* 1(1), 50–66.

Baum, T. (2007) Human resources in tourism: still waiting for change. *Tourism Management* 28(6), 1383–1399.

Buhalis, D. (1998) Strategic use of information technology in the tourism industry. *Tourism Management* 19, 409–421.

Buhalis, D. and Law, R. (2008) Progress in information technology and tourism management: 20 years on and 10 years after the internet. *Tourism Management* 29(4), 609–623.

Cano, M., Drummond, S., Mille, C. and Barclay, S. (2001) Learning from others: benchmarking in diverse tourism enterprises. *Total Quality Management* 12(7–8), 974–980.

Carlsen, J. and Liburd, J. (2007) Developing an agenda for tourism crisis management, market recovery and communications. *Journal of Travel and Tourism Marketing* 23(2–3), 265–276.

Carlzon, J. and Lagerström, T. (1987) *Riv Pyramiderna* (*Tear Down the Pyramids*). Bonniers, Stockholm.

Chesbrough, H., Vanhaverbeke, W. and West, J. (2006) *Open Innovation. Researching a New Paradigm.* Oxford University Press, Oxford.

Dess, G., Lumpkin, G. and Taylor, M.L. (2005) *Strategic Management.* McGraw-Hill, New York.

Gallouj, F. and Weinstein, O. (1997) Innovation in service. *Research Policy* 26(4–5), 537–556.

Goldkuhl, L. and Styvén, M. (2007) Sensing the scent of service success. *European Journal of Marketing* 41(11/12), 1297–1305.

Goodstein, L.D., Nolan, T.M. and Pheiffer, J.W. (1992) *Applied Strategic Planning – a Comprehensive Guide*. Pheiffer and Company, San Diego, California.

Hallenga-Brink, S.C. and Brezet, J.C. (2005) The sustainable innovation design diamond for micro-sized enterprises in tourism. *Journal of Cleaner Production* 13, 141–149.

Hjalager, A.-M. (1998) Environmental regulation of tourism – impacts on business innovation. *Progress in Tourism and Hospitality Research* 4, 17–30.

Hjalager, A.-M. (1999) Technology domains and manpower choice in the restaurant sector. *New Technology, Work and Employment* 14(1), 81–93.

Hjalager, A.-M. (2002) Repairing innovation defectiveness in tourism. *Tourism Management* 23(5), 465–474.

Jackson, T. (1994) *Virgin King: Inside Richard Branson's Business Empire*. HarperCollins, London.

Jones, E., Keeling, D., Davies, R., Hampson, D., Attwell, G. and Hughes, J. (2003) Developing innovation in tourism and hospitality. In: Kusluvan, S. (ed.) *Managing Employee Attitudes and Behaviours in the Tourism and Hospitality Industry*. Nova Science Publishers, Hauppauge, New York, pp. 721–760.

Lynch, R. (2006) *Corporate Strategy*. Prentice Hall, London.

Mattsson, J., Sundbo, J. and Fussing-Jensen, C. (2005) Innovation systems in tourism: the roles of attractors and scene-takers. *Industry and Innovation* 12(3), 357–381.

Mintzberg, H. (1994) *The Rise and Fall of Strategic Planning*. Prentice Hall, New York.

Novelli, M. (2005) *Niche Tourism. Contemporary Issues, Trends and Cases*. Butterworth-Heinemann, Oxford, UK.

Page, S. (2006) *Tourism Management: Managing for Change*. Butterworth-Heinemann, Oxford.

Pikkemaat, B. and Peters, M. (2005) Towards measurement of innovation – a pilot study of the small and medium sized hotel industry. In: Peters, M. and Pikkemaat, B. (eds) *Innovation in Hospitality and Tourism*. Haworth, Binghamton, New York, pp. 89–112.

Rothwell, R. (2002) Towards a fifth-generation innovation process. In: Henry, J. and Mayle, D. (eds) *Managing Innovation and Change*. Sage, London, pp. 115–135.

Schumpeter, J. (1961) *The Theory of Economic Development*. Oxford University Press, New York.

Sigala, M. (2005) A learning assessment of online interpretation practices. In: Frew, A.J. (ed.) *Information and Communication Technologies in Tourism*. Springer, Berlin, pp. 67–78.

Stamboulis, Y. and Skayannis, P. (2003) Innovation strategies and technology for experience-based tourism. *Tourism Management* 24, 35–43.

Sundbo, J., Orfila-Sintes, F. and Sørensen, F. (2007) The innovative behavior of tourism firms. *Research Policy* 36, 88–106.

Tidd, J., Bessant, J. and Pavitt, K. (1997) *Managing Innovation. Integrating Technological, Market and Organizational Change*. John Wiley & Sons, Chichester, UK.

Tribe, J. (2002) The philosophic practitioner. *Annals of Tourism Research* 29(2), 338–357.

Von Hippel, E. (2005) *Democratizing Innovation*. MIT Press, Cambridge, Massachusetts.

Weick, K.E. and Quinn, R.E. (1999) Organisational change and development. *Annual Review of Psychology* 50, 361–386.

Woodroffe, O., Thirgood, S. and Rabinowitz, A. (2005) *People and Wildlife. Conflict or Coexistence?* Cambridge University Press, Cambridge, UK.

chapter 7

The Transformation of Distribution Channels

Enrique Bigné

TOURISM DISTRIBUTION CHANNELS: ROLES AND FUNCTIONS

Tourism suppliers and destinations need to offer their different services to tourists. Distributing tourism is critical for selling the different tourism products and their related services. This includes a group of agents and channels that are characterized by two specific elements: (i) diversity of intermediaries; and (ii) the immense importance of the online channel. On the one hand, the number of intermediaries is multiple; the same as is the case with other markets, but the sequence of relationships between agents is not the traditional one. Habitually, in what is known as the vertical channel, wholesalers buy the product from the manufacturers, and they sell it to retailers, who in turn distribute it to the end consumers. In the marketing of tourist services, however, distribution is carried out by a number of different distribution agents that coexist. These can be the wholesalers themselves (tour operators), the retailers (travel agencies), but also the service providers such as transporters, hotels and others, who carry out the intermediation. The classical system of distribution persists to a considerable degree for some products – especially in tour packages that are not commodities or for tourists who are not Internet users. On the other hand, information and communications technology (ICT) enables tourism service providers to interact directly with consumers, placing enormous pressure on traditional intermediaries (i.e. travel agencies and tour operators). This is critical in the tourism sector, due to the fact that the perceived importance of e-business in tourism is above all sector averages, although this is not the case for microcompanies (e-Business W@tch, 2006). With this, agents avoid intermediaries and also obtain a direct relationship with the customer, which is of great commercial value with respect to the current relationship as well as the future. In this way, for example, a hotel chain can market/sell its products directly by means of the Internet at a price equal to or inferior to the travel agency's price, and build a direct relationship with the customer in order to get to know him/her better and establish a long-term commercial relationship through relationship marketing programmes.

Tourism distribution can be understood on two levels: basic and augmented. Basic distribution is understood as merely intermediation activity: bringing buyers and sellers together. Augmented distribution refers, additionally, to value creation by travel agents. They are in a position to be able to offer something valuable to the supplier's offering. This consists in adding value to the initial offerings. Accordingly, these roles could be seen as being basic, acting as merely distributors or valuable agents offering information and counselling as well as full-range tourism services. In fact, the travel agency's main function is to act as an agent, selling travel products or services on behalf of a supplier. They can put together different basic tourism services such as accommodation and transportation, and other related services such as guided tours, travel insurance, airport transfer, entertainment, sports and leisure activities, and currency exchange, as well as counselling. These basic and derived services can be provided separately or in the form of a full product as package tours.

The travel agencies' role as advisers and especially as resellers has been questioned recently, due to direct selling from suppliers and ICT tools such as Internet and eCommerce. This will be discussed later on, and also in Chapter 13, but the key element that explains their successful role is value. If travel agencies offer value in terms of service, price, availability, information, security or other critical customer dimensions, they will be serving their clients. Otherwise, if a hotel, an airline or other agents give superior value in any dimension, the customers will shift to them. The success of a travel agency depends on customer perceived value (Bigné et al., 2005). For instance, a direct and frequent flight from London to Amsterdam could be offered by a traditional travel agency, an airline call centre or through the Internet. Travellers will choose depending on their perceived value of what each agent offers. Many options are available. Traditional travel agencies could offer accumulating discounts through repeated flights, the Internet could be useful for booking at midnight, and an airline call centre allows flight changes for a traveller abroad.

Tourism distribution can be applied to a variety of tourism services. The following services are the most common ones offered:

- transportation – international and domestic flights, car rentals, rail tickets and cruise lines;
- accommodation – hotel and other accommodation;
- travel insurance – travel insurance policies only, insuring against loss, theft and other damage during vacations;
- currency exchange services and visas;
- guided tours, sightseeing tours, excursions and entertainment tickets;
- specialized services – restaurants, concert or sports tickets, conference registration, ski passes, specific languages or sports training, and others; and
- package holiday – vacation or incentive trips including transportation and accommodation; this may include other services as well, such as entertainment, leisure activities and travel insurance.

These services can be sold by different agents and suppliers for different customers, such as individuals (tourists, business travellers, leisure customers), groups (conferences and major events) and organizations (companies, government institutions and NGOs).

Figure 7.1 shows the relationships between tourism products, distributors and target population. This figure picks up on two main ideas. On the one hand, tourism services can be distributed by travel agencies or by the suppliers themselves, or even by other suppliers that we refer to as cross suppliers. Therefore, some offerers, such as airline companies, distribute their flight services directly through their own offices (offline channel), or by telephone or Internet sales systems (online channel). On the other hand, the different distributors obtain the services from either suppliers or other distributors. Traditionally, travel agencies obtained tour packages – a week

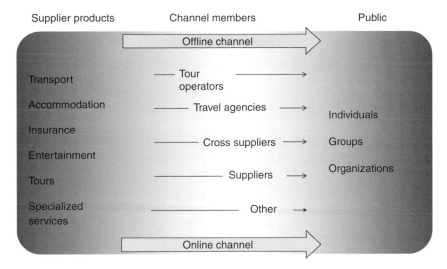

Fig. 7.1. Tourism services, distributors and target population.

in Cancun, for example – from the tour operators. In turn, the tour operators, in order to assemble the product, obtained flight seats, accommodation and other services from a number of different suppliers. Recently, the suppliers themselves have intensified direct distribution, selling their own services and even those of other suppliers through the Internet. In this way, for example, an airline company sells its own tickets and also accommodation, or car rental, thus developing cross selling.

The functions of tourism distribution consist of the following:

- to intermediate in the buying and selling between the buyer and the producer, purchasing in advance or on the spot, and obtaining for this intermediation a commission;
- to prepare complete offerings, known as tour packages; and
- to provide information and advice.

The function of intermediation in the buying and selling between producer and buyer can be carried out in advance in order to assemble tour packages, or at the moment they are requested by the tourist. The difficulty in stocking transport seats or accommodation makes it necessary for tour operators to carry out a follow-up on demand and the use of price as a motivating variable for demand. In situations where sales forecasts are not being met, we often see special offers, popularly known as last minute. This process of price discrimination over a period of time is known as revenue management, and consists of understanding, anticipating and influencing consumer behaviour in order to maximize marginal revenue or profits from a fixed, perishable resource, such as airline seats or hotel rooms.

The function of aggregator and package creator has traditionally been the role of tour operators. This function is also relevant to the tourism industry as it implies a series of benefits such as adjusting the quantity and type of products with consumer demand, and facilitating the searching process and identifying the best products (destinations, hotels, travel experiences and others). The activity of preparing products is carried out in a number of different ways. Focusing on this function, intermediaries obtain accommodation, transport, restaurant and other services in advance, and assemble a tour package, such as for example holidays in a beach destination with meals and direct flight, the price of which is lower than the individual sum total for each service. Here the intermediary, generally a wholesaler, assumes the financial risk derived from the sales obtained and the travel agencies offer the tour product to the tourist, obtaining a commission for each sale.

Finally, the function of providing information and advice is relevant because of the fact that the tourism service is consumed in another destination and generally cannot be tried or checked out beforehand by the final user, or tourist. The information provided by travel agents is based on the knowledge or even on the specialization for certain products, while the advice is established on the basis of the experience and training of these agents. The first models of tourist behaviour were already identifying the critical role of information in the choice of a holiday destination (Moutinho, 1987). The users themselves also develop information and advice on the choice of a tourist service. Word of mouth (WOM) has been reinforced in recent years as a result of the new technologies, such as the Internet and short messages service (SMS) through mobile telephone devices.

As mentioned above, services are marketed though agents or directly by suppliers, through both online and offline channels. Traditionally, the travel distribution role has been performed by tour operators and travel agencies. They are globally connected through computerized reservations systems (CRS) and global distribution systems (GDS), initially created for booking and selling airline tickets. GDS are a worldwide-computerized network with multi-access to a single source database for booking airline tickets, hotel rooms, rental cars and other related services used by travel agents, transporters and hotels.

CRS, initially promoted by the airline companies and the hotels, have gone from being a possible tool for helping tourism businesses, to becoming standardized channels, over which a great number of services related to distribution are carried out. They have evolved to such a degree by bringing together different suppliers, as well as through the incorporation of the Internet. Their principal benefits lie in that they are able to provide immediate information on the availability of seats, rooms, etc., the detailed characteristics of these products and the possibility of making the corresponding reservation.

Within these systems it is possible to distinguish various levels of integration, depending on the number of operators they consist of. Along this line, it is possible to distinguish the following types:

- Reservations centre companies that market the product, generally hotels, of a specific company. These are usually sole distributors. An example of this type is the reservations centre of the hotels of the Accord chain. The group's hotel operations include different brands such as Sofitel, Pullman, MGallery, Novotel, Mercure, Suitehotel, Ibis, All Seasons, Etap Hotel, HotelF1 and Motel6.
- Reservations centres linked to tourist destinations or zones. This is habitual in destinations such as for example visitmenorca.com, or for tourist areas such as ski resorts, like Alpe d'Huez or Baquiera Beret, where not only skiing services are offered, but also accommodation, excursions and other items.
- GDS for distribution of multiple operators of the same category. This acts, for example, for any hotel in any worldwide geographical zone, and different hotels or chains can coexist. Examples of these would be Utell Hotels, which work with over 11,000 hotels in 130 countries and operate through Pegasus.
- Transversal GDS that offer the services of all types of suppliers. The larger GDS are Amadeus, Sabre and Travelport (Galileo, and Worldspan), owned and operated by major airlines, car rental firms and hotel groups, whose main characteristics are summarized in Table 7.1. Recently, the GDS have developed an eCommerce version through the Internet. This has created opportunities for some agents, referred to as new tourism eMediaries, derived from suppliers, such as airlines, Web-based travel agencies (Expedia) and direct sales brands of the GDS such as Travelocity.

Table 7.1. Major global distribution systems (GDS) (Source: GDS websites: Amadeus, 2010; Sabre, 2010; Travelport, 2010).

Name	Created by	Providers available	Locations
Amadeus	Air France, Lufthansa, Iberia and SAS in 1987	500 airlines 80,000 hotel properties 25 car rental companies Other travel provider groups (ferry, rail, cruise, insurance companies and tour operators)	100,000 travel agency locations 34,000 airline sales office locations 36,000 car rental locations
Sabre	American Airlines, all Nippon Airways, Cathay Pacific Airways, China Airlines and Singapore Airlines in the 1960s	400 airlines 76,000 hotels 28 car rental companies 13 cruise lines 35 rail networks 220 tour operators	50,000 travel agencies
Travelport	From 2007 combines Galileo GDS (created by Aer Lingus, Air Canada, Alitalia, Swissair, TAP and United Airlines) and Worldspan GDS (created by Delta Air Lines, Northwestern Airlines and TWA)	450 airlines 83,000 hotel properties 25 car rental companies Over 400 cruise and tour operators 13 major rail networks	63,000 travel agencies

TOURISM DISTRIBUTION CHANNEL MEMBERS

As can be seen in Fig. 7.1, between supply and demand there is a varied combination of possibilities which runs from a long distribution channel in which a number of members intervene, to a direct channel between a supplier and a final purchaser. Additionally, the interactions could take place through an offline channel or through an online channel. The relationships between agents in this latter channel have been given names with specific forms. Activities of businesses serving end consumers with products and/or services are called business-to-consumer (B2C). Business-to-business (B2B) describes commerce transactions between businesses, such as between a manufacturer and a wholesaler or between a wholesaler and a retailer (Bigné *et al.*, 2008). Business-to-government (B2G) is a derivative of B2B marketing. Government-to-citizen (G2C) is the online non-commercial interaction between local and central government and individuals, rather than the commercial business sector G2B.

Traditional tourism intermediaries are classified in three broad categories that reflect their functions: (i) tour operators, which are aggregators, package creators and wholesalers; (ii) outbound travel agencies, which are retailers; and (iii) incoming travel agencies, which are handling agencies in charge of fulfilment at the destination as well as providers of transfers and local excursions. Table 7.2 shows a summary of the activities carried out by each member of the channel before, during and after the trip.

Tour operators

The principal activity of tour operators consists of the preparation and distribution of complete tourism products, by means of the fusion and combination of the components, and this usually includes travel, accommodation, meals and guided tours or excursions. For this reason, the large wholesalers buy some of the components of the products in large quantities, fundamentally airline seats and lodgings. Generally they have a considerable power of negotiation because of their size, concentration and high capacity for purchase, which allow them to enjoy advantageous purchase conditions and resale to the independent travel agencies, which are generally fragmented and of a small dimension. Some of the wholesalers form

Table 7.2. Activities of the members of the channel before, during and after the trip (Source: based on Buhalis and Ujma, 2006).

	Tour operators	Outbound travel agents	Incoming travel agents
Before the trip	Contact suppliers and travel agents Organize charter flights and pre-book accommodation Put packages together Market product	Dispense advice on destinations Identify consumer needs Present available offers to consumers Sell the product and provide documents	Provide links between destination suppliers and tour operators
During the trip	Deliver transportation and supervise delivery by principals such as hotels and attractions Deal with local authorities	Cooperate with tour operators and incoming travel agents on smooth running of holidays Look after customers by providing secure point of contact	Provide transport and local excursions
After the trip	Handle special requests Review the quality of products and services Monitor satisfaction levels	Review the travel experience and received feedback	Improve/change products on offer

part of tourism business groups with a number of lines of business, among which we find tour operators, travel agencies, hotels, airline companies for charter flights and others. Particularly large European wholesalers such as Tui Travel PLC (which includes, among others, Tui, First Choice, Thomson, Nouvelles Frontiers, Atlantica Hotels, Tui Cars and Tuifly) and the Spanish Orizonia Corporation (which includes Iberojet, VivaTours and Turavia as wholesalers, Viajes Iberia as a travel agency, and Iberworld as a charter flight company) are clear examples.

Their specialization is greater in accommodation and transport, and less in other areas such as restaurants. Some wholesalers specialize geographically, or by product type. With large events or conferences, where a high level of very concentrated demand is expected over a specific period, these types of intermediaries operate as sole agents.

Retail travel agencies

Retail travel agencies advise travellers in their travel decision purchases as well as selling tourism services including transport, accommodation, sightseeing tours, car rentals, package holidays and other related services.

There are three different types of agencies. Regarding their location services, they could be outbound travel agencies based in the originating location of the traveller, and inbound travel agents based in the destination and delivering expertise on that location. They tend to specialize in some type of services, such as skiing, safaris or cultural leisure, or in some target groups such as business travellers, as well as other travellers. They can either be independent or part of a large group with many outlets.

Retail travel agencies are the most numerous group within the distribution channel. The ample number of retailers contrasts with the high degree of concentration predominant among the tour operators, which limits their power, especially when they are of an independent type. The degree of specialization by services or by customers does not appear to be habitual in the sector, and, as a result, the degree of differentiation is barely perceived in so far as commercial strategy, range of products and degree of specialization are concerned.

Their income comes from commission on sales, and therefore the volume of business is the most relevant commercial and financial element.

Included among the products they market are:

- Packages coming from tour operators, where the product comes totally defined or defined to a high degree, although more and more flexibility in some aspects such as the type of accommodation or duration of the trip is being seen.
- Basic products that are generally required in the event of a specific demand by the customer – transport, accommodation or others – and those where their position is seen as being in peril as a result of direct sales on the Internet.
- Complementary products – insurance, shows, visits and excursions.

The increasing use of the Internet has generated two contrasting effects. On the one hand, some service providers have developed direct sales of their own products, thus limiting the intermediating role of the traditional agencies. On the other hand, the Internet has opened up opportunities for the appearance of new types of online intermediaries known as eMediaries, and some of the traditional agencies have reinforced their traditional offline sales with online sales. Some examples of online agencies are Expedia, eDreams, Travelocity, lastminute.com and viajar.com. Derived from Internet technology, new agents have appeared such us travel search engines like Trabber, skyscanner and mirayvuela. They are not selling services. These sites use technological tools that generate an aggregate result from other airline sites, including third-party travel agency sites and branded sites maintained by individual travel companies.

Suppliers and cross suppliers

Traditionally suppliers – especially airline companies and hotel chains – have sold their services to end consumers. In this way, for example, the airline companies have sold many seats in their own sales offices or through customer attention telephones known as call centres. In the same way, the hotels have been selling over the phone or directly when a customer arrives at the hotel. This activity has been given impetus thanks to the Internet, which allows for distribution of their services at a global level, accompanied by additional information, special price offers, images or webcam of a hotel, and specific services such as obtaining boarding passes. These added services represent value for the customer, and their function is not that of mere intermediation. The option of direct sale of their services through the Internet represents new opportunities for the distribution of their services on a global level and consequently the non-utilization of other traditional intermediaries.

More recently, these suppliers have come to understand that the role of distribution of services through the Internet does not have to be limited, but rather that they can offer services of other non-competitive suppliers, thus expanding their range of distribution. Indeed, many airline companies are offering services of hotel or car rental reservation, and, in the same way, some hotel chains are offering airline tickets or car rentals or guided tours. Sometimes the origin of this cross selling is a result of their distributing services of other companies that belong to a group of companies in which they are integrated or associated.

Others

In many non-hotel accommodation services, different agents, such as real estate agencies, or even private parties, especially in coastal zones, are carrying out functions of intermediation in the marketing of rental apartments. Even public organizations of a destination have taken on this function in order to develop and regulate the rental of apartments or rural housing.

Some destinations are offering online bookings through their website, redirecting to the service provider's website (see http://www.spain.info/). In some destinations, public organizations such as tourist boards and similar organizations make agreements with airline companies, restaurants, car rental companies, museums and craftwork or gift shops, with the objective of offering discounts, vouchers or other incentives and even certain products such as guided tours through old sections of the city to customers.

TRENDS IN TOURISM DISTRIBUTION ACTIVITY

This section analyses the most relevant tendencies in tourism distribution activity and their implications. In the first part, tendencies of a general type are analysed, and in the second, given the importance of the technological changes in communication, changes in and consequences of ICT in the distribution of tourism products are specifically analysed.

General trends

Distribution in all sectors is witnessing important changes in various directions, which leads to the empowering of channel members. In the tourism sector, certain changes have also taken place in recent years. A number of differences compared with the general distribution system are becoming apparent. A diversity of factors have come to characterize the development of the tourism distribution channel, and these will be briefly mentioned here.

Vertical integration

The process of the integration of diverse distribution links has been showing up in the form of agreements and participation in the share capital of different companies. Vertical integration is the degree to which a firm owns its upstream suppliers and its downstream buyers. This process could be backward when control is for the suppliers or service providers, and forward vertical integration refers to control distribution centres and retailers where their products and services are sold. The former is related to a travel agency that participates in the share capital of airline companies, overland transport companies or hotels. Forward vertical integration takes place when a wholesale agency has retailers at its disposal. In reality, share capital participation in companies, whether this be backward or forward, reflects a clear process of business concentration and of an increase in the power to negotiate, which leads to the creation of large tourism groups which own transportation companies (generally airlines), one or several tour operators specializing by activity or by geographical areas, retail travel agencies and others. This is the case of Globalia, a tourism group that includes an airline (Air Europa), a chain of hotels (Oasis), a retail network of more than 1200 travel agencies in Spain and Portugal (Halcón Viajes and Viajes Ecuador), and tour operators such as Travelplan and Touring Club (a tour operator specializing in Disneyland Resort Paris). Other companies that are a part of the group include Pepecar.com, which is a low-cost car rental company, and a handling company operating under the name Groundforce.

Horizontal integration

Retail agencies are initiating a process of horizontal integration either by means of agreements and acquisitions or by means of franchises. This type of integration is still incipient in the retail agencies, where the independents are predominant.

Technological development

CRS are but a sample of the remarkable technological development in the tourism sector. Together with this, the process of adoption of the Internet and its applications has been unstoppable, bringing about the development of eCommerce in tourism. In addition to online purchasing, other applications are also affecting distribution, such as electronic tickets, online boarding passes, reservation portals, e-mail for communication and others, whose impact have been decisive in tourism (Buhalis and Law, 2008). The Internet has also made possible the integrated development of tools for customer relationship management and supply-chain-management software applications, which allow for the management of one-to-one relations with customers and with suppliers (Bigné *et al.*, 2008). The function that travel agencies carry out as providers of information and advisers (as described in the section 'Tourism Distribution Channels: Roles and Functions') is also being affected by the Internet. In fact, the new communication tools and applications have been grouped together under the denomination Web 2.0, as social networking websites. Among the most well known are Facebook.com, MySpace.com, YouTube.com, Flickr.com, Panoramio.com, Tripadvisor.com and a number of blogs under the label travel 2.0 and tourism 2.0 as travelblog.org, travelpod.com or diariodelviajero.com and foros.blogdeviajes.net, among others. From the supply side, conscious of the strength of the movement, there are also initiatives that have been designed by the destinations themselves, such as 'esmadrid4u' (http://4u.esmadrid.com) or hotels or agencies that offer space to hang tourists' comments. The inclusion of comments, questions or links to certain tourist destinations or videos and photos has served to develop horizontal or between-user information and advice. If the Internet has signified a decisive impulse and changes in tourism distribution, the development of mobile phones is opening up the way to applications for tourism distribution – either through text messaging or by means of Internet connection from the mobile phone. These Internet connections are practically the same as with a computer. The text messages, however, make it possible to locate airport lounges, check flight status, get gate information, check seat and other related services such as weather information. Generally speaking, the technological developments have favoured the processes of the channel agents, but they also allow for customer self-service, providing the service for themselves without employee involvement (e.g. automated teller machines or online ticketing). Finally, barcode and radio frequency identification (RFID) for luggage handling simplifies airline baggage management and improves customer service in terms of reductions in mishandled baggage.

Customization

This is part of the so-called one-to-one marketing, which refers to marketing strategies applied directly to a specific consumer, offering personalized products and service to each one. This approach is just the opposite of mass production. In fact, the role of the travel agencies consists in adding value to their relationship with customers. The value offered resides in the personal interaction, the personalization of the product to the preferences of the customer, and in its follow-up. Travel agencies that act as consultants can interact with their customers, provoking emotions and satisfaction, in contrast to the rationality that the use of virtual travel agencies involves. The personal interaction of the retail travel agencies leads to a higher level of customers knowledge not only about their preferences but also about the context in which the customer will travel, thus facilitating the offering of products that generate higher customer satisfaction. Technology also can be used to improve the efficiency and effectiveness of service encounters through customized service offerings, recovery from service failure and the providing of spontaneous satisfaction through e-mails (Bitner *et al.*, 2000).

ICT and tourism distribution

As pointed out in the study *Trends in European Internet Distribution of Travel and Tourism Services* (Marcussen, 2009), the European online travel market (excluding online sales to customers not living in Europe) may have reached 25% of the total market for travel and tourism services. The direct sellers are becoming increasingly important, accounting for nearly two-thirds of online sales in the European market in 2008. In 2008, the breakdown of the market by type of service was as follows: air travel 54%; hotels (and other types of accommodation) 19.5%; package tours 15%; rail 7.5%; rental cars (and car ferries) 4% (Marcussen, 2009).

As we mentioned above, technology is bringing about important changes in the distribution of tourism services. Specifically, it has brought about two changes that have led to conflict: (i) dis-intermediation; and (ii) re-intermediation. ICT enables tourism service providers to interact directly with consumers, but ICT also makes possible a new type of intermediation for traditional players as well as for newly emerging online intermediaries.

There are a number of ways that intermediation through the use of ICT is affecting intermediaries as well as customers. Increasingly, consumers can undertake their entire tourism product search and booking online, and therefore the role of eMediaries has been changing dramatically. As a result, this has brought about the emergence of a wide range of new tourism eMediaries. The proliferation of eMediaries coming from the tourism suppliers (particularly airlines), traditional and new intermediaries, as well as other types, has brought about an important development in online intermediation. A number of different types of intermediaries can be identified, depending on the service they offer. Some of these offer only information, while others allow for reservations and purchase. Some offer the service of one supplier and others of several suppliers. Among others, it is possible to identify the following types of eTourism eMediaries (Buhalis and Licata, 2002):

- From the supplier side are included the single supplier providers, such as airlines, hotels and car rentals; and the multi-supplier Web pages that have emerged to support airlines dis-intermediating travel agencies. These were airlines (e.g. Opodo in Europe and Orbitz in the USA). Destinations have also developed destination management systems to distribute some services through search engines (e.g. www.spain.info). Even the major GDS are entering the online market by developing interfaces for consumers (e.g. www.travelocity.com owned by Sabre).

- Those originated by intermediaries, either traditional offline agencies that have developed their own online provision or new Web-based travel agencies (e.g. www.expedia.com from Microsoft). There are even some that have opted for specialization, such as the last-minute online agencies.

- Other non-touristic agents are also offering facilities for intermediation. The Internet portals (e.g. Yahoo) and vertical portals specializing in products such as skiing or golf have also developed online travel distribution, often by sourcing their travel content from external online agents and suppliers. Additionally, some media companies such as newspapers and television networks are gradually including eTourism facilities on their sites. A number of tourism blogs and Web pages include search engines and other tools for the distribution of tourism services.

Summarizing, tourists can search for information or book online different services such as flights, hotels, insurance, tour basic packages, and others which come from GDS as well as suppliers' websites and online travel agencies, through various links to Web pages and redirects. In fact, from a tourist perspective, most of the websites are integrated ones that come from internal links to different Web pages of various GDS and suppliers. The relationship between GDS, online travel agencies and integrated websites is shown graphically in Fig. 7.2. The changes

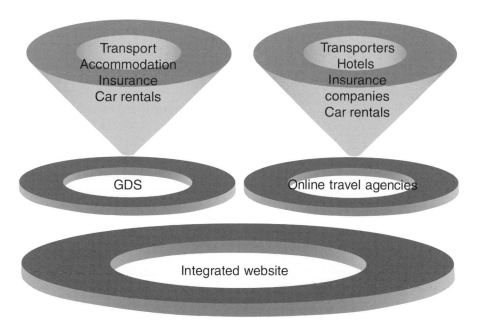

Fig. 7.2. Relationship between GDS, online travel agencies and integrated websites (adapted from Bigné, 2006).

that are happening have not come to an end, as the technological development of the ICTs, as well as the use of these technologies on the part of consumers, continues to increase, and therefore new applications and forms of intermediation are still on the horizon. The implications for the structure of the tourism industry have been analysed by e-Business W@tch (2006), which uses the 'five-forces model', developed by Porter, to discuss and assess e-business implications for the structure of the industry. The 'five forces' are: (i) threat of new entrants; (ii) substitution of products and services; (iii) bargaining power of suppliers; (iv) bargaining power of customers; and (v) rivalry in the market. These will now be discussed.

Threat of new entrants

Current online market developments and technological solutions are becoming popular and are lowering costs for all agents. This will make future business especially difficult for traditional small or independent travel agencies and tour operators. As a result, the existing low barriers enable new market entrants, posing a threat for traditional players, and will bring about an increase in the number of operators in the tourism distribution channel.

Substitution of products and services

New technologies and Web functionalities are modifying in various directions the way products and services are offered. The information activity, which has traditionally been offered by travel agencies, is today accessible through a number of websites belonging to either tourism agents themselves or others. Besides information, on some websites it is also possible to reserve and purchase tourism services, thus favouring customer self-service. Technology even allows for obtaining boarding passes and seat selection for flights online. The obvious advantages of online sales in terms of business hours and sales on holidays add to the difficulties of the traditional offline agencies in being able to compete. New intermediaries, however, have recently come into being, known as aggregators, which have developed websites where it is possible to search out, purchase and redirect the same services of multiple providers and of online travel agencies. This type of eMediaries adds value for the customer as they make it possible to encounter in one website all the different options (from multiple providers and different intermediaries) for the same service (a specific flight, for example).

Bargaining power of suppliers

The online distribution channels contribute to providers being able to carry out the direct sale of their product to the tourist. Therefore, this makes them less dependent on traditional intermediaries in order to sell as well as to manage relationships with customers. The suppliers, conscious of this situation, have not opted in a widespread way for the elimination of the distribution of their products through travel agencies or other agents, but they have reduced their sales commissions. Therefore, service suppliers will continue to work with online and offline intermediaries but under new business conditions, and at the same time will continue to promote direct sales and even cross selling. The bottom line is that distribution via multiple channels is being consolidated, but preference is being given to their own channel. Along this line, some of the hotel chains are advertising that the best price is to be had on their own website.

Bargaining power of customers

The development of the online selling channel increasingly empowers customers to perform an increasing number of tasks themselves. Customers are able to obtain information on their own about destinations, travel offers, flights, view photos or videos, and other things. They can also compare prices, schedules and services that are included. They can then make the reservations, change the reservation, and purchase. Finally, they can act as recommenders through the eWOM. Although with little development so far, it is argued that the **prosumers** are becoming **proksumers** – a designation suggested by Edu William (2010) to refer to those users who carry out through their blogs three activities: (i) *pro*duce – creating knowledge; (ii) br*oker* – distributing, sharing, filtering and recommending; and (iii) con*sume* personalizing information.

Rivalry in the market

As a result of direct marketing on the part of the suppliers, and even the cross selling of other services, the new online travel agencies and the appearance of other new non-tourism intermediaries, competition in the online market is increasing. Additionally, the different players have adopted a global perspective that makes it possible for operators to carry out their functions in many geographical markets. This is due to the growing demand for international destinations as well as the objective of the operators to expand to a global level. In order to do so, it is quicker and cheaper to increase the level of cooperation among service providers. This would explain the appearance of consortiums, alliances and joint websites among providers.

The changes in tourism distribution are increasingly coming about as a result of different forces, but technological development and its gradual adoption by consumers, notably, is to a great degree bringing about these changes in distribution. Many of the changes are already being consolidated, such as online travel agencies. Others, however, are still incipient and require a greater period in order to be able to determine their effective growth. There are some obvious consequences that are arising from this process, such as the following:

1. Innovation in technologies of distribution will continue being key in the future and will serve as a basis for obtaining competitive advantages for those that adopt them. The development of new applications, their extension to mobile phones and television, as well as the development of free software, are foreseen as clear opportunities.

2. Given the fact that the role of the consumer is ever increasing, online applications should concentrate more on customer-oriented solutions. Along this line, and given the low entry costs and the quantity of online operators, the agents of the distribution channel should follow strategies of segmentation and personalized attention or use profiles.

In spite of the fact that the power of the suppliers will be greater, traditional travel agencies will not disappear, but their role needs to be re-adapted. Generally speaking, they will lose market quota in the sale of commodities (e.g. standard flights or individual hotel nights). But, on the contrary, in certain complex or specialized products they will be able to continue supplying perceived value as a result of their greater specialization and knowledge. Their options are varied, and will be analysed in the following section, but the use of communication technologies and personalized customer attention will be key.

STRATEGIC RESPONSES TO THE TRENDS

In previous sections we have shown the functions of the different agents of the distribution channel, the changes they are bringing about and the threats that are arising for each type of distributor. In short, the following conclusions can be identified:

• Direct sales will increase to the degree that the suppliers continue developing online solutions for the marketing of their own products or the products of other agents.

Consequently, their strength in the market will be greater for standard products, and the independent retail travel agencies will be more vulnerable in respect of these products.

- GDS will strengthen the eCommerce version through the Internet. Their proposals will be integrated more and more, offering various types of services such as transport, accommodation, car rentals and others. This will generate two consequences. The first is their increased power, which they will strengthen even more with concentrations and fusions of systems. The development of B2C options through their own websites will provide them with greater power and once again facilitate direct sales. The second consequence is the creation of new opportunities for the intermediaries, especially those derived from the suppliers themselves, such as the Web-based agencies and offline agencies who have developed their online provision. These last operators, however, will need to incorporate added value into their transactions with the objective of being successful in the distribution channel.

- The increased competitive rivalry among the different options will favour the consolidation of aggregator-type travel websites with comparative functions between suppliers of transport or travel agencies, in terms of prices, business hours or other criteria (e.g. www. skyscanner.net). This type of intermediary does not sell the services, but rather informs the end customers about the best purchase options and redirects them to the travel agencies or the airline companies in order to carry out their transactions.

The three conclusions identified lead to a decrease in the role of the traditional retail travel agencies. Travel agencies as the major intermediaries in tourism are faced with a significant challenge. It has been assumed that a profound dis-intermediation is taking place as a consequence of the increasing power of the Internet among the diverse suppliers and the also increasing utilization of online purchasing on the part of the tourists (Dolnicar and Laesser, 2007). Both tendencies lead to a reduced use of the services of the traditional travel agencies in certain products or services. In the face of this threat, two strategic options linked to two generic types of products are emerging. On the one side, in the simple services or products or commodities such as flights between usual places or accommodation, the relevance of the travel agencies in traditional sales will continue to decrease, but they can have opportunities as online intermediaries, either as aggregators of tourist service options, or as sellers, albeit with a high level of dependency on the GDS and suppliers. On the other side, in complex products, such as package tours, specialized trips, business trips or large events, their role will continue being active. Bieger and Laesser (2004) consider that traditional travel agencies will continue to be competitive for the following types of trips: (i) medium- to long-distance trips to destinations in which the travellers cannot draw on previous experience; (ii) medium- to long-duration trips; (iii) complex (sightseeing) and international commodity type of trips (city trips and beach holidays); (iv) trips using commercialized types of accommodation; and (v) trips with a relatively short planning horizon. In short, in the face of dis-intermediation tourism, traditional retail travel agencies need to be present in two opposing strategic options. One of these is to set themselves up as agencies through the Internet with low prices. The other is to incorporate added value to the relationship with the customer and improve the process of service providing, in such a way that the customer obtains more value in the interchange with the agency and is satisfied.

The strategy of specialization is shaping up as being necessary for the traditional and virtual agencies. This specialization works at identifying gaps or places in the market that are not being attended to or which are partially without a complete range of services where advising plays a critical role in the delivery of value and tourist satisfaction. This strategy will allow for a differentiation between agencies along the road of specializing well in certain types of products (such as sports, cultural, training or exclusive), or particular geographical zones, or in types of customers (groups, companies). The majority of travel agencies have not followed a strategy of product specialization, except for some that devote their efforts to business trips, such as Carlson Wagonlit Travel, and some exceptions by product type, such as the tour operator Catai[1] or Made for Spain[2].

The second strategic option for travel agencies is integration. To the degree that the power in the channel is becoming more and more displaced towards the first links of the channel, such as the suppliers, it is necessary to have a certain level of backwards integration. The options are diverse and run from participating in the share capital to joint ventures and long-term collaboration agreements. Not only is the vertical integration increasingly prominent, but also the horizontal. Both lead to the creation of large diversified tourism groups.

In addition to the strategic options of innovation adoption, specialization and integration, management of travel agencies needs to incorporate other elements that favour the satisfaction of the tourist with the services provided by an agency (Millán and Esteban, 2004). The diverse studies on criteria for selection of traditional travel agencies indicate that the most relevant factors in selecting an agency are certain attributes of the service (personnel courtesy, seriousness, credibility and understanding of needs), the price (price–quality relation and price) and WOM communication (Bigné et al., 1995a, b). Heung and Chu (2000) identified six factors that underlie selection of a travel agency in Hong Kong: (i) quality of the interaction; (ii) formal communication; (iii) convenience; (iv) price; (v) characteristics of the products; and (vi) image of the travel agency. Rodríguez del Bosque et al. (2005) identified the most relevant attributes as: (i) functional quality; (ii) the economic dimension; (iii) communication and image; and (iv) service. The variables that are best segmented are: age, family income and marital status (socio-demographic variables) as well as travel frequency and tourist product typology (behavioural variables). Among the principal finds, we should mention that the segment of individuals most advanced in age give greater importance to service and functional quality in their selection of an agency. Additionally, it can be clearly seen that the segment of users with greater purchasing power are the ones that, given their lesser sensitivity to price, attach greater relevance to the service, functional quality and the communication and image of the travel agency as compared with the group with lower incomes. In respect of the behavioural variables, the segments of users that travel more frequently during the year and/or acquire tour packages assign greater importance to the communication and image factor in the selection of a travel agency. This could be due to the greater level of involvement of the individual in the first case, and to the greater level of complexity that the contracting of this type of combined product represents in the second. This motivates the user to look for some solid evidence of the confidence and reliability that the travel agency can offer him/her, the prestige of the travel agency and the recommendations of other customers. The findings of this research reveal the importance of the segmentation of customers in the marketing of tourism services.

Among the various relevant attributes, it is possible to identify two trends that clearly discriminate: the price and quality. Agencies should select as the basis of their positioning strategy the most relevant one, which fulfils two requisites. First, it should be in line with its strategic vision. Secondly, the chosen attribute must be perceived by tourists to be different from competing agencies. Overall positioning based on low prices does not generally incorporate variety and quality of services. Conversely, offering multiple services and high quality does not mean low prices.

The studies reported also show the importance of communication. It is well known that companies may use multiple communication tools. It includes mass media and below the line (i.e. non-mass-communication activities), but also Internet tools (such as the presence at related websites and search engines) are essential. Therefore, an integrated marketing communication approach should be adopted leading to effective communication with customers, based on coordination of all the communication tools.

NOTES

[1] Catai Tours (www.catai.es) has three basic business lines: (i) General Catalogue: cultural trips to 80 countries; (ii) Secret Europe: trips to Europe with special emphasis on seeing Europe in a different way; (iii) Catalogue of Exotic Trips: sun and beach trips to more than 60 islands.

[2] Made for Spain (www.madeforspain.com) organizes exclusive personalized trips in cultural tourism, for foreigners and only in Spain.

REFERENCES

Amadeus (2010) Available at: http://www.amadeus.com/amadeus/amadeus.html (accessed 25 August 2010).

Bieger, T. and Laesser, C. (2004) Information sources for travel decisions: toward a source process model. *Journal of Travel Research* 42(4), 357–371.

Bigné, E. (2006) Las decisiones operacionales de distribución y promoción. In: Parra, E. and Calero, F. (eds) *Gestión y Dirección de Empresas Turísticas*. McGraw Hill, Madrid, Chapter 17.

Bigné, E., Camisón, C., Martínez, C., Miquel, M.J. and Belloch, A. (1995a) Las agencias de viajes: factores de calidad e implicaciones de marketing. In: *V Congreso Nacional de Economía. Economía del Turismo*, vol. 6. December, Economía del Turismo, Las Palmas de Gran Canaria, pp. 189–210.

Bigné, E., Martínez, C., Miquel, M.J. and Belloch, A. (1995b) Perceived quality of the services of travel agencies. In: *Proceedings of 24th Annual Conference of the European Marketing Academy*. European Marketing Academy. May, Paris, pp. 1435–1442.

Bigné, E., Andreu, L., Küster, I. and Blesa, A. (2005) Market orientation and quality: travel agencies' perceived effects. *Annals of Tourism Research* 32(4), 1022–1038.

Bigné, E., Aldás, J. and Andreu, L. (2008) B2B services: IT adoption in travel agency supply chains. *Journal of Services Marketing* 22(6), 454–464.

Bitner, M.J., Brown, S.A. and Meuter, M.L. (2000) Technology infusion in service encounters. *Journal of Academy of Marketing Science* 28(1), 138–149.

Buhalis, D. and Law, R. (2008) Progress in information technology and tourism management: 20 years on and 10 years after the internet – the state of eTourism research. *Tourism Management* 29(4), 609–623.

Buhalis, D. and Licata, M.C. (2002) The future eTourism intermediaries. *Tourism Management* 23, 207–220.

Buhalis, D. and Ujma, D. (2006) Intermediaries: travel agencies and tour operators. In: Buhalis, D. and Costa, C. (eds) *Tourism Business Frontiers. Consumers, Products and Industry*. Elsevier Butterworth-Heinemann, Oxford, pp. 171–180.

Dolnicar, S. and Laesser, C. (2007) Travel agency marketing strategy: insights from Switzerland. *Journal of Travel Research* 46, 133–146.

e-Business W@tch (2006) *ICT and e-Business in the Tourism Industry. ICT Adoption and e-Business Activity in 2006*. European Commission, Enterprise and Industry, ICT Sector Report No. 8/2006. Available at: http://www.ebusiness-watch.org (accessed 25 August 2010).

Heung, V. and Chu, R. (2000) Important factors affecting Hong Kong consumers' choice of a travel agency for all-inclusive package tours. *Journal of Travel Research* 39, 52–59.

Marcussen, C.H. (2009) *Trends in European Internet Distribution of Travel and Tourism Services*. Centre for Regional and Tourism Research. Available at: http://www.crt.dk/uk/staff/chm/trends.htm (accessed 25 August 2010).

Millán, A. and Esteban, A. (2004) Development of a multiple-item scale for measuring customer satisfaction in travel agencies services. *Tourism Management* 25(5), 533–546.

Moutinho, L. (1987) Consumer behaviour in tourism. *European Journal of Marketing* 21(10), 5–44.

Rodríguez del Bosque, I., San Martín, H. and Collado, J. (2005) El proceso de elección de una agencia de viajes: análisis comparativo según las características sociodemográficas y comportamentales de los usuarios. *Cuadernos de Economía y Dirección de la Empresa* 24, 83–102.

Sabre (2010) Available at: http://en.eu.sabretravelnetwork.com/home/about/ (accessed 25 August 2010).

Travelport (2010) Available at: http://www.travelport.com/about/history.aspx (accessed 25 August 2010).

William, E. (2010) ProKsumer. Available at: http://www.eduwilliam.com/?cat=31 (accessed 24 August 2010).

chapter 8

Human Empowerment, Management and Tourism

Jithendran Kokkranikal, Jonathan Wilson
and Paul Cronje

The importance of human resources in a service industry like tourism cannot be overemphasized (Riley *et al.*, 2002; Airey and Tribe, 2005; Fáilte Ireland, 2005; Bolton and Houlihan, 2007). Baum (2002) identifies three major elements of the close association between tourism and people: (i) people as tourists and customers; (ii) people as providers and deliverers of services and facilities; and (iii) people as part of the tourism product and experience including fellow tourists. Right from the conception of a tourism destination, its consequent planning, development, and finally at the cutting edge as the front-line staff people breathe life into this industry. As Fáilte Ireland (2005: 3) rightly observes, 'tourism must look to the people working in the industry to serve as a principal source of competitive advantage'. The uniqueness of skills, know-how and behaviours of its human resource will go a long way in distinguishing the tourism product of a community from its competitors. These attributes of personnel can also be a major source of quality of the tourism product and services, enhancing competitiveness and profit potential of tourism destinations and businesses.

To sum up the obvious, human resource functions are one of the most important components of a service industry such as tourism and a key source of its competitiveness. As Schlesinger and Heskett (1991: 72) argue, capable workers who are well trained, motivated and fairly compensated provide better service, require less supervision and are more likely to remain on the job. Such a workforce can contribute significantly to the long-term competitiveness of tourism businesses, especially for the small and medium enterprises that constitute the bulk of service providers in most tourism destinations. And capable and high performance employees, who contribute to efficiency and productivity and quality, are created in empowered organizations (Hammuda and Dulaimi, 1997).

The aim of this chapter is to analyse the strategic role of employee empowerment in enhancing quality and competitiveness within the tourism industry. Starting with a discussion that reviews some current definitions of empowerment, it intends to arrive at a practical understanding of what empowerment means within the service industry and what this entails. The chapter will also explore supporting disciplines, in the interests of looking towards the future of empowerment and its potential to become a core strategic driving force.

EMPOWERMENT

Empowerment is a strategic approach which has been covered within the fields of generalist management, human resource management (HRM) and organization behaviour. As Smith (1997: 121) states:

> To empower is to give power, to open up, to release potential of people. In these terms it can be viewed as a commonsense activity. Typically, it embraces job involvement, job enrichment, participation in various forms, including suggestions schemes. Essentially the main thrust of empowerment is through having greater autonomy over 'how' jobs are done, carrying with it immense potential for improving productivity.

Empowerment has been variously described:

- 'The act of vesting substantial responsibility in the people nearest the problem' (Barbee and Bott, 1991).
- 'Pushing responsibility and decision-making down the organization to those employees closest to the customer' (Jones and Davies, 1991).
- 'The process of decentralizing decision-making in an organization, whereby managers give more discretion and autonomy to the front-line employees' (Brymer, 1991).
- 'Giving employees the authority to make everyday decisions is the most straightforward aspect of empowerment' (Sternberg, 1992).
- 'Giving employees the power to make decisions that influence organizational direction and performance' (Bowen and Lawler, 1992).
- 'Strategies that strengthen employees' self-efficacy or confidence in accomplishing the objectives of their tasks as set out by managers' (Ugboro and Obeng, 2000).
- 'A cognitive state, a psychologically empowered experience with power-sharing, competence and value internalisation in organisations' (Chang and Liu, 2008).

Thomas and Velthouse (1990) and Spreitzer (1995) describe four dimensions of empowerment: (i) meaningfulness; (ii) competence; (iii) self-determination; and (iv) impact.

- **Meaningfulness** relates to the perception of congruence between a task and the employee's values, attitudes and beliefs. Such task meaningfulness is a major factor in determining job satisfaction.
- **Competence** is about self-efficacy and capability to perform a task successfully. Employees who are confident about their efficacy and competence are likely to perform their tasks well.
- **Self-determination** allows employees to choose the course of action in various task situations and is closely related to a sense of autonomy that they need to feel in organizations.
- **Impact** refers to the degree to which employees can influence events in an organization. In other words, impact is about the level of control an employee has over his or her working environment.

A sense of control is important in creating ownership and job satisfaction. These psychological components of empowerment are closely influenced by the social and structural aspects of the workplace, which include organizational structure, organizational support, access to strategic information, access to organizational resources and organizational culture.

Bowen and Lawler (1995) include personal control over job performance, awareness of business strategies and higher accountability for performance outcomes as the major facets of empowerment. Examining the role of empowerment in service recovery, Hocutt and Stone (1998) describe autonomy and training as two important components of employee empowerment. Autonomy is about allowing employees absolute freedom to do the job, so that, when exceptional incidents occur, they can take decisions without looking for guidance elsewhere. Training is an essential aspect of skills and competence development, without which autonomy will have no meaning. Probably one of the simplest ways of employee empowerment is giving them the choice in how to approach their work (Chua and Iyengar, 2006). The underlying idea in this approach is that choice gives employees a sense of personal control, which can enhance their intrinsic motivation towards their work, resulting in higher morale, creativity and innovation, better performance, greater organizational commitment and lower turnover (Chua and Iyengar, 2006). The rationale behind encouraging empowerment within business organizations can be summarized as attempts to:

- retain work interests;
- increase employee motivation;
- assist employee development;
- encourage fresh thinking;
- increase job satisfaction; and
- reduce labour turnover.

Given these benefits, empowerment could probably be a key strategy to overcome some of the innate human resource issues in tourism, which include: (i) its poor image as an employer; (ii) poor rewards, benefits and compensation; (iii) skills shortages; (iv) concerns about flexibility and innovation; and (v) recruitment, retention and high attrition rate (Baum and Kokkranikal, 2003). These are discussed later in the chapter.

Also, empowerment could be a useful tactic to bring out the best in the stars within organizations: the unsung heroes who manage to make their mark when dealing with customers. However, few are able to share this learning experience among all employees and bring these practices within the formal confines of customer policies. Some argue that their documentation could lose the essence of what actually happened, how it worked and why. The challenge therefore lies in finding a way to faithfully address such rich facets of working life and spread these pockets of tacit learning more widely. Empowerment attempts to provide a positive reinforcement of 'best practice' which encourages staff members to become more active stakeholders.

Points for consideration:

- Why does empowerment even warrant a separate mention – when in our private lives, we wouldn't even give it a second thought? We just do what we can to make our guests happy and we don't even get paid!
- Are we at risk of inheriting many of 'our' management procedures from other disciplines, almost like 'hand-me-downs' – which are ill-fitting, or even worn out?
- If we do make a concerted effort to empower staff: who, where, when, how and, most importantly, what are we letting them do?

EMPOWERING STAFF AND CUSTOMERS

Interestingly, when looking towards the discipline of consumer behaviour, the term *empowerment* is often replaced, or compounded, with the word *choice*. The suggestion is that *empowerment* carries with it the connotation that this choice is restricted by a management function. This being the case, such an overt use of the word may be counterproductive to customer relationship management (CRM) philosophies, which encourage consumers to consider themselves as being central to decisions. However, within the realms of employment, these connotations may serve towards offering necessary structural guidance.

As a cursory note:

> We must also acknowledge that this definition of empowerment hinges more on some notion of accountability than on any wider change in the processes of work and decision making which might be implied by a more active modelling of empowerment. Thus, workers are empowered only in the sense that they have a greater responsibility to act within a narrow sphere directly related to production, and then held to be accountable for their action or indeed their inaction.

(Collins, 1995)

When things go wrong

For failing or stagnant organizations, empowerment is often produced as a cost-effective panacea for the ills that they are currently suffering. However, as with any approach rooted in subjective ad hoc decisions, the propensity for discontentment and disagreements may conversely increase. Once empowerment is adopted as a strategic method there inevitably comes with it the call to justify actions in definable terms. While empowering employees to have more control over their duties may yield short-term benefits, the focus should nevertheless by on implementing such a philosophy over the long term. Within successful organizations, empowerment is a word which may in fact never be considered as employees are simply performing their tasks the best way that they know how. Therefore the overall objective of empowerment is to refine and optimize existing strategic decisions for competitive gains.

Barriers to implementation:

- organizational and consumer cultures;
- skill bases;
- management styles;
- hierarchy and management structures;
- information technology (IT) infrastructures;
- health and safety concerns;
- legislation; and
- experience.

(Continued)

Potential problems resulting from empowering staff:

- lack of willingness to participate;
- self-imposed customer distances;
- turf and ego battles;
- fear or suspicion;
- departure from a standardized and streamlined strategic approach;
- applicability in too few areas to warrant time spent;
- potential to favour some staff over others, leading to discontentment;
- over-customization;
- overemphasis on empowerment, leading to distraction from core duties;
- a mask for lazy management and lax procedures;
- lack of significance in increasing motivation and interest within employees;
- too much control taken away from management; and
- too time consuming.

As organizations have created departments such as finance, human resources and marketing, their individual focuses will inevitably interpret empowerment in different ways – taking into account their immediate and respective accountabilities. Cross-functional management styles, which look to integrate responsibilities, act as agents for addressing these issues. The following of processes takes time and has to be robust enough to overcome any preconceptions that upper management may have, even if well founded.

Class discussion: How would you handle the following objections to empowerment?

- 'It's just an excuse for people to chat.'
- 'It's a waste of time.'
- 'Our staff can't be trusted.'
- 'They don't have what it takes.'
- 'We're encouraging people to do what they want, rather than do what we want.'
- 'Staff just use it to make themselves look good.'

The recent exodus and almost prodigal-son-like return of many call centres to their native countries are testament to the fact that purely financial and resource-based calculations may be short sighted in attempting to increase customer satisfaction. These experiences have encouraged organizations, whether they have stood firm or made an about turn, to focus more of their attention on the softer skills of communication.

(re-)Humanizing services

Within the hospitality and leisure industry, the intangibility of services has been argued as being problematic when looking to ensure consistent excellence. This could be down to an overly mechanistic approach, which is often prescribed when organizations attempt to scale up and control their operations. As hospitality, leisure and tourism are relatively new disciplines (as regards their branding as separate business subjects) the literature at times appears to have been grafted, or at best inspired, by more tangible product management approaches. This is not to say that this approach doesn't produce praiseworthy results. However, there is a risk that an over-reliance on process and procedure may result in neglecting the naturally occurring and potent attributes within the industry.

In short, hospitality, leisure and tourism aim to enact a basic facet of human nature; and their intrinsic value is enjoyed by both staff and customers alike. In addition, they are experience driven, highly emotive and have the power to beguile all in their path. Therefore, the call to implement policies that empower staff is seen as an essential activity which seeks to address not only the efficacy of an organization's corporate strategy but also, more importantly, a deficiency in employees' job satisfaction.

A resulting philosophy from this approach has suggested that employees should be viewed as an organization's **internal customers**. While employees have been viewed as a company's most-valued (not to mention volatile) resource, the contributions of all employees, regardless of position, are now revered as being notable in actively providing significant and informed judgements. The standardization and mechanization of services have necessitated the formalization of every decision. With this being the case, empowerment has sought to ensure that a fan of opinions remains, in order to counteract the risks associated with an over-convergence of decision making. By and large, empowerment exists to promote understanding, in an almost yin-and-yang-like manner, across all facets of the value chain.

A philosophy rooted in empowerment would be of assistance when addressing the relationship between services and products. As services and products extend their offerings, their very nature and terms of engagement are in turn being redefined. Rather than being seen as separate disciplines, each is progressing towards a more convergent, symbiotic state. This carries with it added pressures on employees and management procedures to in turn deliver on increasingly more complicated activities. In addition, the usage of hospitality, leisure and tourism often plays a pivotal role in affording other industries attractive 'sweeteners', rewards, incentives and differentiators, for both consumers and employees. After all, how else can a manager or marketer make the mundane or insignificant seem less so when attempting to attract the masses? As remits expand, so does the appetite for creating bespoke solutions to all of the challenges faced, and some would argue the call to share the burden across several broad shoulders.

Methods of engagement

If empowerment is to be used as an approach that optimizes the differentiating factors in service offerings, the key questions which still remain are, where and how? This has posed challenges when attempting to coordinate coherent management practices which look to implement more innovative approaches:

> most studies on the connection between leadership and individual innovation have explored the role of theory-based leadership styles, originally developed for other purposes such as the assessment of leaders' impact on performance or effectiveness rather than innovation-related outcomes. They did not attempt to develop models aimed specifically at finding out how leader behaviour could stimulate the innovative behaviour of employees.

> (de Jong and Hartog, 2007)

With regard to decision making there are various methods of engagement: (i) a staff-centric approach with either decentralized or centralized decision making (Fig. 8.1a); (ii) a customer-centric approach with either decentralized/centralized or centralized/decentralized decision making (Fig. 8.1b); and (iii) an holistic customer/staff-centric approach involving integrated decision making (Fig. 8.1c).

(a) **Staff-centric approach**

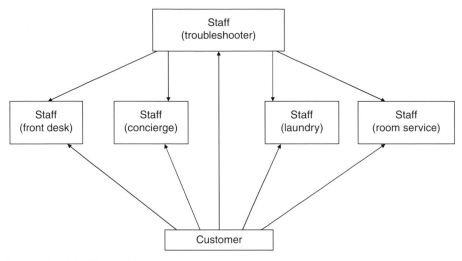

Decentralized decision making

All employees attempt to engage with customers, when appropriate, and are empowered to make decisions. Objection handling and problem solving are centralized and remain largely under the control of management.

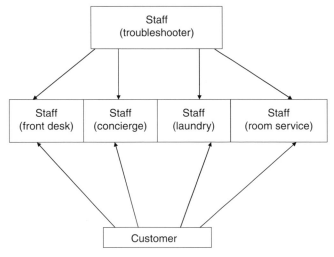

Centralized decision making

All employees attempt to engage with customers, when appropriate, and are empowered to make decisions. They work closely with their colleagues, sharing information and duties. Objection handling and problem solving are largely distributed among subordinates.

Fig. 8.1. Methods of engagement with regard to decision making.

(b) **Customer-centric approach**

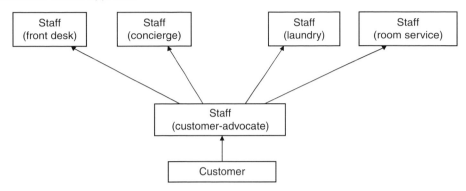

Decentralized/centralized decision making

A key accounts approach is taken here, where the customer is shepherded by a member of staff, allocated to see to most of their needs. This method is largely used when dealing with major customers, or those with specific objections or problems. The benefit to staff is that it shields them from any difficulties of queries, which may overburden them or risk affecting the level of output on their core duties.

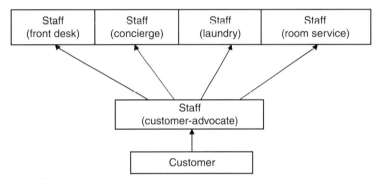

Centralized/decentralized decision making

Following the same rationale from the example above, queries and objections are more similar in their nature across functions. In addition the sharing of knowledge and decision making is present to a higher degree.

(c) **Holistic customer/staff-centric approach**

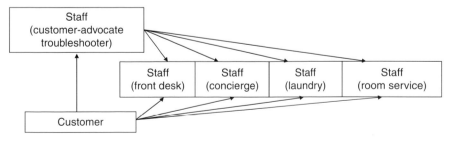

Integrated decision making

This is the highest quality level of interaction for both the employee and the customer. Knowledge and responsibility are shared equally among staff. In addition the customer feels confident that any member of staff can attend to his/her every need.

Fig. 8.1. Continued.

Clearly the holistic customer/staff-centric approach involving integrated decision making is the best option. However, it is perhaps unrealistic and chaotic to assume that everyone can be empowered to the same degree; so following the decision to move to a holistic customer/staff-centric approach to decision making, empowering staff, a screening process is necessary.

Screening approach:

- Where are we lacking?
- Where would it have the most impact?
- Are we in a position to formalize and document these activities (e.g. IT contact management systems, team meetings)?
- Are our staff willing to take part?
- Do our staff have sufficient training and support?
- Do we recognize and reward staff and team achievements; if so, how?
- How much will all of this cost, or save?
- Are we ready to take the plunge?

Strategic planning:

- Isolate empowerment activities to specific areas of service.
- Define the scope for innovation and entrepreneurship.
- Monitor, feedback and review.

Mini case study: 'Firefighting'

The fire service offers an interesting source of reference, which goes beyond the often glibly used business term 'firefighting' – which in fact only paints a partial picture. Staff undergo rigorous training, which equips them with an ability to adopt a fluid approach to a variety of tasks. Firefighters are encouraged to tackle both problems and tasks, based on their proximity to a given situation. Once they are called into action, there is a culture of doing what needs to be done, as soon as possible. This requires:

- thorough preparation beforehand;
- high levels of trust;
- little consultation between staff during a task;
- swift decision making;
- conformity in risk taking;
- Plan 'A' and at least a Plan 'B';
- a style of management which deals with the fundamental during a situation;
- management to focus on the bigger picture during a situation and reflect upon the detail afterwards;
- documented post-preparation; and
- comprehensive debriefing.

Of course, hospitality, leisure and tourism roles do not exact such high levels of risk or intensity, but many have seen their stress levels rise when large numbers of customers suddenly engulf them. The essence of this example is in encouraging the:

(Continued)

- pursuit of calculated evolutionary processes;
- galvanization of staff through their activities;
- suggestion that to optimize performance clear instructions should be given away from the site where the task is to be conducted;
- reduction of stress, confusion and risk during tasks;
- mindset that customers pose little threat to staff; rather, they are the *raison d'être*;
- understanding that customers are a necessary, yet sometimes unpredictable, component to the successful completion of a task; and
- desire to achieve through empowerment, rather than simply historical procedure.

In order to manage people, it is essential to consider their psychological dimensions. We found that providing employees with an empowering experience in conjunction with their training, significantly improved the outcomes of that training, as well as increasing their motivation and satisfaction.

(Kappelman and Richards, 1996)

IDENTIFYING THE KEY CUSTOMERS

'how to communicate with those customers to be clear of their needs and expectations ...' and how to make sure employees 'will meet those needs'.

(Pastor, 1996)

As a comparator, key account management within the field of media may serve towards offering a fresh approach. As with leisure, hospitality and tourism, their dealings are largely concerned with the sale of intangibles. With such large amounts of money changing hands, for highly substitutable and perishable packages, aggressive marketing and price elasticity have always played a vital part. Behind this are account handlers, who are often thrown in at the deep end, but who are encouraged to find creative ways to delight the customer using their own initiatives. Account handlers spend a considerable amount of their time trend spotting and recording details about a customer's habits, likes and dislikes. The rationale is that these pieces of information can be used:

- when crafting effective communication;
- to speculate on future business;
- to avoid potential customer discontentment; and
- to document tacit information which may also be of use to others.

The key to documenting all of this lies in having a contact management system which has the facility to hold this added information in a format that is readily accessible to many. Account managers are trained in the art of unobtrusive open-ended questioning. The questions appear as part of natural conversation and the collection of resulting information is undertaken in a casual manner. Account managers have often recorded anecdotal snippets of information and trivia such as 'doesn't drink alcohol', 'likes going to the opera', 'nut allergy', 'has come down with the flu'. These pieces of information are then used as icebreakers, possible topics of communication or even opportunities to offer additional desirable commercial services. The worthiness of this pursuit hinges on the following:

- an understanding that this information plays a necessary part in optimizing services;
- a culture existing among staff that encourages, celebrates and rewards such practices;

- a willingness of staff to think laterally;
- a desire to delight the customer;
- a fear of misunderstanding customers; and
- a commitment towards looking to convert this information into a commercial gain.

Managing customer expectations

The hospitality, leisure and tourism sectors face an interesting puzzle when addressing aspects surrounding culture. On the one hand, environmental factors steeped in culture are the life-blood of many service offerings to customers. But, on the other, cultures often need to be packaged and restricted in such ways that they conform to neutral universal ideals of optimal service. For example, once a precedent has been set for a consumer (or for that matter an employee) to experience a certain level of service, there exists a pull to make this the norm – or face potential future problems. The global marketplace ensures that employees and customers are becoming more savvy and discerning; which brings with it increased expectations. In addition, staff are faced with consumers who bring with them their own cultural norms and expectations, which they may feel no desire to let go of. After all, the world has been informed of the fact that the customer is there to be served!

Harris (2004) states that:

> It is critical to understand the importance of synergy when working or managing within multinational organizations, their subsidiaries, divisions, and teams. Within such a context, global leaders who promote cultural synergy influence social change in human behaviour and improve system effectiveness.

Language plays a pivotal role in addressing how well people respond to sociocultural environments, as well how they can adapt. Staff should be empowered to use their multilingual skills to build rapport wherever possible. These service industries must attempt to blend their own globally adapted unitarianist values with the wider environment's, without ignoring significant and desirable host cultural factors.

The challenge therefore lies in staff being able to effortlessly manage expectations to a mutually agreeable conclusion – at the earliest opportunity. Many enquiries may in fact be perceived by consumers as being hygiene factors and potentially the root cause of a catalogue of resulting and seemingly unconnected dissatisfaction if ignored. Grumpy consumers have often been dismissed as unnecessarily needy individuals. The majority of customers would argue conversely, that this has been the result of not enough of their rather simple and basic needs being considered soon enough.

There are amusing tales of customers switching to their mother tongue, when playfully looking to try their hand for those added benefits. For example, cultures which seek to engage in barter-based relationships may do so equally upon an initiation from either staff or customers. Staff should be encouraged to entertain these interactions, if at all possible, as they may serve as an opportunity to delight, or at worst avoid future complaints. Sales theory would argue that these touch points suggest potential buying signals, if understood correctly and acted upon.

Following Thwaites's (1999) review of consumer differences, in connection with sports tourism – ranging from culture to languages, attitudes, preferences and behavioural norms – he suggests that 'it is incumbent on management to check for variations that may contribute to friction. Emphasis can then be given to encouraging some segments and discouraging others.' Therefore as a starting point, tools available should also allow for empowerment in these situations, by adding leverage. They can be agreed beforehand by staff consensus and held back – to be applied where deemed appropriate.

Examples of vehicles and tools for empowerment:

- small free gifts;
- tokens of appreciation;
- upgrades;
- discounts;
- compensation (financial, tangible and intangible);
- flexibility in service offering (e.g. extended hours for breakfast in Ramadan for Muslims); and
- freedom to use multilingual approaches; with no suspicion.

Staff should be encouraged to use these to:

- protect prices and money already taken;
- actively win the 'lion's share' of business;
- reward or encourage customer loyalty, leading to an increase in the:
  - recency, frequency or monetary value of an individual;
  - number of recommendations and referrals made;
- speed up customer decision making;
- humanize a service offering; and
- buy customer trust and compliance.

In CRM and key account management an 80/20 rule has been stated as quantifying many interactions with customers. The thinking is that 80% of problems, complaints and enquiries will arise when dealing with 20% of customers. If addressed, these challenges can be converted to encourage the marshalling of customers up the loyalty pyramid. This may result in customers assuming the role of willing ambassadors. The reciprocal benefit of this successful execution may also lead to increased employee motivation and job satisfaction.

HUMAN EMPOWERMENT AND MANAGEMENT IN TOURISM

Having considered key aspects of empowerment as a management practice, we will now turn our attention to its implications for management of tourism. As discussed earlier, characteristics of tourism as a service industry do have implications for the practice of empowerment. As tourism is an amalgam of subsectors such as transport, accommodation, attractions, services and tourism facilitation and each of these, in turn, consists of a number of different groups, virtually all the challenges faced by the sector are a consequence of its structure. For example, the accommodation subsector includes organizations that operate five-star and luxury accommodation, budget hotels, motels, bed-and-breakfast (B&B) units and owner-operated home stays. In addition to this diversity within each subsector, tourism organizations vary according to size (ranging in size from major multinationals to micro, one-person businesses), ownership (public, private, joint venture), location (rural, urban), scale (craft, small and medium, and large) and scope (local, national, international).

Tourism organizations belong within the service sector of the economy (Baum and Kokkranikal, 2003). They are, therefore, very different in the way that they operate and how they are organized from organizations which focus on the processing and production of manufactured goods. There are particular features of service organizations and the services that they provide for their customers which differentiate them from the manufacturing sector. These features establish the parameters within which people can work and are managed in tourism. The characteristics of tourism service operations include the following features.

Intangibility

Most services are intangible in that customers do not receive something physical or tangible in return for their money. Customers purchase experiences and the evaluation of these experiences may include strong subjective elements along with aspects that can be judged objectively. Punctuality of an airline's service can, generally, be measured objectively while the quality of the service offered on board is much more subjective. The human contribution to the delivery of both tangible and intangible aspects of tourism services is core to customer satisfaction and competitiveness.

Perishability

The sales opportunity of an unsold service is lost forever. An unsold airline seat or an empty hotel room is lost revenue and an opportunity that can never be recouped. In other words, services cannot be stored the way that many non-perishable manufactured goods can be held in a warehouse until trading conditions become more favourable. This reality has a major impact on how service organizations, especially those in the tourism sector, organize themselves, particularly with respect to sales and marketing. This feature induces a constant level of stress into tourism operations and this impacts upon employees in that they are constantly required to respond to short-term sales requirements. The operation of effective yield management systems by, for example, the low-cost airlines can reduce this pressure on the individual to a considerable extent.

Tourism services are time and place dependent

Tourism services are frequently prepared/produced, served and consumed almost simultaneously, frequently within sight and with the participation of the customer in a way that is infrequent in manufacturing. The human contribution within this process is critical. Many tourism services must be offered to the customer where they require its delivery and production cannot take place remotely or in a centralized location. Hotels must be located where people want to stay and not where it suits the hotel company to locate its operations. Place dependency impacts on the recruitment and welfare of tourism employees in that frequently they are recruited within the local host community of the tourism operation. This local dimension has implications for skills and training within the workforce and, in some cases, the ability of tourism organizations to deliver some of its services.

Simultaneity and customer involvement in service production

While manufactured goods are produced before they are sold and consumed, services are sold first and then produced and consumed simultaneously (Kandampully, 1997). Simultaneous production and consumption inevitably involve the customer in aspects of the production process, overtly in the case of self-service facilities or restaurants. Fellow customers are also part of the atmosphere or ambience that we buy into when we go to a restaurant or attend a cultural or musical event.

Tourism services cannot be quality controlled at the factory gate

Tourism services are difficult to standardize because they generally require a high level of human intervention for their delivery and are, thus, subject to variability because of the human element. As a result, you cannot return or substitute a service which has been unsatisfactory in the way that you can seek to exchange a faulty good such as an umbrella or personal stereo. Once your experience of a service is concluded, the provider can seek to compensate you for a bad experience but cannot replace the experience.

The human element in tourism service delivery

Human behaviour, whether staff or customer, is unpredictable although good management and effective training should minimize this unpredictability among employees in good organizations. Human interaction at the point of production and service inevitably produces an element of uncertainty that is not faced on the factory floor in manufacturing or, at worst, can be eliminated through effective quality control.

These characteristics of services in general apply within the tourism sector in particular and contribute to the manner in which tourism organizations are structured and operate. They influence the operational culture of organizations and also how they market their services, how their finances are structured and, in particular, the management of people within organizations.

Skills issue in tourism

Baum (2002) has explored the nature of skills in tourism and concluded that the nature and relative level of skills in the sector are determined by the social, economic, political and technological context within which they operate. To talk of tourism as a low skills sector has some validity in the developed world but is meaningless in many developing countries. Likewise, to talk about absolute skills shortages in tourism is something which has relevance in the developed world. In most developing countries, there is no absolute shortage of labour but the skills base that exists in the economy may not be tuned to effective tourism work. In developed countries, skills shortages exist as a result of image problems that the sector may have, as a consequence of demand factors such as seasonality and as a result of changes within the technical focus in education and training programmes within the college system.

Recruitment, retention and turnover

The mobility of staff within tourism is a direct factor of the wider environment, structural and sector-operating characteristics that we have addressed above. Sectors of tourism in some, particularly developed, countries face ongoing challenges to recruit appropriate staff to key positions in the industry, skilled and unskilled. They also face challenges with respect to retaining these staff once they are recruited and reducing what can be very high rates of labour turnover. The impact of variable demand (seasonality), issues of remuneration (see below), unsociable working conditions and generally negative perceptions of the sector for employment contribute to problems faced in this regard. Tourism is also an industry that is seen to be highly reactive to short-term local and international events in terms of its willingness to retrench staff in order to meet short-term financial requirements. The impact on travel and transport sectors in the immediate aftermath of events on 11 September 2001 is a major case in point. Within this environment, potential employees may not wish to risk their long-term security in an employment environment that is perceived to be unstable.

At the same time, the small business environment within tourism means that the recruitment process may not always be conducted in such a way as to ensure the selection of the best and most suitable employees for the job. Limited credence is given to the outcomes of formal education and training while opportunities for workplace development are limited. As a consequence, the recruitment technique of internal promotion is not as widely used in tourism as it could be.

Rewards, benefits and compensation

The popular perception of the tourism industry in many developed countries is that of relatively poor pay (Wood, 1997; Baum, 2006). This is a reflection of a number of factors:

- perceptions of tourism work as synonymous with the large but not necessarily typical hotel and catering subsector;
- the low skills environment of many jobs within tourism;
- limited workplace organization in some tourism businesses although this is not true of, for example, the traditional airline sector;
- seasonal and part-time work;
- the grey or 'tipping' economy within many tourism operations, undermining core remuneration;
- trends to deskill work in tourism through technology substitution; and
- accessible employment for the majority of the population through seasonal and other temporary work.

At the same time, tourism can offer highly remunerated and high-status employment within, for example, airlines. In the developing world, tourism employment may be highly prized and its remuneration, relative to local conditions, competitive with other opportunities in the economy. The experience of newly industrialized states such as Malaysia, Singapore and Taiwan, however, is that, as the economy develops, the attractiveness and competitiveness of remuneration in tourism declines, presenting a real challenge to the sector in meeting its employment needs.

These characteristics of tourism as an industry and employer have major implications to introducing empowerment in the sector.

EMPOWERMENT IN THE TOURISM INDUSTRY

Given the human dimensions of service (Baum, 2006), the competence of the human resource is an important variable in determining not only service quality but the quality of overall visitor experience. Quality management in tourism is about ensuring that tourism businesses can offer distinctive, authentic and higher value holiday experiences (Baum and Kokkranikal, 2003). Quality is also dependent upon value added through a range of human skills during the service encounter, recognition of which has resulted in the adoption of concepts such as managing 'moments of truth' (Carlzon, 1987; Sharpley, 2005) and developing the 'spirit of service' (Albrecht, 1992) by the tourism industry. Carlzon describes a 'moment of truth' as the point of contact between the customer and employee of the company, and these are the critical occasions which determine a customer's satisfaction in a service encounter. Although relatively minor and transient occurrences, 'moments of truth' are make-or-break occasions in service encounters in tourism (Baum, 2002). The visitor–employee encounter in tourism can be mapped with the help of Leiper's tourism system (1995). Leiper (1995) in his geographical system brings out the interaction between tourism demand (travellers in the generating regions) and tourism supply (tourism destinations), tracing the journey through the transit region. Baum (2002) uses this system to scale the intensity of the 'moments of truth' during each stage of the holiday process, starting with the traveller-generating regions and moving through the transit route towards the tourist destination regions and back (Fig. 8.2).

As Fig. 8.2 indicates, typical holiday travel entails a complex range of interactions between the tourist and service providers with varying levels of interaction. Managing this complicated range of interactions requires employees who can think on their feet and are innovative and flexible.

The 'spirit of service', according to Albrecht (1992: 154), is an 'attitude based on certain values and beliefs about people, life and work, that leads a person to willingly serve others and take pride in his or her work'. The spirit of service is about an employee going beyond the normal level of service and making efforts to understand customers and meet their emotional, psychological and physical needs that create the original demand for the service or product.

Buissink-Smith and McIntosh (2001) have identified five characteristics that are essential to demonstrate the 'spirit of service' by employees of tourism organizations. These are: (i) the individual spirit; (ii) the mindfulness spirit; (iii) the energy spirit; (iv) the communication spirit; and (v) the orientation spirit (Table. 8.1).

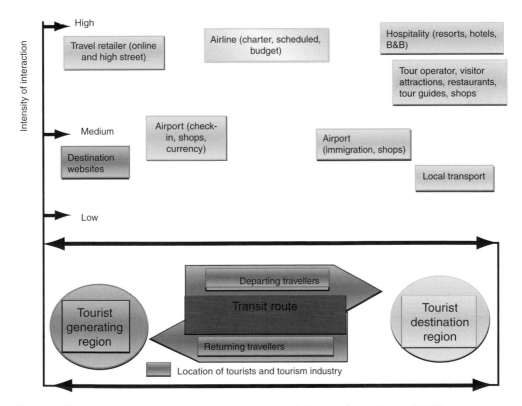

Fig. 8.2. The tourism experiences and encounters (adapted from Baum, 2002).

Table 8.1. The characteristics and skills for the 'spirit of service' (Source: Buissink-Smith and McIntosh, 2001: 83).

Characteristic	Skills
1. Individualism	Being yourself – being physically, emotionally and psychologically 'in' the service encounter. Being able to use your own style, talents and personality and remaining true to yourself Feeling good about yourself and others – positive basic feelings about self, work and other people (self-confidence, self-respect, friendly, interested in others, empathy, resilience, self-control and optimism)
2. Mindfulness	To be mindful – being alert and flexible Feeling empowered – as a state of mind – to be creative, take risks, express personal power, exercise initiative outside the conventional norm
3. Energy	Proactive and willing – motivated, innovative, organized, flexible and open to change – willing to give extra energy and continuously improve and learn Having fun – being a star with the customer is fun – motivated by the intrinsic rewards of the service role
4. Communication	Customer contact skills – active listening, problem solving, complaint handling and analysis of verbal intake Comfortable with all visitors – different cultural perspectives and values
5. Orientation	A customer service-orientation – a commitment to service quality – service-centred and commitment of energies to quality Knowing the big picture – being involved, feeling committed and an awareness of importance of role, job and product knowledge

The foundation of the 'spirit of service' and effective management of 'moments of truth' thus will be a sense of freedom and a range of skills and attitudes that result from and contribute to a belief on the part of the employees that they are empowered to manage customer experiences. Even if an organization is able to recruit skilled and competent employees, their ability to contribute to service quality will depend greatly upon the autonomy and choice available to them to deal with practical aspects of their job without having to look for directions from their superiors (Hocutt and Stone, 1998; Chua and Iyengar, 2006).

Empowering the employees to provide higher quality moments of truth by inculcating the spirit of service seems to be a major strategy towards achieving service quality in the tourism industry (see, for example, Fig. 8.3 adapted from a publication produced by Fáilte Ireland). As Berry (1995: 89) observes, 'Customers may not give extra credit to businesses for doing what they are supposed to do, rather they attach higher value to those that surprise with unusual caring, commitment, and resourcefulness during the service encounter.' Thus the skills and competencies of the employees could be a major variable in facilitating a higher quality customer experience in tourism. Given the variable nature of service experiences and consumer

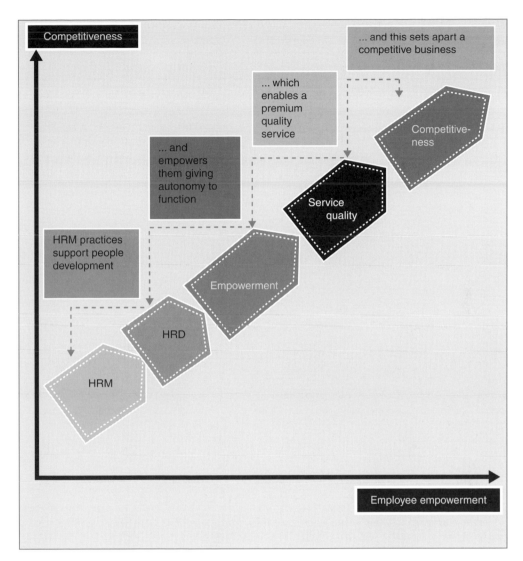

Fig. 8.3. Employee empowerment for competitiveness in tourism (adapted from Fáilte Ireland, 2005). HRD, human resource development; HRM, human resource management.

heterogeneity, it is highly unlikely that a uniform standard set of competencies will be sufficient to meet the ever-increasing needs of more discerning and demanding customers. Flexibility, ability to think and decide on one's feet, and innovation are thus the essential attributes required of employees in the tourism industry. The criteria of good perceived service quality identified by Gronroos (1988) further underline the important role of human empowerment in delivering service quality (Table 8.2). These criteria are: (i) professionalism and skills; (ii) attitudes and behaviour; (iii) access and flexibility; (iv) reliability and trustworthiness; (v) recovery; and (vi) reputation and credibility. These elements strictly belong to the human resource domain. And an empowered set of employees alone are likely to be able to meet these criteria.

Table 8.2. Criteria of good perceived service quality (Source: Gronroos, 1988 adapted by Johns, 1996: 15).

Number	Designation	Description
1	Professionalism and skills	Customers see the service provider as knowledgeable and able to solve their problems in a professional way
2	Attitudes and behaviour	Customers perceive a genuine, friendly concern for them and their problems
3	Access and flexibility	Customers feel that they have easy, timely access and that the service provider is prepared to adjust to their needs
4	Reliability and trustworthiness	Customers can trust the service provider to keep promises and act in their best interests
5	Recovery	Customers know that immediate corrective action will be taken if anything goes wrong
6	Reputation and credibility	Customers believe that the brand image stands for good performance and accepted values

The competitive tourism industry as a service sector largely depends on excellence of service and delivery of an intangible product. The nature of this industry and the satisfaction of customers depend critically on the human factor (Gabriel, 1988) and therefore the way in which tourism and hospitality employees are managed is of critical importance to the employer and customer alike. In this respect many employers have utilized employee empowerment, trusting it will improve responsiveness to customer needs and thereby become more efficient and effective (Rapp *et al.*, 2006).

Empowerment certainly influences the competitiveness of tourism organizations, in that it prepares a platform for better customer relations. Brymer (1991) believes that empowerment is a customer-driven leadership strategy that can separate organizations that really provide a personalized and high quality customer treatment from those who merely talk about providing quality service. Empowerment of employees is an important component of total quality management (TQM) (Sigler and Pearson, 2000). Advocates of TQM believe that, to achieve customer satisfaction, top management should be committed to creating an organizational climate that empowers employees and focuses their efforts on customer satisfaction (Ugboro and Obeng, 2000). These authors maintain that a positive relationship between leadership and commitment and employee empowerment (leading to job satisfaction) with customer satisfaction exist. They maintain that empowerment can hugely contribute to job satisfaction and that employees who do not enjoy the latter cannot provide the required high quality service for customers. In some respects one can refer to this as a circular relationship whereby the organization (top management) can apply empowerment as a means to achieve job satisfaction among front-line staff in order to improve customer satisfaction, which in turn will benefit the organization's objectives. For example, a hotel owner might empower the reception staff to allow tourists early access to their rooms even if the official check-in time is much later. With this responsibility, the staff members experience a sense of added value and their friendly demeanour together with the fact that they could add value to the guests' enjoyment could lead to an increase in guest satisfaction. This in turn could lead to repeat visitors, which will benefit the original objectives of the hotel owner.

Lashley (1996) lists a range of potential benefits to organizations which apply empowerment as a human resource strategy: empowered employees do better work, take responsibility for their own performance, produce more satisfied customers, greater profits and help produce a more competitive organization.

There are, of course, also limitations to empowerment, strengthening the belief that empowerment does not grant employees free reign. Empowerment does not allow for employees to alter prices, product specifications, decor of their workplaces (Eccles, 1993) and gives them virtually no say in the company targets and objectives. For example, an airline employee at check-in might be empowered to allow a customer free excess baggage, but will not be empowered to delay a flight if clients had difficulty in reaching the airport on time. A waiter in a restaurant might be empowered to offer regular customers a complimentary drink, but will not have the power to rearrange the furniture to suit these clients.

The success of the potential benefits of empowerment hinge also on managers' and supervisors' approach towards empowered employees. Employees at all levels should be trained in aspects such as teamwork, problem recognition and problem solving (Ugboro and Obeng, 2000) in order to make good decisions (Sternberg, 1992).

It is believed that empowerment recognizes employee feelings of personal effectiveness and worth (Lashley, 1996) and therefore enhances job satisfaction and overall relationships between employees, customers and managers (Littrell, 2007). Eccles (1993) warns that not all employees are naturally ready for empowerment – many cannot count or read and others may have challenges with honesty and integrity. Empowerment in this sense becomes a rather personal consideration, starting with the existing abilities, skills and attributes of the employee and assessing to what extent, in view of the organization's culture and vision, the employee should or could be empowered.

Most authors on the subject of empowerment agree that, in order to apply empowerment as a human resource strategy, a fundamental shift in managerial power and working practices, as well as attitudes of senior management, is required (Brymer, 1991; Sternberg, 1992; Eccles, 1993; Ugboro and Obeng, 2000; Baum, 2002). Empowerment as a human resource strategy will lead to a more flattened organizational chart than before (Brymer, 1991). As a natural consequence of empowering employees, managers are required to give up some extent of control, although not their accountability. Sternberg (1992), concerned about supervisors' and managers' resistance to empowerment, believes successful empowerment rests with a great relationship of trust between manager and employee.

An empowered group of employees, on the other hand, can also benefit many managers in terms of time saved, developing a better understanding of the customers' needs through feedback from the employee and mutual problem solving. Lashley (2001), one of the leading authors in the field of empowerment in the service industries, identified four forms of empowerment, the first three mainly directed towards front-line or operational personnel and the last one aimed at managers:

1. Empowerment through **participation** – this concerns giving employees some decision-making authority which previously rested with management, such as dealing with complaints, organizing work schedules or meeting unpredictable service requests without reference to managers.

2. Empowerment through **involvement** – this relates to managers gaining from the experiences and expertise of employees and involves techniques such as team briefings, consultation with staff and joint problem solving.

3. Empowerment through **commitment** – employees are encouraged to accept responsibility for the service encounter without necessarily having more authority.

4. Empowerment through **delayering** – here the organizational chart is flattened and layers of management are reduced.

The form of empowerment chosen by the organization will depend on the job at hand, the culture of the company as well as the cooperation of both management and employees. As a general rule, Lashley (1996) stresses that the more unpredictable the demands and needs of the customer (as often perceived in the service industry), the more likely that empowerment of staff will make a positive contribution to the organization. Eccles (1993: 18) states:

> Effective empowerment is thus delivered through a combination of power release and responsibility, with measurable performance criteria to gauge effects. Empowered employees need managerial support rather than being offered fine phrases and then being left to get on with it.

Empowerment should therefore always be applied with great skill and awareness of the management and not merely as a buzzword to keep staff satisfied or to gain competitive advantage.

Empowerment also requires the front-line staff to be equipped with the knowledge and abilities and human resource development (HRD) policies and programmes that provide employees with the skills, attitudes and competence to do their jobs independently (Hocutt and Stone, 1998; Baum, 2002; Baum and Kokkranikal, 2003). Further, empowerment can only happen where there is trust in the positive side of human nature, based on the belief that human beings are capable of being noble and well meaning (Mahesh, 1994). Needless to say, in service industries such as tourism, employee empowerment has been driven by consumer satisfaction, which allows staff to take a leadership role. It also has to be an ongoing process, which requires continuous investment in HRD to update employee skills and knowledge and also to develop a culture of continuous development and lifelong learning (Brymer, 1991; Kokkranikal, 2004).

CONCLUSION

In this chapter, an attempt has been made to examine the strategic role of employee empowerment in enhancing quality and competitiveness within the tourism industry. It started with an analysis of the basic concepts of empowerment and moved on to consider aspects of empowering staff and customers and its practical implications for service industries such as tourism.

The following are a summary of key factors, resulting from the consideration of empowerment as a strategic management function in tourism.

Advantages associated with empowerment

Empowerment:
- is a short- and long-term cost-effective approach;
- is an offensive and defensive technique resulting in:
  - retention of profit centres; and
  - increased profitability;
- optimizes strategy;
- is a long-term strategic differentiating factor;
- is an internal and external marketing tool to attract and retain staff;
- results in the humanization of the work environment;
- reduces gaps between employee and consumer; and
- assists in the movement towards exploring new approaches and markets.

Potential benefit to employees:

- more motivating;
- more interesting;
- a better way to work;
- increased flexibility;
- increased fulfilment;
- easier way to fulfil obligations;
- job enrichment;
- chance to develop new skills;
- opportunity to shape future activities;
- opportunity to demonstrate additional skills; and
- formal recognition of added value contributions.

Potential benefit to customers:

- better experience;
- added value;
- increased feeling of personal worth;
- requests addressed more promptly;
- requests addressed with more relevance; and
- increased personalization of services.

If empowerment is seen as being central to an organization looking to improve both an employee's and a customer's experiences, the challenge lies in coordinating and formalizing an approach which:

- encourages fluid decision making;
- decentralizes management responsibilities;
- relies more heavily on tacit knowledge;
- requires a wider skill set;
- allows for more than one solution to a situation;
- necessitates higher levels of trust among peers; and
- increases individual accountability.

To conclude, there is a strong argument in favour of introducing employee empowerment in the tourism industry, if it is to be consumer and quality driven. And adequately skilled, confident and well-supported and customer-driven employees are essential for the tourism industry in which the workforce has the autonomy to take a leadership role in delivering higher quality tourist experiences.

REFERENCES

Airey, D. and Tribe, J. (2005) *An International Handbook of Tourism Education*, Elsevier, London.

Albrecht, K. (1992) *The Only Thing that Matters*. Harper Business, New York.

Barbee, C. and Bott, V. (1991) Customer treatment as a mirror of employee treatment. *Advanced Management Journal* 5, 27.

Baum, T. (2002) Making or breaking the tourist experience: the role of human resource management. In: Ryan, C. (ed.) *The Tourist Experience*. International Thomson, London, pp. 94–111.

Baum, T. (2006) *Human Resource Management for the Hospitality, Tourism and Leisure Industries*. Thomson, London.

Baum, T. and Kokkranikal, J. (2003) Human resource development for competitiveness and sustainability: a case study of Indian tourism. In: Kushluvan, S. (ed.) *Managing Employee Attitudes and Behaviors in the Tourism and Hospitality Industry*. Nova Science Publishers, New York, pp. 805–832.

Berry, L. (1995) *On Great Service: a Framework for Action*. The Free Press, New York.

Bolton, S. and Houlihan, M. (2007) Beginning the search for the H in HRM. In: Bolton, S. and Houlihan, M. (eds) *Searching for Human in Human Resource Management: Theory, Practice and Workplace Contexts*. Palgrave, Basingstoke, UK, pp. 1–28.

Bowen, D.E. and Lawler, E.E. III (1992) The empowerment of service workers: what, why, how and when. *Sloan Management Review* 33(3), 31–39.

Bowen, D.E. and Lawler, E.E. (1995) Empowering service employees. *Sloan Management Review* 53, 9–16.

Brymer, R.A. (1991) Employee empowerment: a guest-driven leadership strategy. *The Cornell H.R.A. Quarterly* 32, 58–68.

Buissink-Smith, N. and McIntosh, A.J. (2001) Conceptualising the 'spirit of service' in tourism education and training. *Journal of Teaching in Travel and Tourism* 1(1), 79–96.

Carlzon, J. (1987) *Moments of Truth*. Ballinger, Cambridge, Massachusetts.

Chang, L.C. and Liu, C.H. (2008) Employee empowerment, innovative behaviour and job productivity of public health nurses: a cross-sectional questionnaire survey. *International Journal of Nursing Studies* 45(10), 1442–1448.

Chua, R.Y. and Iyengar, S.S. (2006) Empowerment through choice? A critical analysis of the effects of choice in organisations. *Research in Organisational Behaviour* 27, 41–79.

Collins, D. (1995) Rooting for empowerment? *Empowerment in Organizations* 3(2), 25–33.

de Jong, J.P.J. and Hartog, D.N.D. (2007) How leaders influence employees' innovative behaviour. *European Journal of Innovation Management* 10(1), 41–64.

Eccles, T. (1993) The deceptive allure of empowerment. *Long Range Planning* 26(6),13–21.

Fáilte Ireland (2005) *A Human Resource Development Strategy for Irish Tourism. Competing through People, 2005–2012*. Fáilte Ireland, Dublin.

Gabriel, Y. (1988) *Working Lives in Catering*. Routledge, London.

Gronroos, C. (1988) Service quality: the six criteria of good perceived service quality. *Review of Business* 9(3), 10–13.

Hammuda, I. and Dulaimi, M.F. (1997) The theory and application of empowerment in construction: a comparative study of the different approaches to empowerment in construction, service and manufacturing industries. *International Journal of Project Management* 15(5), 289–296.

Harris, P.R. (2004) European leadership in cultural synergy. *European Business Review* 16(4), 358–380.

Hocutt, M.A. and Stone, T.H. (1998) The impact of employee empowerment on the quality of a service recovery effort. *Journal of Quality Management* 3(1), 117–132.

Johns, N. (1996) The developing role of quality in the hospitality industry. In: Oslen, M.D., Teare, R. and Gummerson, E. (eds) *Service Quality in Hospitality Organisations*. Cassel, London, pp. 9–26.

Jones, P. and Davies, A. (1991) Empowerment: a study of general managers of four star hotel properties in the UK. *International Journal of Hospitality Management* 10(3), 211–217.

Kandampully, J. (1997) Quality management in retailing through a concept of 'service-product' design. *Total Quality Management Journal* 8(1), 41–53.

Kappelman, L.A. and Richards, T.C. (1996) Training, empowerment, and creating a culture for change. *Empowerment in Organizations* 4(3), 26–29.

Kokkranikal, J. (2004) Tourism human resource development and sustainability in developing countries. Paper presented at 'Tourism State of the Art – II' organized by the Scottish Hotel School, University of Strathclyde, Glasgow, 27–30 June.

Lashley, C. (1996) Research issues for employee empowerment in hospitality organisations. *International Journal of Hospitality Management* 15(4), 333–346.

Lashley, C. (2001) *Empowerment, HR Strategies for Service Excellence*. Butterworth-Heinemann, Oxford.

Leiper, N. (1995) *Tourism Management*. TAFE Publications, Collingwood, Melbourne, Australia.

Littrell, R.F. (2007) Influences on employee preferences for empowerment practices by the 'ideal manager' in China. *International Journal of Intercultural Relations* 31, 87–110.

Mahesh, V.S. (1994) *Thresholds of Motivation*. McGraw-Hill, New York.

Pastor, J. (1996) Empowerment: what it is and what it is not. *Empowerment in Organizations* 4(2), 5–7.

Rapp, A., Ahearne, M., Mathieu, J. and Schillewaert, N. (2006) The impact of knowledge and empowerment on working smart and working hard: the moderating role of experience. *International Journal of Research in Marketing* 23, 279–293.

Riley, M., Szivas, E. and Ladkin, A. (2002) *Tourism Employment: Analysis and Planning*. Channel View Publications, Clevedon, UK.

Schlesinger, L. and Heskett, J. (1991) The service-driven service company. *Harvard Business Review* 69(5), 71–81.

Sharpley, R. (2005) Accommodation sector: managing for quality. In: Pender, L. and Sharpley, R. (eds) *Tourism Management*. Sage, London, pp. 14–27.

Sigler, T.H. and Pearson, C.M. (2000) Creating an empowering culture: examining the relationship between organizational culture and perceptions of empowerment. *Journal of Quality Management* 5, 27–52.

Smith, B. (1997) Empowerment – the challenge is now. *Empowerment in Organizations* 5(3), 120–122.

Spreitzer, G.M. (1995) Psychological empowerment in the workplace: dimensions, measurement, and validation. *Academy of Management Journal* 38(11), 1442–1465.

Sternberg, L.E. (1992) Empowerment: trust vs. control. *The Cornell H.R.A. Quarterly* 33, 69–72.

Thomas, K.W. and Velthouse, B.A. (1990) Cognitive elements of empowerment: an interpretive model of intrinsic task motivation. *Academy of Management Review* 15, 666–681.

Thwaites, D. (1999) Closing the gaps: service quality in sport tourism. *Journal of Services Marketing* 13(6), 511.

Ugboro, I.O. and Obeng, K. (2000) Top management leadership, employee empowerment, job satisfaction, and customer satisfaction in TQM organizations: an empirical study. *Journal of Quality Management* 5, 247–272.

Wood, R. (1997) *Working in Hotels and Catering*. Routledge, London.

chapter 9

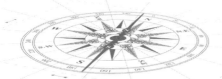

Operations Management in Tourism

Geoff Southern

WHAT IS OPERATIONS MANAGEMENT?

> Operations management is concerned with the design and control of transformation systems to deliver the services, including products, of an organization at the right quality, at the right price, and at the right time.

It should be noted that this definition takes a systems viewpoint of operations. It should also be noted that the 'right quality' is intangible, particularly in the case of tourism, although the price and times are tangibles which are specified at the time of booking a holiday or journey in this sector. Quality is determined by the expectations and perceived delivery level for each of a bundle of factors for each customer. It has been defined as: 'the totality of features and characteristics of a product or service that bear on its ability to satisfy stated or implied needs' (ISO 8042, 1989).

Specifying measurable parameters for artefacts is easier than specifying them for services. Artefacts have shape and size and can be seen and touched by customers, frequently before purchase. Services are more concerned with changes in the state of feelings of customers and as such are intangible to the highest degree. This is particularly so with tourism, where the expectations of customers will be positioned in terms of continuums such as tranquillity to excitement, known to unknown, programmed activities to freedom, simple to complex, and will cover the whole range of human feelings. (The three periods of highest stress in human life are said to be marriage, moving house and going on holiday.) Defining quality in service organizations is therefore no simple matter. This is particularly so in the case of tourism, where the product is bought unseen, except in the case of repeat purchases, and even here the ambience of a location or mode of transport can change year by year. Tourist locations can, in the world of mass communication, become popular overnight and with little development control builders can move almost as quickly. Video and TV can let you see a place, but travel consists of smells, noises, tastes and feelings which sight alone can only hint at. Each holiday or journey booked can be considered as an individual legally binding contract with a vaguely specified product (or 'promise' in legal terms). In fact complaints concerning quality are more likely to surface in the popular press or on broadcast consumer affairs programmes than in law courts, as changes in the state of a customer's happiness are much more difficult to argue. But press and TV items are transient, and even more damage occurs if reports are made on the Internet. These reports remain on public view and tend to be added to. When this happens the tourism company is given very little opportunity to respond, and even if it takes reasonable steps to address the problem its image is already irrevocably damaged.

Case study: Supershuttle New York (Blue Van)

On 1 June Geoff and Marie Southern had checked out of their hotel in New York and were waiting for their transport, a 'Supershuttle taxi', to Newark Airport. They had confirmed the airport transfer arrangements the evening before by phone. The 6-day holiday had been very good, wonderful continuous sunshine, sightseeing, a show Geoff had always wanted to see, and on Broadway, and shopping. But then things started to go downhill rapidly.

Briefly:

- The 'Supershuttle' didn't show.
- The only available transport, a 'black limo' not a 'yellow cab', would only take them for an inflated charge.
- Time was then very tight to make the flight, on fixed-flight no-refund tickets.

It appears that Supershuttle is a franchise company, and the company who hold the New York franchise are called Blue Van. On the Supershuttle website they introduce themselves as:

Welcome to SuperShuttle, the easiest and most cost-effective way to get to and from the airport from your home, office or hotel.

> We are the nation's leading shared-ride airport shuttle, providing door-to-door ground transportation to more than 8 million passengers per year. Our friendly drivers, comfortable vans and reasonable rates take the hassle out of getting to and from the airport in 19 major US cities!
>
> (Supershuttle, 2008)

Back in the UK, and unable to find a customer service point on the Web, the Southerns sent an e-mail to Supershuttle reservations, which was forwarded to Ivy Boatwright, the 'Quality Assurance Rep'. In the letter it was explained that the Southerns had an arrangement to be collected at 3.10 p.m. at their hotel to be taken to Newark Airport. When Supershuttle did not arrive on time the doorman was kind enough to telephone them three times to check what was happening. Twice they said that the van would be arriving shortly. On the third attempt at about 3.55 p.m. they told the Southerns that they should take alternative transport, and that the company would reimburse the cost of this. After some further delay searching for a 'yellow cab' they could only find one 'black limo' driver willing to do this at a price of US$75. (They had a receipt from Communicar Ltd.) They asked how they could claim this, adding that their delay caused them great stress, and hoping that getting reimbursement would not cause them concern.

(Continued)

Case study: Continued.

An e-mail was received from Ivy Boatwright, Quality Assurance Rep. at Supershuttle, asking the Southerns to fax the limo receipt, the confirmation number, and a mailing address in order to receive a cheque for the difference. After a great deal of difficulty sending this information a letter was received from Supershuttle Customer Care Department apologizing for the inconvenience, stating the company's commitment to provide safe, efficient, reliable and convenient transportation to each and every customer, and saying that the company growth and continued success depended on this. They enclosed a cheque for US$41 as reimbursement for the failure to provide proper service.

The question remains as to whether simply refunding the difference between what a journey actually cost and what was paid for the Supershuttle fully satisfies a customer.

It seems the operating systems of Supershuttle leave much to be desired. During this chapter you will be asked questions on the operational systems of Supershuttle (and Blue Van), and you may wish to gather more information on the companies which may guide and support your answers.

Case study questions

What do you think the customer expects of Supershuttle/Blue Van?
How are these expectations created?

Quality standards, with particular reference to the service sector, will be discussed later in this chapter.

The systems view

Operations management owes much to systems thinking, which is central to the concepts of managing change. Interest in managing change arose in the late 1970s and 1980s, when a rapidly changing working environment led to a change in the role of managers. It is associated with a number of developments in management styles and in the socio-economic and technological environment in which management is practised (Paton and McCalman, 2008).

But different people will see the same system in different ways, and the systems may contain subsystems. For example, within a tourist company an employee will see the company as a work provision system, the owners as a profit generating system and the customer as a recreation provision system. Each of these individuals will place the emphasis of their interest in the way specified, and each would define a different boundary for the system. At the same time systems can be structurally very complex, and may need to be considered in terms of an interconnected set of subsystems, or components, related to the functions they fulfil in order to make management possible. We need to take a holistic view of the total system, and relationships within it, and it is therefore necessary to have some way of representing systems. A systems map fulfils this purpose.

The systems map for a typical tour operating company is shown in Fig. 9.1. Senior managers of the organization will draw their system boundary as shown here, or perhaps a little wider if their influence reaches that far. Junior managers will tend to draw their system boundaries at the limit of their section or department. However, the more senior the manager, and the nearer to policy decision making they are, the greater the need to take a higher level, more holistic view of the system. The ability to take what is colloquially known as a helicopter view is of great benefit to a manager, and is represented in Fig. 9.2. All managers will take the

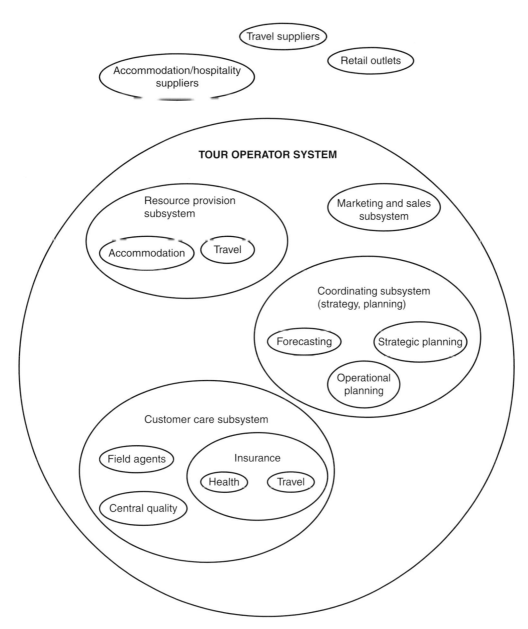

Fig. 9.1. Systems map of a tour operating company.

view of their system and set their system boundary as shown, but more competent managers will take a higher level view which considers the cross-boundary interactions.

It is possible to convert a systems map into another diagram which represents influences between subsystems by adding arrows representing these influences. For instance in our systems map the forecasting part of the coordinating subsystem will influence the strategic planning subsystem, which will in turn influence activities in the marketing and resource provision subsystems. The resulting influence diagram is another useful tool in gaining an appreciation of the operating systems of an organization.

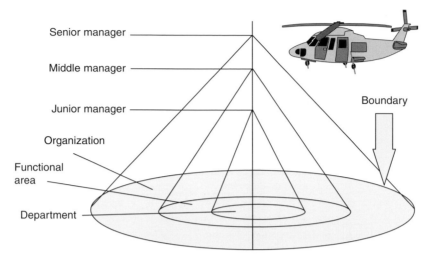

Fig. 9.2. The helicopter view of systems and systems boundaries.

Case study questions (Supershuttle/Blue Van)

What do you think will be the subsystems of:

- Supershuttle worldwide?
- Blue Van New York?

(Use a systems map to illustrate.) How do you think the subsystems influence each other, and what external influences exist?

The systems view of the tour operating company shown in Fig. 9.1 is closely related to the operations management analysis framework which will be introduced later in the chapter, where the subsystems representing resource provision, customer care and coordination will be of particular relevance.

Representing system transformations

Returning to our definition of operations management: 'Operations management is concerned with the design and control of transformation systems to deliver the services, including products, of an organization at the right quality, at the right price, and at the right time', we see that operations management is concerned with a transformation process involving inputs and outputs. This is common to the definition of a system. The transformation process can be displayed by using an input/output diagram which allows us to begin an analysis of the transformation. Here we are not particularly concerned with the transformation mechanism itself, but only with the outputs required and with the inputs necessary to deliver them. The transformation itself can for the moment be considered as a 'black box'.

An input/output diagram for the tour operating company displayed in Fig. 9.1 is shown in Fig. 9.3. Note that inputs to the transformation system consist of tangible items (hotels, travel means and timetables, etc.) and knowledge of these. Output consists of feelings and perceptions created in customers (i.e. intangibles).

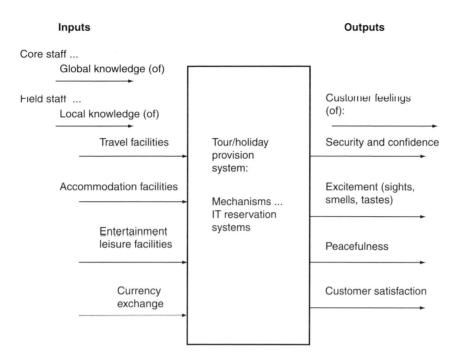

Fig. 9.3. Input/output diagram for a tour/holiday provision system.

Case study questions (Supershuttle/Blue Van)

What will be the inputs and outputs for:

- Supershuttle worldwide?
- Blue Van New York?

(Draw input/output diagrams.)

If we now consider the transformation process and its relationship to systems thinking in more detail, we can see that outputs from one subsystem usually become inputs to another subsystem. Referring back to Fig. 9.1, for example, the outputs from the resource provision subsystem of our tour operating company become inputs to our customer care subsystem, and will provide information inputs into our marketing and sales subsystem.

Activity sequence diagrams expand on the simple input/output diagram by identifying the series of activities involved in delivering the product or service, and are of particular value in a service delivery situation. An activity sequence diagram for the sales subsystem of a typical holiday retail outlet (see Fig. 9.1) is shown in Fig. 9.4. This plots the activities which a customer goes through when selecting and booking a holiday.

Activity sequence diagrams are particularly useful for identifying where value is added in the product or service delivery process, and where cost or effort is expended with little or no value added. Such activities should be eliminated if possible, or combined with value-adding activities if not. An example of this is the trend to eliminate inspection activities by redesigning the value delivery process to eliminate the possibility of defective service and by placing responsibility for quality with the server. This trend correlates closely with

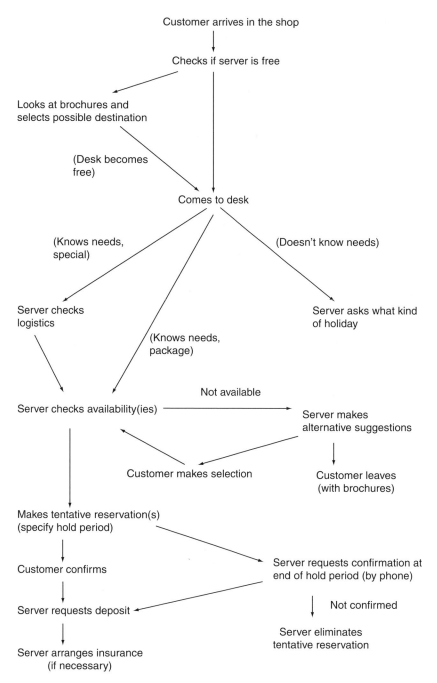

Fig. 9.4. Activity sequence diagram, holiday sales.

a general trend to worker empowerment and job enrichment. In a service situation such as tourism, process flow and activity sequence diagrams are particularly useful in identifying points at which perception of poor quality is created by expecting the customer to queue or wait. In this case attempts must be made to eliminate or decrease the number and length of these delays, usually by careful manipulation of capacity; the techniques for doing this will be described later. Where this is not possible attempts should be made to convert passive waits to active waits. Passive waits can be defined as those where the customer is delayed and feels no progress or action is being taken, or is given no information to justify the delay. Providing information for delayed customers is important to avoid frustration. It is possible to convert passive waits into active waits by providing activities for the customer, preferably useful ones such as browsing brochures in the case described in our earlier activity sequence diagram. It is also advisable to keep the customer advised of progress, for example in the case of holiday bookings (Fig. 9.4) we should let the customer see our computer screen if we are making our computer checks and bookings.

Case study question (Supershuttle/Blue Van)

Draw an activity sequence diagram for the Southerns' return journey to the airport, from booking the pickup time to arrival. Where do you think the points occur that are most likely to lead to a perception of poor quality service, and what can Supershuttle do to prevent this happening?

TOURISM: A SERVICE INDUSTRY

Many of the classic concepts and techniques of operations management have been derived and developed for use in the manufacturing sector. However, tourism is placed firmly in the service sector, and there are fundamental differences between the two which indicate that we must be selective, adaptive and inventive in applying them. The underlying reasons for the differences are concerned with customer expectations and resulting customer perception of value and quality, and with the ability to store the 'value' delivered.

Perishability

A service is perishable, i.e. it cannot be kept in inventory, but is consumed in production. For example, consider a hotel room. What is sold here is the comfort of the room for the night, so if it is not sold on a particular night the potential to sell that room for that night is lost forever. This concept is even more transparent in the case of an aircraft seat, where the opportunity to transport someone is lost if it is empty during a journey.

Consideration of perishability is particularly appropriate in tourism where, apart from the two cases already cited, tour operators tend to buy or take options on travel and accommodation, which if not sold on to customers lead to losses: hence the resulting sale of short-notice holidays at large price discounts.

Heterogeneity

Services produce variable, non-standard output. As a result services cannot be mass produced and pricing options tend to be more elaborate. As a further result of perishability and the inability to mass produce, quality control is primarily limited to control of the delivery process itself, i.e. process control. An indication of heterogeneity in tourism is found to be in the plethora of retail outlets selling a wide range of tour packages, and even tailored holidays, in each location.

Simultaneity

The customer participates in the process of providing the service. As corollaries to this there is high customer contact throughout the service process, skills (or knowledge) are sold directly to the customer, and high personal judgement is employed by the individuals performing the service. Obviously, because of this, service firms tend to be labour intensive and decentralized facilities are located near the customers.

It is obvious in the case of tourism that the service, or any elements of it such as travel, residence, food or recreation consumption, cannot be provided without the presence and participation of the customer. The examples given for heterogeneity also support this aspect.

Intangibility

Services produce intangible output. The quality of the deliverable can only be gauged by the opinion of the customer. This facet is closely linked to both that of heterogeneity and that of simultaneity.

In the case of tourism this is self-evident and was discussed at some length earlier in the section dealing with the definition of operations management and quality within it.

Case study question (Supershuttle/Blue Van)

How does Supershuttle/Blue Van fit the Murdick *et al.* (1990) characteristics of a service organization?

STRATEGIC POSITIONING AND OPERATING SYSTEM DESIGN

Although tourism as a business sector tends to lie at the service end of the manufacturing–service continuum, there are certain elements of it which are delivered using philosophies and techniques which are more akin to those of manufacture. Standard package tours, for example, can be considered as products which are sold to customers as mass-produced goods rather than tailored items. Even where a tour is tailored to a customer's individual wishes it is still likely to consist of elements, such as travel and accommodation, which are readily available 'off the peg', and it is in the combining of these where the true service element is created. Any organization working in the tourist industry will thus be a blend of individual 'niche' service elements at high (or price) and 'mass-manufactured' service elements at low cost (or price). The blend of offerings will be related to the competitive position taken by the organization in the marketplace, which will in turn affect the operating systems of the organization.

The design of the operating system of any organization will therefore depend on the competitive position taken on a continuum ranging from where the design of the holiday or tour is part of the delivery process and each tour will be tailored to the wishes of each customer, to where packages are standardized and the customer chooses one with no variation. The first extreme of this continuum is traditionally known as a process-focused delivery system, or job shop, and the other extreme is known as a product-focused delivery system, or mass delivery.

However, the design of operating systems is not quite so simple and straightforward. Several other ancillary factors also need to be considered in the design process such as consistency of delivering to an agreed specification (standards and timings), level of technology performance and availability of service elements (Krajewski *et al.*, 2007). The inherent variety of choices to be made indicates the importance of carefully and continuously considering the design of a system. The operating environment will change, possibly requiring a strategic repositioning within the competitive priority factors, and thus a repositioning of the operating system on the job shop to mass delivery continuum.

Case study questions (Supershuttle/Blue Van)

Where do you think Supershuttle lies on the competitive position continuum (from individual/niche to mass manufactured/standard)?

Can you identify an alternative airport transport service at each end of this continuum?

What service elements, other than low price, will generate a perception of quality in each of the airport transport services you have identified?

A FRAMEWORK FOR ANALYSIS AND IMPROVEMENT OF OPERATING SYSTEMS

The complexity and degree of choice in the design of operating systems are reflected in an abundance of techniques and methodologies used in operations management. This diversity sometimes overshadows the simple, central purpose of the topic, to deliver goods and services (in the case of tourism primarily services) to the customer. Linda Sprague proposes a five-point framework for the analysis of operating systems based upon consideration of capacity, standards, scheduling, inventory and control (in Devanna and Collins, 1990).

1. Capacity: This is perhaps better titled 'capability' and is the ability to yield output. At a strategic level it is usually measured in the number of units of product or service which can be delivered in a specific time unit. However, at an operational level, where resources are likely to be shared between different products or services, capacity is usually measured in terms of process (plant or equipment) or human resource hours.

2. Standards: Standards consist of work standards and product or service quality standards. Work standards are measures of effort, usually specified in terms of time taken at a reasonable level of work performance which it takes to do a specific task. If the number of tasks to be done is known, then these times can be aggregated to check whether the capacity is available to do them, and this information can also be used to schedule the order of activities. Work standards therefore constitute the data needed to plan the level of capacity needed and the scheduling of the capacity we have. Zeithaml *et al.* (1990), in their service quality model (SERVQUAL), identify five dimenions on which customers measure quality. These are:

- Tangibles: appearance of physical facilities, equipment, personnel and communication materials.
- Reliability: ability to perform the promised service dependably and accurately.
- Responsiveness: willingness to help customers provide prompt service.
- Assurance: knowledge and courtesy of employees and their ability to convey trust and confidence.
- Empathy: the firm provides care and individualized attention for its customers.

The model itself identifies five gaps in an organization's system where quality problems can arise.

3. Scheduling: Scheduling is the planning of the use of resources (or capacity) on a time base to produce a **service delivery plan**. Scheduling has two objectives: (i) to deliver specific products or services at a time agreed with the customer; and (ii) to deliver all products and services at a low cost by full utilization of resources. These objectives often conflict.

4. Inventory: Inventory is the management of flow and storage of physical items necessary to deliver the product or services to the customer. This is of lesser importance in tourism, where the cost of materials is relatively lower than in manufacture. Service industries tend to be labour intensive, and it is here and in capital (travel and accommodation) equipment where most costs are incurred.

5. Control: Control is measuring the performance of the system to the capacity and scheduling plans described above, and the process of planning remedial actions.

This framework is outlined in Fig. 9.5. It provides a useful systematic approach to the analysis of operating systems and will be applied to the tourism sector in the remainder of this chapter. General conceptual issues concerned with each aspect will first be considered, and then quantitative techniques which support the decisions to be made associated with each aspect, *and which are particularly relevant in tourism*, will be described.

OPERATIONS MANAGEMENT DECISIONS

Decisions to be made in operations management consist of two types:

- Those concerned with the design of the delivery system – the service quality levels to be delivered, the level of capability (or capacity) needed to deliver these levels and the way material is managed (i.e. with standards, capacity and inventory).
- Those concerned with the shorter-term utilization of resources, in other words with scheduling and control decisions.

In order to make these decisions and to plan operations, we need to know what tasks need to be done and in what order, how many times each task has to be done and how long each task will take. The activity sequence diagrams already described are useful techniques for analysing tasks and the sequence in which they are done. The traditional forecasting techniques are:

- **Market research** – good for identifying attractive product or service features, not total activity rate, i.e.sales.
- **Delphi** – asking the experts. Good to predict technological or economic changes, but expensive and susceptible to 'groupthink' unless experts are kept separate. Leads to consensus (hopefully). Good for predicting environmental changes.
- **Regression** – finding relationship with a 'causal' variable, the demand for which is known (or accurately predicted by someone else). (Time is not a causal variable, this is time series forecasting – see below.)
- **Time series forecasting** – extrapolation of past activity rates (sales, performance) into the future. Good for short-term forecasts, but beware of environmental changes.

These, and more modern approaches described in Chapters 2 and 4, tell us how many times each task has to be done.

Work measurement and resulting standards (Chase *et al.*, 2001) indicating the time required to complete service transactions or tasks provide the information needed for operational decision making.

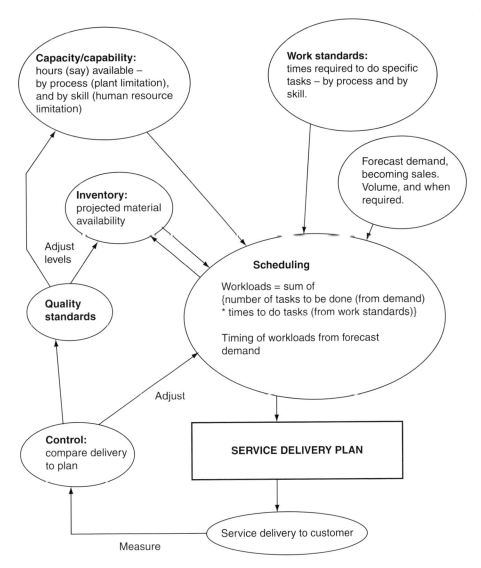

Fig. 9.5. A framework for operations management (after Sprague, from Devanna and Collins, 1990).

Work standards are specified by simple measurement. Many tasks are repeated many times in the course of a working day, and many jobs may be broken down into such tasks. In a hotel, for example, the job of cleaning a room may be divided into:

- change the bedding;
- vacuum the floor;
- clean the bathroom (may be divided further);
- replace bath linen and bathroom accessories;
- replenish the minibar;
- clean away the tea crockery, replace and replenish;
- dust surfaces; and
- spot wipe window and mirrors.

These tasks may be combined in any order or omitted when cleaning a room.

Work study, consisting of work measurement and method study (Chase *et al.*, 2001), may be of value in many situations in tourism: checking in at reception areas, checking in at airports, serving in bars and restaurants, etc. However, it should be stressed that any work measurement exercises undertaken are not to be used for payment purposes. They should be aimed at gaining information for resource planning only, in other words to calculate the necessary staffing levels at various times. Again, this is paramount when the heterogeneous, simultaneous and non-repetitive nature of the tasks is considered, and in many situations it could be argued that in such circumstances the 'analytical estimate' of a skilled tradesman may be both as accurate and as useful, but only if not used for aggregate planning purposes.

QUALITY STANDARDS

While the perception of quality in service delivery and that of an organization is intangible, the creation of that perception will result, at least partially, from a bundle of tangible factors. We can set quality standards for tangible factors that will be an integral part of the design of our operating system. In service situations, because of the heterogeneity and simultaneity involved, these factors are frequently related to service availability and customer waiting times, and can readily be competitive factors, which were identified earlier. In fact, any quality standards specified in an organization should be directed by the competitive stance adopted by the organization. They should also be considered in terms of the concept of order-qualifying versus order-winning criteria related to that stance. (For an order-qualifying criterion an organization must achieve a threshold level to be considered for business; doing better does not increase the likelihood of getting an order. For an order-winning criterion there is no threshold and the better the performance on it the more orders gained.)

Methods of measuring performance to quality standards are also important. Quality factors can be considered as variables or attributes. Variables can be measured on a continuous scale so that a 'degree of error' can be stated, while attributes can be quickly and simply counted. As explained earlier, quality in the service sector is created and measured in the process of delivery, and is often associated with competent completion of the tasks involved in that process. Quality standards, therefore, need to be identified in terms of these tasks, which are related to work standards. In terms of our hotel room cleaning example, the act of cleaning the room before the entry (or return) of a customer might be considered as an attribute. The time between room cleaning (or checking) would be a variable. Both of these would probably be considered qualifying quality criteria. At a more detailed level the acts of changing the bedding and dusting surfaces will be attributes and probably qualifying quality criteria, but the number of spot marks not wiped from a mirror could be considered a variable and an order-winning criterion.

The customer service level which we are seeking to define can only be quantified in terms of tangible quality criteria, and we must seek to identify such factors which are paramount (qualifying) and important (order winning) in satisfying the customer. Examples of tangible measures of quality performance which are appropriate in tourism and in the hospitality sector are given in the Table 9.1. As an organization we must attempt to define an acceptable service level for each of a set of such criteria. The levels will be related to the expectations of the market, and if we reach that expectation then we will qualify to compete in the market. If we exceed that expectation for order-winning criteria we will in all probability win more than our fair share of customers. However, the ability to reach the levels we set depend on the capacity,

Table 9.1. Customer service measures.

Customer service measure	Examples
Percentage of customers we can satisfy with their requirement	Specific requirements may be: journey departure time and means of transport, holiday in specific hotel, brand of drink in a bar, meal in a restaurant
Degree of choice offered	Number of people we can satisfy with an acceptable alternative to the above
Time to be acknowledged	At retail shop counter, hotel reception, bar, restaurant, reception
Time waiting until start of service delivery	Taking details at hotel reception, details or order in retail shop or bar, seated at table in restaurant
Time to be served	Until total service transaction is complete

in terms of skills and capital resources, which we have available at any specific time, which in turn will greatly influence the cost of provision and price we must charge the customer – the final competitive factor from our previous discussion. This is the crux of operations management, and is discussed in the next section on capacity management.

Intangible factors of service quality can only be delivered by people. Any organization must therefore pay careful attention to selection and training of people and to motivating them.

CAPACITY MANAGEMENT

Capacity is the ability to yield output. At a strategic level it is usually measured in the number of units of product or service which can be delivered in a specific time unit. However, this section will concentrate on capacity management at an operational level, where resources are likely to be shared between different products or services. Here capacity, or capability, is usually measured in terms of process (associated with equipment) hours or in terms of human resource hours.

Most major decisions to be made in operations management are concerned with ensuring that sufficient resources are available *when needed* to deliver the level of customer service which is agreed, formally or informally, with the customer. Forecasting is important to find the level of customer-related activity and work standards to convert this into levels of operational activity. Demand for resources is directly proportional to customer-related activity, and in the tourism industry this varies on a cyclic (related to the economy), seasonal and daily basis. This is true of all service situations, but the variation is higher in tourism than most others. The aim of capacity management is to deal with this variation as cost effectively as possible.

There are two extreme strategies for dealing with variation in demand: (i) adjust the capacity available; and (ii) eliminate the need to adjust the capacity available. Very few organizations will use either of these extreme policies, and most organizations will find cost-effective solutions by using a mixture of techniques associated with the extremes.

Methods of adjusting capacity

The following list describes the generic means of adjusting capacity, in the case of tourism equipment and labour availability, and how appropriate they may be.

Subcontracting

Subcontracting can be used to vary the availability of both labour and equipment. It may be employed to add to resources when customer activity cannot be satisfied with in-company resources or to eliminate the need to hold certain resources at all. In the tourism sector both road and air transport provide examples where subcontracting is extensively employed. Many tour companies will have their own transport vehicles but will hire additional vehicles at particularly busy times, sometimes with operating staff included. In dealing with departing passengers at airports a similar mix occurs. Larger airlines will have their own reception staff and 'top up' with personnel from a specialist service company (e.g. Service Air) when necessary; companies who use an airport less frequently will only use the specialist service company, thus in effect sharing the resource with a number of other airlines. Unit costs of subcontracting are naturally higher than those of in-house provision in the short term, and the difference must be optimized against the long-term costs of holding excess resources in quiet periods.

Reschedule activities

Opportunities to reschedule activities in service industries, and particularly in tourism, are limited. Once again, this is because of the heterogeneous and simultaneous nature of the service delivery process. However, there is scope to reschedule activities related to the maintenance of plant and equipment. Major overhauls of equipment can be delayed until the next quiet period, for example at airports and hotels, although in the transport sector such delays are limited more by health and safety legal requirements.

Change workforce size

The workforce size can be changed by employing more staff or increasing hours worked. When a long-term underlying trend in customer activity is recognized then the permanent workforce size can be changed as necessary. This can be done in retrospect following an increase or decrease in activity, or in anticipation if a change in activity is forecast. When the change in activity is short term, then the hours worked by permanent staff can be temporarily changed, or temporary workers can be employed when the activity increases. There is value in employing workers on a part-time basis as working hours are often more easily changed than when a total full-time workforce is employed.

Methods of eliminating the need to adjust capacity

The following list describes the generic means of eliminating the need to adjust capacity and how appropriate they may be in tourism.

Maintain excess capacity

An organization may hold capacity which is above that required at all times by customers, although in most cases the cost of this policy, which will have to be passed on to customers, will be prohibitive. It is still a useful principle to consider applying to the core competencies of any business, in other words the skills or service elements which very few other organizations can provide. Excess capacity held in these core competencies, combined with judicious use of subcontracting and queuing, can create a competitive advantage in the marketplace.

Accept a loss of business

Plan to operate at a known level of activity and accept a loss of customers above this level. This is closely related in most cases to the degree of prestige which the service an organization offers has in the market. If the service an organization offers is specialized, or unique enough, and is in demand for these reasons, then the prestige can be further enhanced by rarity. The organization can then plan to operate at a specific level for a longer period rather than increase the availability of the service: for example, a successful theatrical production may wish to remain in a smaller theatre and extend the run, rather than increase availability by moving to a larger venue or duplicating the production in another venue. Obviously an organization applying this policy will expect customers to queue or wait for the service. The policy will also impact on the pricing policy adopted for the service.

Queuing or waiting

Require customers to queue or wait either in the form of a physical queue or some kind of booking system for the service. Again, reference must be made here to the customer service levels discussed earlier. In the case of a queue, the possibility of customers reneging and the cost of this to the business must be considered. Obviously some customers will not be willing to wait at all for the service so this policy is practically always used in collaboration with that of accepting a loss of customers. Much work has been done on mathematical modelling of queuing situations to derive the times a customer will have to queue in a specific queuing system. These will be described later, but in essence the outcomes must then be compared with the appropriate service levels set by the organization, which in turn are related to the expectations of the market.

Altering demand

Alter the demand pattern by pricing or advertising where the demand pattern varies greatly. An example of this in tourism is in the price of city-centre hotel rooms, which are lower at weekends when there is little demand from the business community. Here the concept of weekend city breaks at 'bargain' prices has been introduced and aggressively marketed. Further examples are in the price of flight tickets and the use of standby systems (also includes queuing) in airlines, and in the relatively high price of holidays during school holiday periods. The objective of this policy is to level demand so that changes in capacity requirement levels are fewer.

Useful quantitative techniques in capacity management

An organization will use a mixture of techniques when attempting to optimize the cost of holding capacity against the customer service level required. There are a number of quantitative techniques which are available to support the decision on which techniques to use and the degree to which each is used. The decision is in two stages. First the level of activity and the probable utilization of resources in terms of likely performance levels must be estimated or forecast. This information can then be used in models which simulate delivery systems and allow the necessary levels of resource needed to be calculated. The two stages therefore involve forecasting and modelling, and there are a number of approaches possible at each stage.

Forecasting

Techniques of forecasting required rates of business activity, time series analysis, regression, Delphi techniques and market research, are described earlier in this chapter.

We will concentrate here on forecasting the output we can expect from a unit of resource. In fact, many of the techniques listed above can also be employed to forecast the performance of resources, for example time series techniques can be used to forecast any continuous improvement resulting from total quality management programmes, and the Delphi technique can be used to forecast any resulting improvements resulting from technology advances in the field of information technology or transport. In addition, much of the information needed for decision making in capacity management comes in the form of work standards derived from work measurement, and many of the techniques associated with this have already been described.

In addition to these forecasting techniques, there are several behaviour patterns in the performance of resources which are of value to organizations. These include learning curves and process life cycles.

Learning curves are concerned with the implementation of a new approach to working or a new operating system. This may involve the training of workers or introduction of some new aspect of equipment, for example a new hardware and/or software computer system. The performance of the new operating system will behave exponentially until reaching a steady state situation. This situation will represent the system operating in terms of standard performance, in terms of the new computer system the average time per transaction reported, or the number of transactions dealt with per hour. Such curves are well established and recorded for various system implementations and must be taken into consideration when change is made to an operating system.

Process life cycles are concerned with the life of a process. Just as products have a natural life cycle of growth, steady state and decline, so a process or piece of equipment also has a life cycle. The failure rate or time out of use ('downtime') is plotted for the life of the process. It is found that there is an 'infant failure' stage where inherent faults or weak elements in the process or system are corrected. The process then settles into a steady state until more parts of the process begin to fail of old age, and the process begins to wear out until it is replaced when the repair costs become greater than the income earned. If, instead of the failure rate, the mean time between failures is plotted, the graph is inverted and becomes similar to the classic product life cycle curve. Again this relationship is well established and has been recorded for many situations where new investments are made. These can be researched and used to predict performance curves for any similar new equipment or system. They may also be used in the design of equipment replacement policy, and depreciation systems in the finance function.

Modelling

Having sourced the data necessary to make capacity decisions there are a number of modelling techniques which will help us to optimize cost of provision to meet the customer service levels we wish to reach for specified quality criteria.

LINEAR PROGRAMMING

Linear programming consists of a set of methods for deciding how to meet some desired objective (e.g. minimizing cost, maximizing profit) subject to constraints on commodities required or resources available. Developed under the auspices of operational research, the generic approach is to specify a mathematical model which represents the limitations imposed by the constraints, and which calculates the costs of system operations and possibly identifies areas of greatest potential cost saving. (The model often takes the form of a set of simultaneous equations which are difficult to solve manually.) Any feasible solution, in other words one which satisfies the constraints but does not necessarily meet the objective, is then used iteratively to improve performance against the objective until no further improvement results from the iteration process.

It is at this point that the model has been optimized and the resulting solution is the best available. One practical example in tourism is in routing transport between locations to maximize the number of passengers carried, which is synonymous with the number of locations reached, and to minimize the distance travelled, which is synonymous with cost. In fact, this example is synonymous with a classic linear programming technique known colloquially as 'the travelling salesman problem'. There are other such techniques in the operations research repertoire which while they may not offer immediate solutions are a useful starting point for solving complex problems of this sort. Computer programs are now available to solve complex sets of simultaneous equations, but the problem still has to be defined in the first instance (Hillier and Liebermann, 2006).

QUEUING THEORY

Queuing theory is concerned with mathematical modelling, using probability theory, of queuing situations which exist in life, for example at airport check-ins, restaurants for tables, self-service restaurants and fast-food outlets. Such models can be used to design the operating system and answer questions related to the level of customer service such as: Can we deliver the service in a time which it is reasonable to expect the customer to queue or wait? It is not necessary to enunciate on the mathematics of the models in detail, but managers should be aware of the nature of the technique, the inputs and outputs of the model, and the alternative choices to be made in the design of the system itself. Questions which need to be considered in the model (i.e. inputs) are:

- What is the service mechanism (e.g. single queue for multiple identical servers, specific queue for each identical server, etc.)? How many servers?
- What is the queue discipline (first come first served/last come first served/shortest operation next (e.g. hand luggage only for flights)/specified priorities (e.g. by class for flights), etc.)?
- What is the nature of arrivals in the queue? This is usually expressed as the distribution of time between arrivals.
- What is the nature of service times, again expressed as a distribution?

With this information it is possible to model the situation, and again there are computer software packages to help us. From the model the following outputs will help us decide whether the system is acceptable in terms of customer service levels:

- the server efficiency, for economic reasons; and
- the customer service level in terms of probability of a queue forming, the average length of queue, the longest queue formed, the average time spent queuing.

With this information we can decide to change the operating system, perhaps in the service mechanism or even by adding or taking away server stations (Krajewski *et al.*, 2007).

COMPUTER SIMULATION

Simulation packages are computer software packages which enable the user to model a set of interconnecting queues. As such they are valuable in modelling very complex flow patterns in organizations, of materials primarily in manufacturing situations and, of particular relevance here, of people primarily in service situations. They are invaluable in modelling the interaction of flow of different people and materials with each other and with the utilization of what are likely to be shared and limited resources for processing them through the system. An example of where they may be applied in tourism is in an airport. In this case arrivals into the system will be:

- Departing passengers arriving at the airport who are separated from their luggage (queue) may then proceed to a general departure lounge through emigration and security checks (queues), then to a departure area specific to their flight (queue), and finally to the aircraft. The luggage, separated from the passengers, will go to a sorting area (queue), to a vehicle designated to go to the owner's flight (queue), and then to be loaded on to the flight.
- Arriving passengers who will go to passport control (international passengers, queue), then baggage collection (queue; the baggage will have been unloaded and delivered to this area, another queue), then to customs control (queue), and finally they leave the system.
- Arriving aircraft, which may have to queue for a landing slot on the runway, then for a disembarking station. They will then interact with the passenger disembarking/embarking systems and with the fuelling and provisioning systems before joining another queue for a take-off slot.

Modelling a situation such as this is obviously complex, particularly if the boundary of the system is widened even more to include the supporting infrastructure of ancillary service provision (shops and comfort provision), public transport, and the airport servicing system such as fuel and provisions. Arrivals of passengers and aircraft will be a complex mix of scheduled activities with 'fixed' times and probabilistic arrival distributions. However, the entire system can be modelled by:

- dividing the system into a set of interconnecting queues, or subsystems in the language of systems theory;
- defining the people or materials (termed entities) which flow through the system and the paths they will take, including where they diverge or combine to become a single entity (e.g. the interrelating paths of passengers, luggage and even aircraft); and
- defining the service mechanisms and service time distributions for each entity at each process, and any interruptions such as mechanical breakdown or sickness of staff which may be expected (i.e. elements of uncertainty) must also be incorporated.

The above are used in the software package to model the airport operating system before simulating the combination of scheduled arrivals and 'bursts' of arrival distributions around the scheduled arrivals on a time base. There will also be an element of uncertainty here, for example late aircraft arrivals, which may also have to be considered.

Outputs from a simulation run using the model will consist of performance indicators for each process in the system in terms of utilization of resources and passenger waiting times. These will indicate points of inefficiency and passenger frustration. The simulation run will also give indications of the performance of the entire system, probably in terms of passenger throughput and aircraft turnaround times.

While the use of this technique has been described in terms of an airport, its value in other facets of tourism, for example in the modelling of a leisure park such as Disneyworld, is self-evident. Here activities are not scheduled and the circumstances of visitors reneging on arrival at a long queue must be considered, but the process of modelling the situation to indicate the need for increase in particular resource availability is still appropriate (Hillier and Liebermann, 2006).

Evaluation of capacity plans: financial modelling

Financial modelling is a tool which must be used to evaluate any resource provision plan we may propose to deliver the required service level to the customer. It enables the outcomes from the resource (capacity) and service level implications resulting from the modelling techniques described above to be considered on a cost–benefit basis. In linear programming the costs of provision will usually be incorporated into the model directly, and when applying queuing and simulation techniques the costs of resource provision will be calculated for the entire system model and compared with the level of service provision delivered so that relatively objective management decisions can be made.

At a more strategic level, financial modelling allows us to evaluate different alternative capacity plans comprising a mix of changing capacity (subcontracting, rescheduling activities, changing workforce size) and eliminating the need to change (carrying excess, queuing, differential pricing) to meet daily or seasonal changes in demand.

Case study questions (Supershuttle/Blue Van)

How will demand for the services of Supershuttle and Blue Van vary?
What capacity constraints will there be?
What policies and techniques can be used to deal with variation in demand?
How will alternative plans to deal with demand variation be evaluated?

INVENTORY MANAGEMENT

The management of inventory is far less important in tourism than the management of equipment or labour, as is the case for most service industries. In tourism inventory consists of materials which are consumed in the delivery of the service, and there is no equivalent of work in progress as required in the manufacturing sector. Material is less important in tourism because:

- the percentage of total operating cost which can be attributed to materials is very small when compared with the share taken by labour, property and capital equipment; and
- much inventory in tourism has a limited shelf life (e.g. that of food, which is very short to medium term; drink; and brochures, which is usually 1 year or season).

As a result of these factors there are fewer savings to be made in improving the management of materials in tourism, except perhaps in ensuring the correct amounts are obtained, than in improving the management of labour and capital equipment. However, shortage of inventory will, in many cases, result in near catastrophic perception of quality; for example, consider a restaurant without a basic foodstuff or a travel agent without popular brochures. Absence of certain materials at the point of service must therefore be considered as order sensitive (or losing) criteria, and is worthy of consideration.

When designing systems to manage material it is worth considering the relative cost of different materials to the organization, and to concentrate on managing the most costly materials, for obvious reasons. The most frequently used technique for doing this is called the Pareto, or more colloquially the ABC, analysis (Krajewski *et al.*, 2007). It plots the cumulative value (or cost) of material held by variety from highest value items to lowest value items. When such an analysis is undertaken it is frequently found that about 20% of the variety of materials, the category A items, are responsible for 80% of the cost, and it is important to manage these materials well as greater savings are possible. It is also found that about 50% of the variety of materials, the category C materials, are responsible for less than 10% of the cost and much less significant savings are to be had by tighter control here. The B category items, of course, fall between the two.

Dependency of demand

Materials can also be generically differentiated in terms of demand for them, and one useful way of classifying materials for the purpose of managing them is in terms of the dependency of demand. Materials may be subject to independent or dependent demand.

Independent demand for an item occurs when demand is influenced purely by the market, and can be said to be independent of the demand for other items. An example of this is the demand for brochures in a holiday shop. Here costs of inventory come from two sources: (i) the cost of acquiring it; and (ii) the cost of holding it. Acquisition costs include the cost of preparing to produce the item and the cost of delivery; in the case of the brochure this would be the cost of preparing for a new print run and delivery, although over a holiday season there would also be the need to recover the cost of preparing artwork at the start of the season and possible obsolescence at the end. Holding costs include storage, insurance and the lost opportunity of invested money. For the holiday brochure, holding costs would mainly result from lost opportunity cost. Optimization techniques are used to minimize the sum of these two cost elements (i.e. the total cost), resulting in the calculation of an economic batch quantity (EBQ; Krajewski *et al.*, 2007), which is used as the basis for designing reordering regimes.

Dependent demand for an item occurs when the demand is dependent on the demand for another item or service activity. For example, when a seat is booked on a flight, then that reserved seat generates the need for meals and drinks, which in turn generate the need for the constituent parts of the meals and drinks.

In dependent demand situations material requirements are defined by 'exploding' the primary requirement, for example the reserved seat, into the dependent material requirements by means of a bill of material (BOM). This may consist of cascading needs through several layers of material, as demonstrated in the reserved seat example earlier. It is then possible to indicate to suppliers a delivery schedule for material. Such methods of material management are termed materials requirement planning (MRP), and they were initially developed in the manufacturing sector where BOMs consist of many more layers than in service industries because of the complexity of product and large numbers of stages of manufacture (Orlicky, 1994).

In practice the MRP process in the tourism sector is usually driven by a timetable in the case of travel, or by a predicted schedule of guest behaviour in the case of hospitality and leisure (e.g. meal and other activity times). This results in the possibility of customers developing close supply chain relationships with suppliers and of sharing information on which material supply decisions are made. The suppliers may even be asked to make material requirement decisions based on planned activities and an extrapolation of previous material requirements for these activities, and then to deliver what they think will be needed.

Supply chain relationships, and the management of them, have been the subject of research in recent years. Models have been designed to test and manage the compatibility of customers and suppliers in terms of operating systems and organizational culture (Macbeth and Ferguson, 1994).

SCHEDULING

As already stated scheduling has conflicting objectives, the delivery of specific products or services at a time agreed with the customer, and the delivery of all products and services at a low cost by efficient use of resources, so again optimization techniques are applied.

It helps a lot if we can level out demand, and in tourism queuing and reservation systems and using price differentials can achieve this. However, having employed these techniques it then becomes necessary to schedule the hours of the workforce so that they are available when the customer needs them. There are a number of constraints to this process, such as:

- The need to match availability with the biological clocks and daily routines of customers, and the travel timetables which these also dictate. This will, of course, include weekend working and working other unsociable hours when customers are at leisure.
- Any legal constraints on the services supplied, such as on the number of safety officers we must have available or the maximum hours worked by vehicle drivers.
- The physiological needs of workers, which are often written into workplace agreements (e.g. limits on consecutive hours or days worked, and time delay before start of next work period).

While constraints such as these limit the operations manager's flexibility in developing workforce schedules, they actually simplify the process of scheduling itself.

The need to work unsociable hours and at weekends often results in the design of a rotating schedule which ensures that the hardships are shared fairly equally among the workforce. In such a system a worker will rotate through a series of workdays or hours, nesting with those of another worker. Systems exist to develop such schedules using simple heuristic rules, and in complex situations computerized workforce scheduling systems are available.

Alternatively the problems of workforce scheduling can be eliminated to some extent, particularly where demand is particularly unpredictable, by having a large number of casual workers on tap. Such workers are often able to turn out at short notice and give the operations planner flexibility in being able to react to short-notice requirements, thus offering the competitive advantage of volume flexibility, and if any workers, full time or casual, have a range of skills then the advantage of service product flexibility is also gained.

Case study question (Supershuttle/Blue Van)

What social, legal and contractual constraints are likely to be in place here?

CONTROL

Having developed a plan in terms of service quality levels to be delivered, resources provided to deliver these service levels, and a schedule of when these resources will be available, systems must now be put in place to ensure that the plan is followed and performs to expectations. In operations management terms this is termed process control, and it is analogous to budgetary control in financial management. It involves the measurement of inputs and outputs, both in terms of quality and in terms of volume, and the comparison of these to ensure that the conversion process is working as expected. It is here where the work standards which were used in the planning process are tested for authenticity. The process is shown diagrammatically in Fig. 9.6, and it should be noted that this is really an extension of the input/output process used earlier to define the transformation process itself.

The secret of good control of operations is in the selection of the output parameters that are closely monitored, and in the selection of the input parameters that affect the outputs,

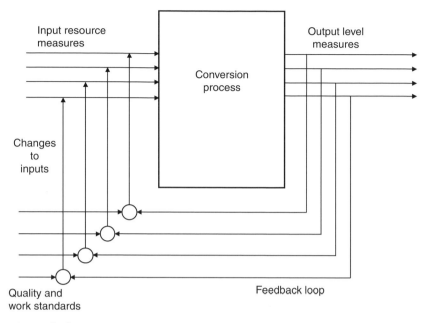

Fig. 9.6. Control of operations – process control diagram.

which must also be monitored. Output measures must be directly related to the quality stand-ards of the organization as dictated by the competitive priority factors on which the organiza-tion competes in the market. Input measures must be in terms of the cost of delivery of the service to these quality standards, usually in terms of effort or work standards. For each subsys-tem of the organization this results in the establishment of several channels to be monitored. In essence, for each output channel monitored (Fig. 9.6), the inputs required to maintain the level of service required at that channel are also monitored. At a comparison point these inputs and outputs are considered to determine:

- if the quality service levels planned are being delivered; and
- if they are being delivered using the planned level of resources.

Deviations from the plan will require actions of two kinds, depending on the reason for the deviation.

If the deviation is a result of a difference in the level of activity from that planned, then we will naturally expect to use more (or fewer) resources than we had planned to use. We will check whether the work standards are still appropriate, and in fact we could also expect some benefits from economies of scale in terms of support functions. For example, if a hotel is working at a higher room occupancy rate than we had forecast then we would expect to need more room servicing labour than we had planned, perhaps as overtime or casual labour. (In management accounting terms this is equivalent to volume variance.) However, we would not expect the supervisory effort to increase as this tends to be a fixed overhead. In this case we would increase the resource input, or more likely acknowledge and endorse the actions the line managers have already taken.

If the activity level is equal to that planned, but we are using more resources than planned, then we must question our work standards on which we are basing our conversion logic. (In management accounting terms this is equivalent to cost variance.) We must then either change the work standards to be more realistic or reconsider the conversion process itself and perhaps re-engineer it to make it better. In the case of hotel room cleaning, where we are using more labour than planned we should first check that the rooms themselves do not vary greatly from our 'standard', then that the cleaners are well supported and they do not spend time seeking cleaning materials or equipment, and finally perhaps that they are not exceeding quality specifications. If there are no discrepancies here, then we can either redesign the room, or the cleaning regime to make it possible to do the tasks in the time planned, or alter our work standards (and readjust our expected profit margins).

In most situations variances from the plan will be caused by combination of different activity rates from those used in the plan, and different conversion rates from those expected. Unravelling this situation is never easy, and it is important to first select the parameters which we must measure to control the perception of quality which we deliver to the customer, and then to put information systems in place which deliver data on both these parameters and the costs of delivering them in terms of effort (man-hours) spent. Only when managers have such systems in place can they expect to control the business.

Case study questions (Supershuttle/Blue Van)

What input/output factors will be used for control in Supershuttle and in Blue Van?
Can (new) technology play a role here?

SUMMARY

1. Definition: 'Operations management is concerned with the design and control of transformation systems to deliver the services, including products, of an organization at the right quality, at the right price, and at the right time.'

2. Organizations are systems. The techniques of representing and describing are invaluable in analysing how they operate and the interdependency of subsystems.

3. Tourism is a service industry. As such its product is perishable, heterogeneous and intangible, and the customer is an integral part of the product delivery process (simultaneity).

4. Organizations should define their strategic market position in terms of established competitive criteria. These then determine the standards to which they operate.

5. Decisions to be made in operations management consist of those pertaining to the design of the operating system (design decisions) and those concerned with the effective short-term utilization of available resources (operating decisions).

6. A useful framework for analysing operations management decisions in organizations, or in parts of an organization, is by considering:

- The service delivery quality standards adopted – these are fundamental to monitoring the factors which create customer perception of the service deliverable at point of delivery.
- Work (or performance) standards adopted – these are fundamental building blocks for planning and measuring economic performance of delivery systems.
- Capacity – to ensure that resources are available to deliver the service-level quality standards at standard work performance.
- Inventory – to ensure that systems are in place to supply materials needed in the service delivery at point and time of need.

- Scheduling – to finalize short-term plans to ensure that available resources are there when needed.
- Control – to monitor performance to plan and to take remedial action when there are deviations from the plan.

Quantitative techniques and qualitative approaches are available to support the management of operations. They should be employed flexibly in the operating context of any specific organization.

REFERENCES

Chase, R.B., Aquilano, N.J. and Jacobs, F.R. (2001) *Operations Management for Competitive Advantage*, 9th edn. McGraw-Hill, London.

Devanna, M.A. and Collins, E.G.C. (eds) (1990) *The Portable MBA*. Wiley, New York.

Hillier, F. and Liebermann, G. (2006) *Introduction to Operations Research*, 8th edn. McGraw-Hill, London.

ISO 8042 (1989) International Standard 8042. International Organization for Standards, Geneva.

Krajewski, L.J., Ritzman, L.P. and Malhotra, M. (2007) *Operations Management: Processes and Value Chains*, 8th edn. Addison Wesley, Reading, Massachusetts.

Macbeth, D.K. and Ferguson, N. (1994) *Partnership Sourcing: an Integrated Supply Chain Management Approach*. Pitman, London.

Murdick, R.G., Render, B. and Russel, R.S. (1990) *Service Operations Management*. Allyn and Bacon, Boston, Massachusetts.

Orlicky, J. (1994) *Material Requirements Planning*, 2nd edn. McGraw-Hill, London.

Paton, R.A. and McCalman, J. (2008) *Change Management: a Guide to Effective Implementation*, 3rd edn. Sage, London.

Supershuttle (2008) Supershuttle home page. Available at: http://www.supershuttle.com (accessed 30 January 2008).

Zeithaml, A.A., Parasuraman, A. and Berry, L.L. (1990) *Delivering Service Quality: Balancing Customer Perceptions and Expectations*. Free Press, New York.

chapter 10

Financial Management in Tourism

James Wilson and Luiz Moutinho

INTRODUCTION AND LEARNING OBJECTIVES

A basic understanding of financial management is essential for managers in the tourism industry. Financial management is central to planning, measuring and controlling many activities and managers that understand and can use this information can act on it more effectively. The learning objectives then focus on those dimensions of financial management most relevant to a manager's effectiveness. This chapter's objectives are:

- to develop an understanding that accounting systems and reports may be adapted to specific management needs;
- to develop a comprehension of the profit and loss statement and the effects of management decisions on it;
- to develop an appreciation of the differences between profit and cash flow and the effects of management decisions on cash flows; and
- to present a perspective on the balance sheet that reveals it relevance for managers.

It is useful to distinguish between differing levels of financial management: (i) some decisions focus on an organization's **strategic** concerns – those that involve major, long-term commitments; (ii) other decisions focus on what may be termed **tactical** concerns – those involving more modest, yet still significant, concerns in the short to intermediate term; and (iii) **operational** financial management is concerned with day-to-day and very short-term issues (Fig. 10.1). It should be noted that these are interrelated for the strategic decisions an organization makes to determine what its shorter-term resources and capabilities may be. Financial accounting is related to financial management, particularly in the short term, where monitoring the financial effects of activities and managing those effectively can be critical.

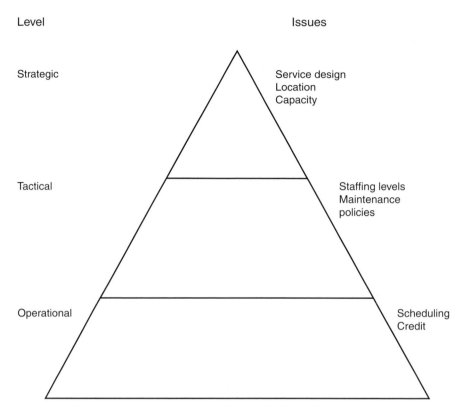

Level   Issues

Strategic   Service design / Location / Capacity

Tactical   Staffing levels / Maintenance policies

Operational   Scheduling / Credit

Fig. 10.1. Financial management: strategic, tactical and operational.

FINANCIAL ACCOUNTING AND FINANCIAL MANAGEMENT

Many of the systems used by financial accountants are useful for management purposes. The prime orientation of financial accounting systems focuses on acquiring information necessary for keeping accounts – tracking sales, cash, stocks, etc. in an organization's day-to-day operations. But, just as an accountant is interested in knowing exactly how much was sold and the incoming revenues for their financial statement preparation reporting on the organization's assets and liabilities, its profits and losses, so too will managers have their own interests in knowing what services are selling, where those sales are occurring, who is buying the services, what prices are being paid, whether a recent sales promotion is having an effect, and a myriad of other aspects of the organization's activities. The financial data may be mined extensively for useful information if the appropriate information systems are in place. And it is a strategic decision to install and operate these systems so that the organization's competitive capabilities are enhanced.

Even relatively small organizations will generate hundreds, if not thousands, of financial transactions in a day. In the past the effort required to collect, extract, categorize and then analyse the information of the greatest use for management has been too onerous. The legally mandated financial controls and reports produced by accounting systems may, through design and implementation efforts that more fully consider the organization's needs, be augmented by further controls and reports that provide better information. Accounting information may now be used as never before to help with a manager's understanding of his or her efforts and their impact.

The fundamental unit of financial activity is a transaction – the exchange of money for goods or services. Financial accounting monitors these and records their effect. When something is purchased the customer surrenders either cash or a promise to pay in exchange for a good or service or for the organization's promise to provide it in the future. No single transaction generally has much significance but when all are taken together and their collective effect is gauged the organization may then understand how well it is doing. With thousands of transactions occurring the volume of data is enormous and its organization and presentation very difficult. Accounting information systems have been developed to handle these demands and to provide summarized reports and controls required to effectively manage the finances. These systems may also be exploited by non-financial managers: operations and marketing managers share an interest in knowing what capacity remains after sales have occurred, and understanding what is selling provides insight into what needs to be promoted and how it might best be used. Finance, marketing and operations all interact and the information vital to one is often just as important within the other functions.

A brief consideration of the profit and loss statement will illustrate the interest managers will have in the financial information acquired and used by accountants. One critical issue and potential problem is that such accounting information only describes what has *already* happened and, while this may be useful for short-term responses in the immediate and near future, its value for longer-term decisions and marketing developments is more limited. Nevertheless, a sound understanding of the past is usually necessary for a well-founded extrapolation or consideration of how future developments might unfold.

Financial statement analysis from a management perspective

The two main financial statements developed by accountants are: (i) the profit and loss statement; and (ii) the balance sheet. These are required by law for all corporations for their annual reports and they are also useful to managers in providing an overview of an organization's operations. From a manager's perspective these are particularly useful when produced more frequently or in greater focus and detail to allow specific questions or issues to be investigated. For example, a profit and loss statement for a particular service or sales region might help in analysing its economic benefit. The balance sheet is rather less useful but some real benefit may be obtained through an analysis of the assets and liabilities that are affected by management initiatives and policies, particularly when strategic decisions involve acquiring long-term assets using liabilities such as debt.

The chief difficulty with most treatments of financial statement analysis is their focus – a consideration of the information from an accountant's point of view rather than that of a manager. Managers of operations, personnel and marketing could find much value in these data if only they were refined in ways to maximize their usefulness in those areas. So long as the preparation of these statements is dominated by purely financial and regulatory requirements, organizations will find they are not extracting the maximum benefits from the data collected. A proactive approach may help design systems that produce information more useful than that seen in the usual sets of accounts produced.

One point to recognize with financial statement analysis is that the information is all historical – it shows the effects of past policies and decisions. In their most commonly seen format they can reveal what happened over the past year (or quarter, if public accounts are produced that frequently). Yet managers will require information more frequently – generally monthly and perhaps even weekly or daily. But even the most current accounting reports will always describe events that have already occurred. This information can be very valuable but it does not necessarily allow marketing efforts to be managed as they are happening.

The profit and loss statement and how managers can use it

The profit and loss statement is perhaps the most useful of the accounting reports commonly used. It summarizes the organization's income from sales, the costs incurred in generating those sales and the overhead expenditures necessary to support the sales activity. This information is presented in a coherent format that allows the different pieces of information to be considered individually and in relation to other relevant issues. A manager may easily see what the sales revenues for the period have been. Going beyond that simple information they may then look at related information: (i) how much the costs of making those sales were; or (ii) how the current period's sales changed from the previous periods; or even (iii) how the current period's sales compare with the same period in a previous year if that is more relevant (as it often is in tourism businesses affected by seasonal factors). The profit and loss statement can be constructed to provide a more precise focus too if necessary – it may be broken down to focus on specific services or regions (and their costs), or any other aggregation in which the manager may have a specific interest in assessing. The information can be acquired and a close working relationship with an organization's accountants can help design systems that allow this information to be easily and effectively collected and reported from the mass of accounting information handled.

Table 10.1 illustrates a common format for profit and loss statements. This also provides a line-by-line synopsis of each entry for management. Besides the raw figures from the profit and loss statement there are a number of relationships that may also be used to explore the organization's performance. These interesting relationships are most often identified through financial ratio analysis, an important tool used by accountants in assessing corporate financial performance. Some of these ratios reflect an organization's competitive and marketing performance and so have a specific relevance to managers.

A frequently used measure of marketing performance and operations efficiency is the gross profit margin: gross profit/sales revenue. This effectively is the difference between the selling price and the direct costs of the goods sold or services provided. The key point to recognize is that this should be considered as showing 'symptoms' of a problem and is not itself the problem. For example: the gross profit margin may fall from one year to the next and raise concern, but without further investigation the most appropriate response cannot be identified from that simple measure. The margin may have fallen because prices have 'softened' due to competitor pressure: (i) price-cutting by existing competition; (ii) improved competing services; and/or (iii) new entrants into the market, etc. Or it could also be due to customer behaviour: (i) tastes may change; (ii) incomes may not rise as expected; or (iii) changes in behaviour as a result of even more general macroeconomic factors such as interest rate changes, inflation or exchange rate variations. The ratio provides an insight into performance, but does not explain why that varies. Explanation requires a closer review of revenues, prices, volume sold, unit costs, etc. – the whole range of factors that affect gross profit.

While selling and administrative expenses are generally presented as an aggregate, an analysis that breaks these down so that the selling costs may be considered on their own is most useful. In this the ratio of selling overheads to sales revenue would be a critical interest. Advertising and other promotions often require expenditure prior to the realization of sales – these fixed costs then need to be recovered by the sales they help generate. If the level of sales is greater than expected then a lower cost:revenue ratio may be seen; if sales are not stimulated as much as desired a lower ratio may be observed. The 'target' or desired ratio may be set arbitrarily or taken from past experience. Differences from the target or past years' experience may again be explained by other factors: (i) advertising costs may be increasing faster than sales revenue,

Table 10.1. Profit and loss statement and implications for management.

Profit and loss statement	Current year (£)	Previous year (£)	Implications for management
Sales revenue	1500	1250	This is the level of sales in monetary terms. Are sales reaching desired levels? Is there a minimum level of sales necessary? Are sales increasing, decreasing or stable? Related questions are: Are revenues per unit sold stable, increasing or decreasing? Is the item's price 'right'? Is it being discounted? Are competitor's affecting sales – and if so is it volume or price most affected? Not only are changes in value considered but also proportionate changes are usually considered too. A £1 million increase in sales might be great for a small company but not so impressive for a much larger one. Comparative changes are important too, for a company may find that its results should not be considered in isolation but also in reference to its nearest competitors and the industry or economy more widely. Thus a set of 'good' results may lose some of their shine if others are doing even better yet, or gain more if those competitors are doing more poorly.
Cost of goods sold	750	650	This reflects the unit costs of the items or services sold. These may include purchase or production costs, distribution costs and direct sales commissions. Are these increasing or decreasing proportionately with sales? These can be a measure of efficiency in production, or a measure of how effectively suppliers are controlled.
Gross profit	750	600	This is also called a contribution margin. This is a broad measure of the profitability of the goods and services sold. Its interest to managers is that it is a better guide for sales promotions than simple price or volume. Increasing the sales of the most profitable services is one financially oriented objective that managers may identify.
Selling and administrative costs	500	400	General administrative costs would be a concern for managers – these represent the office and support staff that facilitate operations; most organizations try to utilize these as efficiently as possible, although there is no direct link between them and the sales volumes achieved. Some marketing and selling overhead costs certainly would be closely considered. These would include such issues as advertising and other promotional costs and their link to sales generated with implications for future marketing effort.

(Continued)

Table 10.1. Continued.

Profit and loss statement	Current year (£)	Previous year (£)	Implications for management
Other fixed costs	100	100	These are usually outside the day-to-day control of managers, though they may be varied over the longer term by investment or disinvestment or changes to the assets base of the organization. Examples of such costs could be items like depreciation of assets, insurance, rent, utility costs, etc. One point to recognize is that investment in new service development may be classified as an overhead in this category. Expanding, or upgrading facilities would generally involve investments that would affect these.
Profit	150	100	This value is how much money is being made from the organization's operations before interest and tax. This is an important number for it represents a measure of the organization's performance independent of the manner in which it has financed itself. Thus two companies might be equally successful in their activities but find that the choices made in financing their operations create cost differentials. This value is thus more suitable for comparisons between periods or companies that finance themselves differently.
Interest charges	50	50	These are the costs of money borrowed to sustain operations. This too may not generally be a concern for managers.
Taxes	50	25	
Net profit	50	25	How much money is made after tax; it is then available for distribution to the organization's shareholders or owners as dividends or profits; or it may be retained to provide additional working capital or money for reinvestment within the business in the future.

yielding a higher cost:revenue ratio; or (ii) a promotion may be more successful in stimulating sales revenues than expected, yielding a lower cost:sales ratio. A disaggregated set of revenues and costs would then attempt to link specific overhead expenditures for a given product's or service's selling, advertising, promotion and development costs to the revenues it yields.

This information may then be compared with the plans previously developed and performance against the plan assessed. Questions may then be posed: Was the plan successfully implemented? If not, what problems were there? (Higher than expected costs?/Delays in promoting the product?/Delays in delivery?/Problems in distribution?) In essence, the effectiveness of the plan and its implementation may be assessed. A proper 'audit' of operations and marketing may then indicate successes to be emulated or failures to be avoided in future plans and activities.

The profit and loss information is just one tool use to manage an organization's operations. It is usually supplemented by a cash flow analysis: managers recognize that profits are only part of the story in running their organizations.

Adjustments to 'profit': cash flow and managing it

The cash flow analysis that follows from the profit and loss statement requires a number of 'adjustments' in order to understand the real impact on the organization's cash position from a period's operations.

Profit is the starting point. But some of the fixed costs deducted generally are depreciation – simply an allocation of past investment in productive assets to the current and future periods with the purpose of more accurately reflecting the true costs of doing business over the life of an asset, rather than forcing all of its costs on to the period when it was acquired. Thus depreciation is a non-cash expense for an organization: one that it has to recognize to properly assess its profitability, but not one that currently costs it any money. Depreciation is effectively money spent in the past that is treated as a current cost, so the true cash position for an organization would look to its profits and add back to them the depreciation previously paid. This generally improves the situation (more cash available for paying debts and other uses), but against that there may be a number of deductions.

It is common for many businesses in the hospitality and tourism industries to face significant overheads costs associated with their facilities, equipment and even the staff they use. In these cases there may be significant benefits to a clear understanding of how sales and demand promotions can affect the overall short-term financial performance of the organization. In these cases financial management can play a significant role.

First, there are inventories to consider. An increase in inventories will require money. These inventories are not shown on the profit and loss statement but will be shown later on the balance sheet. A decrease in inventories has an effect like depreciation: stock created and paid for in the past is currently being sold. Those earlier costs are now shown on the profit and loss as a cost, but they were paid in the past. So current sales of inventories previously created bring in more cash through recovering those earlier costs. In effect the profits from past sales have been stored in inventories until those stocks have been sold off and converted into cash now rather than in the past. Marketing managers should consider inventories as working capital just as accountants do, and ask whether those stocks are being deployed most effectively.

Frequently, managers have to consider the most effective inventory policies for perishables and consumables. In restaurants particularly it is vital to control wastage of food stocks bought in anticipation of sales – a delicate balancing act between having too much and incurring higher costs and having too little and enduring lost sales and/or customer dissatisfaction.

Secondly, there are organizational credit policies to consider. Many organizations will operate using inventories bought on credit from their suppliers. This may be an effective means for raising working capital, but it may be expensive in terms of the cost of the good sold. Supplies acquired on credit might be priced higher than they would be otherwise. Does the organization pay a premium for the easy credit it enjoys? Similarly an organization may offer credit terms to its own customers as a means for stimulating sales. The benefits of increased sales revenues will be reduced somewhat by higher costs of providing credit as well as the cost of the capital used. For example, an organization may sell blocks of its capacity to other organizations at a lower price and with payment due later; as distinguished from sales made to individual customers more irregularly at higher prices and paid for at the time ordered or when the services are delivered. A number of managerial issues arise in these situations.

The working capital employed in an organization's operations will be greatly affected by its marketing policies, and it is useful for managers to understand those effects.

A summary of adjustments is:

$$CASH = Profit + Depreciation - Change\ in\ inventory$$
$$- Change\ in\ creditors + Change\ in\ debtors$$

The profit and loss statement shows the effect of a period's operations on an organization. The cash flow analysis shows the effect of those operations on the organization's working capital – the money it relies on in its day-to-day activities.

But organizations also use buildings, equipment, patents and brands, and capital borrowed or invested for the long term. These are not working capital but are still necessary for the organization to operate. The profit and loss statement simply describes an organization's activity within a specific period, but it existed before that, and will generally continue afterwards. The organization started the period with various assets and liabilities – these are described by the balance sheet. The balance sheet will be changed by the activities described in the profit and loss. Sales (and production) will possibly alter the organization's inventories. These interactions between the profit and loss statement and the balance sheet are also important for management.

Balance sheets and fixed assets used in tourism

The distinction between fixed and current assets reflects the need to distinguish between the working capital used within the day-to-day operations and the marketing efforts of an organization and those assets used to support those operations in the longer term. For example, in a restaurant it is necessary to have both food and the equipment to process and cook it, but the food is inventory that is regularly bought and sold while the equipment remains in the organization's possession. In marketing a similar situation arises: it may be necessary to promote the facilities or services in numerous ways – advertising, discounting, exhibitions, etc. – in the day-to-day activities of the organization but services and facilities also need to be developed.

Management focuses on strategic development of products and services, of brands and customer relationships and numerous other long-term initiatives. Without these developments of what may be considered marketing and operating assets the short-term marketing and operations will be handicapped. These longer-term developments may well have a presence seen in the financial accounts on the balance sheet (Table 10.2 describes the implications). The key issue is whether these have a measurable, marketable value. For example, an organization may purchase a franchise and have the rights to use a brand and products or services in its operations. These represent an asset. Similarly, new facility, product or service development can involve

Table 10.2. Balance sheet and implications for management.

Balance sheet	Current year (£)	Previous year (£)	Implications for management
Fixed assets (at cost less accumulated depreciation)	110,000	120,000	Fixed assets are the long-term capital used by the organization in the form generally of physical facilities – buildings, equipment, shop fittings, etc. Intellectual property like patents is included as are such things as acquired 'rights' to produce products or use a franchise. Whether a 'brand' constitutes a fixed asset is somewhat controversial. And the suggestion that customer relationships too are assets is one totally alien to accounting although any marketing manager would regard these as critical.
Current assets			The basic criterion is whether the asset will last longer than 1 year, or be fully used up or sold in less time
Inventories	25,000	20,000	Inventories are goods produced and held for later sale. They may be created on purpose to decouple sales activities and production processes, or to provide an immediately available supply to support sales. There are two dimensions of particular interest for management: (i) the volume of stock available; and (ii) the variety of stock available. The balance sheet simply shows the total value and a disaggregated view may be more useful. One useful relationship is inventory turnover (i.e. how quickly these stocks could be sold). In service industries such as hospitality and tourism inventories are usually quite small in value – consumables used to support service delivery.
Creditors (less bad-debt allowance)	15,000	10,000	Creditors are customers who have bought on credit and this reflects the money owed to the organization. Credit policies may be a critical issue in supporting sales, with 'loose' credit stimulating sales. Such policies have associated cost: (i) the opportunity cost of the money so lent (it could be deposited in a bank and earning interest); and (ii) a cost is the possibility of non-payment (bad debt). Sales made to larger organizations may suffer from significant delays in payment, so close control of the creditors' turnover period can be important.
Cash and securities	2,000	2,000	These funds are almost immediately available to settle the organization's own debts and liabilities.

(Continued)

Table 10.2. Continued.

Balance sheet	Current year (£)	Previous year (£)	Implications for management
Total assets	152,000	150,000	
Liabilities			Current liabilities are those that will demand payment within 1 year – long-term liabilities are those that do not have to be paid that quickly.
Current portion of long-term debt	6,000	6,000	While the bulk of long-term liabilities do not require payment in the current year there is usually some obligation to service the debt by making periodic payments on the debt. This figure represents the amounts due in the current period.
Debtors	12,000	10,000	The organization may have bought on credit itself. This represents the amounts owed. This may be of some interest to marketing if the credit taken on purchases is reflected in higher purchase costs that will be reflected in higher cost of goods sold in the profit and loss and lower profits.
Long-term debt	20,000	22,000	This is the outstanding balance of the long-term debt excluding the portion currently payable. The long-term debt represents borrowings and reflects the organization's financial strategy – whether to use debt or equity in funding its operations. Debt incurs fixed payments while equity does not.
Share capital	100,000	100,000	Organizations typically have shareholders who have invested. The share capital describes the sums of money so invested.
Retained earnings	14,000	12,000	Retained earnings are profits earned in previous periods that have been kept by the organization for its own investments and to support its future activities. Such profits could have been paid to the shareholders as dividends, but most organizations find that keeping these for reinvestment is more effective than having to raise new equity funding or borrowing.
Total liabilities and equity	152,000	150,000	

expenditure over several years to yield an asset that may then be exploited. This expenditure will often be treated as an expense in the period it is made – there are significant tax benefits in doing so as this effectively shields current profits from taxation. These expenditures may yield later profit streams, so they are in actuality investments.

Similarly, many marketing efforts create brand identities through effort and expenditure over periods of time. These may also be considered to represent an 'asset' in providing an economically exploitable identity. But valuing such expenditure as an investment is difficult: how can a distinction be made between advertising that promotes current sales and its lingering effect in helping future sales? How can such costs be allocated? For the implication is that some of these costs should really be spread over the whole time horizon for which they help sales. If so, then these residual effects need some consideration as an asset just as any other that depreciates over time.

Similarly, many operational activities can promote a particular image and market presence. Consider the role of quality in an organization's image. Relatively small costs in the area of consumables can create disproportionate impressions in the perceived quality of the services offered; as can operational policies such as maintenance that keep a facility at its best appearance, contributing to an image of quality.

Balance sheets are excellent at representing things on the basis of their cost. They are less effective at presenting things in terms of their value. An asset may be carried on the balance sheet on the basis of its purchase price less depreciation, but it may be obsolete and have no monetary value; conversely, another asset may be fully depreciated and thus have no value shown on the balance sheet and yet still be useful for generating income and have value on that basis. This may be true for all the fixed assets of an organization: they are shown on the books at cost less depreciation, and yet the company keeps them because it believes they can all be exploited to yield greater income now and through their life than if sold off.

Many of the intangible dimensions of marketing – building brand identity, customer relationships, etc. and such things as staff skills and loyalty – are almost impossible to effectively value in the first instance. And these can prove even more difficult to convert into a marketable form – how can a customer relationship be 'sold' to another party to realize its value? Should the organization go into liquidation? Thus, many of the financial interests involved create intangibles difficult in the first instance to monetarily value; and impossible to render into a marketable form even if values may be determined. It might be useful nevertheless to think of a 'balance sheet' in which such intangibles have a presence. This cannot replace the true financial balance sheet but ought to serve a parallel purpose – to formally and honestly assess the long-term marketing 'investments' that may be considered assets for any organization.

While a brand may not show up on a financial balance sheet, it may on one used for marketing. However, this forces a number of difficult and potentially unwelcome questions to be confronted, such as: Is this to be valued at cost, or should its exploitable market value be used? Most would argue that some idea of the present value of future benefits should be used but these may not be readily expressed monetarily.

CONCLUSIONS AND SUMMARY

This chapter has presented a perspective on accounting that reveals the financial consequences of common marketing decisions and policies. No marketing manager can ignore the economic effects of their decisions and actions and a better understanding of those should improve both decision making and performance. The chief focus is usually on the profit and loss statement because it reflects sales activities directly and marketing strategy and planning more generally. Simple but important developments like sales revenues and costs can be measured and potential problems recognized. Financial analysis will not provide a solution, but it is a vital tool in identifying symptoms of problems and suggesting avenues for investigation. Relationships too can be recognized – trends in sales or the impact of credit policies on sales. The underlying need to justify marketing decisions and actions in terms of profitability or cost-effectiveness makes a grasp of these relationships most useful.

This has been achieved through the chapter's discussions of:

- the accounting systems reports and their relevance to specific needs;
- analysis of the profit and loss statement and the effects that management actions may have on various elements reported in them;
- analysis of the balance sheet and its relevance for tourism managers; and
- analysis of the differences between profit and cash flow and the effects of various management decisions on cash flows.

FURTHER READING

Haigh, D. (1994) *Strategic Control of Marketing Finance*. Financial Times Management Series. Financial Times, London.

Walters, D. and Halliday, M. (1998) *Marketing and Finance: Working the Interface*. Allen & Unwin, London.

Ward, K. (2003) *Marketing Finance: Turning Marketing Strategies into Shareholder Value*. Butterworth-Heinemann, London.

Wilson, R.M.S. (1999) *Accounting for Marketing*. International Thomson Business Press, London.

chapter 11

Financial Impact of Tourism Marketing

James Wilson and Luiz Moutinho

INTRODUCTION AND LEARNING OBJECTIVES

A basic understanding of financial management is essential for managers in the tourism industry. Financial management is central to planning, measuring and controlling many activities and managers that understand and can use this information can act on it more effectively. The learning objectives then focus on those dimensions of financial management most relevant to a manager's effectiveness. This chapter's objectives are:

- to develop an understanding of the financial effects of management decisions and policies;
- to develop a comprehension of the impact of pricing policies on an organization's financial performance;
- to develop an appreciation of service and product design issues and their relevance to financial performance;
- to present a perspective on the financial consequences of alternatives available for promoting an organization's services and products; and
- to show how the marketing mix interacts with financial management and the impact different elements within the mix may have on an organization's finances.

MANAGEMENT DECISIONS AND THEIR FINANCIAL EFFECTS

Within the tourism industry a useful framework for understanding the financial ramifications of common management decisions may be the 'marketing mix', since marketing is so important for success. This framework provides a comprehensive overview of both operational and strategic issues. One perspective may be seen in Fig. 11.1 (taken from Wilson (1999) and revised slightly), which shows contrasting orientations taken by marketing-dominated companies

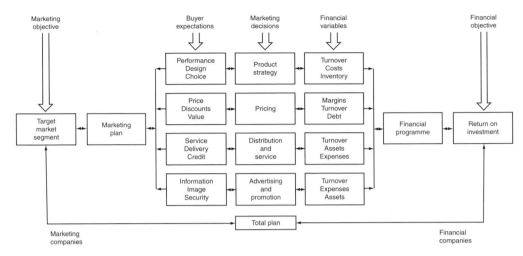

Fig. 11.1. Management versus financial orientations (adapted from Wilson, 1999).

and those dominated by finance. It illustrates the intersection of concerns between general and financial managers, with finance tending to emphasize the right-hand side issues (return on investment and those factors that affect it) and general managers the ones on the left-hand side (market penetration and those related factors). A more balanced view would be beneficial for organizations as a whole – where one or the other dominates the other's concerns may not be given due consideration.

The objective in taking a balanced perspective is to ensure that the relative concerns of both general and financial managers are mutually understood, and that the effects of decisions in each area for the other may be more fully appreciated within the decision-making process. To assist in this a commonly used framework within marketing, 'the four Ps' (product and service, price, promotion and place), will be employed, given the importance of marketing within the tourism industry. These focuses describe the major decisions confronting managers and will thus provide a context for the application of the tools financial analysts may apply.

Product and service

A key decision in any business is the identification and development of products and services for markets. Marketing research and development are essential elements in the marketing mix and may themselves represent a significant demand for finance. Some examples of the activities subsumed in this analysis are those concerned with identifying what services to provide:

- new services or facilities to be introduced, or old ones to be withdrawn or 'improved';
- service product 'ranges', 'lines' and 'portfolios';
- service positioning vis-à-vis competitors, direct competition or differentiation;
- branding; and
- service and facility design/performance characteristics.

This investment is made with a view to potential returns from their successful exploitation later. Similarly, marketing research that helps understand markets and their needs is also clearly a form of investment though quantifying the economic returns of such studies may be virtually impossible. Marketing information does have value but this is derived from its subsequent use.

The following development may then act on this information and yield a new (or updated) service with better potential for being profitable than if no such study were undertaken.

The issue is one of balancing the costs of market research and development against the potential economic benefits. In this there may be a number of analytical tools useful to assist in managing the risks involved in market analysis and for assessing the attractiveness of alternative investments.

New service introduction case

A new service has been developed and is proposed for introduction. The question of its potential profitability and economic attractiveness has been raised. The service will cost £250,000 to introduce inclusive of all necessary equipment, staff training, vendor support, introductory promotions and initial advertising. The service has a 5-year life expectancy and during that time is expected to yield sales revenues of £300,000 in the first year increasing by £100,000 annually until they end in the fifth year, with direct costs of 70% of revenues and allocatable overheads (advertising, back-office support, management, etc.) of £75,000 per annum. The new equipment will be depreciated by £20,000 per annum and have no salvage value at the end of the period. The company pays 40% tax on its profits. Similar projects in the past have been evaluated using a 15% discount rate.

Table 11.1 provides a time-phased analysis of the impact of introducing the new service. It shows the sales revenues in each year based on the starting volume and projected growth, the associated direct production, distribution and selling costs, and the gross profit. The fixed costs for the selling and administrative overheads and depreciation are deducted to yield the profits, from which taxes are deducted to yield the after-tax profits. The cash flow due to the new service is then determined by adding the depreciation to the after-tax profits.

The cash flow generated by the service can then be compared with the costs of undertaking the project. A simple comparison might just total the cash flow from the project and compare

Table 11.1. Time-phased analysis of the impact of introducing the new service.

New product assessment	Financial cost/return (£000)				
	Year 1	Year 2	Year 3	Year 4	Year 5
Sales revenues	300	400	500	600	700
Direct costs	180	240	300	360	420
Gross profit	120	160	200	240	280
Selling and administrative overheads	75	75	75	75	75
Depreciation	20	20	20	20	20
Profit (loss)	25	65	105	145	185
Tax	10	26	42	58	74
Profit (loss) after tax	15	39	63	87	111
Cash	35	59	83	107	131

the total income with the start-up costs: Total income is £415,000, while the start-up costs are £250,000, yielding an apparent net gain of £165,000.

But the difficulty in this simplistic approach is its failure to appreciate that the benefits are spread over a period of 5 years' time while the start-up costs are paid beforehand and could have been earning interest instead. What is necessary is to look at the future cash flows and ask what would be their equivalent value at the time the service was introduced. This value will be lower due to the time value of money. Applying the discounting rate of 15%, the implication is that cash received in 1 year's time would be worth less than its full value. If the organization invested £100 and earned 15% interest on it, in a year's time it would have £115; in 2 years, £132; in 3 years, £152, etc. Conversely, if the company were offered £100 in a year's time that money would be worth only £87 today, for the company might invest that £87 and the interest earned over the year would bring it up to £100. Thus the 'discount factor' of 0.87 would describe the present value of a cash inflow in 1 year's time for a discount rate of 15%. For this service, the projected discounted cash flows are shown in Table 11.2.

The comparison is now much closer – the undiscounted cash flows seemed to be very much greater than the service introduction costs. But this consideration of the impact of time and alternative investments that might be made significantly reduces the economic attractiveness of this proposal. The total discounted income is now reduced to only £256,000 compared with the costs of £250,000 leaving a discounted benefit, the net present value (or NPV), of only £6000. So long as the NPV is positive the proposal is considered viable, but there may well be other proposals with higher NPVs to compete with for limited investment capital.

Price

The price set for a service is one of the most important decisions made. There will be strategic implications but the usual effects relate to short-term volume and profitability. There are

Table 11.2. Projected discounted cash flows.

		Discount factor				
		1/(1.15)	1/(1.15)²	1/(1.15)³	1/(1.15)⁴	1/(1.15)⁵
Discount factor	0.15	0.870	0.756	0.658	0.572	0.497
Cash × discount factor = discounted income (£000)		35 × 0.870 = 30	45	55	61	65
Total discounted income (£000)	256					
Cost (£000)	250					
Net benefit (£000)	6					

a number of alternative approaches to the setting of prices for a company's services. Broadly speaking, these may be categorized as approaches based on accounting, economics or market analysis.

In accounting-based approaches the consideration of costs dominates the analysis. Most typically the focus is on a 'cost-plus' pricing method in which the company first identifies 'the' cost of producing some service and then seeks to obtain some premium over that cost. In most cases the base is the full cost, which includes allocated overheads. The additional mark-up is often a standard one based on historical practice or on industry norms. If the company wishes to achieve a specific gross profit margin, that too may be used to dictate the amount the price should be marked up over the costs of the services bought. This policy may often be seen in retailing in which goods are purchased and then priced using a standard mark-up intended to recover the overheads and provide a profit.

In economic approaches there is a reliance on an economic analysis of both supply and demand curves as seen by the company. In perfectly competitive markets the price is dictated by market factors, and the company would produce until its production costs rise above the price consumers will pay. In monopolistic markets the company would effectively restrict output to increase prices and its profitability. One special case is price discrimination, in which companies would seek to charge different prices to different identifiable groups of consumers so that each group yields the maximum profit possible. One example of price discrimination would be 'peak' versus 'off-peak' pricing – this may have the objective of maximizing profits as well as attempting to shift demand from the peak period to the off-peak periods.

With market analysis the company will generally know its own costs but go beyond those to consider its customers and competitors in determining pricing policy. This may result in a variety of alternative pricing strategies. In practice companies may use 'reference' pricing based on the prices charged by their competitors – and set their price relative to the competitor's, given issues such as perceived quality, availability, etc. Other approaches include a 'skimming' policy, in which a product is introduced at a relatively high price, which is then reduced once those people willing to pay the high price have been satisfied. A similar policy is 'penetration' pricing, in which a relatively low price is charged to achieve a higher sales volume and market share than might otherwise be the case or to attempt to break up existing buying patterns. Such a policy should be considered very carefully since it may induce competitors to reduce their price to retain market share. The consequence of such a response is that neither company may earn the profits it might normally expect.

One interesting development is the idea of target pricing, and target costing based on that information. In this a new service is assessed against consumer expectations, and priced to fall into the range of prices acceptable to consumers. With target costing this analysis is carried one (or several) step back into the organization. If the consumers are only willing to pay a relatively low price for the service, its producers might then ask how the costs may be reduced to allow that demand to be met profitably. This may revolutionize service design, with greater interest in cost as a critical design dimension along with performance, quality and other traditional concerns. In the traditional approach it is usually assumed that the service is defined first and then a price determined for it from consumer behaviour – a more integrated approach sees service design and pricing as interrelated.

All pricing policies have financial implications. Some plainly look at maximizing sales volumes, or sales revenues, and these might be considered as possibly suboptimal since they consider only one aspect of the overall impact. Besides these measures of sales, a well-founded decision should also consider the costs associated with generating sales and the potential profitability.

Breakeven analysis

One of the most basic analyses of pricing is breakeven analysis. In this approach an organization simply needs to identify the fixed costs associated with developing and producing a service, its direct production and marketing costs and the proposed price for which it would sell. The product 'breaks even' when the sales volume yields total revenues that exceed the total costs.

Consider the earlier example. The service had start-up costs of £250,000 and allocated overheads of £375,000 (£75,000 for 5 years) for a total fixed cost of £625,000. The service's direct costs were described as being 60% of revenues, but a more effective approach would consider the actual purchase and production costs instead. These have been estimated as £100 per client. The price initially considered is £165 (providing a mark-up roughly equal to a 60% cost of sales (COS) to price ratio). How many clients would need to be served in order for the organization to break even on this service? The breakeven point would look at the contribution (price − direct costs per client) each client served makes towards recouping the start-up and overhead costs. Each sale thus yields £65 contribution to repaying the £625,000 'invested'. At that rate the company would need to serve some 9616 clients to break even.

Breakeven point: $625,000/(165 − 100) = 9616$

If the projected sales are greater than 9616, the service will yield a profit; if the projected sales are less than that, a loss will result. This breakeven point provides a threshold against which forecast sales can be assessed. In most instances the introduction will depend on exceeding the breakeven point by a healthy margin.

Looking back at the projected sales revenues of £300,000 in the first year, rising by £100,000 annually, we can estimate the first-year sales volume to be roughly 1800, with annual increases of approximately 600 units for a total sales volume over the 5 years of about 15,100 units, well above the breakeven point. This analysis is illustrated in Fig. 11.2.

With the identified relationships the breakeven point is exceeded by roughly 5500 units, yielding a contribution of £65 per unit that becomes profit once the overheads have been fully recovered. The total profit then is £357,500.

ISSUES

This may be used to judge the financial impact of differing prices on the breakeven point − higher prices mean that fewer clients need be served in order to recover the investment. Lower prices would dictate that it would take a longer period. But the process ignores the time needed to generate sales; this is significant for two reasons: (i) future returns should be discounted, particularly if several years' revenues are needed to reach breakeven; and (ii) the time may exceed either the productive life of the facilities used or the service's life cycle.

CAVEATS

The breakeven model is very simple and straightforward in application, but its results need to be carefully considered. Is the volume of sales required to break even a feasible one? In the example the service life was sufficiently long to allow these costs to be recovered, but if its life were much shorter the sales volume would not then be adequate. If the price were much lower, the volume of sales needed to break even might exceed the life of the service substantially.

A further difficulty arises from the use of fixed prices and unit costs. Basic economic theory suggests that prices need to fall in order to induce customers to buy more. The implications are that the total revenue doesn't simply keep increasing at a constant rate, and that

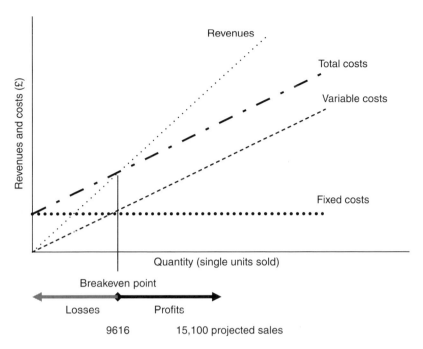

Fig. 11.2. A breakeven graph.

the effect of reducing prices to stimulate further sales would cause total revenues to 'flatten' and fall. Similarly the direct costs might be subject to variations – perhaps exhibiting 'learning curve' effects in which the unit costs decrease as experience is gained and allows for more efficient production. Perhaps the most significant variation for many tourism businesses arises from the limited capacity of their service facilities – their fixed costs then would be quasi-fixed and exhibit a step-like behaviour with fixed increments of capital required to provide capacity increases. This more complex analysis is illustrated in Fig. 11.3.

In this more complex environment the breakeven analysis may still be used, recognizing the effects of the non-linear relationships – the flat fixed costs have been replaced by a set of fixed costs that increase in steps as increases in the sales volume make additional capital investment necessary. The variable cost is no longer a simple line as would be the case for a constant production cost but now curves and becomes 'flatter' as the learning effects reduce unit costs. The total cost is now a stepped curved line, against which the total revenues are plotted as they increase and then decrease to reflect the impact that lower prices and increasing volumes sold have on total revenues. The result is a range of output which allows the organization to break even, below point '**A**' costs exceed revenues, as they do above point '**B**'; but for the points in between '**A**' and '**B**' the total revenues exceed costs and the organization breaks even. The profit maximizing point may be identified where the difference between total revenues and costs is greatest.

Yield management

Yield or revenue management has become one of the most valuable tools for effective pricing decisions in many tourism businesses: it is now common for airlines, hotel chains and car rental companies to use these methods to maximize the revenues that their services generate.

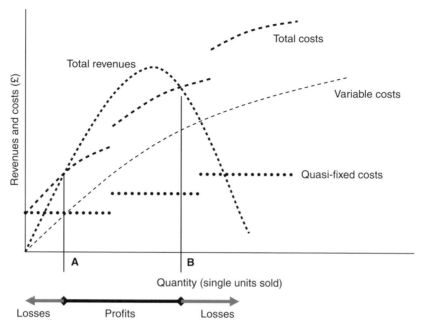

Fig. 11.3. Breakeven graph with non-linear relationships.

The problem is more generally recognized by economists as **price discrimination**: charging different customers different prices for identical goods or services. Yield management strives to charge the right price to the right customers for the right services at the right time. The essential requirements for using yield management are:

1. Limited capacity (a fixed number of hotel rooms, or seats on an aeroplane, etc.).
2. Limited time for use or consumption (hotel rooms and seats on a particular flight cannot be used later).
3. Customers are willing to pay different prices for the goods or services used.

Ideally, an organization would like to charge every customer the maximum price they'd be willing to pay, but competition that drives down prices to an 'equilibrium' that matches marginal consumers with marginal suppliers allows some consumers what's called a 'consumer surplus' (just as it allows the most efficient suppliers a profit) from paying less than they otherwise would be willing to pay. Figure 11.4 briefly outlines this situation. The equilibrium price '**P**' is determined by the intersection of the demand '**D**' and supply '**S**' curves, with the quantity sold then being '**Q**'. However, an individual customer '**q**' might have been willing to pay a higher price '**p**' than the equilibrium; and they thus benefit by the differential between what they'd be willing to pay and the level generally prevalent in the market. In effect, they get a 'bargain', something they want for a price lower than the maximum they'd be willing to pay for it. Sellers would always like to take advantage of this fact, and sometimes such mechanisms as 'blind' auctions (in which bidders must bid without knowing what others are bidding) attempt to get customers to offer their maximum price for the goods and services available.

Yield management is one such mechanism used in the tourism industry to achieve maximum revenues from services that are limited in their available quantities and in time.

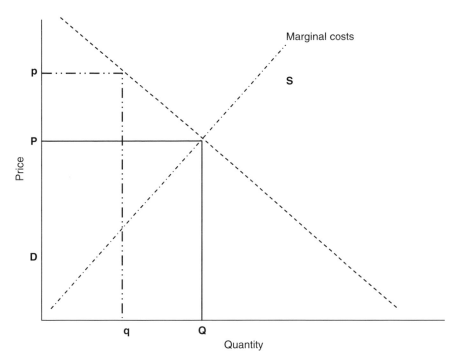

Fig. 11.4. Supply, demand, equilibrium prices and consumer surpluses.

Yield management may be used for off-peak pricing, differentiating between high and low seasons, or when demand might be particularly high due to other factors (or even days, as with a hotel that may charge higher rates when major sporting events or other such events are being staged). This may shift demand from peak periods to the off-peak periods, increasing the revenues with higher prices during the peak when capacity is fully utilized and also increasing revenues from the off-peak when capacity is not as utilized as it might otherwise become.

The timing of sales may be exploited to increase revenues, though this may involve apparently contradictory tactics. One approach may be to offer discounts for early commitments by customers, reserving capacity to be sold at higher prices to those customers that commit to purchases later, as may be seen in the airline industry. In other cases, where expected demand may not be so great as anticipated, surplus capacity may then be sold off very cheaply – even at prices close to the organization's marginal costs simply to generate revenue and contributions to overheads that would otherwise yield losses.

Although yield management systems may be very complex and involve very sophisticated analyses and modelling of consumer behaviour, even relatively small tourism businesses may find it advantageous to act on these insights and thereby improve their financial performance.

Promotion

Promotion involves a wide range of competitive activities used to increase sales and to attract and hold customers. Promotional activities include advertising, public relations and customer-oriented sales promotions. Promotional activities may be directed at customers or at the distribution channel with the intent of increasing demand or to improve service availability. Some promotional activities may involve discounts that affect the revenues from sales, but most are more appropriately considered service-related overheads. The introduction of a new service will typically be accompanied by a number of promotional activities – advertising directed at the service's end-buyers, point-of-sale materials for retailers, training programmes and dealer incentives for wholesalers or intermediaries, etc. These consequently may be considered as overheads that can be allocated to that service specifically though no individual customer or sale can be identified with those costs. If more services are introduced, the organization will have more of these promotional activities to undertake and pay for. Some promotional activities may not be associated with specific services – such things as public relations that have the intent of promoting the organization as a whole rather than any specific service. In those cases the promotional activities would constitute part of the general sales and marketing overheads.

Advertising case

One controversy arises over the benefit of advertising: do organizations really benefit from this expenditure, or not? This issue may be addressed in accounting terms. The analysis proceeds by investigating the impact advertising has on increasing revenues relative to the costs involved in the advertising and supporting those sales.

In the example shown in Table 11.3 the advertising does increase sales substantially – by 20%, a gain of £20,000 in revenues compared with the advertising costs of only £5000. This apparent gain is not actually realized because it ignores the costs of providing the service – the relevant increase is not revenues but instead the gross profits. Advertising has increased these by £2000, which is rather less than the costs of advertising of £5000 so the organization is then worse off despite the increased sales volume and revenues.

Sales incentives case

Sales commissions are frequently used to help motivate staff in their work. These may be considered a direct cost because these commissions are directly linked to the sales volumes achieved – if they increase, so too do the costs of selling the goods. In many cases sales incentives operate on a sliding scale, for example a salesperson may be paid a base salary plus an incentive of 5% for all sales over £10,000/month; 10% for sales over £15,000/month; and 20% on sales greater than £20,000/month. So long as the gross profit margin is greater than 20% the organization will benefit from these incentives.

The increasing sales commission percentages are intended to motivate salespeople; by looking at the midpoint of each sales range in Table 11.4 it can be seen that the sales commissions increase substantially. The profits also increase, though not so much as the salespeople's commissions.

The key is to recognize that the costs of promotion are paid not from the increase in total revenues but from the increase in gross profits. This is true for both fixed-type, general promotional costs involved in advertising, public relations, etc. and for variable-type, sale-specific promotional costs like price discounts and sales commissions.

Other marketing assets, like customer relationship development, may be similarly assessed in terms of their future exploitable value. There may, however, be objections to so doing for such an attitude reduces everything to issues of pounds and pence. But such is the nature of a balance sheet – and numerous other intangible assets of organizations (staff skill and loyalty, for example) are similarly disregarded or treated in a mercenary way.

Indeed, there is much confusion about the concept of value as distinct from cost. A customer may be asked the 'value' of the service they've been provided (or, more to the point, a manager may be asked the 'value' of a customer). In almost every case the customer will

Table 11.3. Impact of advertising on increasing revenue: an example.

Profit and loss (typical month)	Without advertising (£)	With advertising (£)	Implications
Revenues	100,000	120,000	Advertising increases sales by £20,000
COS[a]	90,000	108,000	COS increases proportionately. Note, some promotional activities may involve disproportionate changes – discounting, or higher sales commissions, for example.
Gross profit	10,000	12,000	
Fixed costs			
General overheads	5,000	5,000	The general overheads will not be affected by increased advertising
Advertising	0	5,000	Cost of advertising
Profit	5,000	2,000	
Tax	2,500	1,000	Rate = 50%
Net profit	2,500	1,000	

[a] COS, cost of sales.

respond by saying that the 'value' was the price they actually paid for it. Yet a moment's reflection would show the fallacy of that perspective. The customer chose to exchange money equal to the service's price in order to obtain it, presumably because they valued it more than their money, or the other goods and services they could have bought with that money. This perspective is clear from the basic idea of a demand curve in economics: when prices are high the quantity demanded is low; but as prices fall and the quantity demanded increases those first customers remain and enjoy a 'consumer surplus'. They're able to obtain the product, which they valued so greatly that they were willing to pay a high price for, at the lower prices needed to attract customers not so eager to buy the item. Similarly for producers and supply curves – the most efficient may be able to produce very cheaply; if prices rise they will then enjoy extra profit on those efficiently produced units.

Developing customer relationships can be a costly exercise involving time and effort and even investment in physical facilities to support the relationship and its servicing. The value in terms of current and future sales and profits should exceed current and future costs; otherwise there is no economic justification for it.

Table 11.4. Profitability and sales commission rates.

Profit and loss	Salesperson's basic salary (£)	Salesperson's commission (£)		
		5%	10%	20%
Revenues	5,000	12,500	17,500	22,500
COGS[a] (70% of revenues)	3,500	8,750	12,250	15,750
Sales commissions		125	500	1,250
Gross profit	1,500	3,625	4,750	5,500
Fixed costs	500	500	500	500
Profit	1,000	3,125	4,250	5,000
Tax	500	1,562.5	2,125	2,500
Net profit	500	1,562.5	2,125	2,500

[a] COGS, cost of goods sold.

Customer relationships and their financial impact

Customer relationships are one of the key assets of a business. Each relationship is unique; its value may vary over time in ways which are hard to predict; and customer relationships are not saleable and can be hard to transfer. Valuing a relationship involves collecting data about customer behaviour and having the financial tools to analyse those data.

Arriving at an accurate picture of customer profitability is problematic, particularly where product direct costs are a relatively low proportion of total costs, as is the case in many industries like hospitality and tourism services. In other words, the higher the proportion of indirect costs (facilities, sales expenses, administration and service costs), the more misleading a simple proportional allocation of such costs could be. Different customers use company's resources very differently: for example, capacity requirements, payment terms, order entry, customer and sales support may all vary considerably from customer to customer. Allocating such costs proportionate to volume, as is often done, may well fail to reflect the true pattern of the customer's usage of the company's resources. All sales involve a mix of both goods and services and the costs of *both* must be accurately assessed and allocated between the organization's customers. So long as customers utilize the organization's services proportionately with the volume of sales they generate, then traditional cost allocation methods used by accountants will render fairly accurate allocations of the service overhead costs between customers.

These consider each customer's 'purchase' not as a single entity but instead as a 'bundle' of identifiable goods and support services. Bundling in tourism usually considers the combination of two products or services that may have a natural affinity for the consumer – bed and breakfast in hotels, for instance; or fly/drive in holiday packages. But virtually all primary products or services carry an invisible bundle of supporting services that may constitute some of the cost of producing, selling and delivering the primary product or service. In catering, for example, it would involve the facilities in which the food was prepared, then eaten, and all the cleaning afterwards, etc.

Difficulties arise once customers vary significantly in the services they require in support of the goods bought. In these cases the traditional cost-allocation approaches that treat service support as a general overhead to be distributed evenly across all goods or services produced fails to reflect the uneven distribution of service demands that actually arise. In these cases those customers that place few demands on support service effectively pay more for less, implicitly subsidizing those customers with heavy demands whose price fails to fully reflect that additional service cost. To some extent the variability in service demand may reflect service variability: quality variations, natural variation and the like. These may quite properly be averaged out between customers as a form of 'insurance' in which these expected, but randomly occurring, costs are spread across all customers. But difficulties arise when the variations in the service demands arise not from the product or service sold or its performance but variations in customer behaviour.

For example, some products have a small element of service associated with them. Commodities such as a loaf of bread, bottle of milk or packet of writing paper would be typical examples. For these there is little service involved: the commodity itself offers little variability and both buyer and seller hold well-understood expectations of the product. The service component may exist in ancillary aspects of the product mix – the packaging or delivery of the goods, for example; but the products themselves offer little contention between buyers and sellers. Other products consist almost entirely of services, with few goods involved in their production or consumption. A service such as hairdressing would be a typical example. For this there is little physical product involved: the service itself involves the application of employee's time and skill with little physical product used – in hairdressing there may be small and inexpensive amounts of shampoo, hair gels and mousses, colouring, etc. but the bulk of the effort and cost arise from the staff time used. To the extent that prices may be varied to reflect the effort involved, these relatively fixed labour costs can be effectively allocated between customers – thus a customer that requires twice the labour time of another may be charged proportionately more. But if such pricing differentials are not possible (does it take more time and effort to cut curly or long hair than it does to cut straight or short hair?) then these more labour-intensive services will consume more resource than paid for.

In some markets customer behaviour may vary significantly, with aggressive customers demanding more extensive support *and* lower prices too than more passive customers. These aggressive customers may demand special consideration and service as well as being tough negotiators on price. The balance of power between customer and supplier is likely to affect the profitability of their relationships; the stronger the customer, the more concessions they can wring from their suppliers and the less profitable that relationship may be. This goes beyond the aforementioned desire to break down profit-and-loss-statement entries for overheads into more precise categories for assessing product profitability – at the extreme it goes to the question of the profitability of each product for any given customer. An incorrect allocation of indirect costs can lead to a misleading picture of customer profitability. Some customers are just more costly to serve than others, often as a result of their behaviour.

The role of marketing in this is self-evident, for the price setting in such circumstances may need to shift from easily implemented policies to more difficult pricing schemes based on discriminating between high- and low-service demand customers. The acquisition of the primary goods or services may yield little or no appreciation of the associated services or their costs, and great customer resistance then to any pricing scheme that specifically charges for these. For example, telephone support services that charge customers for the time used are an easily implemented mechanism for differential service pricing. Thus customers that need little support pay little or nothing for these services while more demanding ones do contribute directly and proportionately to the cost of the services they require. In effect, an 'unbundling' of the primary product or service and the telephone support services has been achieved. Managers need to assess customer demands for *both* the primary goods and the services used *and* their associated demands for supporting services, and identify mechanisms for pricing that more fully reflect the true total costs of serving each customer. Where there are significant differentials then mechanisms for unbundling those dimensions susceptible to varying demands may be financially beneficial in generating revenues from those with heavy demands *and* in attracting cost-conscious customers unwilling to subsidize the more intensive service users.

Profit or value?

However, customer profitability – whether in a single transaction or over a relationship lifetime – might not be the best foundation on which to base decisions about customer strategies. As a measure, profit is subject to distortions. Accountants and financial consultants are now arguing that it is value, not profits, that companies should measure. It is possible to perform very well on conventional accounting measures but destroy value. Accounting measures of profit can be misleading, showing apparent growth while providing minimal or negative returns to shareholders. Customer value analysis would serve as a valuable adjunct to traditional accounting measures of profitability.

Traditional profit measures do not necessarily reflect value creation – profits may still occur even if the marginal costs exceed marginal revenues simply because of earlier, even greater profits. The critical difference between measuring performance using accounting profit which reflects **average returns** and using value is that the latter looks at the **specific**, **marginal costs** of serving a customer when calculating returns on the organization's 'investment' in the customer relationship. Value is only created when marginal returns exceed the marginal costs, a more demanding requirement than that of making an accounting profit.

The economic value of a customer

Applying this concept of value creation to customers enables companies to consider the economic value rather than the profitability of their customers. This is particularly important where a company has to make significant investments to serve a customer or group of customers. In order to determine the economic value of a customer, the 'cost of capital' associated with the customer has to be established. This is a function of the direct costs invested in serving that customer, and the rate of return to capital. Customers who require significant individual service (and hence investment) have a higher cost of capital than customers who do not. Using accounting profit rather than a value measure in such cases will tend to overstate the amount of shareholder value the company is creating by doing business with high-investment customers. In this case direct costs of serving a particularly demanding customer are not properly allocated. That is to say, the COS fails to include significant elements of the direct services and support required. If a customer may require additional investment to support their requirements, this too should be considered a cost that can be specifically allocated.

When companies apply this thinking to their customer portfolio, it is likely that they will find a dispersion of customer economic value. It may be that some customers will be yielding more than the company's weighted average cost of capital (WACC), and some will be earning less. It might be thought that, so long as the return on the total customer portfolio is higher than the company's WACC, the company is creating value for its shareholders. However, this thinking is erroneous for it implies that the company may be using more costly finance to serve less-rewarding customers. An economic analysis would suggest that the average returns versus average costs would still be positive for a while *after* the marginal costs exceed the marginal returns and would thus lower the average return. This is a more stringent perspective than the focus on averages. But the company can increase the returns to its shareholders by attracting and retaining more value-creating customers; and also by improving the performance of its existing customers, in particular of those customers that yield less than they cost to serve.

Figure 11.5 illustrates the principle of shareholder value creation. The higher the risk associated with a customer, the higher the return required by the company to create value for its shareholders. Customers in the area below the line may appear to be profitable, but are destroying value. Only customers above the line create value. As Fig. 11.2 indicated, there are many routes to value creation. Nevertheless, there will be times when highly risky customers may fill a role in a well-considered customer 'portfolio', just as highly risky investments may also be included in an investor's financial portfolio.

The cost of capital can be reduced either by reducing the *amount* of capital used in the customer relationship or by reducing the *cost* of that capital. Here the notion of customer relationships becomes important. It may not always be possible to reduce the amount of capital needed to look after a customer, although sometimes customers will agree to bear certain capital costs such as equipment which is used only for a customer's own, bespoke services. However, it may be possible to reduce the cost of capital. The amount that a company has to pay for its equity or debt is a reflection of the amount of risk that investors perceive they are taking on, by lending to that company. If the risk reduces, the cost of borrowing reduces.

It is important not to confuse the cost of capital *used* with the returns on the *use* of that capital. In finance it is common to raise funds for investment in risky projects, and the perceived riskiness of an organization will be affected by the *average* riskiness of the projects in which those funds are invested. If I borrow money at 5%, that is my cost of capital regardless of whether I then invest it in blue-chip shares or the South Sea Bubble, but, if the balance of the investment portfolio includes few blue-chip shares and many speculative investments, that risk will be recognized by investors. Companies in highly volatile markets are naturally riskier

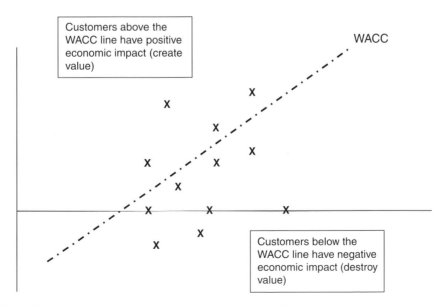

Fig. 11.5. The customer portfolio and value creation. WACC, weighted average cost of capital.

than those in stable markets – with corresponding differences in their costs of capital – returns to equity investors are generally lower for companies in stable markets and higher for those subject to greater fluctuations. While true for markets, this perspective is more difficult when applied to customers.

In the context of a customer relationship, risk is about the *volatility* of the returns from that customer. The more volatile the returns, the more risky the customer. Sudden variability in buying patterns causes difficulties for the organization, and unexpected upswings can be just as difficult to deal with as unexpected downturns. This is just as, or even more, true for large organizations whose facilities may be tied up with other customers and who may have difficulty getting sufficient staff or supporting services in a timely fashion. A customer that buys regularly is more valuable than one who buys the same amount but whose buying pattern is unpredictable. If the variability in demand can be made predictable or controllable, then much of the risk due to the randomness of its occurrence may be managed out of the system. A proactive approach that tries to ascertain customer **intentions** beforehand may be one approach to coping with the natural fluctuations in demand, not by trying to forecast them but instead by trying to obtain early warnings of those variations that create risk.

Implementing relationship management entails certain changes in the way that companies view their customers and manage their contact with them. These are summarized below.

A customer relationship perspective will shift towards customer value analysis and away from product profitability or single-period customer profitability analysis. Value analysis is forward-looking, unlike profit that relies on historical data. Existing management accounting systems may have to be adjusted to accommodate this change. To analyse the economic value of their customers, companies will need to make forward projections of income, costs and risk. This will entail investment in data warehouses to collect and manage customer information and customer-facing technology to facilitate communication.

Positive management of customer relationships as an asset of the business will mean developing customer strategies over the lifetime of the customer relationship. In order to manage all aspects of the value of the customer, these strategies should deal with maximizing returns, minimizing risks and obtaining benefits from the customer relationship (Martin and Ryals, 1999).

Customer relationships do involve significant cultivation and represent a real investment of marketing effort, one that would be worthy of recognition – for there are real, tangible costs to building these intangible but economically valuable and exploitable assets.

Place

Place is the 'P' in the mix that reflects the distribution aspects of marketing: how the product or service gets to the customer – what kind of distribution channel to use, how many outlets or channels should be used, where and when the product should be available. This is particularly true in service industries – location is often the critical strategic decision made in the hospitality and tourism industry, at times completely dominating virtually all other aspects of business marketing and operation. In many cases, the 'place' is a given – a fixed geographical site or location that provides the prime attraction for the business's customers. Frequently tourism businesses operate from a single location and choosing the right one is critical for their success.

With operations that may be spread over multiple sites many of the same location concerns and issues still apply – a poor location is never an attractive proposition for any business, regardless of its size or number of sites or outlets. In expanding from a single to multiple sites there are numerous strategic issues to consider and ideally these additional sites will complement the first in terms of offering a recognized or established service in a new locale, or perhaps extending the current service offerings within a more restricted area – for example, a motel without catering facilities may acquire a nearby restaurant and then offer meals there along with its rooms.

Large-scale, multiple-site operations are frequently found with chains and franchises; these will attempt to provide their customers with a wide coverage through numerous dispersed markets. Again, the location of specific sites is subject to the same considerations as are single-site decisions, but these are also affected by concerns with providing a comprehensive network that covers the major or attractive areas or regions. In these cases the organization will first develop a strategy that identifies those areas for exploitation, and then seek locations within those areas that best meet its requirements. For multiple-site operations there may be significant economies of scale derived from spreading their substantial overheads, administration and marketing costs over a large number of operating units. No one location could provide the marketing capabilities that a chain consisting of hundreds of sites can readily support. A chain operation may allow numerous attractions besides physical convenience to its customers, for example: (i) a brand name with consistent service standards; (ii) pricing policies; and (iii) more efficient handling of service demands. Such consistent chain policies and practices help customers avoid having to make individual arrangements with businesses about which they know little and whose services and pricing policies may be poorly understood.

The place decision is one that may be critical for tourism businesses, both for those that are tied to specific attractions and more generally for those whose market is not so geographically constrained.

CONCLUSIONS AND SUMMARY

This chapter has presented a perspective on the financial consequences of common management decisions and policies. No tourism manager can ignore the economic effects of their decisions and actions and a better understanding of these should improve both decision making and performance. The focus on the marketing mix of price, promotion, place and product/service helps reveal the financial impacts of decisions made in those areas. These financial analyses provide useful tools in considering and choosing between alternatives.

This has been achieved through the chapter's discussions of:

- analyses of the financial effects of management decisions and policies;
- an investigation of alternative pricing policies and their effects;
- an analysis of the implications of service and product design issues for financial performance; and
- a consideration of the financial consequences of alternatives available for promoting an organization's services and products.

REFERENCES

Martin, C. and Ryals, L. (1999) Supply chain strategy: its impact on shareholder value. *International Journal of Logistics Managment* 20, 1–10.
Wilson, R.M.S. (1999) *Accounting for Marketing*. International Thomson Business Press, London.

chapter 12

Strategic Planning and Performance Management

Luiz Moutinho, Shirley Rate and Ronnie Ballantyne

Tourism operators function in a dynamic but volatile business environment. The pace of change in technology, globalization, the economic and social climate, consumer demands and competitive structures among other factors has created an increasingly turbulent environment. To operate under such conditions which present such uncertainties, effective planning processes are critical. Yet many organizations fail to plan. The growth of the tourism industry has been exponential and the rate of growth has encouraged a trend toward short-termism, and yet economic downturns, fluctuations in market demand, increased terrorist activities and unforeseen natural disasters all highlight the importance of a long-term, strategic approach to decision making.

The purpose of this chapter is to outline the importance of strategic planning in managing a company's portfolio of products, in identifying the future profitability of its products and potential products and in developing a plan of activities which address the vision and objectives of the organization. The chapter initially examines the differences and associations between strategic planning and tactical planning before outlining in detail the elements of each of these differing planning processes in the context of the tourism industry. Finally, the aim of the chapter is to consider managing the implementation of strategy as well as the process of monitoring, managing and measuring the performance of strategy.

THE DIFFERENCE BETWEEN STRATEGY AND TACTICS

Long-term plans, particularly those extending beyond 3 years, are generally strategic in nature. In them, the firm's long-term goals such as profit margin, market share and market growth are all identified. These goals are based upon the aspirations for the products and markets of a company and require an independent assessment of future market conditions. The longer term the plan, the further into the future an organization must look and the less reliable available information is. As any consumer behaviourist will tell you, consumer demand is volatile. Current conditions would indicate dramatic change in tourism consumer preferences due to, among other things, social climates, demographic shifts and technological developments. Thus, looking years into the future necessitates the combination of experience, skill and to some extent guesswork. These plans may often be inaccurate and yet they provide desired goals that tourism firms can attempt to attain and/or serve as a benchmark against which they can ascertain the extent to which goals have been achieved. The concept of long-term strategic planning therefore is a crucial part of realizing the vision of an organization, and in a bid to improve the accuracy of strategic decision making many tourism companies are increasingly using scenario planning and computer simulations to make more precise projections and forecasts to help minimize this unknown aspect of the future. Compared with the long-term strategic plan, the short-term plan, more likely an annual plan, is much more operational or tactical in nature, focusing more on the tourism firm's marketing mix and how it will be designed and implemented for each product. The plan should also identify the tourism firm's marketing policy and the expected financial effects on the firm (e.g. promotional costs, expected sales, etc.).

By identifying the difference between the long-term plan and the short-term plan, it has clarified the difference between a tourism firm's strategy and its marketing tactics. The strategy is derived from a firm's goals and is a framework or set of guidelines that a tourism firm will follow in order to attain their goals. A tactic, meanwhile, consists of specific details as to how to execute the strategy. For example, a tourism firm's goals may be to increase market share in Region A by 5% over the next 3 years. The resulting strategy may be to develop a new tourist product line that will allow the company to achieve a dominant share of a certain target market. The tactic may be to develop a tailored and customized product, sell it through a specific type of tourism retail outlet, price it at a particular level and communicate its position to the consumer through the use of a television advertising campaign. The difference between strategy and tactics then is significant and this is summarized in Table 12.1. The purpose of this chapter is to examine these two key parts of the overall planning process and how they should be applied to a tourism context as well as to consider how the performance of strategies and tactics should be best measured.

Table 12.1. Comparison of strategic and tactical planning.

	Strategic planning	**Tactical planning**
Duration	Long term (> 3 years)	Short term (< 1 year)
Done by	Senior management; top marketing management	Marketing and product managers; middle management
Necessary information	Primarily external information	Primarily information from within the firm
Degree of detail	Broad in nature, based on a subjective evaluation	Detailed information and analysis

STRATEGY CHARACTERISTICS

It has been established then that strategies are significantly different from tactics. In developing tourism strategies, it is useful to examine in further depth the nature and characteristics of strategy and the varying levels on which it may be based. Strategy is about identifying the best products and services to compete in the right markets at the right time. To achieve a successful strategy is thus extremely challenging and demands a structured and integrated approach, should be responsive and achievable and should be based upon accurate and rich data.

Rules of strategy

Nevertheless, many tourism operators confuse strategy with tactics, operate in the short term making decisions based on immediate problems and do not consider the longer-term effects of their actions. To ensure a strategic approach is taken, a number of key 'rules' of strategy should be adopted:

- *Limited in number.* Compared with tactics, tourism firms only follow one or two strategies since following too many strategies at once can spread the firm's resources too thinly.
- *Multi department involvement.* Strategy should be high level; however, for it to be successful, it must be integrated and grounded in practice. A strategy requiring new products or new markets needs practical capabilities from across functions, not just marketing. As such, marketing, human resources, design, IT and other departments need to coordinate and integrate in order to achieve one set of goals.
- *Allocation of resources.* Tourism firms must constantly change to keep up with their changing environments. This means that strategies must also change over time and, thus, resource allocation must also change to meet the new strategy requirements.
- *Long-term strategic effects.* Strategy can change the position of the firm and, in effect, changes the firm's foreseeable future. In short, strategic changes may affect a tourism company's performance for years, if not an entire decade. Thus, strategic decisions should be considered. This can only be achieved if appropriate data are gathered, allowing for intelligent, objective and futuristic business thinking. Firms should research and investigate potential changes in strategy with great care, but they should not overlook the need for revising or changing their strategy if the circumstances dictate.

Levels of strategic development

Within an organization, many different types of strategy will exist and they will operate at different levels. Critical to the success of these strategies is the extent to which they are integrated. Tourism businesses are often large organizations composed of many different departments, with each having its own set of goals, norms and methods of operation. Although each department operates as an individual unit, with its own strategy, they are not autonomous. The departments should be an integrated set of units whose strategies are driven by the same corporate strategy and goals. Each department must adhere to the direction of the corporation, while at the same time communicating upwards their particular needs, goals and capabilities. Thus, although the marketing department is constrained by the corporate and business plan, it must develop its own strategies and make its own tactical decisions within the guidelines of the overarching plans. Thus, integration of strategies is a critical success factor for an entire organization. Levels of strategy development can be seen in Fig. 12.1. The development of strategies that link the tourism corporation with its surrounding environment takes place on

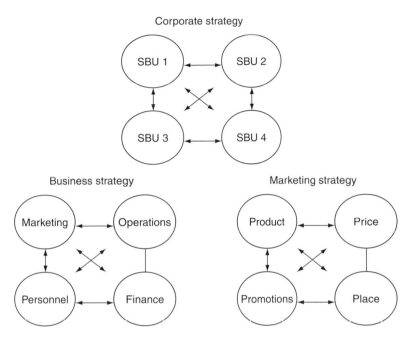

Fig. 12.1. Levels of strategy development. SBU, strategic business unit.

three levels: (i) the corporate strategy; (ii) the business strategy; and (iii) the marketing strategy (Go and Pine, 1995).

Corporate strategy

Corporate strategy provides direction for an organization's strategic business units (SBUs). These units are effectively businesses within a business and should, according to Kotler *et al.* (2010), be defined by customer needs, not products. An SBU is a single business which is led and can be planned for separately. It will have its own mission, products and services, competitors and target customers. Each SBU is usually an operating entity unto itself, and has little contact or links to other SBUs, except through shared ownership of the parent firm. SBUs are also individual profit centres, thus responsible for their own profits or losses. They may operate in similar or completely separate industries from other SBUs in the firm. This is particularly common in the tourism industry, where organizations can house units in the food, transport or hotel industries among others. Although the organization is composed of SBUs, corporate strategists have a goal of increasing the value of the whole firm, not just one SBU. They must have a clear understanding of the economic environments surrounding the industries in which each SBU operates. Once aware of options for future growth and market share, they must devise a corporate strategy to benefit the entire tourism firm. Thus, their strategy may include changes in levels of investment or growth goals for different SBUs. The SBUs must take these corporate strategies and goals and develop their own set of strategies based on top management's general direction and challenges (Hitt *et al.*, 1998). These are known as business strategies.

Business strategy

The business strategy concerns this next level of strategy at the SBU level. The senior managers of each SBU must utilize their resources (operations capacity, manpower, financial capabilities, etc.) in such a fashion that allows them to best attain the desired corporate goals. Although they are developing strategy at a different level, the process that they follow to develop their strategy is similar to that of the corporate level planners. First, they must analyse their individual markets, their competitors, the outside forces that may affect their industry as well as understand emerging consumer trends which affect their products and services. They then develop a strategy based on corporate guidelines that best employs their resources and manages their immediate environment. This strategy is then disseminated to the various departments that make up the SBU. Among other functions, this includes the marketing strategy.

Marketing strategy

From the SBU's business strategy comes the marketing strategy. At this point, the marketing department must decide how the strategy established by the SBU affects the marketing effort. They will utilize the variables of the marketing mix including the tourist product assortment that they offer and how the tourist products are positioned, advertised, priced and distributed, to effectively implement the strategy. In fact, each of these elements of the marketing mix warrants a separate strategic plan. Thus, the tourism marketing manager is responsible for the development of a tourist product strategy, a pricing strategy, a distribution strategy and a promotion strategy. These strategies all become a part of the overall marketing plan.

These levels of strategy present the ideal approach to strategy development. They ensure a cohesive and coordinated approach to long-term decision making for a tourist firm which may comprise of a complex and numerous set of businesses. However, some organizations are yet to see the logic or benefit in planning. These types of organizations tend to be reactive to competitive and environmental forces and spend more time firefighting than developing an identity and direction which guarantees a future. Where planning is undertaken but fails often occurs when an organization develops various plans without a holistic view of the entire organization. One of the most common problems in strategy development is where strategies do not join up because there is no overarching strategy. Only when a corporate strategy drives lower-level strategies will the whole organization move in one appropriate and agreed direction. Likewise a corporate strategy which remains at corporate level will be unachievable. Only when corporate strategy drives the supporting plans of activities will the corporate goals be achieved. Equally beneficial, a corporate strategy which clearly communicates the roles of SBUs, functions and individuals will generate motivation to make those plans successful.

A STRATEGIC PLANNING MODEL

Strategic decisions consist of fundamental choices for the long-term development of the organization. The value and importance of planning increases as customers become more demanding, less loyal and more individualistic in their tastes; as competitors become more numerous and aggressive; and as environmental conditions become more difficult. Having clarified how a strategic plan affects an organization and the levels of strategic planning that exist within tourism operations, it is important to examine the strategic planning process itself. Strategic planning is the development of a long-term plan that best utilizes the resources of an organization within the domain of the organization's mission. The strategic planning process consists of a careful analysis of the tourism organization and the opportunities and threats that competitors and environmental factors may present.

The strategic decisions that are made depend on the focus of the tourism operator, the markets in which it operates and the tourist products that the company offers. They provide long-term direction and generate momentum for the organization. Tactical decisions, on the other hand, are the methods of executing the formulated strategy. The process of tactical planning will be examined in more depth later in the chapter. The aim now is to outline the strategic planning process, which is illustrated in Fig. 12.2.

The strategic planning process consists of five steps that are sequential and linked together. At the completion of each phase, and before continuing to the next phase, progress made should be reviewed and the planners should ensure the plan remains consistent with the tourism company's overall mission. Thus, the feedback loop allows the firm to monitor its progress towards achieving the mission and incorporate changes as needed. Each of these stages will now be explored in more detail.

Phase 1: define the mission

Having clarified the relevance of strategy to organizations in providing direction and stability, it is important to give a context to strategy development; otherwise planners will not know which strategy to pursue in the first place. The corporate vision or mission statement is a means of giving direction to the strategy development process. It is a written statement that reflects the philosophy of the organization. It should sum up what business the tourism company is in and act as a public declaration of the overall purpose of the business. It is a statement that anchors the multitudinous employees, departments and divisions of a tourism firm to one defining direction. It is the firm's *raison d'être.*

Formulation of the mission statement

In formulating the mission statement, the question that tourism firms should ask themselves is: 'What business are we in?' The answer may appear simple at first, but is actually quite complex in most cases. Tourism firms often have various goals and differing SBUs. They grow strategically through franchising, mergers and acquisitions and continually invest money in new product lines. Thus, to capture the business an organization is in is extremely challenging.

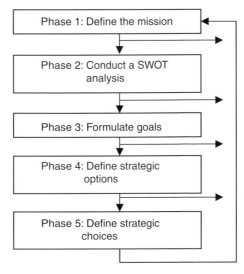

Fig. 12.2. The strategic planning process.

TOO BROAD OR TOO NARROW?

The mission statement should provide boundaries and direction for growth. Thus, it should be neither too broad nor too narrow. If it is too broad, the tourism firm may invest in too many peripheral activities that could detract from its focus. On the other hand, by maintaining too narrow a focus a tourism firm may miss significant opportunities for growth by passing investments that they should consider. Theodore Levitt coined the term marketing myopia to describe this phenomenon. The mission statement must focus the activities of the tourism firm and at the same time provide opportunities to expand, to innovate and to improve. Another danger of a mission statement is that it can become too rigid. Environments change with time. Consumers' tastes change, technology changes, the competitive market changes. If a tourism firm insists on a strict definition of their mission statement that is inflexible, they may also experience difficulty when adaptability is necessary in order to survive. It is easy to see then why mission statements are difficult to develop, adhere to and maintain.

INTERNAL VERSUS EXTERNAL FUNCTIONS

Mission statements not only serve the function of guiding and directing the tourism firm, but also communicate externally what business the firm is in. Many tourism companies have mission statements printed in their annual reports or other communication tools that assist potential investors, customers, community members and other potential stakeholders in understanding the firm and its guiding philosophy. These statements are known as external statements, and they may differ from the internal statements used within the tourism company for the various divisions or subsidiaries. The process of developing these statements is beneficial in itself, in that talking through and arguing a problem may also result in an optimal solution. While managers of the tourism firm are certainly more interested in adhering to an internal statement, the external statements may be used as methods of announcing changes in directions of tourism firms.

STRUCTURE OF THE MISSION STATEMENT

A final note on mission statements concerns their longevity. Tourism firms produce mission statements to act as guides to their travels through the business world. It would not serve the purpose of the statement to have to reformulate it regularly, so it is better for tourism firms to define themselves by the market needs that they satisfy rather than the tourist product they develop. A statement must be developed to weather a changing environment and still be applicable. Typically, a mission statement should serve its purpose for 5–10 years, and some are applicable even longer.

Phase 2: conduct a SWOT analysis

Growth for firms in the tourist industry does not occur without applied effort. Very few tourism firms are in the position of being in exactly the right place at the right time to grasp opportunities for growth. More often, growth is the result of a persistent dedication to striving for pre-established goals and objectives. In order for these goals to be realized, a tourism firm dedicates itself to rigorous planning with the goals constantly in mind. The plan, then, is the engine that drives the marketing department and the rest of the firm towards its goals. But the plan is not functional unless it is based on a reasonable and founded set of assumptions and premises about the environment in which the plan must be implemented. In a bid to achieve this, the first thing that many tourism firms do in the planning process is to complete a SWOT analysis. SWOT stands for Strengths, Weaknesses, Opportunities and Threats, and may also be known as the strategic audit or situational analysis. It is a methodical examination and evaluation of

the internal and external operating environment of the firm. A SWOT analysis is a framew
for assessing the current position of a firm and is derived by asking numerous questions about
the factors that may affect the tourism firm. The types of questions that may be asked are illustrated in Table 12.2. These are not exhaustive and the nature of questions will be determined
by the business the organization is in. The results of this analysis will allow the business to
summarize its current strategic position, in the context of its business environment.

Internal analysis: assessing skills and capabilities

Internal factors of the strategic audit are the factors that can be most readily influenced by the
firm. Funding available for investments, technologies, knowledge and capabilities of human

Table 12.2. SWOT analysis, with the principal questions listed.

Internal analysis	External analysis
Strengths	*Opportunities*
Differentiation possibilities?	Potential new markets or segments to enter?
Sufficient financial resources?	Expansion of the tourist product assortment?
Appropriate competitive strategy?	Diversification into related products?
Good reputation with your clients?	Vertical integration?
A known market leader?	Possibilities to move towards a better
Brilliant strategy for each functional area?	strategic group composition?
Possible scale advantages?	Contact with competitors?
Protected (so far as possible) from strong	Fast(er) growth in the market?
competitive pressure?	Other opportunities?
Unique technology?	*Threats*
Cost advantages?	
Competitive advantages?	Possible entrance of new competitors?
Capacity for product innovation?	Decreasing market growth?
Proven management skills?	Negative government influence?
Other strong points?	Growing competitive pressure?
Weaknesses	Vulnerable to recessions and other economic trends?
No clear strategic orientation?	Strengthening in the negotiation position of
Worsening competitive position?	customers and suppliers?
Ageing facilities?	Changing wants and desires of buyers?
Insufficient profit from …?	Threatening demographic changes?
Lack of management insight and experience?	Other threats?
Shortage of specific skills?	
Bad experience with the implementation of the strategy?	
Plagued by internal operational problems?	
Vulnerable to competitive pressure?	
Bad image in the market?	
Disadvantages compared with competitors?	
Less-than-average marketing skills?	
Not in a position to finance the necessary changes in strategy?	
Other weak points?	

resources, tourist product line and assortment, strength of the marketing plan, sales-force ability and corporate reputation are all variables which the tourism firm can control and on which an analysis of strengths and weaknesses, opportunities and threats should be undertaken. In doing so, the analysis for the SWOT should be realistic. It is natural to rationalize that all of last year's effort resulted in success. But covering up areas of weakness only damages the tourism firm in the long run. By accurately assessing the strategic position, the tourism firm can then best determine how to allocate necessary resources and to locate areas of potential vulnerability.

The internal analysis leads us towards building a tourism company profile. This profile is a snapshot of where the tourism firm stands in that particular time-frame and context. It is a self-explanatory graphic representation of the internal situation of the tourism firm and how it compares with the competition. It provides a picture of the current situation of the company and it can quickly be gauged how potentially successful a particular tourism company can be in its market (Poon, 1993).

External analysis: the world outside the tourism firm

After the tourism firm analyses its internal environment, it must turn its focus externally. This is important since marketing strategies and plans are derived at least partly on what the competitive and regulatory environment will allow a tourism firm to reasonably accomplish. The external analysis should focus on identifying the trends of the environment and how they influence or affect the tourism firm. Ideally, trends or market movements will emerge that will allow the firm to be prepared in advance and be proactive in its tactics via the marketing plan. For instance, a firm interested in moving into a particular tourist product line should be aware of any changes in consumer behaviour that may have an impact on the long-term demand for that product. Watching trends in consumer behaviour, competitive movements and regulatory decision making allows tourism firms to avoid or take advantage of critical situations that may have not been apparent otherwise, thereby increasing the tourism firm's competitive position or minimizing its exposure to potential problems. Recognizing the trends that are vital to a successful SWOT analysis is much easier if the mission of the firm is clearly defined, since a good corporate mission more narrowly focuses the arena of analysis. While our internal search centres around the identification of firm-specific capabilities and influencers – 'internal trends' to a certain degree – the external search will look more closely at environmental opportunities that may exist. By looking outwards, tourism firms may see gaps or opportunities in the market that other firms have not capitalized upon, or gaps that are about to open due to regulatory changes, competitor action or social or economic movements. For instance, the tourism firm that can spot a coming recession may begin to focus on value-based promotions and tourist products sooner than its competitors. Furthermore, a potential threat can quickly be turned into an opportunity for the tourism firm based on swift 'proaction', a skill which will be of increasing importance as tourist-product life cycles shrink and competition intensifies.

Once the SWOT analysis has been completed, a tourism firm has a strong picture of what its capabilities and vulnerabilities are, where it stands in the market when compared with the competition and what potential trends and opportunities may impact upon the tourism firm. Based on this information, a marketing plan can be more accurately formulated.

Phase 3: formulate goals

Once the tourism firm has determined its strategic position based on an evaluation of its strengths, weaknesses, opportunities and threats, it can more readily set appropriate and achievable goals. The tourism firm's goals include the accomplishments and achievements which it aspires to. Strategic goals are high level by nature and tend to relate to revenue growth, customer satisfaction, market leadership, profit levels and operational efficiency. Thus, they are designed to provide overall direction for the organization. Goals and objectives are terms often used interchangeably; however, there is a distinct difference between the two. Strategic goals should inform tactical planning and, within tactical planning, objectives are drawn from the strategic goals. These objectives are the specific aims that must be accomplished to achieve the strategic goals. Objectives will drive the activities that will set the organization in the direction the goals intend. Objectives therefore tend to be more specific and detailed. For instance, a major tourism holding company may have a goal to grow by 12% within the next calendar year. This may translate into an objective to grow 12% within a specific tourist product market targeted at a certain group of customers.

Goals are effective only in certain cases, and many goals, if formulated incorrectly, may even detract from the success of the operation. For example, too aggressive and they will not be supported by key employees or will require the company to take too high a risk. On the other hand, too undemanding and staff will become complacent, eventually losing competitiveness. Table 12.3 illustrates some well-formulated goals and some poorer ones.

For a goal to be effective, a few things should be kept in mind:

1. The goals should be measurable in enough detail to give meaning and direction to those attempting to achieve the goal.
2. The goals should be achievable. No one benefits from goals that are set beyond reasonable attainment. When goals are known to be unreasonably high or even 'impossible' to obtain, then people will sometimes work *less* at trying to achieve them because of their impossible nature.
3. Both long-term goals and short-term goals should be developed. Although the present is important, tourism firms must constantly know which path they are travelling to the future, and make sure present goals and actions are working towards the realization of the future ones.
4. The goals should be ordered in terms of priority to the tourism company. If different SBUs are all chasing widely divergent goals, inefficiencies through a lack of coordination may be experienced as a result. This is the case where one department (e.g. finance) puts its goals first and ignores the needs of other departments (e.g. marketing), which is detrimental to the tourism firm's overall well-being.

Table 12.3. Good and bad examples of goals.

Examples of badly formulated goals	Examples of well-formulated goals
Long term	*Long term*
Our goal is to develop a leading tourist-product development position in the industry	Our goal is to devote at least 20% of gross profit to research between 2000 and 2002, resulting in at least five new tourist products introduced in the market by the end of 2002
Short term	*Short term*
Our goal is to increase sales in 2000	Our goal is to broaden our market share in 2000 from 21% to 25% by opening 22 new travel agencies and increasing our advertising budget by 15%

Phase 4: define strategic options

Guided by the mission statement and goals, the next phase of strategy development is to generate the strategic options for the business plan. To achieve this, each SBU within the organization should be reviewed to allow strategic choices to be made regarding what resources to apply to which SBU, that is, what areas of the firm should be invested in for growth (Kotler *et al.*, 2010). This process of reviewing attractiveness of the SBUs is known as 'portfolio analysis'. Portfolio analysis allows insights into the attractiveness of the SBU's product, market and industry as well as the strength of position that SBU holds in the industry. From there, strategic options can be generated and, following this, decisions can be made based upon how best to apply the businesses strengths to the market opportunities. According to Dickman (1999) portfolio analysis became popular in the 1960s and 1970s when tourist organizations began to capitalize on the growth of the industry through diversification. Coach operators bought hotels, airlines bought travel agencies and, generally, a business's portfolio of products and services became increasingly varied and much more difficult to manage. The concept of portfolio analysis proved to be a popular tool in identifying the best products and market opportunities, and ultimately the best strategic choices for the firm.

The problem for tourism operators, then, is the diversity of products and markets which they serve, the differences between products, their life cycles and their profitability and the fact that resources to invest in products are finite. Decisions must be made regarding the growth, cutback or decline of products to achieve optimal allocation of resources. Two of the most popular portfolio management models include the Boston Consulting Group matrix and the General Electric model, both of which have received criticism and yet are useful techniques in analysing a portfolio of products and understanding their individual contribution and their future potential.

The Boston Consulting Group (BCG) matrix

A simple, two-dimensional matrix created by the Boston Consulting Group (BCG) was developed as a guideline to assist firms who face these investment dilemmas. Also known as the product portfolio matrix, it works well for those firms that have multiple product groups, or a portfolio of products. As shown in Fig. 12.3, the matrix is made up of a horizontal axis and a vertical axis and the four quadrants of the graph that are derived from the axes. On the vertical axis, there is market growth, which is the percentage of annual growth that a tourist product experiences, adjusted for inflation. In this case, we have defined a low growth rate as 0%, a moderate rate as 10% and a high growth rate as 20%, although the distinction between low, moderate and high will vary greatly with the industry and product line. As the growth rate increases, the tourist product requires greater investment to fuel its continued growth. On the horizontal axis, there is relative market share, which is calculated by dividing our market share by that of the three largest competitors within our strategic group. So, if our share was 20% and our competitors' share was 25%, then our relative share would be 80%. Obviously, if we are the market leader, then our relative market share will be greater than 100%. Recall that the higher the share, the greater the differential cost advantage the tourism firm possesses and the better the opportunity for success. By combining these two axes, we can locate and plot almost any market situation. As you can see, the plots (SBUs) will fall into one of the four quadrants identified. We can therefore establish the four quadrants as: (i) stars; (ii) question marks or problem children; (iii) cash cows; and (iv) dogs.

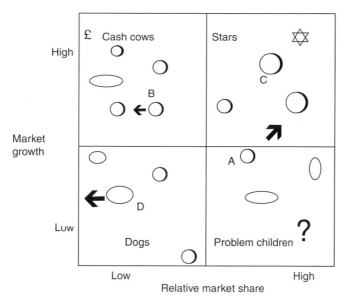

Fig. 12.3. Boston Consulting Group (BCG) matrix. A, B, C and D denote strategic business units.

STARS (HIGH MARKET GROWTH AND HIGH MARKET SHARE)

Stars are tourist products that experience high growth and at the same time enjoy a high share of the market. If a tourist product has a high market share, economic advantages through economies of scale may be realized, which contribute to potentially higher margins and increased cash flows. The extra cash will be required if the tourist product is also growing at a rapid pace. Constant funding is needed to support the additional advertising, promotions and other sales efforts needed to sustain its pace. Having a star tourist product is an excellent position for a firm to be in, but only because of the high market share. Many stars reach a position where the cash generated and the funding required are balanced, easing cash flow management problems. Also, once the rapid growth is complete, the high share suggests that the tourist product may become a cash cow for the firm.

QUESTION MARKS OR PROBLEM CHILDREN (HIGH MARKET GROWTH AND LOW MARKET SHARE)

These are tourist products that are experiencing rapid growth but have little market share to fund their growth, hence the name question mark – it is difficult to know the future of the product. Question marks are found quite frequently in new and uncertain markets. It is unknown what life cycle the tourist product category will have, let alone the firm's actual product. If the tourist product is growing rapidly, it is producing a great need for funding, but with a low market share it has not attained a cost advantage over the competition. So tourism firms must decide how long to fund a product that may have little long-term advantage. Many question marks are funded by the extra cash produced by the cash cows.

CASH COWS (LOW MARKET GROWTH AND HIGH MARKET SHARE)

Cash cows are tourist products that generate a large amount of cash because of their high market share, but do not require additional investment because they are not growing. A typical cash cow may be a tourist product that is a leader in a stagnant or mature market. High market share ensures the economies-of-scale advantage over competitors, but the lack of growth means that the funding is not required to be poured back into the tourist product. Tourism firms like to have cash cows around because they can help finance the growth of other tourist product lines or other projects, also known as cross-subsidization. Cash cows do not have an infinite life, and eventually will experience a decline in sales and market share. But while they are around producing large net cash flows, tourism firms certainly find them advantageous.

DOGS (LOW MARKET GROWTH AND LOW MARKET SHARE)

Dogs are tourist products that are not growing and do not have high market shares. Generally, dogs simply are not good tourist products, or are good tourist products in a product category that has lost its appeal to the consumer. Dogs enjoy few, if any, advantages over their competitors. Although there may be some reasons for keeping this type of tourist product alive (for instance, the continuation of the brand name until major modifications are ready or to round out a tourist product line), the major decision becomes how to divest the firm of this tourist product or drop it from the line. This will be discussed in more detail in the next section.

BCG strategic options

The BCG matrix describes tourist product situations on an individual basis. Of course, the reality is that most tourism firms find that they have different product lines, often within the same SBU, which fit into different categories in the matrix. It is common to have a star, a cash cow, several dogs and a question mark or two all within the same tourist product category. And, just as financial managers seek to diversify to reduce risk through balanced portfolios of financial investment instruments, tourism marketing managers also seek to manage their product situation as if it were an investment portfolio. Tourism firms would ideally like to have a product that is a star, another a cash cow that provides investment funds and a question mark that has the potential to become the firm's next star. And, as identified above, even dogs have their use to the tourism marketing manager, although it may not always be immediately apparent. The important contribution of the BCG matrix is that it provides a template upon which strategy can be built. It illustrates the current position of an organization's products but also the strategic options it has to move forward. Tourism managers have certain control over where their products lie and where they are destined within the product matrix. By increasing investment, it is possible to adjust the growth of a product, or, by cutting price, the tourist product may attain greater market share. The purpose of the BCG matrix is that it is utilized to reveal the opportunities and options which tourism operators have in managing the entire portfolio. Tourism managers should analyse their matrix and plan the path that the tourist product should take to best support the needs of the whole SBU. The path will determine the specific strategy that a manager should utilize in order to attain the goal (Beerel, 1998). Four strategic alternatives are available for the manager:

1. *Build.* Building market share suggests an aggressive growth strategy where market share is more important than profit margins. By focusing on additional target groups or outlets for the tourist product, new customers may be attracted. Question marks are an excellent example of the tourist product type that needs to be supported with a build strategy. Funding for this strategy is not always easy to find since there is some risk involved, but cash cows are a prime source.

2. *Hold.* A defensive strategy that merely maintains or holds market share constant may be required for a cash cow. Cash cows eventually decline, and with the decline goes a tourism firm's source of funding projects. Moves are often made to prop up the cash cow without attempting to gain share.

3. *Harvest.* This is an attractive short-run strategy for tourism firms in need of cash. There is a lag between the cessation of promotional expenditure and the decline in sales of the tourist product. Tourism firms may decide to reap the benefits of past investments by removing support from the product while enjoying the continued sales and cash flows. This strategy is popular for dogs, question marks or even for cash cows that have uncertain futures. But a tourist product will eventually be affected by a decline in promotional support, and firms must be cognizant that there is a cost for pursuing this strategy.

4. *Divest.* Finally, when the tourism firm's financial resources can be better used somewhere else, it is time to escape the market. Tourism firms will often manage this divestment process as closely as a more aggressive strategy, since it is difficult to know just when to discontinue the product. Tourist product lines are kept alive just long enough to sell them off before the brand is either forgotten or tarnished by the poor sales. Other tourism companies may decide to drop the brand name altogether.

An evaluation of the BCG matrix

Although many tourism firms subscribe to the BCG matrix and the accompanying strategies, it has received much criticism. It is important to be aware of the benefits as well as the limitations of this type of technique as there is no model which provides all answers and, as such, it should be used among a plethora of approaches to portfolio analysis.

ADVANTAGES

In adopting the BCG approach, the tourism manager is forced to evaluate the product or SBU on market-share and growth-rate perspectives. This helps ensure the long-term viability of the tourist product, and inhibits management from making decisions in the short term that may damage the overall success of the SBU. The matrix also allows tourism managers to become aware of the product's needs. By analysing the tourist product in isolation, and not comparing it with other products within the SBU, the manager may recognize certain trends (growth may be decreasing while market share remains strong) that would otherwise remain hidden. Finally, as mentioned before, the portfolio approach allows portfolio and resource management. For example, the tourism marketing manager may have several products that can be used to support each other with necessary investment funding (i.e. cross-subsidization). The importance of the total tourist product portfolio of the SBU will be given greater consideration than just the one or two main products.

DISADVANTAGES

While the portfolio approach is worthwhile, it is not easy to achieve. The information needed to build the portfolio matrix for the total market is difficult to gather and painstaking to properly maintain. Some tourism managers may find that it is more trouble to acquire the necessary information than it is worth, though this is a somewhat myopic view. Furthermore, the position and description of the tourist products may be subjective. Even though the tourist product may fall into the quadrant of the cash cow, industries that are under siege may not be strong enough to support the profits that a cash cow should reap. In other words, while the matrix suggests one thing, the uniqueness of the tourist market may suggest another. Finally, recent research has identified that there are some industries that do not necessarily subscribe to the economies-of-scale advantages that the matrix is based on. In many service industries, the costs of producing the service do not change as much with increasing volume to provide the advantageous position and the resultant cash benefits as a product-based industry might. Therefore, use of the matrix should be carefully evaluated as to its fit with the SBU's particular industry (Aaker and McLoughlin, 2007).

An alternative: the General Electric (GE) matrix

In recent years, the General Electric (GE) matrix has become popularized because it can handle some of the shortcomings of the BCG matrix. The BCG matrix tends to simplify things as it has just two dimensions, growth and market share. That said, these are two quite important dimensions. In many cases, there is also a need to assess return on investment, or profit, instead of only cash flow. Furthermore, the GE matrix makes use of some very important qualitative information: primarily how strong the SBU is compared with competitors, and how attractive an investment opportunity a particular industry offers.

This technique is also known as the Industry Attractiveness/Business Strengths matrix. By matching the strength of the SBU or tourism firm with the opportunities offered by a specific market, the matrix gives a suggested direction of how to manage the particular situation. These two dimensions will now be examined in more depth.

INDUSTRY ATTRACTIVENESS

The attractiveness of an industry can mean many things. As a tourism firm looks at an industry in an attempt to gauge investment potential, they may consider: (i) the growth rate of the industry; (ii) the average profit margins experienced by tourism firms competing in the industry; (iii) how many competitors there are; (iv) the strengths of the individual competitors; and (v) the areas or niches in the market that the competitors do not cover. It also incorporates a factor that was discussed in the BCG matrix, economies of scale. Each industry has a unique cost structure that contributes to the ability to attain efficiencies. Table 12.4 provides us with an overview of some of the factors that one should consider when evaluating the attractiveness of a potential investment.

Table 12.4 provides some general characteristics that tourism managers should evaluate. However, not all areas may be of significance for every decision. One possibility is to assign weights to the characteristics that are the most important to the manager. Evaluation can be made of each characteristic on a scale of 1 to 5 and the factors weighted so the combined weights add up to 1. After multiplying the factor score by the weight assigned, tourism managers can sum up the results to score a total value weight. The tourism manager may want to compare this industry score with other industries under consideration to determine which ones are the most attractive from an investment perspective.

Table 12.4. Some criteria for assessing the attractiveness of the sector and the competitive power.

Attractiveness of the sector	Competitive power
Market size	Relative market share
Market growth percentage	Market growth potential
Power position of the suppliers	Quality of the product
Power position of the customers	Brand image
Extent of competition	Location of the tourism company
Average profit margin	Profitability
Threat of potential entrants	Insight into the market
Threat of substitute products	Price competition
Cyclical trends	Contract with the management
Scale advantages	Effectiveness of the sales force

COMPETITIVE STRENGTH

A tourism firm can gauge the competitive strength of its SBU by items such as relative market share, quality, image of the brand and profitability (a more complete list is provided in the right-hand column of Table 12.4). The tourism manager will analyse the strength of his or her SBU in much the same way that he or she determined the attractiveness of the market: by weighting and summing the appropriate factors, an approximation can be made.

DETERMINING THE PORTFOLIO

Next, the tourism manager will plot these two indices to see where the SBU lies on a strengths/industry attractiveness scale (Fig. 12.4). Each number in the matrix represents a tourism firm's SBU. Note that the matrix is divided into green, yellow and red zones. These colours mean much the same thing that a traffic signal might. In the green zone there appears to be a strong match: the tourist market is quite attractive to the firm and the product offering of the SBU is quite strong. Although the tourism manager should evaluate the issue thoroughly, the matrix suggests that this match is too good to pass up, and the firm should go ahead and invest in this market. The yellow zone indicates that the match between the strengths of the tourism company and the attractiveness of the industry is less than optimal, so the firm should proceed with great caution. Finally, the red zone indicates that the industry and the SBU situations are not conducive to investment and the tourism firm should stop and proceed no further.

To conclude the debate on portfolio analysis, given the weaknesses of the techniques, one could question whether the BCG and GE matrices could be used simultaneously. Some tourism firms choose to utilize the BCG matrix first to divide their SBUs into appropriate divisions, and then use the GE matrix for a more detailed analysis and evaluation of potential strategy. Combined, the matrices can provide a relatively thorough picture of the goals and financial consequences that tourism firms face (Deegan and Dineen, 1997).

Phase 5: define strategic choices

This final phase of strategy development is where choices must be made regarding direction and growth for the organization. It is the ultimate decision about strategic emphasis. All phases of strategy development to this point are critical to support this key stage of decision making. The mission communicates the broad vision of the future and the SWOT analysis identifies strategic opportunities and the strategic position of the organization on which the

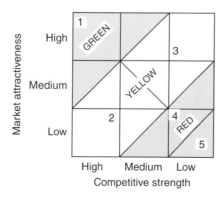

Fig. 12.4. The General Electric (GE) matrix. 1, Hotel chain; 2, rollerblade, fast food; 3, discotheques; 4, casinos/gambling; 5, caravan parks.

goals are based, stating the intended accomplishments. The portfolio analysis generates strategic choices based on strengths and weaknesses of the product portfolio. All this data generation and analysis provide a foundation for the most difficult decision: where to place investment to grow the organization. Igor Ansoff (1957) developed the 'Ansoff Growth Vector' to allow the strategist to identify growth opportunities based upon the research and analysis carried out in the planning process. Ansoff indicated that a firm must question whether growth can be generated from gaining more market share with the current product portfolio in the current markets targeted (market penetration) or whether it can identify and target new markets for the existing product portfolio (market development). Equally, it should consider whether it is possible to develop a new product portfolio targeting current markets (product development) or diversifying into new markets with a new product portfolio (diversification). This is illustrated in Table 12.5.

Deciding which growth strategy to follow is a very difficult one. Successful growth can be very profitable and thus it is tempting to take a more high-risk option, but poorly managed growth can spell disaster to a firm that has not considered the long-term future. Critical to successful decision making is that the choice is informed by rich and accurate data. Each of the strategic choices is now examined in more depth.

Tourist market penetration

When a tourism firm is selling an existing product that it currently offers to an existing market that it already serves, it is pursuing a market penetration strategy. Techniques designed to increase sales will result in deeper market penetration, thus increasing market share.

This can be done in one of two ways. First, market penetration refers to selling more of the tourist product to the existing customer base. This can be accomplished either by increasing the size of the contents or amount that the customer buys, such as airlines using loyalty schemes, or by increasing their usage rate (e.g. going on holiday more times in a year). Secondly, the firm may choose to go with a tourist-market-broadening strategy. This means increasing the number of target customers within the same existing tourist market. New customers are hard to come by when you consider that this usually requires converting them from the tourist brand that they normally purchase. Thus, a penetration breadth strategy is generally more successful in tourist markets that are continuing to grow (Knowles, 1996).

Of course, whether you are going after new customers, a competitor's customers or your own customers, this usually requires a change in the marketing-mix strategy. The promotion of the tourist product could be altered through increased advertising or publicity, better shelf-space displays in the travel outlets or intensified selling efforts. A price change could catalyse sales by offering sales promotions, vouchers or even a reduction in the selling price. Finally, changing the channels of distribution may make the tourist product more attractive. The tourism firm may sell the tourist product in a different type of outlet, online or they may make it available in more remote locations.

Table 12.5. Ansoff's product/market expansion matrix.

Product tourist market	Current tourist products	New tourist products
Current markets	Market penetration	Product development
New markets	Market development	Diversification

Tourist market development

Another method is to develop the tourist market by finding new uses for the product or by selling the product to new target segments. In the Ansoff matrix this means selling the same tourist product to new customers. This may entail finding new segments who have previously not been exposed to the tourist product. Although the tourist product may not change at all, many new consumers are automatically potential customers. A tourism firm may wish to choose a different demographic target segment within the same country, or sell the product to a new institution or industry group, for example.

The problem with this strategy is that, if we consider that a tourism firm may not have much expertise or experience in certain geographical or demographic areas, they may have shied away from the market in the past. Thus, many tourism firms utilize intermediary specialists of some sort who are more familiar with these potential markets. Marketing communications campaigns and distribution channel changes are the two most practicable mix variables to utilize in reaching new tourists.

Tourist product development

This strategy involves altering the characteristics of the tourist product in order to make it more attractive to the same general target market. By increasing the quality of the tourist product, or by offering more of the product (e.g. added attractions, free flights, better-rated hotels, etc.) for a disproportionate increase in price, firms can significantly enhance the value of their tourist products to existing customers. Further, customers that previously were non-users or purchased competing brands may now consider purchase. Typical tourist product modifications include making the tourist product more accessible or changing attributes and features of the tourist product in order to expand its customer base (Laws, 1995).

Diversification

Finally, a tourism firm may choose to make more dramatic changes. By diversifying, a tourism firm attempts to generate new products that they will sell to new customer target groups. Tourism firms diversify for more reasons than to simply increase their sales. There may be a tourist market that they feel offers aggressive growth opportunities for them. Generally, because the market is one that the tourism firm is unfamiliar with, companies will often merge with or acquire a firm that is already competing in the market. This way they gain safer entry into a tourist market, they start with loyal customers to their purchased brand, and they have eliminated one of their potential competitors. Other tourism firms choose to diversify in order to spread the firm's risk among more markets or to smooth out seasonal sales patterns. Table 12.6 illustrates the four primary diversification strategies: (i) vertical diversification; (ii) horizontal diversification; (iii) concentric diversification; and (iv) conglomerate diversification.

VERTICAL DIVERSIFICATION

Vertical diversification (or vertical integration) refers to a tourism firm taking over new markets or product groups within the firm's vertical channel of distribution. Integration can take the form of moving the tourism firm closer to the end user or closer to the product source. When the tourism firm integrates a function between itself and the consumer, it is known as forward integration. Forward integration may include a large restaurant chain such as McDonald's owning the local restaurant as opposed to running it as a franchise. When the tourism firm integrates a function between itself and its suppliers, it is known as backward integration. Integration is not without its risks, however. Many tourism firms are ill-suited to the industries that they integrate with, even though they may seem to match. Generally, tourism firms find

Table 12.6. Diversification matrix.

New tourist products New markets	Current tourist products	New tourist products
Firm is own client	Vertical integration	
Same type market	Horizontal diversification	
Similar type market	Marketing and technology-oriented concentric diversification	Marketing-oriented concentric diversification
New markets	Technology-oriented concentric diversification	Conglomerate diversification

that they can often, but not always, save overall costs through increased control of the channel function, which may contribute favourably to the firm's profits. Therefore, before attempting forward or backward integration, a tourism firm needs to be certain that it has the skills to take on the functions of the channel intermediary that it is buying or replacing.

HORIZONTAL DIVERSIFICATION

Horizontal diversification is diversifying into new tourist products, but targeting your existing customer base as the potential customers. Often firms feel that they have established a brand loyalty with current customers or a certain knowledge of their markets which allows them to introduce new products. An example might be if a travel agent, who normally books holidays, diversifies by purchasing a company selling travel insurance. The travel agent is serving those same customers, but in a new manner. Horizontal diversification can be distinguished from horizontal integration by the newness of the tourist product to the firm. For instance, if the travel agent had purchased a competing travel agency it would have been an example of horizontal integration. The advantages of horizontal diversification are distinct. First of all, the tourism firm is offering an additional product to a current customer base, so not as much effort has to be expended to locate new customers. Secondly, if the tourism firm already has significant knowledge of or familiarity with the customer base's buying habits, then they can be more efficient in the ways that they serve them. But a major disadvantage of horizontal diversification is that the tourism firm has not spread out its risk, as in most diversification schemes. In fact, it may have exposed itself to even greater risk by investing even more in the same tourism market. In the example, if the travel industry endured a serious downturn, then our firm would suffer potential losses from both the travel agent side and the travel insurance side.

CONCENTRIC DIVERSIFICATION

Concentric diversification entails the introduction of a new tourist product to a new but related market. By related we mean that the tourist market must be somewhat similar to the firm's existing market in either a marketing sense (e.g. customers, demographics, needs) or an operational sense.

CONGLOMERATE DIVERSIFICATION

Also known as lateral diversification, conglomerate diversification involves marketing tourist products that are not familiar to the firm, to customers who are not their normal customers. It is so named since it is not unusual for large tourism conglomerates to diversify the risk of their portfolios of SBUs by seeking completely new markets. Further, most conglomerate diversification is achieved by purchasing a company or a division of a company that is already in operation. While this strategy gains a tourism firm a new product line and a new set of customers to serve, it can be quite risky since the new managers usually know very little about the new customer base or the nuances of the new market environment.

Selection of growth strategies

Although there is no specific set of rules or guidelines to direct a tourism company to pick and choose the market growth strategy that will suit it best, following the strategic development process is key to making sound choices regarding growth. The SWOT analysis will help identify the tourism firm's strengths and capabilities. Next, by charting the strength of the tourist market, whether it is growing or in decline, and looking at the strength of the competition, a firm can then determine its actions (Tribe, 1997).

For instance, if a tourism firm is fortunate enough to be in a position where it is strong, the market is growing and the competitors lack particular skills, it can usually attack aggressively by expansion. It may choose to attain a strong anchor position in the tourist market, purchase one or more of its weaker competitors (if allowed by regulators) and then diversify by striving for a more complete path to the customer through vertical integration. Other strategies are also available for other tourist market situations.

TACTICAL MARKETING PLANNING

As outlined earlier in the chapter, it is important to distinguish between strategic and tactical planning. Strategic planning consists of long-term, goal-oriented plans that specify the major directions in which a tourism firm will head over the next 1–5 years or longer. There is little in a mission statement or strategic plan, however, that tells us exactly how the goals will be accomplished. The strategic plan guides tourism companies in the medium to long run, but they must also rely on specific tactics, or a tactical plan, to guide them on a day-to-day basis. Figure 12.5 illustrates a four-phase model of tactical marketing planning. An important element to note is that a tactical plan is not developed in a vacuum. It should be a logical continuation of the strategic planning and the resultant goals. Control is provided at the end of each phase of the strategic plan through a feedback loop to ensure that the plan is still on track and to make any necessary modifications as needed.

Phase 1: conduct a SWOT analysis

The first step a tourism firm takes is to construct a SWOT analysis, which, as outlined earlier in the chapter, is an internal and external analysis of an organization or an SBU. This takes shape in the form of a matrix in which the strong and weak points of a tourism firm, as well as the opportunities and threats facing it, are presented and summarized. Much of the information necessary is available internally. The SWOT analysis covers the market such as the size and nature of the tourist market, the firm's own position in the market and market trends Also included is the position of the competition, the most important market factors, a description of the target group and its usage level and pattern, the business results of prior years, the distribution structure and the firm's own activities (e.g. operators, promotion strategy, etc.).

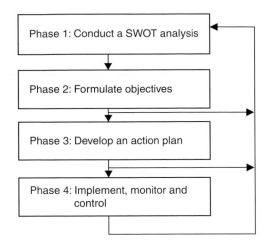

Fig. 12.5. Model of tactical marketing planning.

Phase 2: formulate objectives

The purpose of objectives is to give direction to the activities required to meet the strategic goals. Those who are responsible for developing the marketing plan should include as much detail as possible in formulating the tactical objectives, otherwise it makes little sense to continue with the rest of the phases in the planning process. As one senior manager remarked: 'If you don't know where you want to go, then one way or another you will always arrive there. And as soon as you arrive there, then you won't take the trouble to go any further.' In other words, setting a goal such as 'We will increase our market share' will not challenge a tourism firm to do and achieve as much as a goal such as: 'We seek to improve our market share in the concentrated birdwatching segment in the special interest tourism sector from 10% to 15%.' Once a tourism firm can put its exact tactical plan on paper, then it is ready to develop an action plan.

Phase 3: develop an action plan

Once the tactical goals are known, assets and resources may be allocated. Tourism marketing managers make decisions regarding the marketing-mix elements and how to optimally combine the 4Ps (price, product, promotion and place) in order to attain the established tactical goals. The marketing action plan identifies how the department will accomplish the goals on a step-by-step basis utilizing the 4Ps.

The sequence of events in an action plan is important since tourism firms must integrate their overall efforts in order to effectively achieve their goals. If a tourism firm releases an aggressive promotional campaign that inspires buyers to seek out their product, then they must also ensure that there is enough of their product available to meet this demand. If not, a large amount of promotional money will be wasted and customers dissatisfied. The information in the marketing action plan should be specific enough for employees to know when events are to occur, how much funding will be available to support the events and how they will be carried out. Projected target dates should be established for tourist product introduction, promotional campaigns, operations planning, and all other events that could affect the marketing mix. Of importance are the financial consequences the marketing action plan provides in the form of budgets and projected cash-flow forecasts. Providing accurate sales forecasts (the basis of the financial consequences calculations) is one of the most important and most difficult functions of the tourism marketing department. Decisions to hire, fire, invest and divest are all based on expected sales. But accurate forecasts are difficult to come by because of a lack of necessary information and the general level of uncertainty in tourist markets. Not only do tourism firms not know what their closest competitors are going to do, but they also must estimate general economic and consumer behaviour trends, which is a challenging task. Tourism firms should not only make one forecast based on current data but also make some alternative ones based on different results so they will be ready for any scenario in the market. Finally, the tourism firm needs to specify how it will track and measure the future results and determine if the objectives have been achieved.

Phase 4: implement, monitor and control

As the components of the marketing plan are implemented, careful control methods should already be established. Reviewing goals and expectations and comparing them with results allow tourism managers to monitor the process. If tourist product introductions or promotional campaigns are not producing the results on which forecasts are based, managers must be made aware of the problems immediately through a control and feedback mechanism. Control tools may include sales, share, growth, margins, awareness, tourist product development and consumer intent. But, while control has been established, it will only be beneficial if the tourism firm is willing to adapt to market changes. Few introductions go exactly as planned due to many of the same unforeseen circumstances that make forecasting so difficult. When the control mechanism indicates that things are going off course, the tourism firm must decide what action to take, if any. Although drastic reformulations of the marketing-mix components are unusual, adaptation by the tourism firm to changes in the marketplace is generally called for. Adaptation may be as subtle as extending the advertising schedule for an extra week or two or providing more brochure inventory for certain regions. Further, tourism firms find that adaptations require additional planning in order to reallocate those same scarce resources discussed earlier. This is where the contingency or scenario plans the tourism firm prepared earlier can come into play and save the firm valuable time. Once the plan is implemented, the work has only just begun.

PERFORMANCE MANAGEMENT

The purpose of this chapter was largely to explain and explore the nature of strategic and tactical planning in the tourism industry. It is clear that the process of planning in both the long and the short term is a critical success factor for tourism operators. The climate and environment in which they function are turbulent and the pace of change is such that a framework for day-to-day as well as future decision making is fundamental for survival. The chapter to this point has demonstrated the substantial commitment, time and resources required simply to plan. The data gathering, measurement, analysis, investment decision making and structuring of strategic initiatives are challenging. So too is achieving the total acceptance and respect that the vision is futuristic and that many important things achieved do not immediately result in higher revenues or lower costs.

Nevertheless, the most difficult challenge in strategic planning is to make good investment decisions and this is because, no matter how sound the basis of these decisions, they still represent calculated risks of business investment. As such, perhaps the most important element of the planning process is strategic control. This concept is beyond that of management control of tactical financial decision making; it represents a wider approach to measuring success of overall strategy. Yet this idea of managing performance is not clearly defined nor is it consistently implemented. There has been growing criticism of a reliance on traditional management control which is too narrowly focused on financial measures (Olve *et al.*, 2004). Indeed, calls for more complete reporting on business performance have led to the development of a number of approaches to performance management.

Marketing 'metrics' in performance management

Historically many tourism companies have focused their marketing efforts on attracting and expanding their customer base. As competition has increased and markets have become more volatile – consumers now have the luxury of 'variety seeking' (where consumers can easily switch between the many providers present) and there is increased expectation of return by shareholders – more attention must be given to the monitoring and controlling of the marketing effort. In order to increase efficiency and effectiveness in the delivery of value to the consumer it is paramount that the tourism provider has accurate intelligence to underpin future strategic decision making. These key drivers have led to a growing interest in performance management and marketing 'metrics'.

In simple terms the implementation of marketing strategy is monitored and measured through a series of 'metrics' throughout the different levels of the organization. The challenge is to put in place measures or metrics that truly reflect and help to drive the organization's marketing strategy. Performance management must then focus on identifying the key elements that contribute to the successful implementation of the marketing strategy. Managing these elements will facilitate the attainment of the company's overall strategic aims and objectives. In effect, superior performance and competitive advantage can be obtained.

Historically measures of performance have been overly focused on financial performance – as such they were not known until the planning period was complete – the underlying assumption being that the company had a deliberate and fixed strategy as opposed to an emergent strategy that would respond to both micro- and macro-environmental concerns. As the pace of change has accelerated, key financial measures are now monitored continuously – thus allowing early warning signals to be forecast and be addressed. For example, in terms of profitability, an analysis of any company's financial performance reveals that its profits will group or 'pool' around a discrete selection of opportunities within its overall portfolio. Sustaining high performance over the long term now depends on a company's ability to develop a clear and real-time understanding of its current profit pools, the impact of emerging trends on those profit pools, and potential profit pools (including their timing, magnitude and possible risks) so that the company is always changing ahead of the curve.

Clearly a sound understanding of financial performance is required; however, it must be stressed that seeking the 'solution' exclusively from financial metrics is not enough. Moreover, they may not capture all of the company's strategic objectives and they are not very diagnostic in that they only report the symptoms of underlying problems. As such, the general pattern of evolution of marketing metrics appears to be broadening the portfolio with a miscellany of non-financial metrics. Key marketing metrics have emerged including:

- customer satisfaction;
- loyalty/retention;

- conversion (leading to sales);
- number of new products;
- number of new customers;
- brand product knowledge;
- perceived differentiation; and
- brand salience.

The very nature of some of these areas (i.e. their intangibility) has led to some criticism in terms of the validity of measures and the measurement systems used. Difficulties with non-financial measures are classically related to a lack of statistical reliability, introducing 'measurement error' where a measure does not measure what it purports to measure or where it leads to conclusions which are statistically unsound. Nevertheless, what has been experienced over the last several decades has been a shift of company valuation being based primarily on financial or physical assets of the company to more of the company's intangible assets.

Nearly half of the value of the company is now based on these intangible assets. Three of the most highly valued intangible assets are: (i) intellectual property; (ii) brand (assets associated with the brand account for a large and increasing proportion of stakeholder value); and (iii) company customers. Other recent advances include, for example, lifetime value of customers. Interestingly, marketers often argue that what they do cannot be quantifiable; however, as stated above, as company valuation is increasingly based upon intangible assets the onus will be on marketers to demonstrate returns on marketing investment and, as such, they will need to develop meaningful metrics. Moreover, as marketing metrics become more widespread, they will become the institutional norm. Marketers must measure the 'right things' – but what are those 'right things'? Common sense indicates that the things to measure are the things that make you successful. And what makes a company successful? Simple: delivering value to stakeholders (customers, owners and shareholders, to name the big three). Therefore it stands to reason that ultimately all metrics should be stakeholder-value driven.

Frameworks for measuring performance

As a response to these growing concerns with the narrow focus on financial measurements and the lack of spotlight on the many other aspects of strategic performance, a number of frameworks have been developed in an attempt to better capture all of a company's strategic goals. The 1980s saw an emergence of a number of tools such as Kaizen, total quality management (TQM) and lean production, but still these approaches focused on one issue, ignored organizational and cultural change and failed to encompass critical success factors.

Somewhat of a turning point was achieved by Kaplan and Norton (1992), researchers and consultants, who developed the 'scorecard' approach. The approach is based on the principle that an array of metrics should be utilized not only to measure performance against specific strategic goals but also in the development of the strategic plan itself. In other words, the scorecard should be a driver to the overall vision and strategic thrust of the organization. Furthermore, the metrics employed should be 'balanced', whereby they reflect the focus of the organization and emphasize those activities critical to success, not simply financial measures. Other academics and researchers have also attempted to model performance management processes in a rounded manner such as Maisel's (1992) work on the balanced scorecard, McNair *et al*.'s (1990) 'performance pyramid' and Kennerley and Neely's (2002) 'performance prism'. While these models all take a different approach, the underlying philosophy that performance measures should dictate and encompass all aspects of strategy remains constant.

Thus, the specifics of which measures should be used in performance management are dependent on the context of the organization, its vision and the industry within which it competes. Kaplan and Norton (1996) recommend that financial, consumer profitability, product sales and competence improvement are areas of focus which should drive the choice of performance measures. However, the problem with scorecards is that at corporate, business unit and divisional levels different measures will be relevant to different activities. At the divisional or functional level, care must be taken to ensure that the use of customized measures does not result in developing 'functional silos'; indeed, it may be inappropriate and counterproductive to focus measurement within an individual function. To avoid this, organizations will often create cross-functional measurements based on their value delivery systems or end-to-end business processes. Such thinking has generated new types of scorecards such as the 'Intangible Assets Monitor', which divides intangible assets into external structure, internal structure and competence of people, the 'IC Index', which combines value drivers into a distinction hierarchy, and the 'Inclusive Value Methodology', which that combines financial and non-financial hierarchies of value.

Whatever the approach, there are some rules of thumb: (i) measures should not be set in stone – as the strategy and its goals evolve, so should the measures; (ii) do not implement too many measures which dilute their overall effectiveness, but, equally, too few may be manageable, but they may not encompass the entirety of the strategy; and (iii) ensure that the measures are measurable.

Frameworks for marketing 'metrics'

As mentioned previously, marketers will often argue that what they do cannot be defined by quantitative measurement criteria. Yet the onus is on marketers to demonstrate returns on marketing investment (ROMI). CEOs will only respect the place of the marketing function if the impact of marketing efforts can be seen more clearly.

The marketing profession is being challenged to assess and communicate the value created by its actions for shareholder value. This means responsibilities lie beyond increasing market share and instead with developing and managing market-based assets which are largely intangible (such as customer, partner and channel relationships) and intellectual (such as knowledge about the environment). According to Srivastava *et al.* (1998), market-based assets in turn increase shareholder value by accelerating and enhancing cash flows. If marketing metrics are to be stakeholder-value driven, then they will be increasingly oriented towards share of customer and in terms of customer equity, partner relationships and processes and will include financial as well as marketplace parameters. Of most importance is that they should be stakeholder-led, taking account of the return that stakeholders expect from the firm.

As a means of managing marketing metrics, the 'marketing dashboard' can be used as a marketing measurement platform. It is a tool which requires a single set of performance measures which are applied to different activities at different levels. It pulls together a rainbow of data, key performance indicators, graphic analysis and modelling into a coherent and focused picture which can be disseminated throughout the organization, becoming a shared reference point for everyday decision making. It is a visual display of the most important data required to meet and measure objectives and is captured in one screen for ease of use. In stormy weather, marketers need to learn to 'fly by instrument' and, as such, dashboards should have real-time information.

REFERENCES

Aaker, D.A. and McLoughlin, D. (2007) *Strategic Market Management*, European edn. John Wiley & Sons, Chichester, UK.

Ansoff, I. (1957) Strategies of diversification. *Harvard Business Review* Sep/Oct, 113–124.

Beerel, A. (1998) *Lead Through Strategic Planning*. International Thomson Business Press, London.

Deegan, J. and Dineen, D. (1997) *Tourism Policy and Performance*. International Thomson Business Press, London.

Dickman, S. (1999) *Tourism and Hospitality Marketing*. Oxford University Press, Melbourne, Australia.

Go, F. and Pine, R. (1995) *Globalization Strategy in the Hotel Industry*. International Thomson Business Press, London.

Hitt, M.A., Ireland, R.D. and Hogkisson, R.E. (1998) *Strategic Management and Competitiveness and Globalization Concepts*, 3rd edn. South-Western, Cincinnati, Ohio.

Kaplan, R.S. and Norton, D.P. (1992) The balanced scorecard measurements that drive performance. *Harvard Business Review* Jan/Feb, 71–79.

Kaplan, R.S. and Norton, D.P. (1996) *The Balanced Scorecard*. Harvard Business School Press, Boston, Massachusetts.

Kennerley, M. and Neely, A. (2002) Performance management frameworks: a review. In: Neely, A. (ed.) *Business Performance Measurement: Theory and Practice*. Cambridge University Press, Cambridge, pp. 144–145.

Knowles, T. (1996) *Corporate Strategy for Hospitality*. Longman, Harlow, UK.

Kotler, P., Bowen, J. and Makens, J. (2010) *Marketing for Hospitality and Tourism*, 5th edn. Prentice Hall, Upper Saddle River, New Jersey.

Laws, E. (1995) *Tourist Destination Management – Issues, Analysis and Policies*. International Thomson Business Press, London.

Maisel, L.S. (1992) Performance measurement: the balanced scorecard approach. *Journal of Cost Management* Summer, 47–52.

McNair, C.J., Lych, R.L. and Cross, K.F. (1990) Do financial and non-financial performance measures have to agree? *Management Accounting* November, 28–35.

Olve, N., Roy, J. and Wetter, M. (2004) *Performance Drivers*. Wiley, Chichester, UK.

Poon, A. (1993) *Tourism Technology and Competitive Strategies*. CAB International, Wallingford, UK.

Srivastava, R.K., Shervani, T.A. and Fahey, L. (1998) Market-based assets and shareholder value: a framework for analysis. *Journal of Marketing* 62(1), 2–18.

Tribe, J. (1997) *Corporate Strategy for Tourism*. International Thomson Business Press, London.

chapter 13

eTourism Strategy

Dimitrios Buhalis

TECHNOLOGICAL EVOLUTION AND IMPACTS ON STRATEGIC MANAGEMENT AND MARKETING

Technological tools offer unprecedented opportunities for managerial control and coordination. Information communication technologies (ICTs) should be regarded as the entire range of electronics, computing and telecommunication technologies and all hardware, software and netware required for the development and operation of the 'info-structure' of an organization. The convergence of the Internet and ICTs that has been experienced in the last few years effectively integrates the entire range of hardware, software, groupware, netware and human ware and blurs the boundaries between equipment and software (Werthner and Klein, 1999: 72). Thus, ICTs are an integrated system of networked equipment and software, which enables effective data processing and communication for organizational benefit.

The development of the Internet introduced a whole range of new tools as well as benefits and challenges for organizations (Egger and Buhalis, 2008). The Internet enables the instant distribution of media-rich documents worldwide and revolutionizes the interactivity between computer users and servers. It provides a window to the external world and facilitates the interactivity of organizations globally, instituting an innovative platform for efficient, live and timely exchange of ideas and products. It also provides unprecedented and unforeseen opportunities for interactive management and marketing to all service providers. As a result most business processes had to be re-engineered to take advantage of the new business realities (Hammer and Champy, 1993; Buhalis and O'Connor, 2005). These developments have dramatically changed the ability of organizations to manage their resources, to increase their productivity, to communicate their policies, to market their offerings, and to develop partnerships with all their stakeholders, namely consumers, suppliers, public sector organizations, interest groups, etc. (Buhalis, 2003). Organizations increasingly use ICTs to expand geographically and coordinate their activities regionally, nationally and globally.

In addition, internal systems or **'intranets'** were also developed as 'closed', 'secured', 'controlled' or 'firewalled' networks within organizations or individual departments. Using Internet-standard protocols, and thus offering user-friendly multimedia interfaces, intranets allow authorized personnel to access information, knowledge and mechanisms across the enterprise in order to perform their tasks efficiently. Intranets enable organizations to improve their internal management at all levels by sharing media-rich data and processes, using Internet interfaces. Increasingly enterprises realized the need to formulate close partnerships with their partners and other members of the value chain for the production of goods and services. As a result, they developed '**extranets**', which use the same principles as well as computer equipment and networks to allow access to preselected sections of an organization's data, knowledge base and mechanisms. User-friendly and multimedia interfaces mean that users require limited training for using the systems. As a result, extranets can enhance the interactivity and transparency between organizations and their trusted partners, by linking and sharing data and processes to format a low-cost and user-friendly electronic commerce arrangement. Extranets therefore empower the cooperation between partners by enabling a certain degree of transparency and interactivity. Both partners can enjoy mutual benefits and enhance their efficiency, productivity and effectiveness without compromising on security and confidentiality (Buhalis, 2003; Laudon and Laudon, 2009).

Rapid technological development paradoxically means that the more powerful and complex ICTs become, the more affordable and user friendly they become, enabling more people and organizations to take advantage. Although ICTs are not a panacea and cannot guarantee financial success on their own, when used intelligently they can support the development and maintenance of organizational competitiveness and competitive advantage. Equally, ignoring and underutilizing ICTs can generate significant competitive disadvantages. Using ICTs as a stand-alone initiative is inadequate and has to be coupled with a redesign of processes, structures and management control systems.

Provided that rational and innovative planning and management are exercised constantly and consistently, ICTs can support business success. As a consequence, 'business processes re-engineering' argues that yesterday's practices, traditional hierarchical and organizational structures and habitual procedures are almost irrelevant. Corporations should be able to respond to current and future challenges by having the resources and expertise to design new processes from scratch, in a timely fashion. As a result of the rapid ICT developments, organizations need to convert their operations from business functions to business processes, as well as re-conceiving their distribution channels strategy and, even more importantly, their corporate values and culture (Tapscott, 1996). Perhaps the greatest challenge organizations face is to identify and train managers who will be effective and innovative users of ICTs who will lead technology-based decision making. Intellect therefore becomes a critical asset, while continuous education and training are instrumental for the innovative use of ICTs and the competitiveness of tourism organizations. Certain 'prerequisites' are needed for organizations to succeed in the eBusiness era, namely:

- long-term planning and strategy;
- rational management and development of hardware and software;
- re-engineering of business processes;
- top management commitment; and
- training throughout the hierarchy.

Addressing these prerequisites can facilitate the achievement of sustainable competitive advantage. Constant innovation in applications of hardware, software and network developments means that only dynamic organizations, which can assess the requirements of their stakeholders and respond efficiently and effectively, will be able to outperform their competition and maintain their long-term prosperity. Failure to address these issues can jeopardize the competitiveness, prosperity and even existence of organizations.

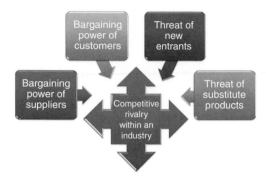

Fig. 13.1. Porter's five forces.

When looking at Porter's (1985) theory, it is evident that the emergence of the Internet affected both the generic strategies and the five forces (shown in Fig. 13.1) in most industries around the world, as it changed the conditions of competition in the marketplace. Porter's (1985) generic strategies demonstrate that organizations can achieve competitive advantage mainly through cost leadership, differentiation or focus on particular markets. His model of industry analysis lies upon the existence of five forces that collectively determine the profitability and intensity of competition in the industry. The strength and impacts of these forces depend upon many factors. The rivalry among existing competitors and the bargaining power of suppliers and buyers represent the current situation in which an organization is found, while the threat of new entrants and the threat of substitutes are based on future expectations. As far as the threat of new entrants is concerned, the Internet had an effect on entry barriers as it altered economies of scale and the amount of capital required for competing within the industry. Rivalry among existing competitors was also affected as technology and the Internet affected differentiation and cost structures as well as switching costs. Changes also appeared to the bargaining power of buyers as the Internet introduced a much higher degree of transparency and lower switching costs. Similarly, a shift in the bargaining power of suppliers has been noticed, as the Internet provided alternatives and reduced the need to buy only from a few powerful suppliers. Finally, the Internet affected substitution as it influenced the relative value/price and reduced switching costs of substitutes (Porter, 2001; Buhalis and Zoge, 2007).

eTOURISM AND STRATEGIC MANAGEMENT

The use of ICTs in tourism is pervasive as information is critical for both day-to-day operations and the strategic management of organizations. Few other industries rely on so many partners to collaborate closely for delivering their products and few other value chains are as elaborate as the one for tourism. 'Tourism is a very information intensive activity. In few other areas of activity are the generation, gathering, processing, application and communication of information as important for day-to-day operations as they are for the travel and tourism industry' (Poon, 1993). Communications and information transmission tools are indispensable to the marketing of the tourism industry (Sheldon, 1997). Tourism products are almost exclusively dependent upon representations and descriptions and the multimedia opportunities offered by the Internet enable tourism organizations and destinations around the world to use the emerging media in order to increase the awareness of their products and also facilitate transactions. Hence the tourism system is *inevitably influenced* by the new business environment created by the diffusion of ICTs and has had to re-engineer a number of processes in the value system (Buhalis, 1998).

eTourism bundles together three distinctive disciplines, namely: (i) business management; (ii) information systems and management; and (iii) tourism. It reflects the digitization of all processes and value chains in the tourism, travel, hospitality and catering industries. At the tactical level, it includes eCommerce and applies ICTs for maximizing the efficiency and effectiveness of the tourism organization. Hence the eTourism concept includes all business functions (eCommerce and eMarketing, eFinance and eAccounting, eHuman resources management, eProcurement, eR&D and eProduction) as well as eStrategy, ePlanning and eManagement for all sectors of the industry, including tourism, travel, transport, leisure, hospitality, principals, intermediaries and public sector organizations. At the strategic level, eTourism revolutionizes all business processes, the entire value chain as well as the relationships of each organization with all their stakeholders.

The tourism industry already uses a wide range of ICT systems. ICTs can provide a powerful tool, which, if properly applied and used, could bring without doubt great advantages in promoting and strengthening tourism industry operations (WTO, 2001). The eBusiness W@tch reports (2006) demonstrate that the tourism industry pioneers eCommerce and it is much more advanced than other economic sectors. Several tailor-made internal-management applications facilitate the management and marketing of tourism organizations. These systems use databases as well as office automation software for inventory control and for generic administration purposes. Knowledge management systems enable organizations to collect information about their functions and to build knowledge on approaches to resolve problems and emerging issues.

The emergence of the Internet provides a window for the organizations to the world and allows them to demonstrate their competencies widely (O'Connor, 1999). As a result, a global electronic marketplace gradually emerges and the vast majority of tourism providers developed Internet interfaces to communicate directly and efficiently with their clientele and partners. Combining loyalty clubs, guest histories and other information held in operation databases provided airlines and hotel chains powerful information, which enabled them to interact with their existing and prospective clientele. Intranets and extranets are increasingly used to offer user-friendly access to employees of organizations while at the same time their authorized partners are able to use company data in order to perform their tasks.

The networking era experienced enables easy access to information and ubiquity, and thus enhances the interactivity between tourism producers or principals (e.g. airlines, hotels), intermediaries (e.g. travel agencies, tour operators) and consumers. In addition, a new breed of intermediaries and tourism enterprises emerged to take advantage of the new capabilities of the Internet. These include electronic intermediaries such as Expedia, Travelocity and Opodo, which have become mainstream providers in a relatively short period of time. New suppliers also emerged mainly because of the new opportunities that the Internet provided and the capability to reach a large market share efficiently and profitably. The main example of that is no-frills airlines that use the Internet to distribute their products dynamically to consumers (Buhalis, 2004). Tourism information and suppliers who are not included in the electronic markets are not that able to address their target markets. Increasingly it is evident that the presentation in the global electronic tourism market and the usability and convenience of the online offering are as important as the actual product itself. As a result, ICTs gradually become a critical determinant of tourism organizations' and destinations' competence. It is evident therefore that the Internet emerges as a mainstream communication and distribution mechanism that gradually alters the structure of the tourism industry as it changes dramatically best strategic management practices (Buhalis, 1998, 2003).

ICTs, and the Internet in particular, support the strategic management of tourism organizations by:

- offering opportunities for differentiation and/or cost leadership;
- empowering internal processes and operational management;
- interacting with prospective travellers and the general public;
- enabling tourism organizations to offer value for time and money;
- allowing a rapid response as an element of competitive advantage;
- empowering decision making;
- expanding market opportunities and the potential for coverage;
- offering opportunities for direct communications with consumers; and
- providing a platform and the essential info-structure for collaboration and transactions between suppliers.

ICTs support all business functions and are critical for the industry's operations as a whole. On the strategic level, tourism organizations have to continuously assess all elements of their external environment, as well as their competition and customer needs, and consequently rein-vent themselves in order to enhance their competitiveness. Through the use of ICTs, tourism organizations can differentiate their offering by having their core product as the basis and then by customizing the final product through adding value according to individual require-ments. ICTs provide the tools for searching and reaching for meaningful and profitable niche market segments, identifying value-added components for the product and promoting the differentiated product through specialized media to particular market segments that would be interested. Cost effectiveness and flexibility are critical assets contributed by ICTs in this process, as they assist cost reductions and efficiency maximization.

eTOURISM: MONITORING THE ENVIRONMENT AND DYNAMIC RESPONSE

ICTs enable tourism organizations to constantly monitor the external environment and act proactively and reactively to maximize benefits. The emerging ICT capabilities provide the ability to collect and analyse information constantly. Tourism organizations need to take advantage of existing data in the organization and use knowledge management, expert systems, artificial intelligence and neural networks in order to develop proactive organizational man-agement. Neural organizations constantly monitor and control their external and internal envi-ronment, identify patterns, trends and developments and take proactive measures to advance their interests. They can take advantage of neural networks to recognize and capture patterns and elements in a sea of data, coming from both the internal and the external environment of organizations, and assist decision makers to design appropriate responses. Interoperable information platforms enable tourism organizations to integrate all their systems, monitor and control their internal processes and external trends. Interconnected processors and networks may run in parallel and interact dynamically with each other in a way that develops knowledge and procedures for dealing with issues and problems before they arise (O'Brien, 1996).

This enables tourism organizations to monitor their external environment and take best action in order to maximize their benefits, supporting tourism and hospitality decision makers, to adopt a very dynamic management or to manage by wire. Managing resources efficiently and communicating with consumers and external partners proactively and reactively can support them in improving their competitiveness. Firms can redesign and repackage tourism products instantly, according to consumer desires, trends and fluctuations. Adding value and specializing tourism products in response to external developments or internal challenges can increase their profitability and explore new market segments efficiently and effectively. Time increasingly becomes more critical, as both consumers and partners will be bombarded with information. Providing the right total solution, at the right time, will be one of the most significant generators of competitive advantage. The strategic benefit emerges from the development of the neural network and the constant update of the system.

eTOURISM: BUILDING COST-COMPETITIVE ADVANTAGE USING ICTS

Porter (1985) clearly demonstrates that competitive advantage can be achieved through product differentiation or cost advantage, either for the entire marketplace or for particular market segments (focus). To the degree that ICTs enable organizations to either differentiate their products or reduce their costs, and therefore their price, they can assist them to achieve competitive advantage, and hence have strategic implications.

Cost advantage can be achieved by using ICTs to maximize the number of travellers served through economies of scale, negotiation with partners and maximizing load factors. Using ICTs to improve efficiency, reduce costs and achieve a price- and cost-competitive advantage is a strategy pursued by many industry players, and particularly those concentrating on the lower-cost sectors such as no-frills airlines. ICTs reduce the time for each process to be completed, and thus minimize the labour cost, but also improve both the interactivity and the reflexes of the organization while reducing the error possibility. It is difficult to assess objectively whether ICTs can contribute to cost reductions and enable tourism organizations to reduce their price accordingly, in order to achieve cost advantage. Nevertheless, ICTs have empowered mass tourism as they enabled the handling of large amounts of information which supported large-scale operations. Consequently, ICTs have enabled the reduction of the price per unit, taking advantage of economies of scale and minimal marginal costs. Only ICT-supported enterprises could increase the operational size of hotels, airlines and intermediaries to capacity levels, which could safeguard economies of scale and cost optimization. Technology supports vertical and horizontal integration of the tourism system and the expansion for tourism value chains, which consequently enhanced economies of scale, operational efficiencies and intra-channel negotiation power, all of which contribute to price reductions.

One of the most common motivations for tourism organizations to develop their Internet presence is to accept direct bookings (eCommerce), and thus to reduce or eliminate commissions and booking fees and other distribution costs as well as dependency on distribution channels. As a result, organizations can, if they wish, pass on savings to consumers, and thus reduce their price accordingly, achieving price competitive advantage. This is clearly evident in the attempted disintermediation of global distribution systems (GDSs). The Internet challenged their position dramatically as both consumers and the travel trade had the opportunity to interact with airlines online without using GDS infrastructure. No-frills airlines totally bypassed GDSs and used the Internet to link with consumers and the trade. Scheduled airlines have also been trying to disintermediate GDSs, especially for the short-haul discounted tickets, in order to reduce their distribution costs. In March 2007, for example, British Airways' (BA) contracts with GDS providers expired without service interruption or BA immediately pursuing a substantially new course, as some in the industry had feared. BA CEO Willie

Walsh explained that the airline industry had struggled to generate levels of profitability that would be deemed acceptable. Other parts of the value chain, including the GDSs, have made operating margins in the double digits. BA has fares in their European operations that start at £29, which, after applying GDS fees (which can be as high as US$7.50 or about £4) and taking out all taxes and charges, leaves BA with a fare of about £2 (Boehmer and Cohen, 2007). The European eBusiness W@tch (2006) suggests that 'sales via Internet platforms bear enormous cost savings for airlines compared to traditional channels via travel agencies, which usually run over GDS'. The report quotes Matthias van Leeuwen, Vice President Sales (Europe, the Middle East and Africa), Lufthansa Systems Group as saying:

> Star Alliance member carriers currently spend an average of 12 US dollars per ticket in GDS fees. Global New Entrants (GNEs) such as G2 SwitchWorks, ITA and Farelogix have indicated to the group that they could offer the same product for 2–3 US dollars per ticket.

Therefore GDSs are forced to rethink their strategies and gradually relaunch themselves as technology platform providers for airlines and other members of the tourism industry.

Developing a cost-efficient eCommerce application and global distribution of multi-media information and promotional material on a 24-hours-a-day, 365-days-a-year basis is also very attractive, as ICTs enable organizations to be permanently available to their markets. The active role of consumers and information seekers in asking for information also ensures that the information targets people with a genuine interest in the product. As a result generic and untargeted campaigns can be eliminated, enhancing the cost efficiency of marketing. For example, prospective travellers would only access information related to their chosen destination. Perhaps one of the less discussed benefits of ICTs for tourism enterprises is their support for their marketing intelligence and product-design functions. Organizations can easily develop targeted mailing lists through people who actively request information and to segment them according to their interests, background-site usage and consumer behaviour. Organizations can collect marketing information from all enquirers. By registering users, tourism enterprises can develop extensive databases of consumers and their preferences and target them accordingly. By tracking the identity of the user as well as what they do once they visit the Web page can also collect valuable marketing research information. The low cost of providing and distributing timely updates of information also provides great flexibility and interactivity with consumers and partners. Once the Internet presence of an organization is established, the marginal cost for serving additional consumers and users is minimal, enabling the organization to benefit from economies of scale and to expand rapidly.

eTOURISM FOR DIFFERENTIATION ADVANTAGE

Tailoring tourism products is not a new marketing technique. **Differentiation strategies** aim to develop unique products and to add value to tourism offerings (Porter, 1985). Differentiation advantage emerges when organizations develop and specialize their products/services to meet the specific requests of consumers. The Internet provides endless opportunities for theming/packaging/customizing tourism products and experiences, as well as for developing specific services and niche products. Tourism organizations can develop and incorporate content in the specific specializations and address the particular needs of their markets. Identifying the entire range of services, information and products required for a niche market can enable organizations to develop integrated themed offerings to support that market.

An example of strategic use of the Internet is Marriott.com, the portal of the Marriott Hotels. It was introduced in 1996 mainly to boost the hotel group's online visibility. Marriott took advantage of the Web to create widespread accessibility to information as well as to facilitate the hotel choice for consumers. The Web also supported the logistics of the purchase process. Although the online travel agencies such as Expedia and the price-comparison websites such as Kelkoo and Sidestep contribute to the commoditization of the hotel product, they also give vital exposure to a huge audience and enable hotel chains to raise their brand awareness. Marriot is using the Internet to support their brand and to achieve product and service differentiation online. Within 10 years, Marriott.com sales have grown at a compound rate of 120%/year from 1996 to 2006. They achieved over US$4 billion in gross sales online in 2006, or about one-third of the group's turnover. About 87% of the Internet sales were booked on Marriott.com while the rest (13%) was from third parties and distributors. The Internet has clearly become the single largest face of Marriott to customers and a key part of their brand experience

On the destination side, Visit London, the London Tourism Board offers a number of sub-websites to address the particular needs of its markets. Young London addresses the needs of young travellers while KidsLoveLondon is addressing the needs of families with children. Although the info-structure utilized is exactly the same, using a comprehensive database and a content management system, different websites are used to provide those particular markets with suitable information and products.

There are endless niche markets waiting to be explored in tourism. They can be segmented according to: (i) activities (e.g. skiers, scuba divers, birdwatchers, etc.); (ii) age groups and life cycle (e.g. young and active, 18–30, families, golden age 50+); and (iii) specific interests and lifestyle (e.g. philatelists, historians, wine enthusiasts, motor sport fans, etc.). The Internet provides the opportunity to target specific markets with special interests at an affordable cost. As they can interact using the Internet, they can declare their interest and request to be kept informed about developments. This will be particularly the case when the Web 2.0 is fully developed, as community-generated content will address the needs of peers. Web 2.0 refers to a second generation of Web-based services based on citizen-/consumer-generated content – such as social networking sites, blogs, wikis, communication tools and folksonomies – that emphasize online collaboration and sharing among users.

The more specific the requirements of the market, the more suitable the Internet is for providing them. This is particularly important for some market segments that have very specific requirements. Disabled people with accessibility requirements, for example, have three major requirements, namely: (i) accessibility of the physical/built environment; (ii) information regarding accessibility; and (iii) accessible information online. The first basic requirement of the disabled traveller market is accessibility of the physical/build environment. Making the built environment accessible will give tourists access to more facilities and services, and the right to choose according to personal preference. Secondly, information regarding accessibility is a fundamental requirement for the disabled traveller market in order to engage in travel. Richness and reliability of information are a key determinant, as information regarding tourism accessibility is highly fragmented and scattered among different industry players. The presentation of the linkages between accessible tourism and transport facilities is of paramount importance. The demonstration of **accessibility paths** within the destination, as well as between the origin, the transit area and the destination, is critical for creating a door-to-door access map. Finally, the third indispensable requirement is the accessibility of information online. Websites that are not designed with Web accessibility in mind cannot support a variety of assistive technologies used by disabled users. Accessibility of information online can provide this market with access to more content and also allows them to personalize their experience (Michopoulou *et al.*, 2007). Tourism organizations and destinations therefore that will be offering comprehensive accessibility information will gain benefits. It is evident therefore that the Internet can assist tourism organizations to differentiate their product by bundling together suitable solutions.

Differentiation can also be achieved through partnerships with clubs and associations, as well as with specialized press and suppliers that can assist in targeting their membership. The Internet empowered tourism firms to develop global specializations and to target their markets, regardless of their location, at an affordable cost. For example, unmissable.com targets a specific market that concentrates on experiences, adventures and special occasions by mediating between suppliers and incentive and corporate travelling companies to offer unique products. ICTs also enabled the development of partnerships with complementary service providers and the establishment of comprehensive value chains, by offering services before, during and after the tourism experience. For example, a golf specializing hotel or tour operator in Bali, Indonesia can provide an interactive Internet page, which can allow guests to undertake a whole range of golf-centred activities and serve to maximize their revenue. Developing partnerships with golf specialist companies and establishing strategic alliances with partners can strengthen their market and enable tourism organizations to add value to their products. Eventually a vertical portal (vortal) can be established based on the different elements brought together.

The emergence of the Internet and the ability of organizations to reach the entire marketplace electronically and cost effectively provide unprecedented opportunities for differentiation strategies. Establishing a global brand name and identity in a niche market is relatively easier in the online era and can be achieved at a fraction of the resources required in the offline world. Consumers from all over the world use the Internet and wait to be impressed by service providers. Providing a comprehensive, valuable and pleasurable experience becomes the key criterion for success. Information becomes a product in its own right, as well as an added-value element and a catalyst for physical products. Bundling relevant and accurate information together increases the value of the product and the benefits to consumers. As a result, it has a positive effect on their willingness to pay and their brand loyalty.

eTOURISM FOR ACHIEVING A FOCUS ADVANTAGE FOR PARTICULAR MARKET SEGMENTS

The **focus** strategy offers differentiation advantage or cost leadership for specific market segments (Porter, 1985). In essence, focus uses one of the two previously discussed strategies for a specific part of the market. Segmentation can be based on customers' location, demographics, consumer behaviour, lifestyle and life cycle or needs. Market segments can be defined and targeted much more precisely than before. Traditional segmentation based on demographics and location can be gradually replaced with more subjective and qualitative criteria such as taste, interests, moods, lifestyle usage of ICTs and personalized preferences. The Internet makes the identification, development and servicing of mini market segments feasible at a fraction of the cost and time required by offline marketing. Responses from online questionnaires and promotional campaigns, as well as tracking of website navigation patterns, enable organizations to cross-reference this information with consumer behaviour from real data. This can support them in developing data warehouses and bringing together and managing their knowledge. Every time consumers log on to the system, organizations can collect useful information about their needs, preferences and factors determining their behaviour. Adjusting interfaces, Web pages, offerings and enhancing their interactivity, organizations can reflect on the most critical factors that influence consumer behaviour. Being able to cross-tabulate data and analyse them against the behaviour of individual consumers can provide an unprecedented wealth of information, which can enable organizations to develop mini segments and customize their offering accordingly. Looking into the frequency of checking particular flights, the affiliated products examined and the booking behaviour of users may enable an airline, for example, to add a new route or to develop innovative packages or even to target the market segment of one by adding individualized value to their offering. BMI is practising this principle: for exactly the same flight on a London to Brussels trip, tickets cost between £29 and £284 depending on the level of service and flexibility required. Prospective customers are offered the opportunity to book any of these fares, which are flexible according to demand levels and a powerful yield/revenue management system. By offering transparent information on the level of service and flexibility available, BMI focuses on a number of different markets that have dissimilar requirements and ability to pay.

The emergence of mobile devices as Internet terminals will enable organizations to offer specialized products interactively to different market segments. Location-dependent technologies will recognize the position of consumers and will provide local products that will suit not only the location and local conditions but also the preferences of the consumer as defined in their preferences. New business models, such as priceline.com, effectively enable consumers to declare what they wish to purchase, and at what price, and then aim to identify potential suppliers who are willing to offer that product. In that sense, ICTs empower consumers to develop the marketing mix of the products that they wish to purchase and search in the marketplace for suitable suppliers.

eTOURISM FOR ACHIEVING TIME-COMPETITIVE ADVANTAGE

Time becomes another source of competitive advantage, as deprived-of-time consumers increasingly appreciate value-for-time and efficiency in the process, often more than differentiation or cost advantages. Time and efficiency will eventually overtake both cost and differentiation for several market segments as a critical factor for purchasing products. Websites that are simplified and at the same time comprehensive, which enable consumers to complete a transaction in a few minutes and within a few clicks, already enjoy great competitive advantages, and thus their organizations emerge as winners of the electronic battle. Thus, consumers appreciate saving time during the information seeking and reservation process through efficient and interactive mechanisms. Many intermediaries already take advantage of that and bring a wide range of travel products to consumers. Visiting Expedia.com for example, consumers can have access to a one-stop shop for all their travel requirements such as flights, hotels, car rentals, holidays and business trips. Everything is bookable in a few clicks and travel documents are electronically delivered. Several added-value services are also readily available such as airport guides, currency converter, *World Travel Guide* and access to the *Rough Guides*, arrivals and departures of airlines, fare tracker, flight timetables, etc.

Interestingly a number of travel-specific meta-search engines emerge, such as Kayak, Kelkoo and travelsupermarket, to enable consumers to aggregate content from multiple websites. Figure 13.2 demonstrates how Kayak aggregates content from a plethora of suppliers and intermediaries and enables consumers to filter results according to their specified criteria. Content aggregation will be providing more efficient customer information and will allow people to filter information effectively.

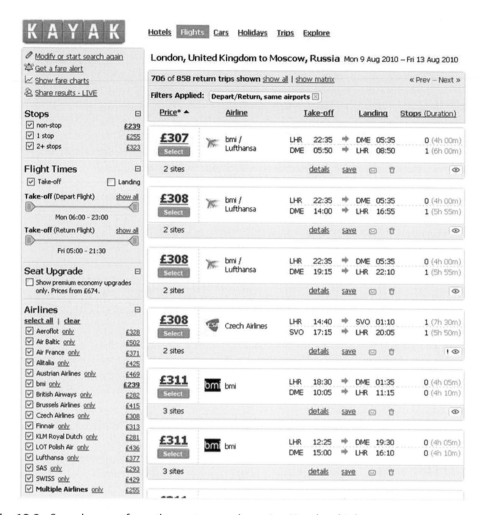

Fig. 13.2. Sample page from the meta-search engine Kayak, which aggregates content from a plethora of suppliers.

eTOURISM FOR SUSTAINABLE COMPETITIVE ADVANTAGE

The emerging ICT tools introduce new capabilities, which consequently provide new opportunities as well as major challenges for all players. Newcomers, such as Kayak, lastminute.com, Expedia.com and priceline.com, challenge all tourism intermediaries and suppliers as they introduce new and flexible business models, increase transparency and gradually increase their market share dramatically. Although technology can support the competitiveness of organizations, it is difficult to offer sustainable competitive advantage. Increasingly hardware and software become standardized and often easily available to all players through application service providers (ASPs) (Paraskevas and Buhalis, 2002). Most Star Alliance airlines now use common technological platforms even if they compete on several routes. Internet innovations are also widely visible and they are often copied within a short period of time by competitors. Sustaining competitive advantage therefore in the long term is one of the most difficult challenges organizations have to face.

Developing mechanisms to sustain competitive advantage in the long term can only be achieved by adopting dynamic and innovative practices that will enable tourism organizations to constantly outperform their competitors. Competitor tactics as well as demand trends can increasingly be monitored online, in real time. Organizations can take advantage of the instantaneous interaction facilitated by the Internet and electronic mail and address the need of their clients at the right time. Inevitably competition will be intensified and may force smaller and technologically disadvantaged players to lose considerable market share.

Similarly to many other innovation diffusions, one of the most difficult challenges for tourism organizations is deciding when to enter the competitive arena and how much to spend on their online strategy. Pioneering technological solutions often means that organizations take greater risks and have to explore a fairly difficult field. In return they can hope to capture a significant market share that will enable them to increase their profitability in the future. In contrast, being a latecomer may be less risky in terms of investment and ICTs but it is more complex to attract customers and develop relationships once those are established with other organizations.

It is becoming increasingly obvious that the utilization of the range of available ICTs and the Internet will be determining the scale and scope of tourism business globally. It will also define the potential for geographical and operational expansion of a tourism organization. ICTs are instrumental in a number of strategic decisions for tourism organizations and they are gradually one of the key strategic considerations for tourism planning and development at both the micro and the macro level.

ICTs should support and serve the business plans and models of tourism organizations, rather than the other way round. Equally, unless decision makers appreciate the importance of the ICT capabilities and opportunities emerging, they will be unable to inform their business models and plans or achieve their full potential. Hence a close integration between ICTs' potentials and business models is a prerequisite for the successful tourism organization of the future.

REFERENCES

Boehmer, J. and Cohen, A. (2007) BA, GDSs Still Talking: Business As Usual Despite Much-Hyped Contractual Expiration. *BTNonline* magazine. Available at: http://www.allbusiness.com/transportation-communications/transportation-services/4160695-1.html (accessed 29 August 2010).

Buhalis, D. (1998) Strategic use of information technologies in the tourism industry. *Tourism Management* 19(3), 409–423.

Buhalis, D. (2003) *eTourism: Information Technology for Strategic Tourism Management*. Pearson (Financial Times/Prentice Hall), London.

Buhalis, D. (2004) eAirlines: strategic and tactical use of ICTS in the airline industry. *Information and Management* 41(7), 805–825.

Buhalis, D. and O'Connor, P. (2005) Information communication technology – revolutionising tourism. *Tourism Recreation Research* 30(3), 7–16.

Buhalis, D. and Zoge, M. (2007) The strategic impact of the internet on the tourism industry. In: Sigala, M., Mich, L. and Murphy, J. (eds) *ENTER 2007 Proceedings*. Ljubljana, Slovenia. Springer-Verlag, Vienna, Austria, pp. 481–492.

eBusiness W@tch (2006) ICT and e-Business in the Tourism Industry. Sector Impact Study No. 08/2006, European Commission. Available at: http://www.ebusiness-watch.org/studies/sectors/tourism/documents/Tourism_2006.pdf (accessed 28 August 2010).

Egger, R. and Buhalis, D. (eds) (2008) *eTourism Case Studies: Management & Marketing Issues in eTourism*. Butterworth Heinemann, Oxford.

Hammer, M. and Champy, J. (1993) *Reengineering the Corporation: a Manifesto for Business Revolution*. Nicholas Brealey, London.

Laudon, K. and Laudon, J. (2009) *Management Information Systems*, 11th edn. Prentice Hall, Upper Saddle River, New Jersey.

Michopoulou, E., Buhalis, D., Michailidis, S. and Ambrose, I. (2007) Destination management systems: technical challenges in developing an eTourism platform for accessible tourism in Europe. In: Sigala, M., Mich, L. and Murphy, J. (eds) *ENTER 2007 Proceedings*. Ljubljana, Slovenia. Springer-Verlag, Vienna, Austria, pp. 301–310.

O'Brien, J. (1996) *Management Information Systems: Managing Information Technology in the Networked Enterprise*. Irwin, Chicago.

O'Connor, P. (1999) *Electronic Information Distribution in Tourism and Hospitality*. CAB International, Wallingford, UK.

Paraskevas, A. and Buhalis, D. (2002) Web-enabled ICT outsourcing for small hotels: opportunities and challenges. *Cornell Hotel and Restaurant Administration Quarterly* 43(2), 27–39.

Poon, A. (1993) *Tourism, Technology and Competitive Strategies*. CAB International, Wallingford, UK.

Porter, M. (1985) *Competitive Advantage*. Free Press, New York.

Porter, M. (2001) Strategy and the Internet. *Harvard Business Review* 103D (March), 63–78.

Sheldon, P. (1997) *Information Technologies for Tourism*. CAB International, Wallingford, UK.

Tapscott, D. (1996) *The Digital Economy: Promise and Peril in the Age of Networked Intelligence*. McGraw-Hill, New York.

Werthner, H. and Klein, S. (1999) *Information Technology and Tourism – a Challenging Relationship*. Springer, New York.

World Tourism Organization (WTO) (2001) *eBusiness for Tourism: Practical Guidelines for Destinations and Businesses*. WTO, Madrid.

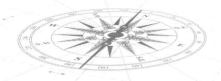

chapter 14

Process-based Management in Tourism

Geoff Southern

In this chapter we will be looking at process thinking in travel and tourism, referring to much of the academic and populist literature on the topic. We first consider what is meant by a business process and the act of 're-engineering'. We then describe management movements that led to the early 1990s' breakthrough in business process re-engineering (BPR), and other developments since then. Finally we consider the role and relationship of the traditional functions of management (finance, organizational behaviour and human resource management, operations management and marketing).

Throughout the chapter cases will be used to relate the concepts, theories and techniques of process thinking to tourism.

WHAT IS A PROCESS?

Most texts on BPR begin by defining what a business process is.

Peppard and Rowland resort to the dictionary for their definition: 'a continuous and regular action or succession of actions, taking place or carried out in a definite manner and leading to the accomplishment of some result; a continuous operation or series of operations' (*Oxford English Dictionary*, as quoted in Peppard and Rowland, 1995: 6). But this definition is qualified by adding that the accomplishment might just be simple safe retention of goods (storage), and they question whether this is a process. They then say that organizations adopting a process approach may find that it is sometimes difficult to figure out why many steps exist at all.

Armistead and Rowland, in *Managing Business Processes: BPR and Beyond*, also refer to a dictionary: '(a) a series of actions or proceedings used in making, manufacturing, or achieving something; (b) progress, course; (c) a natural or involuntary operation or set of changes' (*Collins Dictionary*, 1996, as quoted by Armistead and Rowland, 1996: 57). They also narrow their definition, arguing 'in an organizational context the first is best' (Armistead and Rowland, 1996: 58).

Turning to the seminal papers on BPR we get the following definitions for a business process: (i) 'a collection of activities that takes one or more kinds of input and creates an output that is of value to the customer' (Hammer and Champy, 1993: 35); and (ii) 'a set of logically related tasks performed to achieve a defined business outcome' (Davenport and Short, 1990). While there is general agreement on the definition of a process, and on the need for BPR, the views of these two teams of experts on how to get to a 're-engineered' state differ appreciably. Hammer advocates a 'big bang' approach, starting from a clean sheet and suggesting that we 'don't automate: obliterate' existing processes and systems. He believes that it can only happen from the top down, and that it can never happen from the bottom up. Davenport stresses the compatibility of BPR with more incremental approaches to change such as continuous improvement within total quality management (TQM). Davenport also seems to emphasize that technology is a driver of change, while Hammer considers it to be an enabler, although both come from a background in technology (Watts, 1994b).

Hammer and Champy in their first text (1993) cite four recurring processes, defining them by a change of state:

- concept to prototype;
- prospect to order;
- order to payment; and
- inquiry to resolution.

These processes mirror Porter's earlier work on the generic value chain, where the primary activities of inbound logistics, operations, outbound logistics, marketing and sales, and service are supported by the activities of firm infrastructure, human resource management, technology development and procurement (Porter, 1985).

They may have to be modified in tourism, but we also propose four recurring activities:

- informing potential customers of travel products;
- getting sales;
- delivering travel products; and
- coordinating activities.

While we define these as primary processes in tourism we also recognize that there are many sub-processes, some of them within the primary processes and others providing an overlap between them. We have defined three secondary processes:

- **Targeting past customers** is currently termed customer relationship management (CRM), and covers the overlap between 'informing potential customers' and 'getting sales'. This concentrates on building client relationships and ensuring return customers.
- **Preparing customers** for their tour covers the overlap between 'getting sales' and 'delivering travel products'. This creates customer expectations and informs clients of their responsibilities, factors that relate to the SERVQUAL 5 gap service quality model of Zeithaml *et al.* (1990).
- **Developing service products** could possibly be designated as a primary process, but it has been placed between 'delivering travel products' and 'informing potential customers' as it relies on input from both of these, and when a new (or improved) product has been designed needs action from both to implement.

The relationship between our primary and secondary processes is shown as a process map in Venn diagram form in Fig. 14.1.

Considering the relationship between Hammer's generic processes and our tourism process model:

- Hammer's 'prospect to order' has been modified to form two processes in tourism: 'informing potential customers of travel products' and 'getting sales'. We argue that these are fundamentally different processes with a degree of overlap; indeed, Hammer appears to overlook our first process to some extent.
- Hammer's 'order to payment' corresponds to our 'delivering travel products', but we have placed payment between 'getting sales' and 'delivering travel products' on the grounds that in tourism customers pay upfront before the product is delivered.
- Hammer's 'inquiry to resolution' process has been divided into the sub-processes 'enquiry system' and 'complaints procedure', and we believe they fit into 'getting sales' and 'delivering travel products', respectively.
- We believe that, in tourism, Hammer's 'concept to prototype' constitutes 'developing new products'. These are primarily in terms of destinations and transport, although new ancillary products (e.g. insurance and currency exchange) may also be added to an organization's product portfolio. These are, perhaps, relatively less important in tourism than in other commercial sectors such as manufacture.

The 'coordinating activities' process has been added to Hammer and Champys' set of processes. We have emphasized it and made it central in our model. Within this process exists

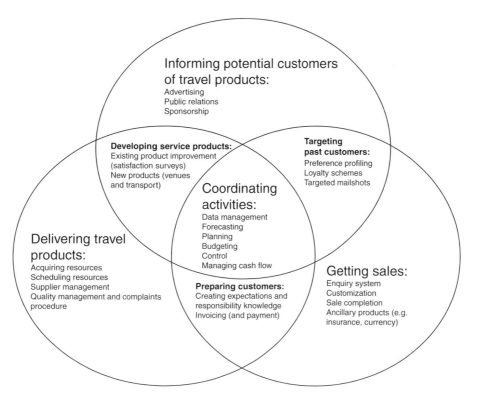

Fig. 14.1. Process map for a tourism company.

the means of developing strategy and delivering it by providing and maintaining necessary resources. Hammer and Champy, and indeed Porter, place less explicit emphasis on it in their models, although it is obviously implied.

Our 'tourism' generic processes will be used as the framework for the remainder of this chapter, and will offer opportunities to elaborate on what process-based thinking offers to a re-engineered organization. In addition case studies falling into one or a combination of these seven categories will be used to illustrate benefits to be gained.

WHAT IS BPR?

Having defined what a business process is we can now define 're-engineering'. The most cited definition is that of Hammer and Champy (1993): 'Re-engineering is the fundamental rethinking and radical design of business processes to achieve dramatic improvements in critical, contemporary measures of performance, such as cost, quality, service, and speed.'

In 1994 Hammer was asked to respond to people who say there is actually nothing new in BPR (Watts, 1994a). He began his response by saying 'I'd say they're probably right!'

Indeed, the established techniques of system analysis and development are described and called upon in many BPR texts. These include techniques of work study (method study and work measurement) begun by Taylor and Ford in the 1920s, TQM concepts and techniques from the 1970s, and systems theory and change management material from the 1980s.

Hammer called upon TQM to illustrate his view of the novelty of BPR, saying:

> Re-engineering borrows two concepts from the quality revolution, namely the focus on customers and the notion of process. They are not original to re-engineering. Those I think, go back a long way, but certainly they are the fundamentals of the quality revolution. What's new about re-engineering is its radical nature. The notion of a clean sheet … So that's what I think is really distinctive and new about it.
>
> Watts (1994a)

But at the same time Davenport had a less radical view, and saw a greater role for existing management concepts and techniques in the analysis of processes and implementation of new or amended ones. In response to Hammer he says:

> he [Hammer] takes a very strong view of the differences and almost the opposition between re-engineering and the more incremental approaches to change – things like quality and so on. My experience has been very much that these are very compatible approaches to change and in fact most organizations end up mixing and matching and combining them, even on a single project.
>
> Watts (1994b)

Developments after the mid-1990s have mainly focused on supply chain management and performance management, both supported by rapid development in technology. In supply chain management Porter's concept of the value chain has been exploited and the effectiveness and efficiency of supply chains have particularly been improved by better technology. Perhaps in tourism we should be talking about supply networks rather than supply chains, as leisure providers will call upon a larger number of suppliers and suppliers will service a larger number of customers than in other sectors. In performance measurement the balanced scorecard approach (Kaplan and Norton, 1996), concentrating on developing measures to support improvement, has been introduced.

However, in these developments, the underlying principles of BPR are still being applied. The underlying principles are:

- **concentrating on processes** and the change in mindset from specialist (knowledge-based) functional silos to cross-functional completion; and
- **focusing on customers** throughout the organization's supply chain.

WHAT MAKES BPR HAPPEN?

BPR is fundamentally a systems change process. Of particular importance in both the managing change and the BPR literature are the reason and imperative for change. In a technique attributed to Lewin, and developed further by others (e.g. Paton and McCalman, 2008) the forces driving and restraining change are analysed to determine the nature of the change. All agree that change only happens when driving forces are greater than restraining forces. Paton and McCalman differentiate between internally and externally generated change, demonstrating that the latter is more difficult to apply and control. The BPR literature, on the other hand, concentrates on a need to do BPR resulting from changes in the environment in which the organization operates, usually on a re-engineer-to-survive basis. This is a useful starting point when considering what makes BPR happen.

Unpublished work by the author considered 12 companies who claimed to have re-engineered their organizations, and found three types of driving/enabling forces that made BPR happen: (i) internal factors; (ii) external factors; and (iii) changes in technology.

An example of **internal factors** is the appointment of a new CEO, as happened when a new principal at the University of Glasgow was appointed who immediately began to restructure the organization on the basis of processes in a search for efficiency and effectiveness. However, even here it can be argued that changes in the financial environment and increasing expectations of both students and funding bodies are the real driving forces behind the restructuring exercise, as recognized by the new principal.

External factors include changes in the environment such as changes in the law or the economy. Other changes in the marketplace, such as new market entrants or a change in customer needs or expectations, are also included here.

One major development in **changes in technology** is the development and expansion of the World Wide Web, enabling improvements in communication systems. Other examples include satellite positioning and tracking systems for logistics management, and new product developments such as i-players and flat-screen TVs. The question of whether changes in technology drive process re-engineering or just enable a good idea to be implemented is an interesting one.

Of the 12 companies considered 11 were driven by legal and/or market changes (three had both), and only one company was driven by internal factors, a fear of losing core skills. In all cases the presence of a strong committed CEO was important as an internal driver once the external threat was recognized.

EXAMPLES OF BPR IN TOURISM

This section will briefly describe a number of examples of BPR and then comment on them in terms of the process changes (referring to the 'tourism' categories defined earlier), whether the change was radical (Hammer) or evolutionary (Davenport), and the driving forces.

Online reservations

This process is now well established and requires no explanation, except perhaps to consider it in the context of process thinking. It represents the re-engineering of the customer acquisition process, using new technology (the Internet) to cut agents out of the traditional supply chain and allowing the resulting savings to be passed to the consumer either as lower prices or as discounts for using the more direct purchasing route.

Larger organizations such as no-frills airlines (Ryanair, easyJet, Southwest), economy hotel chains (Holiday Inn, Travel Lodge), car rental companies (Hertz, Budget) and package holiday companies (Thompson) have developed their own websites. Many of these organizations use links from their websites to those of a network of allies offering complementary services; for example, almost all airlines provide a link to car-hire-company and hotel-chain websites offering services at the customers' destination.

Smaller organizations such as family-owned hotels can sign up to an independent travel website (e.g. bargainholidays.com), frequently geographically based (e.g. Visitmalta.com), that acts as an intermediary between clients (the hotels) and consumers (hotel guests) and offers secure money transfer transactions. Thus financial security is maintained on both sides of the contractual agreement, concluding the 'deliver' (order fulfilment) process.

Table 14.1 comments on this example of online reservations in terms of the process changes.

Malabar Beach Hotel

In 1985 Chris Voss reported a case in service management that is worthy of review in the context of process thinking (Voss *et al.*, 1985). The Malabar Beach Hotel was, at the time, in decline and needed to, paraphrasing the words of Hammer, 'radically design its business processes to achieve dramatic improvements in critical, contemporary measures of performance, such as cost, quality, service, and speed'. The hotel owner decided to follow the, then novel, marketing concept of a 'no-money' holiday, where customers pay an inclusive fixed fee upfront to cover all accommodation, leisure and consumable costs of the holiday, plus a profit for the company. The change in policy had implications for all generic processes:

- **Developing service products**: The service product of the hotel had to be changed from a traditional US-style room-letting or half-board (UK-style) offering, with all other purchases individually billed to each guest, to one where a single payment entitled a guest to all food, alcoholic drink and leisure amenities of the hotel. The new regime had implications for all other generic business processes.
- **Getting sales**: For example, on careful consideration of tourist segments it was decided families would benefit least from the proposal, and single young people would be the most difficult to deal with. It was therefore decided to limit customers to established couples, and the owner entered a franchise agreement with an appropriate hotel group.
- **Delivering travel products**: In terms of food and alcoholic beverage availability the no-money regime allowed the hotel to limit choice of menu and bar offerings, but to offer better quality food on average and branded drinks. Economies of scale resulted. Leisure activities had to be upgraded as guest expectation of both availability and variety increased, and pre-booking systems were introduced to create a perception of fairness. In fact the financial 'drive' of the hotel changed from a series of departmental profit centres trying to attract spending from customers, to a series of cost centres attempting to delight customers with a better-than-expected service, but still controlling food and drink consumption.

- **Coordination**: The focus of coordination and control activities therefore switched from profit maximization and individual billing, to material and leisure activity volume control, given a minimum service quality specification. In fact control of the business was simplified. Some problems were predicted with staff motivation, given the propensity for guests not to tip. Greater care was taken in selecting and training staff, and appropriate salary adjustments were implemented. Input from the 'couples' franchise was useful here, based on the experience of franchise sister companies. Profits were more easily forecast in the short term from the booking system, and resource management in bars, restaurants and other leisure activities became easier to plan. In addition data management was greatly simplified, as indicated by the comments above.

Table 14.2 comments on this example of the Malabar Beach Hotel in terms of the process changes.

Table 14.1. Online reservations: comments in terms of the process changes.

Aspect	Commentary
Process re-engineered	While this is primarily a re-engineering of the 'getting sales' process, the data management sub-process (within the 'coordination' process) supports it. The information gained frequently immediately contributes to the forecasting sub-process (again within the 'coordination' process), and thus to the 'delivery' process by allocating or acquiring operational resources. It also contributes to the 'coordination' process as input to budget development and control.
Radical or emergent change?	It could be argued either way. Direct selling (i.e. cutting out agents or retailers) was established as early as the 1950s when John Bloom began selling low-cost washing machines to people who replied to newspaper adverts (Wikipedia, 2010). (The lowering of credit restrictions was also a factor here, and hire-purchase was invented.) So direct selling here is not radical. In addition most organizations listed above started by running traditional agent selling and Web-based selling in parallel, but easyJet and Ryanair now sell solely by electronic means; perhaps that was a radical step, and technology became an enabler to fully control their ticket distribution.
Driving forces	The original driving force was probably the expansion of the travel market, a direct result of economic growth, presenting opportunities for more people to travel and for companies to grow. However, increased competition then became the driving force, with direct electronic selling enabling companies to cut prices and hence increase sales and profits at the expense of travel agents. In the case of transport companies, improvements in technology and electronic banking then enabled this to develop further into ticketless systems and elimination of check-in procedures.

Table 14.2. Malabar Beach Hotel: comments in terms of the process changes.

Aspect	Commentary
Process re-engineered	This case represents a report of BPR in hindsight (the theory followed the practice), perhaps supporting Davenport's views. It also represents a case of 'total' BPR (after Hammer?), and a demolition of 'functional silo' thinking. Thus a multitude of business processes covering all aspects of Fig. 14.1 were re-engineered.
Radical or emergent change?	For the individual company this was a radical change in everything they had done before, from selling and the market segment to service delivery and budgetary accounting systems. However, within the industry it can be seen as an emergent trend, and the company was able to draw on new franchise partners to help with the changes.
Driving forces	These were entirely financial; they were making a loss, but having decided to go for the no-money proposal this drove all resulting changes in the generic processes. As far as technology was concerned the internal accounting system was simplified and selling was transferred to a franchise operator, so the complexity of internal IT systems was lowered. Hence, as far as the fundamental change was concerned, changes in technology had no real significance.

easyJet/hotels/cruises

easyJet has taken the expansionist route of creating core products that meet and anticipate customer needs, and has created new companies within a holding group offering no-frills hotel rooms, car hire and cruises to complement its low-cost flights. All group companies can be accessed through the easyJet Web pages. They have also collaborated in the production of reality TV programmes that create low expectations of remedial action if customers do not comply with check-in and baggage requirements, and that can be considered to educate potential customers in company processes. In comparison Ryanair has concentrated on its core product, low-cost flights, but has developed network relations with hotel chains and an international car hire company, all of which can be accessed via the Ryanair Web page.

Table 14.3 comments on this example in terms of the process changes.

Hong Kong pan-Pearl River Delta (PRD) tourism market

In May 2005 an announcement in tdctrade.com described opportunities for Honk Kong tourist organizations in its nine neighbouring mainland China provinces.

As a tourist venue Honk Kong emphasizes its urban characteristics as an international hub for commerce and air connections. These characteristics complement those of its neighbour's relatively unexploited ecological, cultural, historical and ethnic tourism attractions. Hong Kong is also endowed with extensive experience in tourism management, services and promotion.

Under a regional cooperation agreement signed on 3 June 2004, the nine provinces and Hong Kong and Macau have agreed to promote regional cooperation in tourism, and to

Table 14.3. easyJet/hotels/cruises: comments in terms of the process changes.

Aspect	Commentary
Process re-engineered	The 'getting sales' process was re-engineered to widen the product portfolio and create a single one-stop shop for customers, a (customer-focus) primary principle of BPR?
Radical or emergent change?	This was an emergent step-by-step approach as new services were introduced. Banks cross-sell financial products in the same way.
Driving forces	The driving force was an internal drive for greater profits, enabled by improvements in IT systems and company skills in employing them.

jointly formulate development and marketing strategies and hence build a strong branding for tourism in the region. The agreement aims to build an international tourist belt in the PRD by creating a barrier-free tourism zone. Companies are allowed to open branch offices freely, and reputable travel companies are encouraged to launch intercity operations.

Prior to this initiative, tourism organizations in Hong Kong had been limited to organizing mainland-bound package tours. They can now participate directly by forming joint ventures with their mainland counterparts, operating without geographical restriction. They can also engage fully in the construction and operation of hotels and restaurants, and set up wholly-owned engineering consulting companies in support of tourism development. Hong Kong, as a world-class performer in tourism, is well placed to facilitate the development of tourism in the wider region.

Table 14.4 comments on this example of the pan-PRD tourism market in terms of the process changes.

THE ROLE OF TRADITIONAL TOURISM MANAGEMENT FUNCTIONS IN BPR

Let us now consider the relationship between the traditional functions of management and our generic business processes, in other words where the work was done and who was primarily responsible.

- **Informing potential customers** (of travel products) was, and still is, primarily the concern of the marketing function, supported by the delivery and service product development processes to inform the organization of customer preferences to best direct marketing expenditure.
- **Targeting past customers** (or CRM), although part of the marketing function, is a growing specialist activity in its own right, recognizing that knowledge of customers and the development of loyalty to an organization can vastly reduce the cost of getting a sale.
- **Getting sales** is the responsibility of the sales department, although in the past this has been paired with the marketing function in many organizations. However, with technological development and increased customization of products, especially in the tourism industry, this is becoming increasingly recognized as a separate area of expertise.
- **Preparing customers** (for their trip) falls between the marketing (including sales) and delivery processes. It informs customers what to expect on their trip, and also of their

Table 14.4. Hong Kong pan-PRD tourism market: comments in terms of the process changes.

Aspect	Commentary
Process re-engineered	'Getting sales' and 'delivering travel products' were the processes that were re-engineered to create a wider portfolio.
Radical or emergent change?	This was a radical change requiring political backing (enabled perhaps by the transfer of sovereignty of Hong Kong from the UK to China in 1997).
Driving forces	The driving forces were for greater regional profits following the transfer of power, and possibly to draw Hong Kong into central Chinese national culture.

responsibilities on such aspects as visa, passport and health insurance requirements. It will also inform them of additional attractions they may wish to visit and may offer to sell tickets for these (in addition to products they have purchased already). In terms of service quality this process is very important and is represented by one of the gaps in the SERVQUAL 5 gap customer service model.

- **Delivering travel products** was, and still is primarily, a concern of the operations function, consisting of subsystems to define resource needs, acquire resources (travel seats, accommodation), schedule use of resources, and ensure that quality standards are maintained. It works on estimates of organizational activity levels from marketing, delivered via the coordination process (or strategic planning function).
- **Developing service products** is usually undertaken in most organizations by a specialist department calling upon expertise from all departments on a need basis, or by a cross-functional team drawn from existing departments. In tourism, however, completely new products that compete on pure innovation are rare and there is a continuous development of existing products or a move into new destinations or ancillary products.
- **Coordinating activities** is traditionally undertaken by strategy and finance departments. The operating mechanism for this, at least in the short to medium term, is the budgeting process, where inputs come from marketing (activity levels) and operations (resource costs).

SUMMARY

- BPR is the 'fundamental rethinking and radical design of business processes to achieve dramatic improvements in critical, contemporary measures of performance, such as cost, quality, service, and speed' (Hammer and Champy, 1993).
- BPR draws upon concepts and techniques from other management strands of thought. It encompasses ideas from, for example, systems thinking, TQM and supply (and value) chain management.
- BPR takes a holistic approach to management which concentrates on processes while also focusing on customers.
- The author of this chapter has identified four primary generic business processes: (i) informing potential customers of travel products; (ii) getting sales; (iii) delivering travel products; and (iv) coordinating activities. Three secondary (overlapping) generic business

processes were also identified: (i) targeting past customers; (ii) preparing customers; and (iii) developing service products.

- These encompass traditional functions of management, but put into practice a culture of cross-functional completion rather than one of specialist-silo mentality with responsibility handovers.

REFERENCES

Armistead, C. and Rowland, P. (1996) *Managing Business Processes: BPR and Beyond*. Wiley, Chichester, UK.

Davenport, T. and Short, J.E. (1990) The new industrial engineering: information technology and business process redesign. *Sloane Management Review* 31, 11–27.

Hammer, M. and Champy, J. (1993) *Reengineering the Corporation: a Manifesto for Business Revolution*. Nicholas Brearley, London.

Kaplan, R.S. and Norton, D.P. (1996) *The Balanced Scorecard: Translating Strategy into Action*. HBS Press, Boston, Massachusetts.

Paton, R.A. and McCalman, J. (2008) *Change Management: a Guide to Effective Implementation*. Sage, London.

Peppard, J. and Rowland, P. (1995) *The Essence of Business Process Re-engineering*. Prentice Hall, Hemel Hempstead, UK.

Porter, M.E. (1985) *Competitive Advantage: Creating and Sustaining Superior Performance*. Free Press, London.

Voss, C., Armistead, C., Johnston, B. and Morris, B. (1985) *Operations Management in Service Industries and the Public Sector*. Wiley, Chichester, UK.

Watts, J. (1994a) The business change and re-engineering interview: Dr Michael Hammer. *Business Change and Re-engineering: the Journal of Corporate Transformation* 1(4) (Spring).

Watts, J. (1994b) The business change and re-engineering interview: Tom Davenport. *Business Change and Re-engineering: the Journal of Corporate Transformation* 2(1) (Summer).

Wikipedia (2010) John Bloom (businessman). Available at: http://en.wikipedia.org/wiki/John_Bloom_(businessman) (accessed 13 October 2010).

Zeithaml, V.A., Parasuraman, A. and Berry, L.L. (1990) *Delivering Quality Service: Balancing Customer Perceptions and Expectations*. Free Press, New York.

FURTHER READING

Armistead, C. and Rowland, P. (1996) *Managing Business Processes: BPR and Beyond*. Wiley, Chichester, UK.

chapter 15

International Strategies in Tourism

Eduardo Parra-López, Vanessa Yanes Estevez
and Mercedes Melchior Navarro

INTRODUCTION

In recent times, the tourism environment has undergone many changes. Tourism companies find themselves in an increasingly competitive environment and, whether or not internationalization is and will continue to be an advantageous step for any company, it seems reasonable to think that it is an opportunity that should at least be explored. Porter (1991) indicated that firms achieve positions of competitive advantage through processes of innovation, which is understood not only as new technologies but also as new ways of doing things, such as by means of internationalization, for example.

International competitiveness in tourism

It is difficult to define the concept of international competitiveness in tourism because it is a complex variable that depends on the characteristics of its country (or region) of origin and other environmental factors. Perhaps we should start by mentioning that the national (or regional) characteristics of national tourism firms can hinder or facilitate their international development.

If we examine the reasons for the international activity of a tourism company, historically, they are based on the economics theory in that, in line with the macroeconomics theory, trade between nations occurs because each country has a competitive advantage in the production of one or several products. The nation has been described as one of the key elements in internationalization. The specialization of nations and the reasons why some countries focus on the production of certain goods or are more competitive in the production of those goods have been widely addressed in the economics literature but not in the tourism literature. Therefore, the following paragraphs address some issues of international competitiveness that lead to tourism internationalization.

Research into international competitiveness in tourism has evolved over the years and there are several theories that analyse which variables explain international trade. The first of these focused on the country, its competitive advantage, and the whys and wherefores. Then, in the area of the economic theories of international trade, research was aimed at explaining the patterns of that international trade.[1] After the work of Porter (1991), other theories appeared, based on the company as the principal figure. Those works considered that it is the firms, not the countries, that constitute the part that is, or is not, internationally competitive. It was then considered that nations specialize in certain sectors. That thinking came to be called the Competitive Advantage of Nations Theory.

Those authors designed a model labelled the double diamond, which they considered an extension of the national diamond designed by Porter (1991) (see Fig. 15.1). This new model considers not only the characteristics of the home country but also the attributes of the country that is its most important trading partner. Later, Dunning (1993) developed a multiple diamond model that not only considered the characteristics of the home country but also observed determinants of a series of neighbouring countries and the role of multinationals.

In short, the usefulness of the theory of international trade can be highlighted since it contributes to explaining what could be produced competitively in a specific place or tourist destination, which direction a tourism firm should take to produce a product efficiently, and whether or not government practices could interfere in the flow of trade between countries.[2]

Heckscher (1919 cited in Ingram and Dunn, 1999) and Ohlin (1933) developed the factor proportions theory, which was no longer based on the work factor as the principal determinant but provided a model proposing that a country's competitive advantage stemmed from the relative abundance of resources and the intensity of their use through technology.

However, the 1960s saw a great change in the international scenario: multinational firms played an increasing role in international trade and the theories that had, as far as possible, explained trade were no longer valid. As a result, new theories were proposed in an attempt to explain international trade. Those new theories would be called the neo-technological theories. The principal exponents included Posner (1961), Hufbauer (1966), Vernon (1966), Hirsch (1967 cited in Bajo, 1991), Kravis (1970), White (1974), Jacquemin (1982), Krugman (1994) and Krugman and Obstfeld (1994). In most cases, those theories shared the relaxation of the hypothesis of perfect competition and attached special importance to the role that national

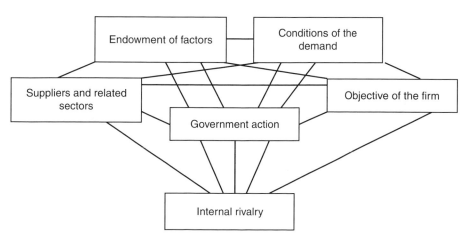

Fig. 15.1. National diamond (Source: based on Canals, 1991).

technological differences play in the generation of comparative advantage and in international trade and, similarly, in the processes of tourism internationalization.

In the 1990s, those theories were no longer able to explain trade because the conditions of the international context had changed once again. It was Porter (1991) who indicated that firms attain positions of competitive advantage by means of innovation processes, understood not only as new technologies but also as new ways of doing things. He created four large factors as determinants of the competitiveness of nations, 'Porter's diamond'. However, although the contributions of Porter (1991) have also been unable to explain trade because his diamond has limitations, they have been of great importance to the current explanation of international trade in tourism.

Those initial aspects led to the proposal of new approaches to the international process in the tourism industry. The promotion of international tourism will improve with a deeper and more precise knowledge of what drives firms in the tourism sector to initiate and maintain the process of geographical expansion and of the variables that affect business decisions in that direction. Moreover, there must also be more knowledge of the pattern of behaviour in the development of the process. Following the classification established by Young et al. (1991), there are various approaches to the internationalization of firms and these are: (i) a sequential approach; (ii) an economic approach; and (iii) a business strategy approach (see Table 15.1).

In the case of contextuality, the sequential approach is more applicable to tourism firms that are taking their first steps in the international context with little or no experience, for example small and medium firms. With regard to the criticism that the sequential approach receives, the fact that firms cannot follow the Uppsala model in its entirety does not invalidate the basic hypotheses of the model.

Finally, to conclude the theoretical aspects, if a tourism firm is considering internationalization, it should analyse two modes of entry, in line with Jarillo and Martínez (1991): (i) exporting; or (ii) overseas production. The difference between these two is that, in the former, only the tourism product is exported, while, in the latter, not only is the product transferred but also resources, knowledge and/or technology.

Focusing on the economic aspects, for example transaction costs (e.g. Buckley and Casson, 1981), two types of overseas production can be distinguished. In this case, the distinction is between direct investment abroad and the option of granting a licence. As a general rule, exporting implies production in the tourism firm's home country and selling the products in the overseas market with more or less involvement of the firm (depending on the use of intermediaries in the home country, host country, etc.).

As previously highlighted, in the economic approach, each mode of entry has a different impact on the variables, that is: (i) the level of resources committed; (ii) the degree of risk taken; (iii) the level of control over the operations; and (iv) potential profit (Root, 1987; Agarwal and Ramaswami, 1992). Therefore, the modes that entail committing a greater amount of resources have the advantage of permitting greater control over the operations, which must have positive effects on the potential profit. However, the commitment of more resources will also mean having to bear a greater economic risk.

Factors determining a commitment to tourism internationalization

After analysing the internationalization process of firms in the tourism sector and proposing that the internationalization process is usually sequential for most small and medium tourism firms, the next step is to identify the factors determining the export activity, with special emphasis on internal factors, particularly the demographic characteristics of the decision makers, which will be addressed in greater depth.

Table 15.1. Classification of approaches to the internationalization of the firm (Source: the authors, from the analysis of the different approaches).

Approach	Schools/theories	Characteristics
Sequential approach	Uppsala Innovation School	1. A sequential or phased model 2. Defence of the sequential process and not of internationalization 3. Exclusion of firms with vast leisure resources and organizations with accumulated experience (Johanson and Vahlne, 1990)[a]
Economic approach	Transaction Costs Theory	1. Importance attached to the international strategy 2. Intermittent approach: indicates a lack of feedback and the possibility of development[b]
Business strategy approach	Business Strategy Theory	1. Based on continuous dialogue between the organization and its environment 2. The Root model (1987): the firm takes into account both the internal and the external factors when deciding on the mode of entry

[a] Taking these exceptions into account, it is understood that the concept of the tourism internationalization process is a sequential strategy of approach to overseas markets that is mainly applicable to small and medium firms in the sector that are taking their first steps in international business (Young, 1987). Also, see the works of Kim and Hwang (1992).
[b] In light of the previous conclusions, it can be stressed that the internationalization process is and will be a highly complex phenomenon that can only be understood if the context in which it takes place is considered. The environment in which today's tourism firm moves, as well as the internal variables that influence the process, can be so different that it is very difficult to follow any general rule (Buckley, 1995).

The factors influencing the export commitment of companies in general, including those in tourism, can be grouped into two broad categories: (i) business or internal; and (ii) environmental or external (Aaby and Slater, 1989; Alonso and Donoso, 1994, 1998). However, it should be remembered that the content of each factor has not always been defined in the same way (factors are addressed in greater depth in the section 'Strategic Analysis as a Key to Internationalization in Tourism' of this chapter). There is no single classification of these determinants since, while some may coincide in general, they sometimes differ in the variables that are considered. Thus, some authors classify export determinants as factors in the environmental context and those in the business context (Aaby and Slater, 1989; Alonso and Donoso, 1994, 1998). Environmental factors should be understood as cultural, political, social, macroeconomic, etc., while the business factors are those key aspects of the firm's strategy and organizational capabilities that are under the firm's control and are necessary for the export activity. Within the determinants in the business context, other authors, such as Kamath *et al.* (1987), differentiate between the characteristics of the firm itself and those of the decision maker.

Although the most frequent criterion to classify determinants of commitment to exporting is the differentiation between business or internal factors and environmental or external factors, Alonso and Donoso (1994: 114) establish that 'it is, however, necessary to add a third important factor: the analysis of *management* attitudes and aptitudes'.[3]

Thus, a tourism firm's inclusion of exporting in its strategic behaviour does not solely depend on it having the capability to compete in overseas markets: the business and environmental factors must also be present since they are what decisively change the scope and quality of the decision. In this respect, while the tourism literature on strategic behaviour is fairly recent, the idea of seeking the internal foundations of a tourism firm's competitiveness is not. It is the core of the resource-based approach originally proposed by Penrose (1959), who defined the firm as a set of production resources, some physical or tangible and others human.

The importance of internal factors in explaining the export behaviour of firms is highlighted by Cuervo García (1993: 363) when he stated, in relation to sources of competitiveness, 'it is the heterogeneity of firms that ultimately explains sustainable competitive advantages and results'. The review of the analysed works revealed a series of internal factors in the tourism firm that are associated with commitment to internationalization, and three types of research works on that commitment:

- those focusing on the analysis of the internal factors that influence the tourism firm's decision to enter overseas markets;
- those focusing on the differences in the internationalization commitment of a group of tourism firms wishing to produce abroad; and
- those focusing on explaining tourism firms' intentions to internationalize or to increase international activity.

The following section examines the key strategic aspects in the internal and external analyses and their importance to internationalization.

STRATEGIC ANALYSIS AS A KEY TO INTERNATIONALIZATION IN TOURISM

To merely follow trends is surely not one of the best 'strategic choices', especially in the case of internationalization, which is growing in importance and particularly in complexity (Corfu and Nistoreanu, 2006) and, in some circumstances, constitutes a necessary step for the tourism firm's long-term competitiveness and even survival (Ruzzier and Konecnik, 2006).

However, the key is: (i) to have clear objectives to be achieved; (ii) to constantly analyse the external factors; (iii) to be aware of the organization's strengths and weaknesses; and (iv) to implement and control the direction to take. Those stages form part of the strategic process and help the firm to be successful and so attain international competitiveness. Moreover, circumstances such as changes in customer preferences, advances in technological resources, increased concentration and rivalry and the relaxation of entry barriers occur in a stage of sector maturity and make it more complicated to solve any problem (Reichel, 1983).

Thus, tourism firms must apply strategic management as the system of philosophy not only to lead them to positive results but also to survive in the sector.

In the vast majority of the lists of phases in the strategic process (Johnson and Scholes, 2001), the first phase is usually strategic analysis. This entails seeking and processing relevant information about the internal and external characteristics of the firm. This enables the firm to identify not only the environment opportunities that its strategy should exploit – such as the presence of a new international destination or the change in its customers' preferences – but also threats whose negative impact must be minimized – such as the possible country-related risk (the country risk analysis tries to identify idiosyncratic sources of potencial volatility in a country's political, economic or social environment (Di Gregorio, 2005)). With regard to the internal analysis, this diagnosis should enable the firm to identify its strengths, in other words, the strategic resources and capabilities that will support its expansion, and its weaknesses, the factors that need improvement.

The importance and application of the strategic orientation are crucial in the case of a strategy like internationalization, which is considered one of the most solid ways to promote the firm's international competitiveness while strengthening its position in the national market (Ramón, 2002a). It is also the first step towards globalization, generally understood as a process that takes the company's presence to the world stage (Pine and Go, 1996). Thus, as mentioned in the previous section, the determinants of international activity are basically classified as internal factors and environmental or external factors (Aaby and Slater, 1989; Alonso and Donoso, 1994, 1998). Another, more recent, study that should be mentioned is that of Brotherton and Adler (1999), which focuses on the strategic choices of international hotel companies. These authors' 'strategic constellation' includes the key internal and external factors which must be considered, to a greater or lesser extent, in determining the most appropriate international strategy, which ranges from **standardization** (internally focused) to **customization** (externally focused and more consumer-oriented), depending on the level of customer participation and the degree of differentiation of the strategies (Table 15.2).

Table 15.2. The strategic constellation (Source: adapted from Brotherton and Adler, 1999).

Internal factors	External factors
Costs	Competitors
Organizational complexity	Cultural diversity
Product/service conceptualization	Corporate image and credibility
Standards and conformance	Customer participation
Centric orientation	Competitive conditions
Internal change	Channels of distributions
Coordination and control	External communication
Capabilities and competences	Markets and customers
Capacity management and asset productivity	Environmental change and complexity
Product/service configuration	Revenue potential and cash flow
Internal communication	

It is patently clear that strategic analysis is not only important in taking the internationalization decision but also crucial throughout the rest of the process, such as in choosing the way to compete in the new circumstances. Therefore, it is necessary to expand on how to carry out that strategic analysis, and its implications.

Strategic analysis of the environment

As well as the above, the importance of undertaking an accurate analysis of the environment in tourism is supported because it leads to improved results (Olsen *et al.*, 1994). It is even more critical in the case of internationalization since most of the determinants that have been examined are external factors (Perks and Hughes, 2008).

It is precisely the environmental scanning that helps a firm in the key decisions in its internationalization process, which is no more than to identify the international destination in which a market opportunity exists, and generally follows customers' likes and demands. This analysis could be facilitated by the Porter approach (1991), known as the diamond, and its identification of the factors that lead a country to success in a determined sector. Thus, the choice of destination country in the internationalization strategy will, in part, depend on the result of the strategic analysis of the following determinants (Porter, 1991):

- **Conditions of the factors** – such as training, aptitudes and experience of the workforce specialized in the sector, physical resources (water, climate), geographical location, knowledge of tourism and its importance in the country, the amount and cost of the capital available to finance the tourism sector, the transport system, communications network, generalization of the different methods of payment, health infrastructures, modernization of public works, and the presence of the home country's authorities or commercial offices. If the current situation of the factors is not ideal, the firm should consider what the possibilities are and the cost of creating or remedying what is lacking, for example human resources training or communications.
- **Conditions of the demand** – the demand for the tourism service in the home country, in terms of its composition, quantity and quality, is usually one of the factors that determine the advantages for international firms to establish themselves in the host country. Thus, if internationalization is to be successful, it is absolutely essential to characterize the possible segments that exist or their potential for growth. This analysis must also consider the distribution channels and their suitability. However, it is particularly important to remember that the greater part of the internationalized firm's customers are often its customers in the home country who are seeking its image and reference in another country that they visit. It could be the case that a hotel chain positioned in the 'small city hotels' segment could well capture additional customers in the new country but perhaps a large part of the demand comprises regular customers who have a brand reference and, wherever they go, they seek hotels in the same chain.
- **Related support sectors** – this would include the diagnosis of suppliers and related sectors, industrial machinery suppliers, the construction and installation sector, car rental, the agrifood sector, the development and promotion of outdoor sports and cultural activities (e.g. the actions taken by France to improve its competitiveness because China is going to overtake France as the world's leading tourism destination (see Box 15.1)). However, Porter (1991) gives special value to the possibility of innovation and perfection in these sectors. In that case, if the firm to be internationalized has bargaining power over a firm in the support sector, it could specify the requirements of the products

---

Box 15.1. France prepares to be overtaken by China as the world's leading tourism destination

France is preparing to take action to improve its competitiveness. One step will be the adaptation of its categorization of hotels to the international format. In turn, the Head of French Tourism has indicated that there will be a programme to promote cultural tourism, which will include promoting the Loire Valley Chateaux Route and organizing occasional activities and ecological excursions. Improvements will also be made to the 'canoe route for young people' in the south of the country, the spa facilities in the Ardèche and to the ski stations in the French Alps. Another of France's attractions, its cultural events, including the film festivals in Cannes, Toulouse, Deauville and Biarritz, and the Avignon Theatre Festival, will be a focus to attract tourists.

Source: adapted from Hosteltur (2008a)

---

it needs and make that sector be competitive since it would also be to its own advantage. However, in the early stages, the safest option may be to trust in the suppliers in the home country. For example, a hotel may open in a new destination and indicate to a textile company the type of fittings that it needs, specifying the design and the requirements of quality and composition of the most suitable fabrics for ease of washing, ironing and durability.

- **The firm's strategy, structure and rivalry** – the country's social norms or history make it important to analyse their possible implications for the ways of managing firms in the target country. These aspects include worker attitudes towards management and vice versa, individual and group behaviour, the attitude towards learning, as in the case of languages, the rivalry between domestic firms that puts pressure on firms to innovate and improve, and the possible presence of 'national champions' that make it difficult to enter and remain in the country.

External factors that influence the entry mode

Once the destination has been selected, another extremely important decision must be taken: the choice of entry mode into the foreign country and the desired level of commitment and control. In making that decision, a number of external elements that influence it must be considered (internal factors that affect the mode of entry are considered in the section 'Internal strategic analysis'). In the diagnosis of the environment, the decision makers have to pay special attention to the following factors, since they influence one of the most important phases of the internationalization process (Ramón, 2002b; Quer *et al.*, 2007):

- **The target country risk** – this includes the social, legal, economic and political traits of the target country and is usually used to identify potential sources of volatility and **downside-risk** in order to avoid investments in high-risk situations (Gregorio, 2005). Thus, a firm considering an internationalization strategy must analyse the political stability and government system of the new country, public safety, the situation of the currency and the financial system, the risk of the nationalization of property and businesses, food and health and safety, etc.
- **The cultural distance** – (or the way in which the way of life in the home country's inhabitants differs from that in the target country) this includes such aspects as the predominant values of society, customs, language, education and the dominant religion.

- **The target country's level of economic development** – this is important since adequate necessary infrastructure, the efficiency of communications together with the development of the new information and communications technologies are essential for simplifying and streamlining the strategy, especially in its initial implementation.
- **The presence of foreign investment** – this is important since it indicates that the public administration and organizations in the target country have experience of similar processes and do not need to design specific procedures and rules.

In spite of the complexity of an environmental analysis for a firm operating on an international scale, internationalized tourism firms are more aware of the importance of such an analysis than those operating only in a national context (Olsen *et al.*, 1994).

The process of environmental scanning

Apart from the results of the environmental scanning, the very process of carrying it out also provides firms with intellectual stimulation and helps in the development of a proactive attitude (Costa *et al.*, 1997). Thus, the process should be seen as a succession of activities and phases, the development of which maximizes the profits for the firm. Some of the recommended phases (Costa and Teare, 1996) are: (i) specify the firm's information requirements; (ii) specify the relevant sources of information; (iii) select the participants in the process of analysis and allocate tasks; and (iv) develop a process of information storage, processing and distribution.

SPECIFY THE FIRM'S INFORMATION REQUIREMENTS

In order to develop a process that is as efficient as possible, and considering the limited rationality of individuals (Simon, 1947), the firm will have to specify the data that it needs about the target country (legislation, infrastructure, risk, political system) as well as about its customers, the competitors already operating in the country and those who may follow the same strategy as the firm.

SPECIFY THE RELEVANT SOURCES OF INFORMATION

Once its information requirements have been specified, the firm must decide where to obtain that information by assessing its reliability, its cost and the time it will take to obtain it. For example, in the case of country risk, the firm must consider which indicator to use since the large international banks have departments specializing in the analysis of that risk, and there are specialist agencies and consultancies such as Credit Risk International, Institutional Investor and Euromoney (Gregorio, 2005).

In the case of information about customers' tastes and preferred international destinations, the firm will be able to use existing information (e.g. statistics from public institutions) or conduct a postal survey, use the satisfaction questionnaires available in hotel rooms or opt for short in-depth interviews.

Sometimes, tourism managers say that they do not conduct an exhaustive analysis of the environment because they are not sure of the reliability of the source used (Olsen *et al.*, 1994), and most firms in the sector prefer to implement an informal process (West and Olsen, 1989); hence, the importance of this phase.

SELECT THE PARTICIPANTS IN THE PROCESS OF ANALYSIS AND ALLOCATE TASKS

Once the previous stages have been defined, the next step is to identify the individuals or groups that will take part in the process. In order to facilitate the process, the participants should comprise those individuals more directly related to the sources of information to be used or those with some experience of or link with the target country.

DEVELOP A PROCESS OF INFORMATION STORAGE, PROCESSING AND DISTRIBUTION

The effort made up to this point serves for nothing if the information is not interpreted and conclusions reached that aid the decision-making process. Therefore, the information must be stored, processed and delivered to whoever needs it so that it can be fully exploited both now and in the future.

Although these stages and levels of specification are desirable, the reality is that research has revealed that international hotel chains follow somewhat different guidelines to scan their environment (Olsen *et al.*, 1994). In this respect, most of the analysis activities focus on the short term and identify customer needs and the development of new products by competitors as the principal sources of threats.

Tools for conducting the external analysis

Some of the tools that may be useful in conducting the external analysis are:

- **Typology of environments by means of cognitive maps** – this is based on Duncan's (1972) typology of environments. The objective of this technique is to diagnose the environment according to the uncertainty perceived by individuals. To that end, the technique considers the perceptions of the complexity and dynamism, as components of uncertainty, of the most relevant variables. After they have been evaluated, they are represented on a graph whose axes will measure the perceptions of both dimensions (Oreja-Rodríguez and Yanes-Estévez, 2007).
- **Analysis of sector rivalry** – this perspective of the environmental scanning analysis focuses on the task environment and aims to test the negotiating power and influence of the five components that comprise it (according to Porter, 1982), namely: (i) suppliers; (ii) customers; (iii) current competitors; (iv) potential competitors; and (v) substitutive products. In the internationalization strategy it is particularly important to know the tastes and preferences of current customers since, most of the time, they are the ones the firm pursues in the international expansion of its activities and they are considered one of the principal sources of threat (Olsen *et al.*, 1994).
- **Strategic groups or the analysis of the most direct competition** – belonging to a group implies having the same perspective of how to compete in the sector (Leask and Parnell, 2005). Thus, this tool offers the ability to obtain information about the most direct competitors, the rivalry within each group and the differences between groups, as well as the possibility of identifying the barriers for each group and the opportunities or unoccupied segments (Johnson and Scholes, 2001). The characteristics used to identify the strategic groups must be those that distinguish one group of firms from another and are really relevant to the sector under analysis. For example, in the case of the accommodation sector, we could apply geographical expansion, the market segments in which the firm acts, quality of the products offered or the size of establishment.
- **Scenarios** – the creation of scenarios is a technique that is suited to the tourism sector since it is recommended to aid decision taking in uncertain environments (Schoemaker, 1995; Goodwin and Wright, 2001; Walsh, 2005). According to Goodwin and Wright (2004), the scenarios are based on the assumption that, in an uncertain environment, it is best to identify the principal uncertainties and propose a set of possible future uncertainties. Thus,

while the objective of the scenarios is important, it is sometimes equally or more relevant that the firm acquire knowledge and abilities throughout the entire process. Hence, these hypothetical scenarios permit us to consider and test the viability of the internationalization strategy in different future scenarios.

Internal strategic analysis

Apart from identifying the opportunities and threats, the firm also needs to know its potential ability to face this new environment, in other words, the means at its disposal and those that it lacks. Therefore, it is equally important to conduct an internal analysis that enables us to consider not only the strengths that the firm must exploit but also the weaknesses and deficiencies that it must solve.

In an environment like that of tourism, with its uncertainty and rivalry, the firm's resources and capabilities become a more solid and stable basis for the achievement of a competitive advantage. The firm should not so much ask what needs it must satisfy but rather what it is able to offer (Grant, 1996) for its strategy to be successful in the long term and in the new destination. This is even more important when the already established international firms are developing increasingly complex strategic orientations and the number of firms competing internationally is growing (Litteljohn and Beattie, 1992).

With regard to the internal environment, the firm must evaluate its available resources and capabilities according to the extent to which they meet the requirements to be a possible source of competitive advantage, such as being relevant, inimitable, rare and non-substitutable, etc. (Grant, 1996). Moreover, the firm must aim to ensure that the identity of the resource or capability that generates this position of competitive advantage is not revealed, so that the strategic resources and capabilities are 'invisible to competitors' (Tampoe, 1998).

Some of the following techniques could be used for the diagnosis of the internal environment.

'Audit' and evaluation of resources and capabilities

Sometimes, the firms themselves are not aware of their potential and, consequently, do not exploit it. Therefore, we believe that, for the internal diagnosis, the tourism firm itself can conduct a simple but important exercise of self-analysis and so be able to identify each resource and capability that it has at its disposal in order to examine whether they could constitute a possible strength to support its internationalization strategy. The firm would have to evaluate the following groups of resources and capabilities (Wernerfelt, 1984; Barney, 1991; Grant, 1996):

- **Tangible resources** – such as physical resources (land, facilities, machinery and stores in the destination country) and financial resources (liquid assets and debt capacity), which are the easiest to identify and evaluate.
- **Intangible resources** – which comprise technological and human resources, reputation and organizational resources. Although the study and evaluation of these resources are more complex, they constitute the principal source of competitive advantage for firms. Firms implementing an international strategy tend to rely on their available human resources to undertake their overseas operations (Yu and Huat, 1995). Therefore, it is important to ask about the difficulties they perceive in being transferred (e.g. language, personal and family situation, adaptation to a new culture and society) and their attitude to, and availability for, assignment to head the new project. China would be one

example where it is perfectly clear that the success of international operations depends on the technical competence and cultural adaptation of the expatriate managers (Yu and Huat, 1995).

- **Organizational capabilities** – defined as the firm's ability to perform a specific activity, they are the result of the combined application of resources. Among these capabilities, we can highlight the innovation capability, organizational capability in a foreign country and, given the ever-increasing competition, the managers' capability to recognize international opportunities (Dimitratos and Jones, 2005).

Strategic profiles and benchmarking

Profiles add the possibility of benchmarking or making a comparison with some reference, for example the firm's situation at a prior date, the sector leader or firms in the same strategic group or sector. For example, Grupo Hotusa is not going to expand into Spain because when they benchmark themselves against companies that already operate there they cannot compete (see Box 15.2).

Internal factors that influence the entry mode

One of the most important decisions in internationalization is the choice of entry mode into the foreign county, and a number of internal factors that influence it should be considered (Ramón, 2002b; Pla and León, 2004):

- **Firm size** – this factor is one of the principal features that stand out among the internal characteristics of firms and has most influence on the internationalization strategy (Ruzzier and Konecnik, 2006) and the managers' perceptions (Johnson and Vanetti, 2005). Aspects such as the negotiating power with governments, the necessary financing and the availability of management resources that large companies enjoy facilitate their implementation of an international strategy. Thus, according to the literature (Quer *et al.*, 2007), such firms seem to be able to make a stronger commitment by choosing the mode of entry.
- **International experience** – although each country and process may have its own peculiarities, there is no doubt that previous experience of an international strategy means that the firm internalizes the past experiences that serve as references, acquires knowledge about the necessary information, where to look for it and what sources to use, as well as about the stages to be developed, its own shortcomings and its reactions to certain unexpected events.

Box 15.2. Grupo Hotusa: committed to the holiday segment, but outside Spain

Having opted mainly for the city segment, the firm has no intention of ignoring the holiday segment. 'We have begun something in Mexico, in the Tulum area ...' and, asked whether that would not also be the line to follow in Spain, the spokesperson indicated that 'any case where that occurred would be an exception', and explained that 'There are chains with great experience and a long tradition and they are doing it very well. For an organization without long experience to compete on that ground would surely mean that it was the underdog.'

Source: adapted from Hosteltur (2008b)

- **Competences** – these become more difficult to imitate and contribute more to the achievement of a competitive advantage as their intangibility, due to orientation to service, and organizational complexity increase (Erramilli *et al.*, 2002).
- **Strategic and control factors** – the main factors to consider are the importance attached to economies of scale, reservations systems, the trade name and investment in training.

INTERNATIONAL STRATEGIES IN TOURISM

The internationalization of the firm in general and the tourism firm in particular is accompanied and conditioned by the development of a series of organizational decisions that are necessary to support these strategies. The relationship between strategy and structure has been a topic that is especially relevant from the contingent theory that explains the need for contextual conditions (including the environment), organizational strategies and organizational components fitting for the effective and efficient achievement of the proposed objectives. In an international context, there are additional factors due to the problems of control and coordination together with the actions of the agents in foreign markets.

Askenas and others (1995: 273) consider that firms committing to globalization have to address a number of critical challenges, They have to:

- establish a workable global structure;
- hire global supermanagers;
- manage people for a global environment;
- learn to love culture differences;
- avoid parochialism and market arrogance;
- design a unifying mechanism and a global mindset; and
- overcome complexity.

Hult and others (2007) stress that, for a firm to internationalize, it must: (i) design global coordination mechanisms; (ii) facilitate the flows of knowledge and resources between organizational units; (iii) manage the interdependencies of the operations in different countries; (iv) exploit economies of scale in the different processes; and (v) cultivate a global view within the organization, which, together with the corporate culture, will provide the organizational structure with the cohesion that is necessary in a geographically dispersed company. The choice and design of an appropriate organizational form will be conditioned by factors that include the internationalization strategy and the mode of overseas entry.

Choice of the international entry mode

The mode of entry to a foreign market is defined by Root (1987) as 'an institutional arrangement that makes possible the entry of a company's products, technology, human skills, management, or other resources into a foreign country'. There are two principal ways for a firm to expand internationally: (i) the equity-based entry mode; and (ii) the non-equity-based entry mode. Within equity-based modes, the choice is between wholly-owned operations or partial-owned-equity joint ventures, while, within non-equity-based modes, the choice is principally between different contractual agreements. As already mentioned, the choice of entry mode depends both on external factors (country-specific factors such as country risk, cultural differences, level of economic development of the foreign country and the country's openness to global business) and on internal factors (firm-specific factors such as varying degrees of resource commitment, risk exposure, control, profit return).

Traditionally, total ownership ensures control over management and profits as well as over such important aspects as quality and knowledge in the provision of the service, with their implications for brand positioning. However, in the new business scenario and given the complexity, competitiveness and uncertainty that firms face when they become geographically dispersed, the last two decades have seen the strong emergence of two new modes based on collaboration between firms, namely: (i) **joint ventures**; and (ii) strategic alliances such as the **management contract** and the **franchise**. Table 15.3 shows how entry modes are classified by ownership characteristics and Table 15.4 outlines the management control for the different modes of ownership.

Table 15.3. Entry modes: classification by ownership characteristics (Source: adapted from Sharma and Erramilli, 2004: 3).

Ownership by entrant	Mode
Full	Wholly owned subsidiary (acquisitions, mergers and wholly owned new ventures)
Partial	Joint ventures
None	Contractual modes (management contract and franchising)

Table 15.4. Dimensions of management control in equity and non-equity modes (Source: adapted from Contractor and Kundu, 1998: 330).

	Mode			
Control	Fully owned	Partly owned	Management contract	Franchise
Daily management and quality control[a]	Strong control	Weak control	Weak control	Non-existent control
Physical assets[b]	Strong control	Weak control	Non-existent control	Non-existent control
Tacit expertise[c]	Strong control	Weak control	Weak control	Weak control
Codified strategic assets[d]	Strong control	Strong control	Strong control	Strong control

[a] Daily operational and quality control in each hotel property.
[b] Control over physical assets or over the real estate and its attendant risks.
[c] Control over tacit expertise embedded in routines of the firm.
[d] Control over codified assets, such as a global reservation system and the firm's internationally recognized brand name.

One of the most important decisions that a firm must face when committing to enter new foreign markets is the choice of organizational form that supports that strategy (Mutinelli and Piscitello, 1998). In the current hotel sector, non-equity modes are at least as widespread as equity modes since the capital-intensive resources (such as installations) can be separated from the resources based on knowledge or management experience (Contractor and Kundu, 1998).

Globalization strategy and multi-domestic strategy

The challenge for all firms in their internationalization is to find the best balance between local adaptation and global optimization. In that respect, Daft (2004) identifies two types of strategy: (i) the globalization strategy; and (ii) the multi-domestic strategy.

The **globalization strategy** is one in which the firm works in a standardized fashion across all its locations, both in the design and in the production of the product and in the market strategy. The aim is to achieve economies of scale and efficiency by proposing a coordinated global operation in which standards, suppliers, technology and other aspects are shared. The structure that supports this type of strategy is a divisional structure by products, where the product/services divisions take responsibility for all the operations related to their product (planning, organization and control of production distribution), including those on an international scale. In that way, the divisional managers conveniently organize the international operations that concern their product. Thus, they focus on global objectives and the strategy provides them with a clearer view of competence and response to changes in the global environment.

This design is particularly indicated for firms with technologically similar products that can be standardized to be sold worldwide, which means cost efficiency (especially in production) and improved transfer of resources and competences, including technology and innovation, between geographical regions (Johnson and Scholes, 2001). However, it entails one great disadvantage in that it ignores the peculiarities and needs of each country or region; communication and coordination problems arise and the different product divisions of the same parent company may even end up competing with one another operating in one country.

The **multi-domestic strategy** seeks to compete in each country independently of the others, with the prime objective of adapting to and reflecting the idiosyncrasies of each market. A global geographical structure divides the world into regions and a division with full control of the functional activities in its area is established in each of them. This formula is usually adopted by firms with lines of mature products with stable technology who focus on offering custom-made products to meet better the specific needs that require a local and regional response.

The main disadvantage of this structure is related to the parent company seeking global control since it would require great planning, a good information system to coordinate the activities of the different independent geographical divisions with full autonomy in their regions, as well as the design of relations and processes that facilitate the flow of knowledge and resources between those units. Sharing a culture and some corporate values, the use of multicultural teams and recognition of the contributions of the different subsidiaries can often improve coordination and communication.

The management contract

A management contract is a long-term agreement between the owners of the real estate and a firm that takes on the day-to-day management. For example, if a hotel chain wishes to enter foreign markets, this type of contract enables it to maintain a certain control over the management and quality of the establishment while it contributes the knowledge, experience, processes and standards of the chain, which enables it to maintain control over its brand and image. For the hotel chain, this entails less risk of leakage of tacit knowledge since, although the operational personnel are hired locally, the management posts are designated by the international chain.

Barceló grows by 25% in the USA by acquiring 17 more hotels

Barceló Crestline, the USA subsidiary of the Barceló Hotels and Resorts Group, has added 17 hotels to its portfolio. This operation means that the Majorcan Hotel Chain has increased its US offer by 25% and now manages 70 properties in the USA, a key territory in the Group's expansion. Barceló has acquired the management contracts of the North American company Tidewater Hotels and Resorts. It represents the largest addition of assets in the history of Barceló Crestline. With the purchase of the management company Tidewater Hotels and Resorts, the Barceló Group has acquired the management of 17 hotels in North Carolina and Virginia.

Source: adapted from Cincodías (2008)

The owner of the establishment does not take operational decisions but in all important respects, including financial, retains ownership. In return for its services, the management firm, in this case the hotel chain, receives a sum stipulated in the contract that is often linked to revenue and performance. The owner receives the residual profits after expenses. In general, such an agreement implies maximizing the return on investment for both parties. For a hotel chain, the main advantage of this non-equity mode of entry is the possibility of international expansion with no great initial investment and access to new markets or products without great requirements of capital. The management contract is one of the formulas most used by hotel chains in their national and international expansion. For example, 46% of the beds of the Sol Meliá hotel chain in 2006 were under this regime (Fig. 15.2).

The franchise
The franchise is a long-term agreement under which the owner of a brand, for example a hotel chain (the franchiser), licenses another firm (the franchisee) to use its brand name or a certain

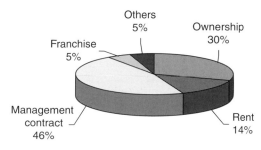

Fig. 15.2. Portfolio of Sol Meliá hotel chain indicating the proportion of the company that is owned, franchised, under management contract, rented or other. (Source: Sol Meliá, 2006).

form of management and practice in the provision of a service, under specific conditions or within determined limits. In exchange for that licence, the firm pays the hotel chain fees or a percentage.

In this case, control of the management and quality, as well as ownership of the assets, remains in the hands of the franchisee. A fundamental decision is the choice of the 'right partner in foreign nations' (Geringer and Hebert, 1991). One of the principal reasons why international chains might not opt for the franchise in its international expansion is the difficulty of transmitting know-how, professional skills and abilities and the application of standards of quality and conduct common to all hotels in one brand, especially when there is a considerable cultural difference in the country of the franchisee. When the chain franchises, it loses control over those intangible resources.

In light of the above, franchise contracts have evolved to include customer expectations of the service. The franchiser has increased its control over product standards to favour its brand or image, which also benefits the franchisees, to whom the brand and image that they are paying for are also important. The advantage to the chain lies not only in the high fees that it charges, but also in controlling and achieving economies of scale on a global scale in 'logistics, supplies, architectural design, reservations, training and brand recognition' (Contractor and Kundu, 1998: 331). The advantages of this type of contract to the franchisee comprise: (i) the right to use a brand; (ii) access to supply or distribution channels through the franchiser; and (iii) the business consultancy service that it receives, which is especially important for firms with little experience in the market.

Organization networks

In order to be able to address today's competitive environment, strategic alliances in the form of international joint ventures have become a widespread mode of entry into overseas markets. These formulas for cooperation aim to respond to the high costs and risks associated with internationalization. In general, the objective of an international joint venture is to combine the complementary resources of existing companies. Those resources may be financial, technical and human as well as intangible resources, such as know-how.

In principle, many of the activities that a firm's internationalization process entails could already be defined as network activities since the firm forms systems of relationships with foreign agents, such as customers, suppliers, competitors and governments (Welch and Welch, 1996). As the firm internationalizes, the number and the strength of these relationships between different network agents increase.

Many firms outsource or subcontract those activities that do not constitute core competences, thus forming a broad network of relationships and cooperation agreements with other firms or individuals. These multiple cooperative links have introduced new, flexible organizational forms to respond to the increase in the internal, external and spatial complexity that the firm faces and that obliges it to reconsider:

- Activities that are to be subcontracted or outsourced and activities to be produced by part of the firm – one of the first business decisions to be taken is which activities are essential to the firm and, therefore, must be retained in-house, and which activities would have greater value if they were produced outside the firm.
- The problem of differentiation and integration – just like an individual organization, the network has to assign roles and responsibilities and design the necessary mechanisms to coordinate and manage the interdependencies in order to tackle the increased complexity (teams, integrated information systems, meetings, etc.).

- The problem of control and trust – as in the case of non-equity-based modes, for the firm that internationalizes, the joint venture entails a greater loss of control and higher external dependence than internationalization based on ownership of the resources.
- A multi-domestic strategy – this favours the joint venture and the non-equity-based modes since they constitute low-cost strategies to enter foreign markets.

NOTES

[1] Among the models of perfect competition, the works of Adam Smith (1937), David Ricardo (1821), Heckscher (1919 cited in Ingram and Dunn, 1999) and Ohlin (1933) stand out; the works of Posner (1961), Hufbauer (1966), Vernon (1966), Hirsch (1967 cited in Bajo, 1991), White (1974), Krugman and Obstfeld (1994), Kravis (1985), Bajo (1991) and Culem and Lundberg (1986) stand out among the neo-classical models; and Porter (1991) for the competitive advantage of nations model.

[2] Adam Smith (1937) developed the theory of economic growth, where trade is free and without limits, countries will produce goods and services in which they are more efficient and production will be destined for consumption and export: this provides an absolute advantage. The rest of the goods and services will be imported since it will cost more to produce them than to buy them. Thus, growth and competition become stronger and the economies grow. David Ricardo (1821) agrees with the theory of the specialization of countries, but qualifies Smith's theory in the sense that the advantage is not absolute and the productivity of the work factor is the only production factor, which is used for the manufacture of goods. Each country specializes in the goods for which productivity is relatively higher.

[3] These same authors state that another perspective could consider this factor [management attitudes and aptitudes] to be one of the firm's competitive resources, but that its more subjective than objective nature, its relative autonomy compared with the other factors and its decisive influence on the firm's behaviour indicate that it should be treated differently (for an in-depth view of the concepts, see Alonso and Donoso, 1994: 115; also consult the empirical works of Bilkey, 1978; Axinn, 1985; and Aaby and Slater, 1989).

REFERENCES

Aaby, N. and Slater, S.F. (1989) Management influences on export performance: a review of the empirical literature 1978–1988. *International Marketing Review* 6(4), 7–26.

Agarwal, S. and Ramaswami, S.N. (1992) Choice of foreign market entry mode: impact of ownership, location and internalization factors. *Journal of International Business Studies* 27, 7–23.

Alonso, J.A. and Donoso, V. (1994) *Competitividad de la Empresa Exportadora Española*. Instituto Español de Comercio Exterior, Madrid.

Alonso, J.A. and Donoso, V. (1998) *Competir en el Exterior: La Empresa Española y los Mercados Internacionales*. Instituto Español de Comercio Exterior, Madrid.

Askenas, R., Ulrich, D., Jick, T. and Kerr, S. (1995) *The Boundaryless Organization. Breaking the Chains of Organizational Structure*. Jossey-Bass Inc., San Francisco, California.

Axinn, C.N. (1985) An examination of factors that influence export involvement. PhD thesis, University of Michigan, Michigan.

Bajo, O. (1991) *Teorías del Comercio Internacional*. Antoni Bosch, Barcelona.

Barney, J. (1991) Firm resources and sustained competitive advantage. *Strategic Management Journal* 17(1), 99–122.

Bilkey, W.J. (1978) An attempted integration of the literature on the export behaviour of firms. *Journal of International Business Studies* 9(1), 33–46.

Brotherton, B. and Adler, G. (1999) An integrative approach to enhancing customer value and corporate performance in the international hotel industry. *Hospitality Management* 19, 261–272.

Buckley, P.J. (1995) Barriers to internationalization. In: Buckley, P.J. (ed.) *Foreign Direct Investment and Multinational Enterprise*. Academic Press, London, pp. 79–106.

Buckley, P.J. and Casson, M.C. (1981) The optimal timing of foreign direct investment. *Economic Journal* 91, 75–87.

Canals, J. (1991) *Competitividad Internacional y Estrategia de la Empresa*. Ariel, Barcelona.

Cincodías (2008) Barceló grows by 25% in the USA by acquiring 17 more hotels. Available at: http://www.cincodias.com/ (accessed 7 June 2008).

Contractor, F.J. and Kundu, S.K. (1998) Modal choice in a world of alliances: analyzing organizational forms in the international hotel sector. *Journal of International Business Studies* 29(2), 325–358.

Corfu, A. and Nistoreanu, P. (2006) Insights into the internationalization of tourism firms. *Amfiteatru Economic* 8(19), 46–51.

Costa, J. and Teare, R. (1996) Environmental scanning: a tool for competitive advantage. In: Kotas, R., Teare, R., Logie, J., Jayawardena, C. and Bowen, J. (eds) *The International Hospitality Business*. Cassell, London, pp. 12–20.

Costa, J., Eccles. G. and Teare, R. (1997) Trends in hospitality: academic and industry perceptions. *International Journal of Contemporary Hospitality Management* 9(7), 285–294.

Cuervo García, A. (1993) El papel de la empresa en la competitividad. *Papeles de Economía Española* 56, 363–378.

Culem, C. and Lundberg, L. (1986) The product pattern of intra-industry trade: stability among countries and over time. *Review of World Economics (Weltwirtschaftliches Archiv)* 122(1), 113–130.

Daft, R.L. (2004) *Organization Theory and Design*, 8th edn. Thomson, London.

Di Gregorio, D. (2005) Re-thinking country risk: insights from entrepreneurship theory. *International Business Review* 14, 209–226.

Dimitratos, P. and Jones, M. (2005) Future directions for international entrepreneurship research. *International Business Review* 14, 119–128.

Duncan, R. (1972) Characteristics of organizational environment and perceived environment uncertainty. *Administrative Science Quarterly* 17, 313–327.

Dunning, J.H. (1993) *Multinational Enterpriser and the Global Economy*. Addison Wesley, Wokingham, UK.

Erramilli, M., Agarwal, S. and Dev, C. (2002) Choice between non-equity entry models. *Journal of International Business Studies* 33(2), 223–242.

Geringer, J.M. and Hebert, L. (1991) Measuring performance of international joint ventures. *Journal of International Business Studies* 22(2), 249–263.

Goodwin, P. and Wright, G. (2001) Enhancing strategy evaluation in scenario planning: a role for decision analysis. *Journal of Management Studies* 38(1), 1–16.

Goodwin, P. and Wright, G. (2004) *Decision Analysis for Management Judgement*. John Wiley & Sons, Chichester, UK.

Grant, R.M. (1996) *Dirección Estratégica. Conceptos, Técnicas y Aplicaciones*. Civitas, Madrid.

Gregorio, D.D. (2005) Re-thinking country risk: insights from entrepreneurship theory. *International Business Review* 14, 209–226.

Hosteltur (2008a) France is preparing to be hit by China as the first tourist destination in the world. Available at: http://www.hosteltur.com (accessed 7 September 2010).

Hosteltur (2008b) Amancio López: 'We want more international, with formulas of leasing and management.' Available at: http://www.hosteltur.com (accessed 7 September 2010).

Hufbauer, G.C. (1966) *Synthetic Materials and the Theory of the International Trade*. Duckworth, London.

Hult, G.T., Cavusgil, S.T., Deligonul, S., Kiyak, T. and Lagerström, K. (2007) What drives performance in globally focused marketing organizations? A three-country study. *Journal of International Marketing* 15(2), 58–85.

Ingram, J.C. and Dunn, R. (1999) *Economía Internacional*. Limusa, Mexico.

Jacquemin, A. (1982) Imperfect market structure and international trade, some recent research. *Kyklos* 35, 75–93.

Jarillo, J.C. and Martínez, J.I. (1991) *Estrategia Internacional, Más allá de la Exportación*. McGraw-Hill, Madrid.

Johanson, J. and Vahlne, J.E. (1990) The mechanism of internationalization. *International Marketing Review* 7(4), 11–24.

Johnson, C. and Vanetti, M. (2005) Locational strategies of international hotel chains. *Annals of Tourism Research* 32(4), 1077–1099.

Johnson, G. and Scholes, K. (2001) *Dirección Estratégica*. Prentice Hall, Madrid.

Kamath, S., Rosson, P.J., Patton, D. and Brooks, M. (1987) Research on success in exporting: past, present and future. In: Rosson, P.J. and Reid, S.D. (eds) *Managing Export Entry and Expansion*. Praeger, New York, pp. 398–421.

Kim, W.C. and Hwang, P. (1992) Global strategy and multinationals entry mode choice. *Journal of International Business Studies* 23, 29–53.

Kravis, I. (1970) Trade as a handmaiden of growth: similarities between the nineteenth and twentieth centuries. *Economic Journal* 80, 850–872.

Kravis, I. (1985) Services in world transactions. In: Inman, R. (ed.) *Managing the Service Economy: Prospects and Problems*. Cambridge University Press, Cambridge, pp. 135–160.

Krugman, P.R. (1994) *Rethinking International Trade*. The MITT Press, Boston, Massachusetts.

Krugman, P.R. and Obstfeld, M. (1994) *Economía Internacional: Teoría y Política*. McGraw Hill, Madrid.

Leask, G. and Parnell, J.A. (2005) Integrating strategic groups and the resource based perspective: understanding the competitive process. *European Management Journal* 3(4), 458–470.

Litteljohn, D. and Beattie, R. (1992) Corporate structures and expansion strategies. *Tourism Management* 13(1), 27–33.

Mutinelli, M. and Piscitello, L. (1998) The entry mode of MNEs: an evolutionary approach. *Research Policy* 27, 491–506.

Ohlin, B.G. (1933) *Interregional and International Trade*. Harvard University Press, Cambridge, Massachusetts.

Olsen, M., Murthy, B. and Teare, R. (1994) CEO perspectives on scanning the global hotel business environment. *International Journal of Contemporary Hospitality Management* 6(4), 3–9.

Oreja-Rodríguez, J.R. and Yanes-Estévez, V. (2007) Perceived environmental uncertainty in tourism: a new approach using the Rasch model. *Tourism Management* 28, 1450–1463.

Penrose, E.G. (1959) *The Theory of Growth*. Wiley, New York.

Perks, K.J. and Hughes, M. (2008) Entrepreneurial decision-making in internationalization: propositions from mid-size firms. *International Business Review* 17, 310–330.

Pine, R. and Go, F.M. (1996) Globalization in the hotel industry. In: Kotas, R., Teare, R., Logie, J., Jayawardena, C. and Bowen, J. (eds) *The International Hospitality Business*. Cassell, London, pp. 96–103.

Pla, J. and León, F. (2004) La internacionalización de la industria hotelera española. *Papeles de Economía Española* 102, 193–206.

Porter, M. (1982) *Estrategia Competitiva*. Compañía Editorial Continental, Sociedad Anonima, Mexico.

Porter, M.E. (1991) *La Ventaja Competitiva de las Naciones*. Plaza and Janes, Barcelona.

Posner, M.V. (1961) International trade and technical change. *Oxford Economic Papers* 13, 323–341.

Quer, D., Claver, E. and Andreu, R. (2007) Foreign market entry mode in the hotel industry: the impact of country and firm-specific factors. *Tourism Management* 16, 362–376.

Ramón, A.B. (2002a) La internacionalización de las empresas turísticas. *Economistas* 92, 31–44.

Ramón, A. (2002b) Determining factors in entry choice for international expansion. The case of the Spanish hotel industry. *Tourism Management* 23, 597–607.

Reichel, A. (1983) Strategic management: how to apply it to firms in the hospitality industry. *Service Industries Journal* 3, 329–343.

Ricardo, D. (1821) *On the Principles of Political Economy and Taxation*, 3rd edn. John Murray, London.

Root, F.R. (1987) *Entry Strategies for International Markets*. Lexington Books, Lexington, Massachusetts.

Ruzzier, M. and Konecnik, M. (2006) The internationalization strategies of SMEs: the case of the Slovenian hotel industry. *Management* 11(1), 17–35.

Schoemaker, P.J.H. (1995) Scenario planning: a tool for strategic thinking. *Sloan Management Review* 36(2), 25–40.

Sharma, V.M. and Erramilli, M.K. (2004) Resource-based explanation of entry mode choice. *Journal of Marketing Theory and Practice* Winter, 1–18.

Simon, H. (1947) *Administrative Behaviour*. MacMillan, New York.

Smith, A. (1937) *Inquiry into the Nature and Causes of the Wealth of Nations*. Modern Library, New York.

Sol Meliá (2006) Annual report. Sol Meliá, Palma de Mallorca, Spain.

Tampoe, M. (1998) Getting to know your organisation's core competences. In: Ambrosini, V., Johnson, G. and Scholes, J. (eds) *Exploring Techniques of Analysis and Evaluation in Strategic Management*. Prentice Hall Europe, Hertfordshire, UK, pp. 607–621.

Vernon, R. (1966) International investment and international trade in the product cycle. *Quarterly Journal of Economics* 80, 190–207.

Walsh, P.R. (2005) Dealing with the uncertainties of environmental change by adding scenario planning to the strategy reformulation equation. *Management Decision* 43(1), 113–122.

Welch, D.E. and Welch, L.S. (1996) The internationalization process and networks: a strategic management perspective. *Journal of International Marketing* 4(3), 11–28.

Wernerfelt, B. (1984) A resource based view of the firm. *Strategic Management Journal* 5, 171–180.

West, J.J. and Olsen, M.D. (1989) Environmental scanning, industry structure and strategy making: concepts and research in hospitality industry. *International Journal of Contemporary Hospitality Management* 8(4), 283–298.

White, L. (1974) Industrial organization and international trade: some theoretical considerations. *American Economical Review* 64, 1013–1020.

Young, S. (1987) Business strategy and the internationalization of business: recent approaches. *Managerial and Decision Economics* 8, 31–40.

Young, S., Hamill, J., Wheeler, C. and Davies, J.R. (1991) *Penetración y Desarrollo en los Mercados Extranjeros*. Plaza & Janes, Barcelona.

Yu, L. and Huat, G.S. (1995) Perceptions of management difficulty factors and expatriate hotel professionals in China. *International Journal of Hospitality Management* 14(3/4), 375–388.

Index

Page numbers in **bold** refer to information in tables, figures or boxes.